S0-AXN-630

Human Adaptation to Extreme Stress

From the Holocaust to Vietnam

The Plenum Series on Stress and Coping

Series Editor:

Donald Meichenbaum, *University of Waterloo, Waterloo, Ontario, Canada*

COPING WITH LIFE CRISES
An Integrated Approach
Edited by Rudolf H. Moos

COPING WITH NEGATIVE LIFE EVENTS
Clinical and Social Psychological Perspectives
Edited by C. R. Snyder and Carol E. Ford

DYNAMICS OF STRESS
Physiological, Psychological, and Social Perspectives
Edited by Mortimer H. Appley and Richard Trumbull

HUMAN ADAPTATION TO EXTREME STRESS
From the Holocaust to Vietnam
Edited by John P. Wilson, Zev Harel, and Boaz Kahana

A Continuation Order Plan is available for this series. A continuation order will bring delivery of each new volume immediately upon publication. Volumes are billed only upon actual shipment. For further information please contact the publisher.

Human Adaptation to Extreme Stress

From the Holocaust to Vietnam

Edited by

JOHN P. WILSON
ZEV HAREL
and BOAZ KAHANA

Cleveland State University
Cleveland, Ohio

PLENUM PRESS • NEW YORK AND LONDON

Library of Congress Cataloging in Publication Data

Human adaptation to extreme stress.

(The Plenum series on stress and coping)
Bibliography: p.
Includes index.
1. Post-traumatic stress disorder. 2. War—Psychological aspects. 3. War victims—Mental health. I. Wilson, John Preston. II. Harel, Zev. III. Kahana, Boaz. IV. Series.
RC552.P67H86 1988 616.85'21 88-22497
ISBN 0-306-42873-3

A Division of Plenum Publishing Corporation
233 Spring Street, New York, N.Y. 10013

Printed in the United States of America

To our wives . . .
Diane, Bernice, and Eva

Contributors

Roland M. Atkinson, Psychiatry Service, Veterans Administration Medical Center, Portland, Oregon

Elizabeth C. Clipp, Geriatric Research Education and Clinical Center, VA and Duke Medical Centers, Durham, North Carolina

Yael Danieli, Group Project for Holocaust Survivors and Their Children, 345 East 80th Street, New York, New York

Glen H. Elder, Jr., Department of Sociology, University of North Carolina, Chapel Hill, North Carolina

Phyllis Ehrlich, Benjamin Rose Institute, Cleveland, Ohio

Mary C. Grace, Department of Psychiatry, University of Cincinnati College of Medicine, Cincinnati, Ohio

Bonnie L. Green, Department of Psychiatry, University of Cincinnati College of Medicine, Cincinnati, Ohio

Zev Harel, Center on Applied Gerontological Research, Department of Social Service, Cleveland State University, Cleveland, Ohio

Mardi J. Horowitz, Center for the Study of Neuroses, Department of Psychiatry, Langley Porter Neuropsychiatric Institute, University of California, San Francisco, California

Edna J. Hunter, Hunter Publications, P.O. Box 81391, San Diego, California

Boaz Kahana, Department of Psychology, Cleveland State University, Cleveland, Ohio

Eva Kahana, Elderly Care Research Center, Department of Sociology, Case Western Reserve University, Cleveland, Ohio

J. D. Kinzie, Department of Psychiatry, Oregon Health Sciences University, Portland, Oregon

Fran Klein-Parker, Comprehensive Psychiatric Services at Southfield, Southfield, Michigan

Robert S. Laufer, Department of Sociology, Brooklyn College, Brooklyn, New York

Robert J. Lifton, John Jay College of Criminal Justice, City University of New York, New York, New York

Charles R. Marmar, Center for the Study of Neuroses, Department of Psychiatry, Langley Porter Neuropsychiatric Institute, University of California, San Francisco, California

Michael J. Maxwell, Vietnam Veterans Readjustment Counseling Center, Portland, Oregon

Erwin Randolph Parson, Parson Associates, Inc., P.O. Box 14015, Albany, New York

Michael E. Reaves, Psychiatry Service, Veterans Administration Medical Center, Portland, Oregon

Tena Rosner, Elderly Care Research Center, Department of Sociology, Case Western Reserve University, Cleveland, Ohio

Steven M. Silver, PTSD Program, Veterans Administration Medical Center, Coatesville, Pennsylvania

Tom Williams, Post-Trauma Treatment Center, Aurora, Colorado

John P. Wilson, Department of Psychology, Cleveland State University, Cleveland, Ohio

Foreword

This book is one additional indication that a new field of study is emerging within the social sciences, if it has not emerged already. Here is a sampling of the fruit of a field whose roots can be traced to the earliest medical writings in *Kahun Papyrus* in 1900 B.C. In this document, according to Ilza Veith, the earliest medical scholars described what was later identified as *hysteria.* This description was long before the 1870s and 1880s when Charcot speculated on the etiology of hysteria and well before the first use of the term *traumatic neurosis* at the turn of this Century.

Traumatic stress studies is the *investigation of the immediate and long-term psychosocial consequences of highly stressful events and the factors that affect those consequences.* This definition includes three primary elements: event, consequences, and causal factors affecting the perception of both. This collection of papers addresses all three elements and collectively contributes to our understanding and appreciation of the struggles of those who have endured so much, often with little recognition of their experiences.

Traumatic stress incorporates many other areas of study, many of which are represented in this book. They include, for example, post-traumatic stress disorder studies, victimology, suicidology, stress and coping, Nazi Holocaust studies, disaster studies, bereavement studies, crisis theory/intervention, phobia studies, burnout, and stress management studies, learned helplessness studies, substance abuse studies, rape and other victims of violence studies, and elements of the more general fields of study such as disaster psychiatry/psychology/sociology.

I have noted that any substantial and sustaining field of study can be identified by eight criteria. Briefly, the criteria for a true field of study must include a body of knowledge and standards of practice that are subsumed within (1) a history, (2) professional organizations, (3) publications, (4) theory, (5) measurement, (6) research methodology, (7) intervention technology, and (8) actions affecting policy and the judicial system. This volume makes an important contribution to the field of traumatic stress in that it addresses in some way most of these criteria.

The purpose of this volume is to present the latest research-based insights about human adaptation to extreme stress, particularly those emerging from war. More specifically, the central goal of the book is to provide a source book for some of the major theoretical, research, and clinical contributions to war-related traumatic stress that have emerged over the last 40 years. It is too early to tell if the book has reached these ambitious goals. It will most certainly be an extremely important reference for scholars and practitioners in this new field of study, however.

This collection represents the culmination of hundreds of hours of effort over 2 years. Most of these chapters were originally presented at a conference at Cleveland State University in 1986. They were carefully assembled by an experienced and able editing team who are all professors at Cleveland State University. John P. Wilson is widely recognized for his work with Vietnam veterans, particularly in diagnosis, assessment, and forensic psychology. In addition, he enjoys an excellent reputation as a personality and social psychologist as coauthor, with Joel Aronoff, of a highly popular textbook in this area.

Zev Harel is also a professor of social service and director of the Center on Applied Gerontological Research. Like his co-editors, Harel is a nationally known scholar in stress, coping, and the aging process in the elderly. Boaz Kahana is professor of psychology, former chairman of the psychology department at Cleveland State University, and a nationally known gerontologist, especially in the area of assessing coping styles in the elderly. Recently, Harel and Kahana completed a cross-sectional study of Holocaust survivors in Israel and the United States.

The 16 chapters represent a wide variety of scientific disciplines, theoretical orientations, and highly stressful events. Among the common threads that link them together are the perception, processing, adaptation, assessment, and treatment of highly stressful life events. These are the same factors that are common to the presentations made at the annual conference of the Society for Traumatic Stress Studies and to the articles that are published in the society's *Journal of Traumatic Stress.* Together, these themes have firmly established the field of traumatic stress as critical to a world replete with global trauma.

Among the unique features of this collection is the important contribution in the first chapter by Robert Jay Lifton, a cofounder of the society and its journal. This chapter pulls together many of Lifton's seminal and influential contributions to our knowledge of traumatic stress.

In many ways, Lifton speaks for all of us in the field when he says in the beginning of his chapter that as we "gather as an intellectual and moral community in connection with our concern about traumatic events and post-traumatic responses, we seek to have good emerge from the bad." His chapter paradoxically focuses on the deeds of the bad, the Nazi doctors, because, as he notes, by doing so we can more fully understand and appreciate and perhaps prevent what has happened to their victims. Clearly, all psychological traumata are experiences, and we need to understand the psychology of both the victims and the victimizers to more effectively ameliorate and prevent both.

Throughout this collection are other gems of theoretical insight and empirical generalizations too numerous to cite within the space limited to me. This is certainly an intellectually stimulating book. Yet, it is also a book full of compassion, beginning with Lifton's essay and ending with a call for more proactive programs and policies in the Epilogue. By presenting new ideas and approaches to understanding and helping victims of extreme stress, these scholars are helping to insure that good will indeed emerge from the bad.

CHARLES R. FIGLEY

Purdue University
Lafayette, Indiana

Preface

This book is one of a plethora of new books on traumatic stress responses that have emerged in recent years in a rapidly growing field that is examining this phenomenon in many traumatized groups that include survivors of war-time stress and other victims of traumatically stressful life experences. *Human Adaptation to Extreme Stress: From the Holocaust to Vietnam* is primarily focused on war-related extreme stress. The book is organized into three sections, on theory, research, and treatment. The contributors to the book represent a multidisciplinary effort to understand war-related traumatic stress and its impact on life-course development, the aging process and the diverse forms of coping, and post-trauma adaptation. The survivors studied in this book include the victims of the Nazi Holocaust and their children; Cambodian refugees who survived the genocide of the Khmer Rouge regime; Vietnam veterans, including those held as prisoners of war; a cross-section of aging World War II veterans who were originally part of the Oakland Growth Study; Native American Vietnam veterans, and the Buffalo Creek Flood disaster victims. The latter group was included because the ability to conduct a 14-year follow-up study on this population presented unique conceptual and methodological opportunities to inquire into social-psychological and psychiatric issues that are both generic and indigenous to research in the field of traumatic stress.

The book was born out of a serendipitous mutual interest by the editors in the study of extreme stress. In the early 1980s, Zev Harel and Boaz and Eva Kahana began discussing the feasibility of conducting an empirical investigation of adaptation, aging, and coping in survivors of the Nazi Holocaust living in the United States and Israel. At that time, the Kahanas were living in Detroit, Michigan, and Zev Harel was living in Cleveland, Ohio. In 1984, Boaz and Eva Kahana accepted the opportunity to become chairpersons of their respective departments at Cleveland State University and Case Western Reserve University in Cleveland, Ohio. By then, the research on the sociological, psychological, and gerontological consequences of the Holocaust was underway with support from the National

Institute on Mental Health. During the same period of time, John Wilson and Zev Harel began exchanging perspectives on post-traumatic stress disorder and the recovery process from extreme stress experiences. It was then only a matter of time until our converging interests gave birth to a series of collaborative efforts. Thus, in 1985 we decided to organize *An International Conference on Human Adaptation to Extreme Stress: From the Holocaust to Vietnam* to examine recent developments in theory, research, and treatment in the area of post-traumatic stress. After 1 year of planning, the conference became a reality on April 4–6, 1986, and was held at the International Conference Center of Cleveland State University. This volume is the outgrowth of that conference and the scientific interchange that occurred then.

There were two primary sponsors for the conference, and we wish to thank them for their institutional and financial support that was provided for the organization of this conference. First, the administration of Cleveland State University was both cooperative and generous in supporting the various facets of this conference. We are especially thankful to Georgia Lesh-Laurie, dean of the College of Arts and Sciences, for her consistent support. We are also thankful to Provost John Flower for his welcoming address and enthusiastic endorsement of the aims of the conference. Additionally, Dan Meyer, director of Conference Services, was tireless in overseeing all aspects of the 3-day event. Second, The Society for Traumatic Stress Studies, under the executive leadership of Scott and Jackie Sheely, provided financial support and invaluable administrative services. We are appreciative of their dedication to the society and its goals of furthering knowledge about the human effects of extremely stressful life events.

During the conference, which was dedicated to Vietnam veterans, many students in the College of Arts and Sciences volunteered to help with the various tasks that insured a smooth running of the conference. Of special merit were the efforts of the local area Vietnam Veterans, especially Bob Knestrik, a former Green Beret, who donated a hospitality suite that provided food and beverages to conference participants. Their generosity and involvement greatly helped to create good will and comraderie among everyone.

We are grateful to the staff and students of the Center on Applied Gerontological Research and the department of psychology for their assistance with the organization of the conference and preparation of this book: Sue Roberts, Sharon Kryza, Giacoma Farhat, Denise Steeley, Renee Wiltshire, Barbara Graelle, Raynette Boggins, and Lynn Viola. All of them were most conscientious and devoted to seeing that the work progressed and got done on time. A special acknowledgment extends to Alice Walker, a graduate student in stress studies at CSU, who insured the careful editing of the chapters and the completion of this manuscript.

Finally, we thank all of the authors who contributed the chapters in this book. Our goal to prepare a state-of-the-art book on theory, research, and treatment, which will significantly enhance knowledge and understanding of extreme stress consequences and aid professional efforts to help the readjustment of stress victims, was well served by the authors. We hope that this book will further stimulate the pursuit of knowledge for the purposes of reducing and ameliorating the consequences of stress and for the prevention of trauma, wars, and holocausts in the future.

Contents

Human Adaptation to Extreme Stress

I

Theory

Part I of this book contains five chapters that explore the central theoretical, conceptual, and methodological issues in the field of traumatic stress studies. In the first chapter, Robert J. Lifton has synthesized the major aspects of his work from his landmark research on the survivors of the atomic bomb at Hiroshima to his most recent study, *The Nazi Doctors.*

Lifton's special chapter in the book is rich in its theoretical formulations of the impact of traumatic events on the self-structure and psychic processes of the survivor. The 10 central principles of psychoformative theory are presented as a groundwork by which to understand how it is that humans struggle with and ultimately transform individual and collective traumata. Among the principles of psychoformative theory are those that are now part of the diagnostic criteria for post-traumatic stress disorder, such as psychic numbing, survivor guilt, death immersion and reenactment of traumatic life events. Additionally, the chapter includes a concise review of psychoanalytic perspectives of traumatic stress reactions and their serious limitations when applied to the understanding of post-traumatic adaptations. Lifton argues that most, if not all, psychological theories have ignored the importance of death imagery and death encounters in their formulation of the self. In his theory, Lifton suggests that there are core themes among survivors that include the need to confront the death encounter and then to transform the experience in a way that renews the self with enhanced sense of vitality. The chapter concludes with a discussion of the concept of doubling, or the formation of a part self, which individuals create to overcome death anxiety and guilt in situations of extreme stress and conflict. Lifton employs the concept of doubling to explain how it was that Nazi physicians in the death camps like Auschwitz could violate their Hippocratic oath to participate in mass killings of innocent people. These two extreme forms of adaptation, doubling and transformation, complement theoretical formulations concerning the processing of the experience *during* the stressful events as well as afterwards.

Doubling is a cognitive resolution whose adaptive process is different than physiological and emotional modes of coping with extreme stress.

In Chapter 2, Robert Laufer discusses the relationship of war trauma to identity formation and life-cycle development. This chapter is unique because it is a sensitive and well-reasoned blend of sociological, social-psychological, and psychological conceptions about the role of wars and war trauma in the context of society and in the lives of veterans.

One of the central tenets of the chapter is that wars disrupt the process of identity formation and development. Moreover, Laufer argues that in more recent wars, such as the Vietnam War, because of its nature and the way society related to it, the actual exposure to atrocities in warfare may produce a radical fragmentation in individual identity. This fragmented self Laufer labels the *serial self,* which is discontinuous to the prewar identity and self-structure of the veteran. But not only is the serial self in intrapsychic conflict with the prewar self, it also disrupts life-course development because it interferes with the epigenetic process of ego development and with the defining elements of personal and social identities.

Laufer further proposes that modern societies contribute to the formation of a serial self in war veterans because, in the nuclear age, modern technological warfare has essentially made the warrior role obsolete. And with the conflict between the civilian identity and warrior identity, the veteran finds it difficult to subscribe to the norms of a peaceful society. Thus the identity formed during war, the warrior state of disinhibition, killing and exposure to atrocities, gets frozen in time epigenetically and then leads to serial self-structures that coexist with the prewar self-structure. Similar to Lifton's concept of death immersion, Laufer writes that "the war self develops under the aegis of the death principle and is never able to free itself from the premature encounter with death or its preoccupation with death and survival. . . . The war self episodically attempts to dominate the adaptive self at moments of vulnerability in the life course and in so doing creates intrapsychic discontinuities and dualities that are inherently conflicted." Laufer's work complements Lifton's theory and shows the need for more systematic studies of the consequences of the death encounter (loss of comrades, killing, exposure to atrocities) on the processing of those experiences throughout the life span.

In Chapter 3, Eva Kahana, Boaz Kahana, Zev Harel, and Tena Rosner discuss the topic of coping by the major theorists and researchers such as Selye, Lazarus, Haan, Appley, and Trumbull and Vaillant. The authors note that when evaluating the effects of extreme stress in the lives of survivors, it is important to go beyond the pervasive and often uncritical assumption that extreme stress invariably leads to long-term psychological damage. Coping is a multidimensional and multifaceted phenomenon that is mediated by many other variables, such as personality styles, social resources, and economic opportunities.

Because the authors are presently involved in an extensive cross-cultural, cross-sectional analysis of Holocaust survivors living in the United States and Israel, they chose the Holocaust experience to illustrate the difficulties and complexities in conceptualizing coping with extreme stress. To begin, they note that the Nazi Holocaust was a genuine evil and that all rules of morality, values, and decency were not operative in the death camps. Thus, to attempt to survive such evil, those interned had to have the will to live. The authors propose that self-preservation is a powerful motive that creates the energy to cope with the many extreme stresses found in the concentration camps.

After reviewing the literature on Holocaust survivors, most of which are clinical case reports and not scientifically controlled research studies, the authors develop a model of the coping mechanisms used by the internees in the Nazi death camps. The model includes the following components: (1) motive for survival, (2) cognitive responses, (3) coping behaviors and (4) outcome variables. For example, for those persons who had no will to live, their cognitive response might include fatalism, acquiescence, and a death wish that, in turn, might produce passive compliance and, in some instances, suicide. An outcome of this sequence would then be depression, learned helplessness, or death. On the other hand, where the victims had a will to live (no matter what the reason), they would be prone to such cognitive responses as hope, psychological detachment, fantasies of retaliation, or splitting of the self. The coping responses associated with these forms of cognitive restructuring would include (1) vigilance and attempts at mastery of the situation, (2) compliance with the persecutors, (3) manipulations of various sorts, (4) active resistance, (5) altruistic behavior, (6) cooperation and collective support and (7) aggression. If successful beyond the starvation and killing of the Nazis, the individual would live and become a survivor. Finally, the chapter concludes with a comparison of coping theory and research in normal situations versus those under conditions of extreme stress. This chapter offers a conceptual approach to the understanding of the ways individuals in extreme stress conditions perceive, process, and cope with the immediate dangers and challenges of life-threatening environments. It also offers insights on the ways that survivors of extreme stress are able to come to grips with these experiences and continue living in the poststress years.

In Chapter 4, Charles Marmar and Mardi Horowitz discuss the theoretical and conceptual rationale that underlies the diagnosis and phase-oriented treatment of post-traumatic stress disorder (PTSD). They begin the chapter with a review and update on the DSM-III-R changes in diagnostic criteria for PTSD. There then follows a concise but complete review of war-related research on extreme stress that includes war veterans, Holocaust survivors, and the Japanese survivors of the atomic bombing of Hiroshima.

The third section of the chapter includes a discussion of Horowitz' phase-oriented model of stress response. The normal and pathological sequence of stress recovery is presented, and case illustrations usefully demonstrate the symptom patterns of traumatized persons who are stuck in either the avoidance or intrusion stages of stress recovery. Moreover, Marmar and Horowitz note that oscillation between the avoidance and intrusion phases is both common and indigenous to severe cases of PTSD as ego controls modulate symptom expression. In chronic cases, it is noted that distortions in basic character structure can occur and transform personality functioning in nature.

The last section of the chapter presents a short-term (12 sessions) program of psychotherapy to treat PTSD. The authors contend that the time-limited therapy has at least three major goals: (1) to rapidly establish the therapeutic alliance, (2) to counter the tendency toward oscillation between avoidance and intrusion and (3) to reestablish the normal stress recovery process. Each of the 12 sessions is explained in light of these goals, and finally the chapter concludes with a discussion of how personality styles influence PTSD symptom expression and resistance in psychotherapy. This chapter shows that well-formulated theoretical and conceptual models of stress response syndrome provide an excellent basis by which to design intervention and treatment approaches to alleviate maladaptive stress response.

In Chapter 5, the last chapter in Part I of this book, Bonnie Green and Mary Grace present a lucid analysis of conceptual and methodological issues in working with survivors. They begin their chapter by noting the important fact that research or clinical work with survivors is a highly sensitive issue. Researchers especially need to appreciate the special status, concerns, and areas of vulnerability in survivors that may have emanated from a traumatic experience. Victims are typically reluctant to talk about their involvement in a trauma for fear of being judged or misunderstood in terms of the complexities of coping with extreme stress. In this regard, Green and Grace suggest that it is important for the researcher to gather the person's narrative of the traumatic event prior to further inquiry via questionnaires or diagnostic interviews. An empathic interviewer who is willing to listen to the survivor's narrative in a sensitive, open, and non-judgmental manner can build rapport and trust that may very well increase the validity of the data gathered.

The authors suggest that in the field of traumatic stress studies, two genres of questions are being addressed at this time. The first set is nomothetic in nature. It concerns general principles about traumatic stress reactions. For example, what is the nature and sequence of the recovery process? The second set of questions concerns idiosyncratic and individual differences in adaptation to stressful life events. Included here are questions about differences between traumata, differences in recovery environments, and individual differences in response to similar stress exposure. Green and Grace go on to suggest that in order to get meaningful answers to the two classes of questions, at least five methodological factors are important: (1) the nature of the sample, (2) the types of data collected, (3) the definition of the traumatized population, (4) the criteria used to define stress and (5) the timing of the research program. In the last part of the chapter, all of these factors are illustrated in a 14-year follow-up study of the Buffalo Creek Dam disaster. Among the many interesting results is the finding that persons with more bereavement were more likely to refuse participation in the follow-up study. Along with the progress noted before, conceptual and methodological approaches in studies of extreme stress need to identify other limitations. For example, there are few longitudinal studies of survivorship, and most current studies are based on selected populations that come to the attention of mental health professionals or those who are volunteers. In both of these cases, there is limited generalizability of the findings unlike that afforded by longitudinal studies.

1

Understanding the Traumatized Self

Imagery, Symbolization, and Transformation

ROBERT J. LIFTON

INTRODUCTION

When we gather as an intellectual and moral community in connection with our concern about traumatic events and post-traumatic responses, we seek to have good emerge from the bad. Although I feel this is especially true in my work, which involves so many destructive, indeed evil, events, I think it is also true for all of us. The logical aspect of that paradox for us is that, as we pursue our work, we seek the moment when our work is less necessary. We seek and work toward the cessation of destructive events on a massive scale, such as the Holocaust, the Vietnam War, or Hiroshima. As a result, we must keep a watchful eye on perpetrators, even as we pursue our work to help victims and survivors. At the same time, we have to keep a sharp moral and psychological distinction between victimizers and victims. In that regard, I refer to my own study of Vietnam veterans, *Home from the War* that I subtitled *Vietnam Veterans: Neither Victims nor Executioners* (Lifton, 1973). This reflects my understanding, as I began to work with Vietnam veterans, that they had been cast into the two roles that Camus warned us never to assume. Those with whom I worked subsequently struggled courageously to extricate themselves from both the roles of executioner and victim. One does not want to be a victim any more than one wants to be a victimizer.

ROBERT J. LIFTON • John Jay College of Criminal Justice, City University of New York, New York, New York 10003.

In retrospect, as I consider my earlier work involving victims of Chinese thought reform and survivors of the nuclear attack on Hiroshima (Lifton, 1976a), I have come to realize, especially through my present work with Nazi doctors, that if we want to understand what has happened to victims and cope with post-traumatic stress reactions, we must understand more about the deed of the victimizers. Moreover, that understanding must include some of the psychology of victimizers, even as we seek to understand the victims. In this sense, we not only seek to help people but also to do things that take a stand against the victimizing process.

GENERAL PRINCIPLES OF PSYCHOFORMATIVE THEORY AND POST-TRAUMATIC STRESS REACTIONS

1. *Life/death paradigm and symbolization in the self.* From my own work, as well as from that of others, I have derived 10 fundamental principles that can inform us in our research and treatment of post-traumatic stress disorder (Lifton, 1976b). First is the principle of the life/death basis and the recognition that, in the most artificial and harmful way, the issue of death traditionally has been omitted from post-traumatic stress. Although people acknowledge death as an issue, conceptual resistance to death is coupled with a general cultural resistance to the idea of death. In my work with Nazi doctors, I have recognized that victimizers as well as victims experience death immersion. In the case of the Nazi doctors, some of their behavior was a means of warding off their own death anxiety. Certainly, the issue of death is central conceptually and in every other way, and our task is to confront death personally and conceptually. The more that we do this, the more effective our work will be.

2. *The concept of being a survivor.* The second principle, which is a direct corollary to the first, is the concept of the survivor, and, again, death is a key. The clear point is that *survival is an achievement.* Moreover, survival has a dialectical nature. The survivor has different alternatives. He or she can remain locked in numbing, or he or she can use that survival as a source of insight and growth. We all seek the second choice in our work. The principle of survival keeps us on a normative level because we know that if one survives something, this is not of itself pathological.

3. *The human connectedness of survivors.* Third is what I refer to as the ultimate dimension (Lifton, 1976b). We know that trauma involves very immediate and painful nitty-gritty experiences, and we know some of the symptoms as post-traumatic stress disorder. But there is also a dimension in post-traumatic stress disorder that involves larger human connectedness. If we review some of our experience with Vietnam War veterans and other groups who have undergone severe trauma, we find in each case a struggle to reinstate a larger human connectedness or a sense of being "on the great

chain of being." This is one of the most poignant and difficult struggles that accompanies the recovery process. We symbolize immortality—our historical and biological connectedness to those who have gone before, those we assume will follow. We do this through our limited life span, whether through children, our works, our influences, or through nature, or through some spiritual principle, or even through experiences of transcendence.

When we experience radical discontinuity in an immediate way, in the intrapsychic self, the self is dislodged from its forms. Janet described this in the nineteenth century, and Freud later addressed it within the context of depth psychology. This experience of vulnerability to dissociation and splitting in this acute or radical discontinuity at this immediate level renders the self susceptible to doubling.

Although prior characteristics of the self are of enormous importance in the outcome of any kind of post-traumatic stress reaction, the experience and our knowledge of radical discontinuity teach us that dissociation can be created in anybody. Moreover, severe stress can make contact with some prior vulnerability to dissociation, to splitting, to discontinuity, which exists to some degree in everyone. Although the degree of vulnerability to discontinuity and dissociation may vary in each of us, some such vulnerability is part of the human condition.

4. *Post-traumatic stress disorder (PTSD) as a Normal Reaction to Extreme Stress.* Fourth is the normative principle. *The post-traumatic stress disorder is a normal adaptive process of reaction to an abnormal situation.* Understanding this leads to a greater acceptance, on the part of both the therapist and the person who has undergone that post-traumatic stress reaction, of his or her situation and symptoms.

5. *Survivor guilt and self-condemnation.* Fifth is the issue of self-condemnation. Self-condemnation is the source of what we call psychological guilt, which occurs in people who experience extreme trauma and in post-traumatic stress disorders or survivor reactions. I refer to this as a paradoxical form of guilt because, sometimes, one can condemn self more as a survivor or victim than as the victimizer because the victimizer may numb himself or herself.

This self-condemnation is associated with a combined extreme sense of helplessness at the time of the trauma and what I call *failed enactment.* That is, at the time of the trauma, there is a quick and immediate sense that one should respond according to one's ordinary standards, in certain constructive ways, by halting the path of the trauma or evil, or helping other people in a constructive way. Neither of these may be possible during extreme trauma. At the very most, the response that is possible is less than the ideal expectation.

I speak of this as failed enactment because some beginning, abortive image forms toward that enactment in a more positive way that is never possible to achieve. One can then describe the idea of an image as a schema for enactment that is never completed. The response to this incomplete enactment can be perpetual self-condemnation.

When we say that a survivor or somebody who has undergone stress some time ago is "down" on himself or herself, we may be referring not to a sense of guilt but rather to self-condemnation that is related to that lingering failed enactment and to a residual, traumatized "self" that is still to some degree in that state of helplessness. In other words, the entire functional self is still in that state of helplessness and failed enactment, and the self in that state brings about self-condemnation. The recovery process involves transcending that traumatized self.

6. *Emotional vitality*. The sixth principle is that of feeling versus not feeling. I suggest that the standard psychoanalytic defense mechanisms are less discrete than we claim. They overlap to a great extent, and they relate to feeling and not feeling. This whole issue of dissociation originally described by Janet is central to post-traumatic stress reaction and survivor experience.

7. *Psychic numbing: Discontinuity in the self*. This central concern in our work takes us in turn to a seventh principle, namely psychic numbing. Psychic numbing stops the symbolizing or formative process. The mind needs the nourishment provided by the continuous process of creating images and forms in order to function well. In extreme forms of psychic numbing such as dissociation, the symbolizing process is interrupted and distorted. In that way, psychic numbing becomes a key, or at least a lever, to looking at this cessation or interruption of the psychic process, the radical discontinuity, that so characterizes post-traumatic stress disorder. Analyzing this formative process and applying it to post-traumatic stress disorder is a very hopeful dimension because it is perpetual. If one sees that continuous process, then one can move beyond the traumatized self and radical discontinuity.

8. *The search for meaning*. This brings us to the eighth principle—the principle of meaning. Although psychiatrists and psychologists have sometimes declined to use the term *meaning* on the grounds that it cannot be defined scientifically, we must find a rigorous way of analyzing it because, without addressing this idea of meaning or inner form, we cannot understand post-traumatic stress disorder. Again, meaning must take place at two levels—the proximate level, in which one is struggling with issues of connection and separation, of movement and stasis, and of integration versus disintegration, or integrity versus disintegration, and the aforementioned ultimate level at which one is struggling with issues of larger human connectedness. We have witnessed a person coming out of severe stress reexamine his or her sense of meaning about such phenomena as the goodness or badness of human beings, about whether human beings are really tied to each other, and whether we can trust any connections that we have in our lives. This supports my assertion that we cannot really address the issue without those questioned meanings.

9. *The moral dilemmas of trauma.* The ninth principle is the moral dimension. War neurosis has been defined as a refusal to die coupled with a refusal to kill. That double refusal was the beginning of wisdom for many Vietnam War veterans and points to the importance of the moral context in which behavior occurs. Did the man who refused to fire at My Lai, who kept his gun faced to the ground, very visibly demonstrating that he refused to fire, commit abnormal behavior? Was he a victim of combat neurosis? Or, did he exhibit an admirable form of restraint that took unusual personal courage? I believe it was the second. In that sense, the moral context played a fundamental role.

Having addressed these symptoms, I now assert that part of our function is to legitimize the right to have some of these symptoms within the context of trauma. We fulfill that function by accepting and helping people with these symptoms.

At the same time, I think we need to render illegitimate some of the destructive or traumatic situations that create the symptoms. In our discourse, in our relationship to patients, and in our public positions on relevant issues, our moral stance toward destructive behavior is bound up with the effectiveness and the humanity of our work with victims and survivors.

Although this is much more valid in massive, destructive, evil forms of trauma, as opposed to the kind of trauma that occurs in the natural history of human experience, such as the loss of a parent or another loved one, we nevertheless must legitimize the symptoms and the reaction in this case without necessarily trying to delegitimize the trauma itself, as we would do in other forms of massive traumata.

10. *Transformation of the self.* Finally, in looking at all these issues, I return to a psychology of the self. I refer not to the present, popular psychology of the self (as espoused in the works of Heinz Kohut) but rather to the the overall sense of self, which has constituted an increasing emphasis in the last 10 or 15 years on psychoanalytic psychiatry and psychology and has enabled us to unite these various dimensions. This unification is essential in order for us to see the dialectical nature of the survivor and the capacity of staying numbed, as opposed to a capacity not only for insight, but even special forms of illumination, which a survivor can have as perhaps no one else can.

Any claim to psychological insight must be tested against disorder. I believe that psychoformative theory, the principles around death and continuity, can contribute to understanding the major psychiatric syndromes. Yet at the clinical and conceptual heart of psychiatry, death-related issues have been most neglected and here too, overall symbolizing principles are required most.

There are certain advantages in formulating a consideration of the traumatic syndrome. Over time I have developed several strong convictions about this general psychological area: direct, intense psychological trauma—perhaps even adult trauma in general—is a kind of stepchild in psychiatry. An exploration of the psychology of the survivor is crucial to understanding such trauma (Lifton, 1976a). The study of adult trauma and survival has direct bearing on issues around death and death imagery in ways that shed much light on both psychiatric disturbance and on our contemporary historical condition.

PSYCHOANALYTIC CONTRIBUTIONS TO UNDERSTANDING POST-TRAUMATIC STRESS SYNDROMES

We have learned to find models in early childhood experience for later adult behavior. But there is a beginning sense in psychiatry that a reverse process may be just as useful. Intense adult trauma can provide a model, at least in terms of understanding, for the more obscure and less articulated traumata of early childhood. This reversal was not unknown to Freud (1955). And it is the basis for the image model of the human being as a perpetual survivor—first of birth itself and then of "holocausts" large and small, personal and collective, that define much of existence—a survivor capable of growth and change, especially when able to confront and transcend those "holocausts" or their imprints (Lifton, 1976b).

War Neurosis as a Paradigm of Adult Traumatic Stress Reaction

The adult traumatic experience, in the form of war neuroses, played a very special part for Freud in his conceptual development in general and in his ideas about death in particular. Freud gives special attention to war neurosis and the concept of trauma in connection with his elaboration of the death instinct in *Beyond the Pleasure Principle* (1955). That book is a crucial one in Freud's opus. James Strachey, for instance, tells us (in his editor's note for the Standard Edition) that "in the series of Freud's metapsychological writings, *Beyond the Pleasure Principle* may be regarded as introducing the final phase of his views" (Jones, 1953). Robert Waelder, a distinguished second-generation Viennese disciple of Freud, has noted that: "It is probably not accidental that this short work was written soon after World War I . . . [when] Europe was full of shell-shocked soldiers; one could see them shaking in the streets" (Waelder, 1967).[1]

[1]Wealder goes on to explain: "Some of them had merely been exposed to the 'ordinary' experience of trench warfare; others had been subjected to more particular experiences of concentrated shock, such as, for example, being suddenly covered by a load of earth in an explosion—they had barely escaped being buried alive" (p. 222).

By then a number of psychoanalysts had worked professionally with such people. The Fifth International Psycho-Analytic Congress, held in Budapest in late September 1918, had in fact included a symposium, The Psycho-Analysis of War Neuroses, from which a small book eventually emerged.

Yet the impact of the traumata of World War I on Freud and his movement has hardly been recorded. World War I (as well as his personal affliction with cancer) had considerable bearing on Freud's elaboration of the death instinct and his preoccupation with it in his later, speculative books, and Europe's grotesque death immersion had an equally significant impact on Freud's attitudes toward his own life and toward his struggling psychoanalytic movement. He cared more about the movement than he did about his individual existence. The war's traumata to the movement (personal and professional deprivations, various forms of separation and isolation, as well as the deaths of friends and family members) must have been perceived as a struggle for survival. And although Freud had relatively (for him) unproductive periods during the war, he also had bouts of extraordinary creativity. There can be little doubt that he and many of his followers were energized in some degree by their survival, though it is difficult to say at what cost. It is quite likely that the war's many levels of destruction accelerated the spread of psychoanalytic influence throughout the world. Few other groups could offer as compelling an explanation for both the mass killing and the psychological consequences of war. More fundamentally, massive trauma subverts existing systems of symbolization and tends to bring about in its victims a hunger for explanation or formulation, though it also stimulates (perhaps more frequently) an opposite tendency toward a covering-over that requires static closure. Freud's movement undoubtedly encountered both kinds of war-linked responses, but it was the receptivity that was new and especially important. There is also the possibility that this psychoanalytic survival of World War I reactivated earlier death anxieties in the movement and contributed to its fearful sectarianism and antagonism to heretics. (We can take it to be more than coincidence that, in an important letter written by Freud to Ernest Jones in February 1919, an interesting discussion of the nature of traumatic neurosis was followed directly by the sentence: "Your intention to purge the London Society of the Jungish members is excellent" [Jones, 1953].)

The Problem of Adult Traumatic Reactions to Freud's Instinct Theory of Behavior

Clearly, the war experience raised important theoretical questions for sensitive theorists like Freud. These had to do not only with the nature of homicidal destruction but also with the trauma and neuroses that could be observed in its wake. The problem for Freud was to assimilate these experiences into his already well-developed theoretical system, which meant assimilating them to instinct theory in general and to the libido concept and the sexual origin of the neuroses in particular Freud (1964).

To be sure, Freud could point out with some pride that earlier psychoanalytic emphases on psychogenic origins of the symptoms of any neurosis, the importance of unconscious impulses, and the part played by psychic gain through or "flight into" illness had been vindicated by widespread observations on the war neuroses. But, at the same time, he was clearly troubled by the fact that those observations had done nothing to confirm psychoanalytic theory to the effect that "the motive forces which are expressed in the formation of symptoms are sexual and that neuroses arise from a conflict between the ego and the sexual instincts which it repudiates" (Freud, 1964). Freud's response to the challenge was ingenious if a bit convoluted and characteristically illuminating beyond its conceptual claim. In two of his writings devoted to the question of war neuroses and in a few letters written at the end of World War I, one to Jones in particular, Freud acknowledged the importance of the external trauma but at the same time associated war neurosis with "internal narcissistic conflict" (Jones, 1953). By invoking his newly evolved theory of narcissism, of libido directed not at another person but at one's own self, Freud could at least place this form of traumatic neurosis within the general realm of libido theory. Although Freud was not always entirely clear on the subject, the essence of his argument was that traumatic neuroses of peacetime (railway accidents and other injuries in which there remains considerable neurotic overlay) can be explained by means of sexual energy or libido becoming fastened to the particular organ or to the body or ego in general, whereas traumatic neuroses of war included that narcissistic process along with an added dimension of "the conflict . . . between the soldier's old peaceful ego and his new warlike one . . . [which] becomes acute as soon as the peace-ego realizes what danger it runs of losing its life owing to the rashness of its newly formed, parasitic double" (Freud, 1964).

That argument carries Freud beyond mere libido theory toward a concept of meaning. The conflict within the self has to do with what one is willing or not willing to die for, and one's "fixation to the trauma" includes a "compulsion to repeat" elements associated with it as a form of mastery or integration. It was, in fact, precisely this compulsion to repeat that Freud described as violating the "pleasure principle" (according to which the quest for pleasure is always a central motivation) and carrying the organism "beyond the pleasure principle."

The Stimulus Barrier as a "Protective Shield" for the Ego

Moreover, it was in discussing these questions that Freud emphasized a principle of a "protective shield" by which he meant a kind of psychic skin necessary for the important everyday function of keeping out external stimuli that might otherwise overwhelm the self or ego (Freud, 1964). Hence, "*protection against* stimuli is an almost more important function for the living organism than *reception* of stimuli." He could then define "as 'traumatic' any excitations from outside which are powerful enough to break through the protective shield." And traumatic neurosis became "a consequence of an extensive breach being made in the protective shield against stimuli" (Freud, 1955). Freud could then see in traumatic neurosis something close to a retrospective model for neurosis in general and even for individual acts of repression that may or may not contribute to neurosis.

Not only did Freud make traumatic neurosis a retrospective model for neurosis in general but he did so around a concept of blockage of stimuli or what could be called diminished feeling or psychic numbing. The protective shield carried out that function toward outside stimuli but, for stimuli arising from within (instinctual impulses or primary process), there had to be an analogous pattern (what Freud called the "binding" of excitations). And "a failure to effect this binding would provoke a disturbance analogous to a traumatic neurosis." That failure, incidentally, makes necessary the compulsion to repeat and the operation of the psyche outside or beyond the pleasure principle. Freud is saying the same thing when he concludes his essay on war neuroses with the observation that "we have a perfect right to describe repression, which lies at the basis of every neurosis, as a reaction to trauma—as an elementary traumatic neurosis." Here Freud associates neurosis with a feeling disorder arising out of the organism's attempt to block excitations caused or released by trauma. This stress on the struggle against feeling reverberates throughout his work. Although Freud did not speak of what we have been calling death imagery, he did associate this struggle around excitation and feeling (as encountered in traumatic neurosis) with his argument for a death instinct. Traumatic neurosis became a cornerstone for neurosis on the one hand, and Freud's death-related conceptualizations on the other. In this juxtaposition, Freud came closest to creating a death-oriented psychology.

But, at that point, Freud called forth his own protective shield in order to place the traumatic neuroses within libido theory. To do so, he had to ward off the potentially transforming influence of death on *theory,* on our understanding of human experience. Freud's conceptual shield was his invocation of the concept of narcissism. That concept approaches conflicts within the self in terms of libido or sexual energy "lodged in the ego." Freud could claim that such "ego libido" was released by trauma and could no longer be adequately "bound" or constructively contained. Similarly, he invoked the concept of narcissism to explain psychological patterns in schizophrenia and, to a lesser extent, those in severe depression or melancholia. In all three conditions, Freud used the idea of narcissism or intense, unmanagable self-directed sexual energies to explain actual processes of disintegration and related death equivalents. In that way, Freud could not only reaffirm libido theory but collapse his own observations on meaning (in traumatic neurosis, conflicts over what one will die for) and impaired feeling (the protective shield and related internal blockage or "binding") into a mechanistic-quantifiable energic principle. Yet, the beginnings he made in sorting out these death-related struggles around meaning and feeling have by no means been lost.

Kardiner's Conception of Traumatic Neuroses: Ego Contraction and Symptom Formation

Abraham Kardiner (1959), for instance, who has distilled much of psychiatric thought on the traumatic syndrome emerging from World War II, began with Freud's explorations of trauma. But by emphasizing his own and Rado's view of "neurosis as a form of adaption," he was able to stress the need "to unravel the sense behind the symptomatology" as well as issues around feeling and numbing. Concerning the letter, he spoke of a "shrinking" of the ego, of the organism's "shrunken inner resources," and above all of "ego contraction" that interferes with virtually all areas of behavior. Kardiner combined this stress on "ego contraction" with the equally important emphasis on "disorganization rather than regression." Contraction and disorganization—what we would call numbing and disintegration—lead readily to the symptom complex, acute or chronic, that just about everyone has observed: fatigue and listlessness, depression, startle reactions, recurrent nightmares, phobias and fears involving situations associated with the trauma (what Rado calls "traumatophobia"), mixtures of impulsive behavior and unsteadiness in human relationships, and projects of all kinds (including work or study) that may take the form of distrust, suspiciousness, and outbursts of violence.[2] A convergence of observations suggests that severe threats to the organism produce patterns of stricture that have relevance for a wide variety of psychiatric impairments.

What Kardiner neglected, however, is the place of death and death anxiety in the traumatic syndrome (see Lifton, 1976b). His advances depended upon bypassing instinctualism. But, as in the case of much revisionist work, rejecting the death instinct became associated with neglect of death. The neglect is striking in traumatic neuroses, where death is so

[2]Like Freud, Kardiner is struck by resemblances between extreme forms of the traumatic syndrome and schizophrenia but in terms of these principles of contraction and disorganization rather than narcissism and libido theory. Kardiner's thinking closely approximates our own:

> Traumatic neurosis is a disease very closely related to schizophrenia, both from the point of view of central psychodynamics and from the ultimate withdrawal from the world which it set in motion. The deteriorations undergone in both conditions have a striking resemblance to each other. In a manner of speaking, the traumatic neurosis is a kind of persecutory delusion. The persecutor is, however, the outer world. *The entire syndrome is produced by what appears to be a prominent device in the establishment of schizophrenia, namely, ego curtailment* [italics added]. This "ego curtailment" or contraction is associated with what other observers have called "a chronic state of over-vigilance . . . which seriously affects [many combat veterans'] lives." (1959, p. 247)

close. An evolving view puts the death back into traumatic neurosis. As early as 1953, Joseph D. Teicher entitled a paper on the subject, "'Combat Fatigue' or 'Death Anxiety Neurosis,'" advocating the latter. Teicher associates his advocacy of "death anxiety neurosis" with classical emphasis on the importance of guilt toward the dead, as intensified by prior guilt from "fantasied murder" (feelings toward one's father, for instance in asociation with the Oedipus complex). But when he goes on to say that "in the neurotic form of fear of death, the sufferers are afraid to die and afraid to kill; in their illness they avoid death and murder," we find ourselves at first nodding in agreement but quickly sensing that there is something wrong in the way he is putting things. What is right about the approach is its direct stress on dying and killing, its relationship, that is, to death. What is dubious about the statement is its equation of fear of dying and killing as a *neurotic* state. What Teicher means, of course, is that these fears become incapacitating and therefore associated with "death anxiety neurosis." But the reader's impulse is to say, "Well, if that is the case, the world could use a good bit more of such a neurosis, or a modicum of its symptoms: if not fear, at least reluctance, to die or kill in military combat." The problem here is the reference point of disturbance or neurosis, a matter that turns out to have considerable importance. Both Kardiner and Teicher wrote from the vantage point of World War II, sometimes referred to as "America's last good war." It was, of course, a dreadful war: Its "goodness" lay in the American combination of decisive success and equally deserved moral clarity. So evil was the enemy—at least the Nazi enemy—that to annihilate him could only be perceived as virtuous. Consequently, those soldiers who broke down, who were "afraid to die and afraid to kill" on behalf of this crusade, could be quite comfortably viewed as neurotic.

Not so in the case of the Vietnam War two or three decades later (see Lifton, 1973). That war, for American participants, was ambiguous in the extreme. Its combination of doubtful justification, absence of structure (as a counterinsurgency action in which the enemy was nowhere and everywhere), and consequent frequency of killing or even massacre of civilians all contributed to various forms of confusion and reluctance to fight. Under those conditions, moral revulsion and psychological conflict became virtually inseparable, sometimes in the form of delayed reactions.

Months or even years after their return to this country, many Vietnam veterans combined features of the traumatic syndrome with preoccupation with questions of meaning—concerning the war and, ultimately, all other areas of living (Archibald, Long, Miller, & Tuddenham, 1962).[3] Most of these men were not incapacitated by their symptoms and could not be

[3]The official incidence of traumatic neuroses has been observed to be lower in Vietnam than in World War II. But, as a number of observers have pointed out, these statistics are misleading because they neglect the delayed reactions and nonclinical manifestations of pain and resistance (Lifton, 1973).

called "neurotic" (Sajer, 1971). Indeed, their anxiety, guilt, and anger could serve animating functions in terms of both introspective and "extrospective" (outward-looking or social) exploration. They seemed to need those emotions for their assimilation of the pain and confusion they had experienced. The traumatic experience, or at least elements of it, had a constructive function for them. And in many of these cases, both the syndrome (or some of its components) and the doubts about the war began with a confrontation that broke through existing patterns of numbing and evoked images of dying or killing in Vietnam. An approach to traumatic syndrome should focus on death and related questions of meaning, rather than requiring us to invoke the idea of "neurosis." This death-centered approach suggests a moral dimension in all conflict and neurosis.

THE DEATH IMPRINT AND THE PSYCHOLOGY OF THE SURVIVOR

The psychology of the survivor helps us greatly here. The survivor is one who has come into contact with death in some bodily or other psychic fashion and has remained alive. There are five characteristic themes in the survivor: the death imprint, death guilt, psychic numbing, conflicts around nurturing and contagion, and struggles with meaning or formulation. Each of these has special relevance for traumatic syndrome, and, in combination, they affect survivors at both proximate and ultimate levels of experience.

Core Themes of Survivors and Victims: The Death Imprint

The death imprint consists of the radical intrusion of an image feeling of threat or end to life. That intrusion may be sudden, as in war experience and various forms of accidents, or it may take shape more gradually over time. Of great importance is the degree of unacceptability of death contained in the image—of prematurity, grotesqueness, and absurdity. To be experienced, the death imprint must call forth prior imagery either of actual death or of death equivalents. In that sense, every death encounter is itself a reactivation of earlier "survivals." The degree of anxiety associated with the death imprint has to do with the impossibility of assimilating the death imprint—because of its suddenness, its extreme or protracted nature, or its association with the terror of premature, unacceptable dying. Also of considerable importance is one's vulnerability to death imagery—not only to direct life threat but also to separation, stasis, and disintegration—on the basis of prior conflictual experience. But predisposition is onlv a matter of degree: If the threat or trauma is sufficiently great, it can produce a traumatic syndrome in everyone, as was largely the case in the man-made flood disaster at Buffalo Creek, West Virginia, in 1972 (Lifton & Olson, 1976).[4]

The survivor retains an indelible image, a tendency to cling to the death imprint—not because of release of narcissistic libido, as Freud claimed, but because of continuing struggles to master and assimilate the threat (as Freud also observed) and around larger questions of personal meaning. The death encounter reopens questions about prior experiences of separation, breakdown, and stasis as well as countervailing struggles toward vitality; it reopens questions, in fact, around all of life's beginnings and endings. So bound to the image can the survivor be that one can speak of a thralldom to death or a "death spell."

The death imprint is likely to be associated not only with pain but also with value--with a special form of knowledge and potential inner growth associated with the sense of having "been there and returned." The death encounter undermines our magical sense of invulnerability by means of its terrible inner lesson that death is real, that one will oneself die—and this vies with our relief at no longer having to maintain that illusion. The result can be comething resembling illumination.

Death Guilt

Affecting the outcome and the degree of anxiety is the extent of the sense of grief and loss. In severe traumatic experience, grief and loss tend to be too overwhelming in their suddenness and relationship to unacceptable death and death equivalents for them to be resolved. And many of the symptoms in the traumatic syndrome have precisely to do with impaired mourning, or what Mitscherlich had called "the inability to mourn." What is involved in our terms is the inability to reconstruct shattered personal forms in ways that reassert vitality and integrity.

Thus the death imprint in the traumatic syndrome simultaneously includes actual death anxiety (the fear of dying) and anxiety associated with death equivalents (especially having to do with disintegration of the self). This powerful coming together of these two levels of threat may well be the most characteristic feature of image response in the traumatic syndrome (Lifton, 1976b).

The extraordinary power of this imagery—its indelible quality—has to do not only with death but with guilt. What is extremely important, in

[4]The flood resulted from corporate negligence in the form of dumping coal waste in a mountain stream in a manner that created an artificial dam, which eventually gave way, killing 125 people and leaving 5,000 homeless. I consulted with two law firms concerning questions of psychic damage (or "psychic impairment") and, together with Eric Olson, conducted extensive interviews with Buffalo Creek survivors and found that virtually all of those we examined showed significant traumatic effects.

addition to ultimate threat, is the limited capacity to respond to the threat and the self-blame for that inadequate response.

We have stressed the importance of the image for motivation, its anticipatory quality in the sense of providing a "plan" or "schema" for enactment. But in the face of severe trauma, precisely that process is radically interrupted. The soldier whose buddy is suddenly killed or blown up right next to him, for instance, experiences an image that contains feelings not only of horror and pity but an immediate inner plan for action—for helping his comrade, keeping him alive, relieving his pain, perhaps getting back at the enemy—or at least a psychic equivalent of any of these forms of action. But under the circumstances—and all the more so in a massive immersion in death (as in Hiroshima and the Nazi death camps)—both physical and psychic action are virtually eliminated. One can neither physically help victims nor resist victimizers; one cannot even psychically afford experiencing equivalent feelings of compassion or rage. Freud raised this kind of issue in trauma when he drew an example from children's play in which he emphasized that "children repeat unpleasurable experiences . . . [so] that they can master a powerful impression far more thoroughly by being active han they could by merely experiencing it passively." And Erikson has similarly stressed the severe psychic consequences of inactivation as opposed to the capacity for activity in any threatening situation. The inactivation of which we speak is within the image itself and therefore a violation of the kind of psychic flow one can ordinarily depend upon. One feels responsible for what one has not done, for what one has not felt, and above all for the gap between that physical and psychic inactivation and what one felt called upon (by the beginning image formation) to do and feel.

The image keeps recurring, in dreams and waking life, precisely because it has never been adequately enacted. And there is likely to be, in that repetition, an attempt to replay the situation, to rewrite the scenario retrospectively in a way that permits more acceptable enactment of the image—whether by preventing others from dying, taking bolder action of any kind, experiencing strong compassion and pity, or perhaps suffering or dying in place of the other or others. In that way the hope is to be relieved of the burden of self-blame. But whatever actual recovery and relief from guilt one achieves depends much more on the capacity to grasp and accept the nature of one's inactivation under such circumstances.

From this standpoint, we can take another look at survivor or death guilt. We have mentioned the survivor's fundamental inner question: "Why did I survive while letting him, her, or them die?" It is a relatively simple step to feel that by having so failed in one's image actions at the time, "I killed him." Or that "if I had died *instead,* he, she, or they would have lived." This last feeling may in part reflect the psychic death one did actually undergo—the extreme stasis or numbing accompanying one's inactivation in the face of death and threat—and the related sense that subsequent resumption of vitality in the absence of true enactment (mostly in the form of preventing the dead from dying) is wrong. Death guilt ultimately stems from a sense that until some such enactment is achieved, one has no right to be alive.

One could define the traumatic syndrome as the state of being haunted by images that can neither be enacted nor cast aside. Suffering is associated with being "stuck." Hence the indelible image is always associated with guilt, and, in its most intense form, it takes the shape of an image of ultimate horror: a single image (often containing brutalized children or dying people whom the survivor loved) that condenses the totality of the destruction and trauma and evokes particularly intense feelings of pity and self-condemnation in the survivor. To the extent that one remains stuck in such images, guilt is static, there is a degree of continuing psychological incapacity, and traumatic syndrome can turn into traumatic neurosis. But there is also the possibility of finding something like alternative enactment for the image that haunts one, of undergoing personal transformation around that image. In that sense, the very association of guilt with the traumatic syndrome makes possible a transforming relationship to its indelible imagery. And here are the beginnings of a psychological explanation for religious visions of realization and moral growth through suffering.

Only part of oneself feels discomfort at having survived—the experience is also associated with relief, even joy or exhilaration. These feelings can, in turn, contribute to additional guilt. The 'oy at having survived remains tainted by its relationship to that gap between image and enactment, between the excruciating, demanding picture one had constructed and the muted, devitalized, limited actions and feelings one could muster.

In all this, self-condemnation strikes us as quite unfair. The traumatized person seems to have to endure the additional internal trauma of self-blame. This is why there is a "paradoxical guilt" experienced by victimized survivors. This guilt seems to subsume the individual victim–survivor rather harshly to the evolutionary function of guilt in rendering us accountable for our relationship to others' physical and psychological existences. This experience of guilt around one's own trauma suggests the moral dimension inherent in all conflict and suffering. We have no choice but to make judgments about trauma and our relationship to it. Just as there is an inseparability between psychological and moral dimensions of guilt, we may say the same about all psychological disturbance. Psychological pain always includes a moral judgment; moral judgments express psychological conflict and realization.

In that sense there is no such thing as a value-free mechanism in either traumatic syndrome or any form of neurosis or psychosis. If we can speak of evolutionary purpose, we may say that the capacity for guilt was given us so that we might imbue all behavior, perhaps especially pain, with an ethical dimension. There is no denying the enormity of the cost, of the secondary pain via the guilt itself. That cost is starkly visible in the "paradoxical guilt" of the traumatic syndrome, which in turn has bearing on equally "unfair" forms of guilt in many different neurotic and psychotic conditions. In such states, we observe the destructive manifestations of an emotion necessary to humanity, of the emotion concerned with critical self-judgment. And we come to suspect that beyond guilt itself, neurotic and psychotic versions of it are also integral to the human condition.

Psychic Numbing

At the heart of the traumatic syndrome—and of the overall human struggle with pain—is the diminished capacity to feel, or psychic numbing. There is a close relationship between psychic numbing (including its acute form, "psychic closing-off") and death-linked images of denial ("If I feel nothing, then death is not taking place") and interruption of identification ("I see you dying, but I am not related to you or your death"). The survivor undergoes a radical but temporary diminution in his or her sense of actuality in order to avoid losing this sense completely and permanently; he or she undergoes a reversible form of symbolic death in order to avoid a permanent physical or psychic death. From the standpoint of formative process, those patterns can be understood as expressions of an internal decision of the organism concerning investment and, therefore, experience of feeling. When made under conditions of acute trauma, that "decision" is neither voluntary nor conscious.

Freud was acutely aware of such issues. This awareness is reflected in a passage from *Civilization and Its Discontents:*

> No matter how much we may shrink with horror from certain situations—of a galley slave in antiquity, of a peasant during the Thirty Years' War, of a victim of the Holy Inquisition, of a Jew awaiting a pogrom—it is nevertheless impossible for us to feel our way into such people, to divine the changes which original obtuseness of mind, a gradual stupefying process, the cessation of expectations and cruder or more refined methods of narcotization have produced upon their receptivity to sensations of pleasure and unpleasure. Moreover, in the case of the most extreme possibility of suffering, special mental protective devices are brought into operation. (Freud, 1961, pp. 55–56)

Freud (1919) is referring to acute and chronic forms of psychic numbing, in response to the most extreme kinds of trauma. Because he abruptly terminates these observations ("It seems to me unprofitable to pursue this aspect of the problem any further"), I had previously thought that Freud was making a special case of these extraordinary situations of what have been subsequently called "massive psychic trauma" and contrasting them with ordinary existence. But more careful study of the context suggests that Freud is actually making a relativistic statement. The preceding sentence, in fact, reads, "Happiness . . . is something essentially subjective," and Freud was cautioning against making too many assumptions concerning the effects of what we would consider the most extreme forms of trauma on people whose situation was quite removed from our own. He was suggesting that a process of "narcotization" or numbing might well prevent these people from experiencing anything like the degree of pain we might think we would experience. This reading suggests that Freud had a sensitive awareness of the adaptive nature of psychic numbing and of its importance for the whole gamut of human experience. There is perhaps implicit here also an important distinction between this kind of "gradual stupefying process" and more sudden kinds of traumata for which the organism is totally unprepared.

This passage was surely consistent with Freud's earlier observations about the "protective shield" and the extent to which the sense organs not only receive stimuli but "include special arrangements for further protection against excessive amounts of stimulation and for excluding unsuitable kinds of stimuli." To place all this within his instinctual cosmology, however, Freud (in a passage with which we are already familiar) subsumed this narcotization or numbing to the operation of the death instinct in maintaining the "Nirvana principle":

> The dominating tendency of mental life, and perhaps of nervous life in general, is the effort to reduce, to keep constant or to remove internal tension due to stimuli. [Freud went on to say that] our recognition of that fact is one of our strongest reasons for believing in the existence of death instincts. (Freud, 1955, p. 32)

And he saw this as an alliance between the pleasure principle, operating to reduce the internal tension caused by stimuli of various kinds, and the death instinct. Where this reduction of stimuli could not be considered exactly pleasurable, it was the latter, the death instinct, that took precedence in guiding the organism toward its own demise, in being "concerned with the most universal endeavor of all living substance—mainly to return to the quiescence of the inorganic world." Via instinctual theory, Freud is doing something interesting here. He is suggesting that a struggle with, or primarily against, feeling is the most fundamental characteristic of the human mind. In one place he suggests that in traumatic neuroses the compulsion to repeat derives from the earlier inability to experience feeling appropriate to the trauma—so that repetitive dreams about the traumatic experience "are endeavoring to master the stimulus retrospectively, *by developing the anxiety whose omission was the cause of the traumatic neurosis*" (Freud, 1955, italics added). This is close to what we call *failed enactment,* here a matter of feelings that should have been but were not experienced. But where Freud goes on to see this compulsion to repeat as itself we would emphasize the struggle to assimilate the destructive or annihilating force into prior, or else altered, mental structures.

For the numbing in severe versions of the traumatic syndrome consists of *the mind being severed from its own psychic forms.* To explain this process let us consider two quotations:

> The whole situation around me was very special . . . and my mental condition was very special too. . . . About life and death . . . I just couldn't have any reaction. . . . I don't think I felt either joy or sadness. . . . My feelings about human death weren't really normal. . . . You might say I became insensitive to . . . death. (Lifton, 1976a)

> We were all too exhausted to react, and almost nothing stirred our emotions. We had all seen too much. In my sick and aching brain, life had lost its importance and meaning, and seemed of no more consequence that the power of motion one lends to a marionette, so that it can agitate for a few seconds. Of course, there was friendship . . . but immediately behind them (two close friends) there was that hole full of guts, red, yellow, and foul smelling; piles of guts, almost as large as the earth itself. Life could be snuffed out like that, in an instant, but the guts remained for a long time, stamped on the memory. (Sajer, 1971)

The first quotation is from a Hiroshima survivor, the second from a former soldier in the German infantry during World War II. In the case of the Hiroshima survivor, the overwhelming trauma was the experience of the bomb and its immediate aftermath of grotesque death immersion. The German soldier had experienced years of perpetual death-linked trauma. Their tone is strikingly similar in its combined suggestion of desensitization toward death and the annihilation of physical and psychic life. In order to dissociate itself from grotesque death, the mind must itself cease to live, become itself deadened. The dissociation becomes intrapsychic in the sense that feeling is severed from knowledge or awareness of what is happening. To say that emotion is lost, whereas cognition is retained is more or less true but does not really capture what the mind is experiencing. What is more basic is the self's being severed from its own history, from its grounding in such psychic forms as compassion for others, communal involvement, and other ultimate values. That is what is meant by the mind's being severed from its own forms. And that severance, in turn, results in the failed enactment and guilt we spoke of previously. This kind of process was described even before Freud by Janet under the concept of *dissociation.* It includes not only stasis in the sense of inactivation but also disintegration in the sense of a coming apart of crucial components of the self. To be sure, that disintegration, like the stasis, is partial and, to a considerable degree, temporary—in fact, is in the service of preventing more total and lasting forms of disintegration. But we can say that this dissociative disintegration characterizes the psychic numbing of the traumatic syndrome and is at the heart of that experience.

There is a close relationship between the phrase used by a Hiroshima survivor, "a feeling of paralysis of my mind," and a Buffalo Creek survivor's sense, in explaining his isolation from people around him, "Now . . . it's like everything is destroyed." Those two comments refer respectively to patterns of stasis and disintegration and suggest important elements of separation as well. For all three death equivalents are important in the dissociative disintegration of the traumatic syndrome. As a consequence, psychic action, the essence of the formative-symbolizing process, is virtually suspended, and the organism is in a state of severe desymbolization. In that sense, psychic numbing undermines the most fundamental psychic processes. That is why we can speak of it as the essential mechanism of mental disorder.

The Problems of Intimacy, Nurturance, and Suspicion of the Counterfeit

These manifestations of psychic numbing are directly responsible for the two additional survivor struggles we have not yet discussed, those around suspicion of the counterfeit and quest for meaning. The survivor struggles toward—and in a way, against—reexperiencing himself or herself as a vital human being. Conflicts over nurturing and contagion have to do with the human relationships he or she requires for that revitalization, and with their impaired state. The survivor experiences feelings of weakness and special need, along with resentment of help offered as a reminder of weakness. Any such help is likely to be perceived as counterfeit. This is not only because of its association with weakness but because prior forms of dependency in human relationships have proven themselves unreliable; one's human web has been all too readily shattered, and in rearranging one's image feelings, one is on guard against false promises of protection, vitality, or even modest assistance. One fends off not only new threats of annihilation but gestures of love or help. Part of this resistance to human relationships has to do with a sense of being tainted by death, of carrying what might be called the psychic stigma of the annihilated. This stigma, which victims have always experienced, is usually explained around the idea of self-concept: If one is treated so cruelly, one tends to internalize that sense of being worthless. To modify and add to that principle, we could say: Having been annihilated and "killed," one feels oneself to have become part of the entire constellation of annihilation and destruction, to be identified with—live in the realm of—death and breakdown. The whole process, of course, is intensified by others' fear of the survivor's death taint. He or she becomes associated in their minds with a constellation of killing and dying that, should one let him or her get too close, endangers "ordinary healthy people." That is, associations to his or her experience can activate latent anxieties in others concerning death and death equivalents.

The struggles around nurturing and contagion are directly related to an insufficiently appreciated survivor emotion, that of perpetual anger and frequent rage. We discussed various kinds of survivor anger, rage, and violence, as directly related to a sense of inner death and a desperate effort at vitality. The survivor seems, in fact, to require his or her anger and rage—and all too often, violence—as an alternative to living in the realm of the annihilated. Many have noted that anger is relatively more comfortable than guilt or other forms of severe anxiety; it can also be a way of holding onto a psychic lifeline when surrounded by images of death.

The Task of Reformulation: Transformation and Reanimation

Maybe that is something of the way we live all the time, but in the case of severe trauma we can say there has been an important break in the lifeline that can leave one permanently engaged in either repair or the acquisition of new twine. And here we come to the survivor's overall task, that of formulation, evolving new inner forms that include the traumatic event, which in turn requires that one find meaning or significance in it so that the rest of one's life need not be devoid of meaning or significance. Formulation means establishing the lifeline on a new basis. That basis includes proximate and ultimate involvements. The survivor seeks vitality both in immediate relationships and ultimate meaning, the one impossible without the other. Some Hiroshima survivors, for instance, could reanimate their lives around peace movement activities, which offered a sense of immediate activity in like-minded groups and ultimate significance within which their otherwise unassimilable experience could be understood. If the world could receive a valuable message from Hiroshima, that is, and they could be the agents and disseminators of that message, then what happened to them could be said to have a larger purpose. The same principle applies to Nazi death-camp survivors in their struggle to establish and participate in the State of Israel. More typical is the quest for vitality around direct biological continuity—the tendency of many survivors to reassert family ties and reproduce and thereby assert biological and biosocial modes of symbolic immortality. In any case, the ultimate dimension, the struggle for resurgent modes of symbolic immortality, is crucial to the survivor, though rarely recognized as such.

Without this kind of formulation, the survivor remains plagued by unresolved conflicts in the other areas mentioned—by death anxiety, death guilt, psychic numbing, and immobilizing anger and suspicion of the counterfeit. Numbing in particular, the desymbolizing center of the traumatic syndrome, is likely to persist. For to overcome that numbing, new psychic formations that assert vitality and one's right to it must evolve.

BEYOND THE DEATH ENCOUNTER: CONFRONTATION, REORDERING, AND RENEWAL

A student of people with grief reactions around survival once spoke of their need for "emancipation from bondage to the deceased" (Lindemann, 1944). Even where deaths have not occurred, the survivor of a traumatic situation requires parallel emancipation from the bondage from his or her own inner deadness. In neither case does emancipation mean total severance but rather the creation of imagery that maintains fidelity to the end or to one's experience of inner deadness, fidelity in the sense of remembering what the experience entailed and including its excruciating truths in the self that is being recreated. What one does with feelings of self-condemnation or guilt is crucial to the outcome. *There is a three-stage process available to the survivor of actual or symbolic death encounter, consisting of confrontation, reordering, and renewal* (Lifton, 1973). The second of these stages, reordering, is likely to be dominated by struggles with guilt and especially with converting static to animating forms of guilt. Confrontation, in the sense of recognizing the threat to existing forms and allowing for a certain amount of necessary dissolution of them, must precede those struggles. And for them to bear fruit they must be followed by renewal at both proximate and ultimate levels, and, equally important, in centering arrangements that integrate these levels. But without guilt-associated struggles around fidelity to the dead and the experience of deadness and to oneself as a witness, no such renewal or formulation is feasible.

A major difficulty here is the literalism the survivors impose upon themselves in viewing their death encounter. So terrifying and awesome do they find it, so demanding are their requirements of fidelity to it, that they may bind themselves to what they take to be its absolutely unaltered reality and permit themselves no psychic movement from that perceived reality. But where that is the case, the "reality" they lock themselves into is a false one because perception of any experience is achieved only by inner recreation of it. And the literalism they impose upon themselves turns out to be a form of numbing in the area of image formation, a suppression of psychic action. To be literally bound to a traumatic experience is to permit oneself no psychic vitality in relationship to the experience itself and to limit vitality in other areas of life as well. This near sanctification of the literal details of the death immersion was a considerable barrier to writers and artists attempting to give form to Hiroshima. The same issue affects every survivor within the confines of his own psyche. Here we may speak of a vicious circle in which death guilt and death anxiety reinforce numbing, which, in turn, holds one to suspicion of the counterfeit and to a relationship to the death immersion that is literalized and unformulated, which, again in turn, leaves one naked to death anxiety and death guilt.

To break out of this vicious circle in the direction of formulation, survivors must find a balance between appropriate blaming (which may indeed include considerable anger toward those who bear some responsibility for the traumatic events) and scapegoating (total concentration on the target for anger in a way that continues to literalize and inhibits assimilation of the experience). They must look backward as well as forward in time. Their tendency to claim a personal "golden age" prior to the death encounter can, it is true, distort, but may also serve as a source of life-sustaining imagery now so desperately required. To be forwardlooking, to be receptive to experience that propels one toward the future, one must assemble those image feelings available to one that can assert, however tenuously, the continuity of life.

THE NAZI DOCTORS: THE CONCEPT OF DOUBLING IN RESPONSE TO EXTREME STRESS

I turn now to the subject of perpetrators and, more specifically, to my work with Nazi physicians. The doctors with whom I worked were involved not only in experiments but also in direct supervision of killing at Auschwitz and other camps. They did selections; they went to the gas chamber; they supervised the insertion of the gas; they were responsible for declaring people dead and for having the gas chambers opened. They also did selections in camp; they did selections on medical blocks, reversing healing and killing in an almost literal way. They were part of a vast project—which was put forward in theory, a kind of biomedical theory that was central to Nazi belief—of killing in the name of healing. One cannot kill that many millions of people without a claim to virtue, a healing vision. This is the ultimate paradox of the Nazi movement—the combination of terror and brutality on one hand and visionary idealism on the other. We must understand this combination in order to comprehend the Nazi movement itself. The fact that physicians were at the center of this paradox points to the biologized nature of the regime. As one doctor told me, "I joined the Nazi party the day after I heard Rudolph Hess declare that National Socialism was nothing but applied biology." The movement saw itself as healing the Nordic race, in a biological way, and doctors were crucial to the process, both in direct, personal ways and in sterilization and so-called "euthanasia," or the killing of mental patients. Moreover, they were symbolic figures, biological activists, carrying out this biomedical vision.

Interviews with both Nazi doctors and many observant and sensitive survivors of Auschwitz have led me to attribute their behavior to the principle of doubling, or the formation of a part self, which ultimately becomes an entire and considerably autonomous self. Although the two selves are interacting parts of a holistic self, a dialectic exists between them when autonomy connects with the considerable autonomy of the second self.

Second, is the holistic principle. The second self functions fully as a whole self; for this reason it is so adaptable and so dangerous. It enables a relatively ordinary person to commit evil. It has a life/death dimension, in which the perpetrator overcomes his or her own death anxiety by involvement in the killing of others.

Another function of this doubling is the avoidance of guilt, or in the case of perpetrators, the transfer of conscience. The conscience becomes associated with the group, with the sense of duty, and with an adaptation to the Auschwitz milieu, so that the self can protect itself from the feelings of conscience over what it *should* feel guilty about, namely its involvement in killing other people.

Doubling represents a way of adapting to evil. Indeed, it is part of the genius of adaptation of our species, which has carried over into adapting to evil. By doubling one can sufficiently overcome conflicts in order to commit acts of evil. In the case of the Nazi doctors, once one made a decision to stay in Auschwitz, then one had to double if one were to adapt to that environment.

We can view Auschwitz as an institution that operated on doubling. Moreover, the institution needed and was provided with a certain degree of ideology, including degrees of anti-Semitism. This belief system, accompanied by extreme numbing and various mixtures of omnipotence and impotence, led to the creation of that Auschwitz self, while maintaining a sense of professional identity as physicians. Thus the doctors conducted experiments in an effort to remain doctors, when in reality they were killing. Sometimes they supported medical work carried out by prisoner–physicians. They saw themselves as physicians who were performing very technical tasks; in so doing they developed tunnel vision regarding their actions.

Auschwitz prisoners also underwent doubling. Many Auschwitz inmates, whom I interviewed said things such as "I was a different person in Auschwitz. I really was. I was a completely different person." They were suggesting a different self-formation, this time in the name of the preservation of life. Although the purpose and moral judgment differ drastically, the process has some parallels.

Looking back at some of my own and others' work with Vietnam War veterans, we might recall the words of Philip Kingrey, who wrote in his book, *The Labyrinth of Fear,* that "threat made me threatening. I was two of myself, one human and the other inhuman. I delighted in destruction, and yet was a healer." He struggled with two sides of himself, the way in which any person put into an atrocity-producing situation might struggle in trying to heal. In the early 1970s, a Vietnam War veteran told of a dream in which "I was arguing with myself. There were two separate selves, and one of them finally shot the other, so that I shot myself." Here a tremendous and painful kind of doubling process occurred, in which the dream was expressing a powerful impulse to end the doubling in some way but was unable to do so in a constructive manner. Instead, the dream served as an opportunity to look at the violence and to move toward a more nonviolent resolution, albeit through a violent act in the dream itself.

THE PROTEAN PRINCIPLE

In conclusion, the experience of an extreme situation really is an assault on and a threat to the entire self. This is the wisdom of theory focused on the self, as articulated by Kohut and Erikson, as well as by Harry Stack Sullivan and, much earlier, Otto Rank. To this we must add a formative principle, as I have previously described—one of continuous psychic action. Furthermore, we must add what I call the Protean principle, after the Greek god Proteus. This Protean principle involves something that is historically influenced and has to do with the multifaceted nature of our lives, the way in which we can move from involvement to involvement or have multiple images that are sometimes contradictory, simultaneously in our heads, because of various historical forces to which we are exposed. Such forces include the breakdown of the kinds of classical symbols that hold us to a more narrow life pattern in the past, as well as the influence of the mass media, which can be considerable, in making contact with areas of the self that need not only be superficial.

Given the formative principle and the Protean principle in connection with a focus on self, we can look at post-traumatic disorders, struggles, and survivor reactions in terms of a self-process that is very specific to that traumatic situation. We then are better equipped to look at the process in which people can move in and out of the traumatized self or in and out of symptoms, feelings, or positions with respect to the trauma. As I have stated, moving out of that traumatized self into some reintegration of the self constitutes the recovery process.

The post-traumatic stress reaction can be understood as an effort to restore or create anew the reintegration of the self. The residual symptoms are, on one hand, adaptive; their presence implies their necessity. We struggle with the ambivalence toward the extent to which we want to eliminate these symptoms, because, although they are a problem, they also represent adaptation. Again, the symptoms include evidence of residual doubling, which is a continuing adaptation. Indeed, perhaps one never loses a sense of that traumatized self fully, but one masters it and integrates it into a larger sense of self. Overcoming that doubling is very much the reintegrative and therapeutic process.

Often the unfinished psychological work has to do with not only a new enactment to compensate for that failed enactment at the time of the trauma, in order to eliminate self-condemnation, but also moving out of that entire holistic double self toward a more integrated self. In contrast, for example, the *Rambo* phenomenon is a superficial and malignant mass media effort to chart a false direction of integration, where integration is not present. It is a reintegrative process, through violence along with a replay of failed enactment that is absolutely made literal. In the *Rambo* film, we see the replay of the Vietnam War, and as the film says, "this time, we win." It is very externalized, harmful, and ultimately a false claim to reintegration.

Finally, we can say that the same phenomenon of the formation of a second self can contribute to mass murder in ways that I have described previously. At the same time, it can, in a different guise and in a different moral context, contribute to survival and to the enhancement of life. But doubling and the conditions for doubling are our adversary in our work. Moreover, within the moral context of the work that we do, we are confronting the adversary all the time in our efforts to bring about reintegration. Indeed, our efforts toward that goal, toward contributing to reintegration of the self, require that we grasp the nature of the adversarial forces of disintegration and take our stand against them.

REFERENCES

Archibald, H. C., Long, D. M., Miller, C., & Tuddenham, R. D. (1962). Gross stress reaction in combat: A 15-year follow-up. *American Journal of Psychiatry, 119,* 317–322.

Freud, S. (1919). *Zur psychoanalyse der kriegneurosen.* Leipzig: Internationaler Psychoanalytischer Verlag.

Freud, S. (1955). *Beyond the pleasure principle* (Standar ed., Vol. 18). London: Hogarth Press.

Freud, S. (1961). *Civilization and its discontents.* New York: W. W. Norton.

Freud, S. (1964). *Introduction to psychoanalysis and war neuroses, including appendix, "Memorandum on the electrical treatment of war neurotics"* (Standard ed., Vol. 27). London: Hogarth Press.

Jones, E. (1953). *The life and work of Sigmund Freud* (Vol. 2, pp. 253–254). New York: Basic Books.

Kardiner, A. (1959). Traumatic neuroses of war. In S. Arieti (Ed.), *American handbook of psychiatry* (Vol. 1. p. 256). New York: Basic Books.

Lifton, R. J. (1973). *Home from the war.* New York: Simon & Schuster.

Lifton, R. J. (1976a). *Death in life.* New York: Touchstone Books.

Lifton, R. J. (1976b). *The life of the self.* New York: Simon & Schuster.

Lifton, R. J., & Olson, E. (1976). The human meaning of total disaster: The Buffalo Creek experience. *Psychiatry, 39,* 1–17.

Lindemann, E. (1944). Symptomatology and management of acute grief. *American Journal of Psychiatry, 101,* 141–48.

Sajer, G. (1971). *The forgotten soldier.* New York: Harper & Row.

Teicher, J. D. (1953). 'Combat fatigue' or 'death anxiety neurosis.' *Journal of Nervous and Mental Disease, 117,* 232–42.

Waelder, R. (1967). Trauma and the variety of extraordinary challenges. In S. S. Furst (Ed.), *Psychic trauma* (pp. 221–234). New York: Basic Books.

2

The Serial Self

War Trauma, Identity, and Adult Development

ROBERT S. LAUFER

INTRODUCTION

Research on the effects of war on human adaptation in the post-war period among veterans shows that it is the direct experience with the trauma of war which is decisive for subsequent psychosocial development over the lifeline (Archibald & Tuddenham, 1965; Brett & Mungine, 1985; Brill & Beebe, 1955; Card, 1983; Elder & Clipp, Chapter 6 this volume; Foy, Sipprelle, Rueger, & Carroll, 1984; Frey-Wouters & Laufer, 1986; Futterman & Pumpian-Midlin, 1951; Green & Lindy, 1985; Laufer, 1985; Laufer, in press; Laufer, Yager, Frey-Wouters, & Doneallan, 1981; Laufer, Gallops, & Frey-Wouters, 1984; Laufer, Brett, & Gallops, 1985; Laufer, Gallops, & Joyce, 1985; Lindy, Grace, & Green, 1984; Wilson & Krauss, 1985; Yager, Laufer, & Gallops, 1984). These studies of World War II and Vietnam veterans show that the life trajectories of individuals were fundamentally altered as a result of direct exposure to the various traumata of war. The evidence of enduring pathogenesis as well as the alterations of the life course requires that we examine the process through which the traumata of war impact on personality functioning and the vicissitudes of the life course development.

Conceptually we will approach the issue of life-course alteration through exposure to warfare from the perspective of personality and social structure (Pitts, 1961) and psychosocial theories of development and adaptation (Erikson, 1968; Freud, 1953; Goldberg, 1980; Haan, 1977; Levin-

ROBERT S. LAUFER • Department of Sociology, Brooklyn College, Brooklyn, New York 11210.

son, Darow, Kleen, Levinson, & McKee, 1978; Lifton, 1967, 1973, 1986; Vaillant, 1977; Wilson, 1980). Our point of departure is that the environment of war and civil, peaceful societies are radically different and psychologically at odds. One implication of this reality is that the process of going to war and subsequent adaptation may require radical breaks, sequential in nature, between self-systems as a consequence of participation in distinct social systems. Thus, one of the central problems for the individual who experiences this discontinuity is the adaptation of the fractured self after immersion in conflicting normative social systems over the life course (also see Parson's concept of narcissistic injury to the self, Chapter 11, this volume).

The veteran population with which we are concerned is usually relatively young, usually in their 20s when they went to war. In World War II, the average age of the veterans was 26, and in Vietnam it was about 20. Thus, in this chapter, we will be concerned with the impact of war trauma on the lifeline for men in their 20s, that is, the period of early adulthood. Limiting the analysis to this age group is necessary because the age at which traumatization occurs plays an important role in determining its long-term effects (Wilson, 1980). Furthermore, although people of all ages are victimized in wars, our data base for interpreting the impact of war is far better for the age group we propose to examine than any other age strata in Western societies, if for no other reason than the quality of data gathered on Vietnam veterans for over a decade.

THE ROLE OF WAR IN WESTERN SOCIETIES IN THE TWENTIETH CENTURY

The twentieth century stands alone in the annals of human history for its savagery and the brutal and fatal human toll it has exacted through its wars. In no century in the accumulated history of humankind has war taken such a massive toll on human life. Although survivors of World War II are still numerous in the West, they are outnumbered today by generations that have never known war, or the majority of whom have never experienced war. Despite this fact and the subsequent wars in Korea, Vietnam, the Middle East, Central America, and Africa, veterans represent a unique minority of those age cohorts. Over the last 40 years, the West, including Japan, has moved progressively closer to developing the capacity to destroy the world while making the experience of warfare ever more remote for the vast majority of its citizenry. Warfare, however, still rages in much of the rest of the world, often abetted by the economic and political support of Western societies that publicly abhor war at home.

In spite of the reality of warfare, the idea that war is an aberration, not normative, has continued to gain ground. The most recent version of the

American Psychiatric Association's *Diagnostic and Statistical Manual of Mental Disorders* (DSM-III, APA 1980), defines war as out of the range of normal human experience. The contradiction between war as an aberrant condition and the policy of sending men and women off to experience the grotesque realities indigenous to war has a profound and often distressing effect on those who survive.

The definition of warfare, as out of the range of normal human experience, at least in the West, has developed slowly over the decades of the twentieth century (Fussel, 1979; Wohl, 1979). In the past, war was thought of as part of the "natural" relations between societies in conflict and warriorhood an important aspect of male identity. That concept of man and society has, with dramatic exceptions such as Fascism and Nazism, generally been waning during the twentieth century. Today, however, no matter how prominent its presence on the world scene, war is regarded as an aberration precisely because it raises the specter of a nuclear holocaust.

In the nuclear age, the idea of war as aberrant has become central to survival of the species and quite possibly to the ability of political leaders and ordinary citizens to function in the world of everyday life. Clearly, to some political leaders, the function of nuclear weapons is to deter war and the "logic" of the enhancement of nuclear armories is often presented in terms of the MAD (mutual assured destruction) theory. Most recently, we have entered an era of defensive nuclear technology as a "panacea" for preventing the unthinkable called strategic defense initiative (SDI). Whether it is the language of MAD or SDI, it should be clear that the massive expansion of nuclear research and arsenals operates within a theoretical-conceptual framework that is supposed to provide both political and scientific leaders as well as the general body politic with the assurance that there will not be war. It is no longer an understatement to assert that leaders who would publicly acknowledge nuclear warfare as an acceptable alternative would be regarded as pathological. Whether or not the hidden agendas include pathological elements that cannot be reconciled to the end of global warfare in the nuclear age as an acceptable component of international politics remains to be seen. In human terms, however, we may have reached the point where war no longer has a legitimate psychological role for the warrior. Theoretically, at least, this position has deep implications for those who now fight wars and are exposed to its trauma.

The contradiction between warfare as an anachronism and the role of warfare in the history and prehistory of the human psyche should not be overlooked. The urge to dominate and liberate the self from constraints remains rooted in the human psyche. Alternatively, Lorenz's (1966) concern with psychobiological roots of human aggression transformed into warfare in human society reminds us of the powerful roots of the warrior identity and the proclivity in human society to engage in warfare as a means of demonstrating dominance. In this sense, one might argue that

Nazism and Fascism, ideologies of the deed and violence, reflect resistance to the threat technologically grounded civilian society posed to the survival of the warrior society and warrior identity as a viable component of mature adulthood. Viewed from this perspective, the aggressors in World War II, in a fashion horrifying beyond comprehension, were to the idea of civil society in the advanced technological age what the Luddites were to early technology. Unfortunately, the destruction of Nazism and Fascism did not eradicate the urge toward warfare in the modern world. The point about culture lag is relevant here. Technology, and not just the technology of destruction but the technology of production, has made warfare an increasingly dysfunctional mode of interaction between societies. Therefore, the role of the warrior in these societies has been rendered meaningless, except for political expediency. And yet, if Lorenz's ethological view is correct, the biological urge toward dominance is still a motive that must be readapted to today's world.

It is also useful to understand that we do not ignore the increasing role of armaments in the world, nor the role of military men in the political systems of the most powerful societies on earth. It is important to point out, however, that, except in localized conflicts, the massive arsenals of weapons are useless, and it is increasingly the soldier as administrator rather than the warrrior who is raised to eminence.

Our point here is to emphasize that human emotional and cognitive structures sustain, in an anthropological sense, perceptions of "outsiders–enemies" that can in principle only be satisfied through violent modes of subjugation of the stranger, that is, warfare. It is the contradiction between the emergent integrated and interdependent international civilian social order and the persistence of an archaic appendage, the warrior mentality, that constitutes one of the central problems of the modern world. In this perspective, then, when men are sent off to war, their *reintegration* into civilian society is inherently problematic for the general population but particularly difficult and complex for the returning soldier–veteran. The fundamental reality of warfare is that the veteran is systematically stripped of his public identity as a warrior, whereas the experience of war is permanently burned into his psyche, no matter what the character or nature of the war. The resulting contradiction between the civilian identity that evolves from the warrior, itself based on the repression of civilian adolescent identity is never fully resolved. From the perspective of life-course ego development, the root of the problem is that increasingly veterans of war live in an environment where the warrior experience primarily plays a traumatic role in adult development. Therefore, the central problem that this chapter explores is the implication for individual identity (self-systems) for those caught up in the vortex of war in societies in which the warrior has become an anomaly and war defined as deviant or aberrant.

THE SELF AND WAR

Erikson (1968), Kohut (1971), and Lifton (1976) have developed distinctive theories of the developmental structure of the self, but their interpretations of the relationship between the individual and environment share certain commonalities. Wolf (1980), working within the tradition of Kohut's self-psychology, and Erikson argue that the developmental process depends on an evolving relationship between the self-system and a symbol-constructing and symbol-enforcing social matrix. Erikson (1968) and Wolf (1981) argue virtually identically that "identity . . . depends on the support which the young individual receives from the collective sense of identity characterizing the social groups significant to him: his class, his nation, his culture," (Erikson, 1968, p. 89) and, according to Wolf (1980):

> Setting aside, for the moment, any particular age-appropriate form of self-object need, one may compare the need for the continuous presence of a psychologically nourishing self-object milieu with the continuing physiological need for an environment containing oxygen. It is a relatively silent need of which one becomes aware sharply only when it is not being met, when a harsh world compels one to draw breath in pain. And so it goes also with self-object needs. As long as a person is securely embedded in a social matrix that provides him with a field in which he can find the needed mirroring responses and the needed availability of idealizeable values, he will feel comfortably affirmed in his total self with its ambitions and goals. In short, he will feel himself strong and, paradoxically, relatively self-reliant, self-sufficient and autonomous. But if by some adversity of events this person should find himself transported into a strange environment, it will be experienced as alien and even hostile, no matter how friendly it might be disposed to him. Even strong selves tend to fragment under such circumstances. (p. 128)

Lifton's recent approach to the self in *The Nazi Doctors* (1986) uses the concept of "doubling" to deal with the problems of identity in concurrent but distinct environments, which are at least culturally antagonistic. The doubled self is the self that can function effectively in these antagonistic social matrices by completely separating the selves. Subsequent to the elimination of one sociocultural system, the concentration camp, the doubled self persists, but only the historically social self is active in everyday life. The other self is cloistered in a destroyed social milieu; and only if forced into memory does the other self emerge, but even then it remains essentially encapsulated.

These theories of the self all focus on the continuity of the social matrix as a prerequisite for development of healthy adult personality, that is, active mastery of the environment where there is "a unity of personality" that permits the individual to accurately perceive the world and himself or herself (Jahoda, 1950). Lifton's concept of doubling takes this sociological insight to its extreme conclusion, that is, he argues that theoretically and empirically it is feasible that self-systems are so entirely embedded in social structure that the structural constraints, the self's need to be integrated into and supported by class, nation and culture, permit the construction of two totally encapsulated self-systems that can function without reference to each other in antagonistic social matrices.

The relationship between the self and the environment, and especially the issue of continuity in the developmental process that allows the self-system to master the environment, is central to the idea of unity of personality or coherent and healthy ego identity. The question that emerges in the literature on massive psychic trauma is the impact of the tearing of the relationship between self and environment on post-traumatic personality.

The literature on conceptual approaches to the impact of warfare on personality indicates that the major theorists and theories (Freud, Horowitz, Kardiner, & Spiegel, Kolb & Multalipassi, Krystal & Lifton) argue that there is a lasting impact of the experience on the life course (Brett & Ostroff, 1985). All of these theories are grounded in empirical research on the survivors of war. A central feature of these theories of post-traumatic stress is the imprinting of the experience on the individual and its disruptive impact on later life. Whether we take Freud's view of the impact of memories and defense against the painful effect, Lifton's argument of psychic numbing and doubling, Kolb and Multalipassi's conditioning approach, or Krystal's and Kardiner and Spiegel's view of adaptive failure of the stimulus barrier, all of these theories argue that once the personality is subjected to extreme stress, that trauma becomes embedded in personality and that there is an interactive relationship between the memory of the trauma and subsequent stages of adult development.

Thus, the literature on post-traumatic stress argues that the traumatization is not integrated readily into the personality or self-system of the survivor. If we reflect for a moment on conceptualizations of the self discussed before this should not be surprising. Indeed, we would argue that a plausible interpretation of self and post-traumatic stress theories is that it is the exposure of the self-system to a hostile enviornment that fundamentally undermines the ability of the maturing organism to unfold its potentialities, which shatters the self-system. It seems plausible to argue that, once the social milieu that nurtures self–object relations is radically transformed, a new set of self–object relations must be built and that the self/identity/personality that emerges in that context will derive its structure from the social matrix in which it is embedded. The fundamental problem in a traumatizing social matrix is that the self-system of survivors will be partially grounded in the traumatic milieu. The problem that we propose to explore is the relationship between the self-system of the traumatic social matrix and the post-traumatic self-system that must necessarily be grounded in culture and conventional society. The interplay between self-systems grounded in antagonistic social systems within the personality system of the survivor through the remaining years of adulthood, the lifeline, constitutes a major dilemma in modern societies that requires further exploration. This formulation of the discontinuity of the self and society forms the framework within which we will explore the issue of the development of the adult self of the survivor.

CONCEPTUAL FRAMEWORK

The central assumption of the chapter is that personality is constrained by social structure. The self emerges within a social system and through the process of socialization the child evolves into an adult through a process that requires the internalization of the dominant values, norms, and behavior patterns of the society. The self that emerges from this process reflects the particular way they have integrated the existing sociocultural system.

From our perspective, the fundamental issue is that those values and norms learned in childhood and adolescence provide a foundation for the transition to adulthood. In the twentieth century, however, childhood and adolescence has become a more complex process because of rapid social and technological change. Further, socialization processes increasingly have been organized around civil society. Thus, the warrior identity has played a diminishing role in Western socialization. Considered in this way, the norms, values, and self-systems of civil society are increasingly incompatible with those of war. However, generations of young men have been sent off to war.

The emphasis on civilian identity in the socialization process also increasingly precludes the idea that children will grow into warriors, though not into peacetime soldiers. Soldiering in Western societies is not supposed to lead to warring. First and most important, soldiering is, for the vast majority of men and women, an interregnum between adolescence and adult life. At best it takes up a few of the early adult years; and in many instances it provides an opportunity for less privileged youth to have a moratorium from early career demands. The soldier identity, like the student identity, is a transitory one. Only a fraction of the men and women who enter the military make it a lifetime career. The function of the military in these societies is to deter war, not to fight wars. With two notable exceptions, the Korean and Vietnam wars, this scenario reflects the experience of people who have served in the U.S. military from 1945 to the present.

THE TRANSFORMATION OF THE CIVILIAN TO WARRIOR

Wars require that we change the identity of the men we send to fight them. In order to change identity, we alter the social structure in which the soldier fights. The most fundamental structural alteration we impose on soldiers at war involves the reorganization of the basic societal objective from life enhancement to life taking and life threat. The actuality of killing within an organized unit that legitimatizes the taking of life and constructs its reality around killing on a day-to-day basis fundamentally alters the ego and self-concept of individuals. The civilian identity forged as it is within a social structure that operates on a life-giving principle is, regardless of military training, unprepared for the reality of existing within a social structure organized around the death principle. This is especially true in contemporary Western cultures that emphasize the vitality of youth and its unlimited potential. The problem is further exacerbated by long life expectancy in these societies. Young men in their 20s can, without the intervention of war, anticipate another 50 years of life. Thus warfare attacks the prewar adolescent identity and forces a premature encounter with death than would normally be the case in the life cycle (Laufer, 1985; Parson, 1985; Wilson, 1978, 1980). The normative identity, self-system, and ego mechanisms that are forged by the structure of the warfare society's preoccupation with the death principle, its isolation and total system quality, and its threat to normal aging at the point of entry into adulthood stand in sharp contrast to the late adolescent prewar self-system and the postwar adult self.

THE TRANSFORMATIVE EXPERIENCES OF WARFARE

Why do we refer to exposure to warfare as a transformative experience? First, it is outside the range of normal human experience, as DSM-III's description of post-traumatic stress indicates. To us, that also implies that it is an experience that the individual cannot be phenomonologically prepared for by training, discussion, or simulation (Brende & Parson, 1985; Hendin & Haas, 1985; Schnaier, 1982; Van Deventer, 1983). Cognitive preparation, even if it is accompanied by sophisticated simulation, usually is not designed to overwhelm the self-system. It is unlikely that it produces the *level* of neurophysiological release similar to threatening or traumatizing environments. Undoubtedly, in the actual context of warfare, there is an interaction between neurophysiological and psychosocial mechanisms that produces changes in the self-structure described before. Stated simply, there is no preparation for immersion in death and the exposure to catastrophic stress.

In training, as this marine indicates, the emphasis on killing is not especially frightening:

> In basic training I felt wonderful. I felt physically perfect, mentally alert. . . . Naturally there was a certain amount of brainwashing that goes

through basic. They would constantly pound it into you that you have to kill to survive. You know, you are going to Vietnam and you are going to fight a war and all you are going to do is kill, kill, kill, kill.[1]

However, training and reality expose you to very different emotional stress as a navy veteran so eloquently illustrates:

I arrived in the middle of the night . . . and we bounced along in trucks forever to get . . . to camp. The next day I woke . . . in a 15 × 32 tin-roof hut. . . . That morning within hours of my first awakening I saw more than I wanted to see. I felt a sense of hopelessness, of being overwhelmed by the physical fact that a 17-year-old kid is really in Vietnam and that there are bullets being fired.

Warfare, as an army man elaborates, is also the realization that you are now in a place where it is no longer a game:

What did I first feel? Panic! The realization you are so far away from anything that you could even come close to calling your own. The mass of troops . . . massive equipment . . . it is all mind-boggling. The realization that you are not a little kid any more playing cowboys and Indians. . . . The reality is there. There was no turning back.

Second, the key issue not addressed in DSM-III is that warfare is not an event but a process. Thus for most soldiers and civilians caught up in war, traumatization is repetitive, often continuous for long periods of time. By long periods of time, we mean anything from weeks to months, though in some cases exposure to extreme stress persists over years. As a marine describes his response to the repetitive exposure to trauma, "I was always scared. Whenever you got pinned down." An army infantryman provides a graphic illustration of the traumatization of war as a process rather than a single event:

The first time I was wounded I walked in a mine field. The whole platoon walked in it. So we had to probe our way out of there. It took us about an hour and a half to get out of the place. The second time I was wounded was when we got overrun. That was December 22, 1968. The night of the 22nd we were dug in underground . . . and all hell broke loose. We were surrounded. There were 350 of them and only 64 of us. The only thing that held them off was that we had the perimeter dug in so good and we had wire around it. By the time we got air support, they were in on us, about 40 or 50 of them were in the perimeter. We had to fight 40 or 50. . . . That was the night I got wounded. I lost a number of friends, 15 guys.

[1]All excerpts from case histories used in this chapter come from the *Legacies of Vietnam* study (Egendorf, Kadushin, Laufer, Rothbart, & Sloan, 1981).

Thus, the environment of warfare has a developmental component that requires that the individual attempt to construct a self-system that is functional within the context of war.

Third, warfare is constructed around killing and dying and therefore stands in direct opposition to the fundamental developmental structure of the self experienced prior to entry into the milieu of warfare. Furthermore, the death and dying is not simply of the enemy, but of one's friends and comrades as well as the self. Thus, individuals actively pursuing war or caught up as protagonists in warfare must for some period of time cease to exist in a normal developmental sense. The negated self, or the self in flux, must necessarily become a central component of selfhood during the period of immersion in an environment where death is the guiding teleological principle. Fundamentally the self-system must seek a structure that offers some hope for survival while at the same time accepting death as possible, logical, and even necessary, or finally as a meaningful release. Indeed, the dominant response to the war experience reported by Vietnam veterans in *Legacies of Vietnam* was the need to survive (56%). An illustration of the this comes from an army veteran who did survive:

> I only thought about my own survival. Every time somebody got killed I was just glad it was not me lying there. . . . Getting out safe was the only thing on my mind. I changed so much in Vietnam. I became selfish and hard and scared.

Fourth, we talk of warfare in geopolitical terms, but for those involved it is largely personal. The personal experience we discuss as combat is a cacophony of madness and fear portrayed in the aftermath in film and/or print as organized, but imagistically retained in memory in its raw and uncut fury, accompanied by rage, fear, and terror. In a fundamental sense, although language helps convey some component of the experience, it ultimately fails, as we have indicated, because it cannot bring together the complex of simultaneous emotions nor the process of acculturation to the environment. Film is often more misleading because it provides the *appearance* of the act while missing the reality of war. The self-imagery, which is what DSM-III focuses on as the traumatic event, is better understood as the fragments of the warrior self that survive in memory in indelible imagery. Two veterans recall in rather similar ways the shadowy character of warfare, the initial feelings of exhilaration and then depression. First, a navy veteran recalls:

> It was just before dusk. I guess you would call it twilight. We just kind of stumbled on the Vietcong and fortunately for us they had their weapons laying on the ground. We had ours on our person. This one gook reached for his automatic weapon and I shot him. . . . The first instant that it happened it was like a flow of adrenalin or whatever, I felt great. It gradually sank in and

made me sick. And then the next day I found out the kid was only 14 and that did not help.

An artillery man discusses his experience:

> We were outnumbered in an ambush and surrounded by the Vietcong. I had to fight my way out and I do recall having hit several Vietcong by the way in which their shadows, their outlines fell to the ground. This was at night, not in daytime. I first felt great. Later it hit me and the effect was one of depression, one of a nonfuture, discontent.

Thus, soldiers retain frozen frames of the "killer" self that can either haunt their daytime memory or nighttime nightmares or they can attempt to repress, block, or transform those fragments of the self. In either event, a considerable amount of energy has to be invested in the self created during war.

Fifth, warfare is not only the momentous clashing of men's destructive capabilities between military forces in combat. It is also the cold-blooded pre- and postcombat destruction of the enemy and civilians. An infantryman noted:

> I was a squad leader at that time and a few guys in my squad had captured a Vietcong. He was unarmed and instead of bringing him to intelligence, turning him in as a prisoner, they executed him. A couple of guys held me down as I screamed for them not to do it. . . . They murdered him right there in front of me.

At other moments frustration yields acts of revenge at those closest at hand. One veteran explained why he could kill both in and out of combat: "I got to the point where I started to get a kick out of killing. . . . After seeing what they do to someone you are on line with. They turned you very cold towards the people we were fighting against."

Finally, among men who have lost any sense of the world of the living, some soldiers kill simply from habit, to experience or reexperience power, and some for pleasure. We call them psychopaths in the civilian world, but military organizations have found uses for such men over the centuries, and they are part of every war. One veteran recalled:

> Our support unit had captured some medical personnel . . . most of them were women, nurses. And we had this captain . . . and he told these women, maybe ten to fifteen, if they didn't give the information that he wanted, he was going to turn the whole unit loose on them. . . . The nurses were beaten and raped and eventually killed because they wouldn't give information.

Such savagery permeates war and is not the province of a particular side. Indeed, our point in this chapter is the degree to which war is a psychological reality unto itself and it is the self that must adjust. The veteran who says he got to the point where he got a kick out of killing also described the environment that brought him to this state:

> We were looking for another squad that was missing for two months. We found what was left of them. Their bodies were of course decayed, left out in the sun, their I.D. cards were nailed to their foreheads, to their skulls.

Sixth, it is the survivors, civilian and military, who become living symbols in war zones of the grotesque. Literature and film capture this aspect of war well because characters become metaphors for the distortion of "normal" human emotions, personality, and physical appearance. The last aspect of the grotesque is the easiest to illustrate because we are all familiar with the legless, armless, and faceless survivors of wars. However, the grotesque is also exemplified in personality and captured well in *Apocalypse Now,* where all the living characters are grotesque and no longer related to a comprehensible civilian world. This film captures the grotesque and bizarre aspect of emotion and personality central to warfare rather than describing the war or those fighting it. This aspect of the Vietnam War is central to virtually all the literary efforts to describe this war. As the design of war is the repetition of killing until one party is subdued, the grotesque in a war of any duration becomes a normal part of the cosmology of warfare.

Finally, there is survivor guilt. In all wars, there is loss among those involved in the killing. The enemy also kills, and the dead are often friends, buddies, or partners who died instead of the self. Who dies at a given moment and who lives is often random chance. One step forward or one step backward and a different body lies dead or disabled. Sometimes a friend's favor, walking point or taking a patrol or standing guard, results in death or the cheating of death. Death is final, and so are disabling wounds. Unlike children playing war games, the combatants cannot yell "Uncle," and say the game is over. The memory of death at the doorstep threatens the self and raises the question of "why should I survive and the other die." The broken connection cannot be repaired, and the survivor self must endure the surviving. As one survivor recollects, the pain and rage are often "beyond endurance":

> When we were out on the river, we were hit three times and they sunk our boat. There were twelve men aboard and only four of us made it back. It happened so suddenly, I heard a mortar round hit. I went upstairs and there were dead people lying everywhere. I found the captain, his legs blown away. I found my buddy, he was lying over the 50 caliber, dead. I pushed him off and then I went crazy. I just started shooting at the beach, . . . at anything that moved.

The significance of survivor guilt is its impact on the relationship between personality and social structure. For some veteran/survivors, survivor guilt becomes a dominant intrapsychic theme that in principle precludes participation in successful interpersonal and social relationships such as marriage, parenthood, or careers. Clearly, self-punishment can permeate all aspects of living. These seven factors, we would argue, constitute the foundation of a transformation of the self that, once experienced, become a permanent part of the self-system, the biography, that is carried in the lifeline until death.

COPING WITH REENTRY INTO CIVIL SOCIETY

The transition from being combatant to being a survivor in civilian society poses a series of problems. As we have indicated elsewhere, the initial transition can for a number of years be quite difficult. In the lexicon of our times, it has been called readjustment. Readjustment is not, however, a lifelong process. The evidence from recent research on Vietnam veterans (Laufer, Gallops, & Joyce, 1985), World War II veterans (Elder & Clipp, Chapter 6 this volume), and Dutch Resistance fighters from World War II (Institute Psychiatrie, 1986; Op den Velde, 1985) indicate that the impact of the stress of war is for a significant portion of the exposed population a lifelong process. Indeed, there is evidence in the Dutch literature of a curvilinear pattern of war-related pathology, that is, men and women who in the immediate postwar period exhibited war-related stress symptoms that subsequently went into remission during their 30s and 40s show evidence of disturbance in their 50s. Thus it is clearly more than an issue of readjustment. The use of such terminology indeed obfuscates the issue and inhibits our understanding of the process by which the self created in war adapts to life. Indeed, Vaillant's (1977) notion of adaptation is a far more appropriate approach to postwar adult development because this term implies that there are multiple paths of human adaptation to extreme stress.

The early period of readjustment is nonetheless important in our attempt to understand the interactional relationship between self-systems developed in the matrix of war and those that evolve in the postwar adult years. The evidence suggests that, in the early stages of readjustment, there is profound confusion and disorientation associated with the effort to assume once again the self-system of civilian society. In part, it appears that one pattern of adaptation is to repress the war experience and pretend that the developmental pattern of the prewar self can be picked up (developmental arrest). As one veteran noted:

> I am trying to forget . . . the whole deal in Vietnam. . . . [I was] a lot different than before I went in. All my friends when I got out said that I was not

> right—"There is something wrong with you, man." . . . It is just like three years of a big void—a black spot in my life. I just cannot remember, or don't care to, what happened. It is like I was dead for three years there.

Three veterans less committed to repressing the trauma but no less confused by it, provide additional insights into the transition from the world of war to civilian society:

> I stayed to myself. I felt very guilty. . . . I was totally confused in terms of right and wrong. I came back with less pride than when I went there.

> All I had experienced was how to make a bomb, how to kill somebody, or how to shoot a rifle, and so I felt kind of lost. . . . A lot of people say I was changed. I was quiet when I went into the service and I got more violent.

> I think a rehabilitation program where they teach a person how to live around civilian people again . . . is a good one. Teach them how to be a human being with human rights . . . people do forget when their mind is in an uproar. Kind of analyze him to see if he is capable of handling civilian life.

The evidence indicates that regardless of the strategy employed to cope with the reentry problem, there is the emergence of a considerable degree of disorder in the lives of war veterans in the period after returning to civilian life. Although only a small proportion require institutionalization, the evidence suggests that there is a range of vulnerabilities among those exposed to high levels of war stress. Our own research, cited before, showed a rather low correlation between mental health and other indicators of pathology such as substance abuse or postservice arrest, employment problems, or divorce. If one takes into account the proportion of men who showed evidence of disturbance on one or another dimension of adult functioning, the conclusion that appears inescapable is that a majority of the war-stressed veteran population experiences the return to civilian society as problematic.

THE POSTWAR ADULT DEVELOPMENTAL PROCESS

From our perspective, the evidence of the last few years indicates that the disruption of the war experience persists in the lives of veterans exposed to the trauma of war (Archibald & Tuddenham, 1965; Elder & Clipp, Chapter 6 this volume; Green & Lindy, 1985; Laufer, Gallops, & Joyce, 1985; Kahana, Kahana, & Harel, 1986). Vietnam veterans who sought access to programs for helping veterans with serious long-term employment problems were overwhelmingly a population that had extraordinarily high levels of exposure to war trauma. These men are now in their late 30s or early 40s. Data from other sources also indicates that there is a chronic and episodically disturbed population of war survivors. There is also evidence that, although not all survivors of war are prone to pathology, the war experience contributes to the patterns of stress in social relations among survivors and their families even in the absence of diagnosable pathology (Bergman & Jucovy, 1982; Haley, 1977, 1986; Laufer & Gallops, 1985; McCubbin, Dahl, Lester, Benson, & Robertson, 1976; van der Kolk, 1986).

ADAPTATIONS OF THE SELF IN WAR AND POSTWAR ADULT DEVELOPMENT

We have argued that the immersion of individuals living in modern societies into the milieu of war constitutes a break in the developmental process so fundamental that an other self must be created and that the other self cannot be fitted into the mature adult identity of the civilian social order of these societies. We would argue, however, that the antagonistic selves are in communication with each other. The nature of the interaction process will be discussed later. However, we need to elaborate the historical and developmental basis of our conceptualization.

Our conceptualization of the self is grounded in an interpretation of the modern world as increasingly demarcating the boundary of civilian society and war. To some, that may seem odd as it is clearly the case that the weaponry of warfare is aimed at the destruction of civilian society. Military conquest increasingly over the last hundred years has come to mean the destruction of the opposition civil social order.

However, we have argued, warfare historically was seen as part of the normal, if extraordinary, pattern of interaction between social systems. Indeed, we find that one of the main purposes of the United Nations now is the maintenance of international peace and security and that to the end "to take effective collective measures for the . . . suppression of acts of aggression." True, there have been since 1945 enough military confrontations to leave untold millions of victims of warfare. Nonetheless, the fundamental shift in societal interaction, in principle and increasingly in practice, from military to nonmilitary modes of conflict resolution has taken place and has a considerable impact on individual maturation.

Furthermore, modern advanced societies take as a first-order principle that between the major powers, the only war that can occur is nuclear war and that form of warfare is so utterly destructive that it cannot really occur, that is, the expanded weaponry of destruction is a deterrent that cannot and will not be used. Thus, in theory these societies are immune from war and no longer need to take war into account vis-à-vis their own populations. Furthermore, although these societies do not in practice reject the use of force in Third World areas, such intervention is generally viewed as a pitfall to be avoided and a threat to sociopolitical stability. Furthermore, the occurrence of such events is relatively rare. Thus, in general, the role of warfare as a socially acceptable and central aspect of industrial social systems has been dramatically diminished.

In the advanced industrial nations, the principled renunciation of warfare as a legitimate means of conflict resolution has had an enormous impact on the theory and practice of childhood and adolescent socialization and adult development. In our view, it is the developmental issue that is paramount in understanding the relationship between the self-systems of war and civil society.

Human development theories deal with normal development as if adolescent and adult development does not include the issue of exposure to warfare. The issue of nonpathological development in the aftermath of the experience of warfare, where warfare is treated as part of the developmental lifeline, is not included in either the psychology, psychiatry, or sociology of adult socialization. Our point is simply that with the exception of Lifton (1976), there is no theory of adult development that takes into account either empirically or theoretically the role of war as a systematic component of the adult lifeline.

We are suggesting that current research efforts are ignoring a fundamental shift in modern culture, the transition to understanding war as pathology rather than a normal component of social intercourse between societies. The failure to focus on this transition contributes to the second omission: an effort to understand the normative structure of warfare and the personality/self-systems that are consistent with warfare. Finally, of course, the previously mentioned problem leads us to pay inadequate attention to the differences between functional personality/self-systems in war and civil society and how these self-systems interact in the life course of individuals who have experienced war, usually in early adulthood, and must thereafter developmentally adapt to civilian society. It is our contention that any understanding of the role of warfare in the developmental process of adulthood must take as its point of departure the problem of a truncated war self, the self created in war which is blocked developmentally at the point of reentry into civil society and the developmental (adaptive) self, the self-process that adapts to the events and stages of the adult lifeline.

THE SERIAL SELF AND POSTWAR ADAPTATION

The populations most affected by the structure of war are those most directly exposed for extended periods of time to the death, mutilation, and systematic human, social, and environmental destruction of warfare. The issue is not simply individual psychopathology as a function of the inability to integrate the warrior identity into the civilian self. That problem clearly exists and has been amply documented. Rather, we suggest that, even within the population that learns to function effectively, that is, where there is no evidence of psychopathology, the relationship between the war self constructed under the dominance of the death principle cannot be fully or easily integrated with the adaptive civilian self of the postwar world.

Our hypothesis is that the core experience of the war exists in a vacuum and cannot be used to validate subsequent stages of the life course but can disrupt the lifeline (Van Dyke, Zilberg, & McKinnon, 1985). The war self is located in a distinct historical milieu, constrained in a narrow chronological period in the individual's biography, and is arrested developmentally. The last point is of particular importance. The adaptation of the self that took place for the war self to emerge is frozen in time epigenetically. The war self is therefore a truncated self that survives in a timeless dimension of biographical time, able neither to evolve, integrate, nor disintegrate. It is fixated on that moment in biography when it developed to allow the individual to function within the parameters of the social order of warfare. Further, the *war self* develops under the aegis of the death principle and is never able to free itself from the premature encounter with death or its preoccupation with death and survival. The power of the war self derives from the fact of survival in the face of death, and its threat to the adaptive self is especially vigorous when the self is threatened. Thus, we would argue, the war self episodically attempts to dominate the adaptive self at moments of vulnerability in the life course and in so doing creates intrapsychic discontinuities and dualities that are inherently conflicted.

The adaptive self, on the other hand, is the developmental self that seeks to integrate the individual's identity across biographical time. Thus it is historical and not time-bound. We are arguing, however, that the process of identity integration is incomplete vis-à-vis the war self. The inability to fully integrate the war self into the adaptive self is a product of the radical discontinuity of social structures in which these self-systems initially emerge.

Life transitions occur throughout the life course. Thus the adaptive self is episodically vulnerable, in the civilian context, to the "pathology of the war self." This suggests, in our view, that adaptation to life through the life course is structurally unstable. This instability is rooted in the coexistence of antagonistic self-systems, the war self and the adaptive self. The interaction between these antagonistic selves over the life course at points of transition we label the *serial self* because the adaptive self is serially vulnerable to the war self.

Pathology clearly is an important, but not inevitable, consequence of a serial self-system. Indeed, the pathology among the survivors of war has been amply documented, and the serial self is a self-system that is poised at the edge of pathology throughout the life course. We would suggest that such phenomena as post-Vietnam syndrome, post-traumatic stress disorder and the persistence of vulnerability to pathology in war survivors reflects the precarious relationship between self-systems in the survivor population(s). Our main point, however, is that pathology is the expression of the antagonistic relationship between the war self and the adaptive self where the war self comes to dominate. The struggle between these self-systems is part of the legacy of war and is central to the lives of those who become survivors whether or not there is evidence of traditionally conceived psychopathology.

The concept of the serial self also provides us with an insight into the evidence found in the literature that, for war-traumatized veteran survivors, there is a lifelong struggle of coping with their sense of apartness from civilian peers, exhibited simultaneously by the determined effort to communicate the uncommunicable, as illustrated by both memoirs, novels, plays, films, and scholarship by the survivors about their experience and by the larger silence of the majority of the survivors in their intimate social networks. Further, we would argue, the serial self is expressed in the propensity of survivors to seek solace in the company of their own. For, as we have tried to suggest, the serial self is a self-system nurtured in the womb of inhuman catastrophe, and only those who must survive in a civil world and who have also entered through the portal of the most desolate circle of hell can comprehend its phenomenological reality. The need for such communion, although a necessary condition for the mastery of the war self, is not a sufficient condition. The reader should not mistake the argument that those who have existed outside our "normal" social system must, of necessity, find each other for the often popularized notion that only the traumatized can help the traumatized. The issues are separate. Although we recognize the first claim, the second is a recipe for disaster for it furthers the isolation of the survivors and mitigates against their ability to cope with stress of the serial self, that is, the prospect of a fulfilling life span in a world that remains dominated by social and personality systems foreign to the nature of war.

SUMMARY

The experiences of war consume a significant proportion of the individual's biography, are deeply traumatizing and fixating in the immediate context and in the aftermath of war. The clinical picture that has emerged from the literature of war survivors provides ample evidence of the pathological legacy of war. Our point, however, is that, unlike the clinician who argues that the fixating trauma can be resolved through insight, we are arguing that, whereas clinical or social intervention may certainly ameliorate symptom expression and contribute to greater self-understanding, the social transformation of the role of warfare in society means that postwar development is systematically vulnerable to the antagonistic relationship between the encapsulated war self and the adaptive self of civil society—the serial self.

The problem of seriality is that the war experience and the adaptation of the self that took place for the warrior is, in contemporary society, frozen in chronological and developmental time, in the late teens or early 20s, and in social space, there is no subsequent experience with warfare. This means that, unlike adult identity in civilian society, there is no development of the self that could give meaning to the experience of war through the lifeline.

The war experience can become less salient and/or less disruptive in the aftermath of the war through clinical treatment of symptoms or, in some cases, by society socially adjusting its treatment of the survivors. Fundamentally, however, the unresolved traumatic elements of the war experience's lasting contribution is the disruption of the life course at crucial life transitions or as a result of subsequent stressful life events.

In summary, war creates the serial self with which individuals must then struggle throughout the remainder of their lives. In our view, there is no possibility that survivors of war can escape a dialectical reality. The possibility we do see is that the adaptive self can be strengthened so that it may generally have the upper hand in the struggle survivors endure throughout the developmental process.

REFERENCES

American Psychiatric Association. (1980). *Diagnostic and statistical manual of mental disorders* (3rd ed.). Washington, DC: American Psychiatric Press.

Archibald, H. C., & Tuddenham, R. D. (1965). Persistent stress reaction after combat: A 20-year follow-up. *Archives of General Psychiatry, 12,* 475–481.

Bergman, M. S., & Jucovy, M. E. (Eds.). (1982). *Generations of the Holocaust.* New York: Basic Books.

Brende, J. O., & Parson, E. A. (1985). *Vietnam veterans: The road to recovery.* New York: Plenum Press.

Brett, E. A., & Ostroff, R. (1985). Imagery and post-traumatic stress disorder: An overview. *American Journal of Psychiatry, 142,* 417–424.

Brett, E. A., & Mungine, W. (1985). Imagery and combat stress in Vietnam veterans. *Journal of Nervous and Mental Disease, 173,* 309–311.

Brill, N. Q., & Beebe, G. W. (1955). *A follow-up study of war neuroses.* Washington, DC: Veterans Administration Monograph.

Card, J. J. (1983). *Lives after Vietnam: The personal impact of military service.* Lexington: Lexington Press.

Egendorf, A., Kadushin, C., Laufer, R. S., Rothbart, G., & Sloan, L. (Eds.). (1981). *Legacies of Vietnam* (Vol. 3). Washington, DC: U.S. Government Printing Office.

Erikson, E. (1968). *Identity, youth, and crisis.* New York: Norton.

Foy, D. W., Sipprelle, R. C., Rueger, D. B., & Carroll, E. M. (1984). Etiology of posttraumatic stress disorder in Vietnam veterans: Analysis of military and combat exposure influences. *Journal of Consulting and Clinical Psychology, 52,* 79–87.

Freud, S. (1955). *Moses and monotheism.* New York: Vintage Books.

Frey-Wouters, E., & Laufer, R. S. (1986). *Legacy of a war: The American soldier in Vietnam.* New York: M. E. Sharpe.

Fussel, P. (1979). *The great war and modern memory.* New York: Oxford.

Futterman, S., & Pumpian-Midlin, E. (1951). Traumatic war neurosis five years later. *American Journal of Psychiatry, 108,* 401–405.

Green, B. L., & Lindy, J. D. (1985). *Prediction of delayed stress after Vietnam: A summary of preliminary study findings.* NIMH Final Report. Cincinnati: University of Cincinnati.

Goldberg, A. (Ed.). (1980). *Advances in self-psychology.* New York: International Universities Press.

Haan, N. (1977). *Coping and defending: Processes of self-environment organization.* New York: Academic Press.

Hendin, H., & Haas, A. P. (1985). *Wounds of war: The psychological aftermath of combat in Vietnam.* New York: Free Press.

Haley, S. A. (1977). When the patient reports atrocities: Specific treatment considerations of the Vietnam veteran. *Archives of General Psychiatry, 30,* 191–196.

Institute Psychiatrie (1986). *Literatuuronderzoek Medische causaliteit bij oorlogsgetroffenen 1940–1945.* Unpublished manuscript. Rotterdam: Erasmus Universiteit.

Jahoda, M. (1950). Toward a psychology of mental health. In M. J. E. Benn (Ed.), *Symposium on the health personality,* Supplement II: Problems of infancy and childhood, transactions of fourth conference. New York: Josiah Macy Foundation.

Kohut, H. (1971). *The analysis of the self.* New York: International Universities Press.

Laufer, R. S. (1985). War trauma and human development. In S. Sonnenberg, A. Blank, & J. Talbot (Eds.), *The trauma of war: Stress and recovery in Vietnam veterans.* Washington, DC: American Psychiatric Press.

Laufer, R. S. (in press). The aftermath of war: Adult socialization and political development. In R. S. Sigel (Ed.), *Handbook of adult political socialization: Theory and research.* Chicago: University of Chicago Press.

Laufer, R. S., & Gallops, M. S. (1985). Life-course effects of Vietnam combat and abusive violence. *Journal of Marriage and the Family, 47,* 839–853.

Laufer, R. S., Yager, T., Frey-Wouters, E., & Doneallan, J. (1981). Post-war trauma: Social and psychological problems of Vietnam veterans in the aftermath of the Vietnam war. In A. Egendorf, C. Kadushin, R. S. Laufer, G. Rothbart, & L. Sloan (Eds.), *Legacies of Vietnam* (Vol. III, pp. 19–44). Washington, DC: U.S. Government Printing Office.

Laufer, R. S., Gallops, M. S., & Frey-Wouters, E. (1984). War stress and trauma: The Vietnam veteran experience. *Journal of Health and Social Behavior, 25,* 65–85.

Laufer, R. S., Brett, E. A., & Gallops, M. S. (1985). Patterns of symptomatology associated with post-traumatic stress disorder among Vietnam veterans exposed to war trauma. *American Journal of Psychiatry, 141,* 1304–1311.

Laufer, R. S., Gallops, M. S., & Joyce, K. (1985). *Opportunities for intervention: Employment needs of Vietnam veterans in New York City.* New York: New York City Vietnam Veterans Memorial Commission.

Levinson, D., Darow, C., Klein, E. B., Levinson, M. H., & McKee, B. (1978). *The season's of a man's life.* New York: Knopf.

Lifton, R. J. (1967). *Death in life: Survivors of Hiroshima.* New York: Random House.

Lifton, R. J. (1973). *Home from the war.* New York: Simon & Schuster.

Lifton, R. J. (1976). *The life of the self: Toward a new psychology.* New York: Basic Books.

Lifton, R. J. (1986). *The Nazi doctors.* New York: Basic Books.

Lindy, J. D., Grace, M., & Green, B. L. (1984). Building a conceptual bridge between civilian trauma and war trauma: Preliminary psychological findings from a clinical sample of Vietnam veterans. In B. A. van der Kolk (Ed.), *Post-traumatic stress disorder: Psychological and biological sequelae* (pp. 43–57). Washington, DC: American Psychiatric Press.

Lorenz, K. (1966). *On aggression.* New York: Harcourt, Bruce and World.

McCubbin, H. I., Dahl, B. D., Lester, G. R., Benson, D., & Robertson, M. L. (1976). Coping repertoires of families adapting to prolonged war-induced separations. *Journal of Marriage and the Family,* 461–476.

Op Den Velde, W. (1985). Postraumatische stres-stoornis als laat gevolg van verzetsdeelname. *Nederlands Tijdschrift Voor Geneeskunde, 129,* 834–838.

Parson, E. R. (1985). Life after death: Vietnam veterans struggle for meaning and recovery. *Death Studies, 10,* 11–26.

Pitts, J. R. (1961). Personality and the social system. In T. Parsons, E. Shils, K. P. Naegele, & J. R. Pitts (Eds.), *Theories of society* (Vol. 2, pp. 685–716). New York: The Free Press of Glencoe.

Schnaier, J. A. (1982). *Women Viet Nam veterans and mental health stress: A study of their experiences and post traumatic stress.* Unpublished master's thesis, University of Maryland, College Park, MD.

Vaillant, G. E. (1977). *Adaptation to life.* Boston: Little, Brown.

van der Kolk, B. A. (1986). The psychological consequences of overwhelming life experiences. In B. A. van der Kolk (Ed.), *Psychological trauma* (pp. 1–30). Washington, DC: American Psychiatric Press.

Van Deventer, L. (1983). *Home before morning.* New York: Beaufort.

Van Dyke, C., Zilberg, N. J., & McKinnon, J. A. (1985). Post-traumatic stress disorder: A thirty year delay in a World War II veteran. *American Journal of Psychiatry, 142,* 1070–1073.

Wilson, J. P. (1978). *Identity, ideology and crisis: The Vietnam veteran in transition* (Vols. I and II). Washington, DC: Disabled American Veterans.

Wilson, J. P. (1980). Conflict, stress and growth: Effects of war on psychosocial development among Vietnam veterans. In C. R. Figley & S. Leventman (Eds.), *Strangers at home: Vietnam veterans since the war* (pp. 123–166). New York: Praeger.

Wilson, J. P., & Krauss, G. E. (1985). Predicting post-traumatic stress syndromes among Vietnam veterans. In P. Kelly (Ed.), *Post-traumatic stress disorder and the war veteran patient* (pp. 102–147). New York: Brunner/Mazel.

Wohl, R. (1979). *The generation of 1914.* Cambridge: Harvard University Press.

Wolf, E. S. (1981). On the developmental line of self–object relations. In A. Goldberg (Ed.), *Advances in self psychology.* New York: International Universities Press.

Yager, T., Laufer, R. S., & Gallops, M. S. (1984). Some problems associated with war experience in men of the Vietnam generation. *Archives of General Psychiatry, 41,* 327–333.

3

Coping with Extreme Trauma

EVA KAHANA, BOAZ KAHANA, ZEV HAREL, and TENA ROSNER

INTRODUCTION

In an effort to address research challenges posed by the study of coping with extremely stressful life events, this chapter will outline a conceptual framework provided by a dynamic consideration of immediate and long-term coping with trauma and will consider the relationship of coping to psychological well-being. Although we consider such a fremework to be useful and necessary, we will also point to limitations of current research in operationalizing such a framework, especially as it relates to extreme stress and long-term adaptation. Specific illustrations of the suggested paradigm will be provided from the literature and from our study of coping efforts of Holocaust victims during the period of victimization and by survivors in the aftermath of the Holocaust.

OVERVIEW OF STRESS AND COPING RESEARCH

The broad questions of human adaptation or adjustment have been central to theoretical formulations dealing with personality, social behavior, and mental health (Horowitz, 1986). Social and behavioral scientists have long been interested in the human tendency to seek homeostasis

---

EVA KAHANA and TENA ROSNER • Elderly Care Research Center, Department of Sociology, Case Western Reserve University, Cleveland, Ohio 44106. **BOAZ KAHANA** • Department of Psychology, Cleveland State University, Cleveland, Ohio 44115. **ZEV HAREL** • Center on Applied Gerontological Research, Department of Social Service, Cleveland State University, Cleveland, Ohio 44115.

(Cannon, 1939) and the adverse consequences of the inability to achieve desired equilibrium (Selye, 1956).

A commonly accepted definition of stress continues to elude researchers despite the fact that the need to define one's terms in systematic research is an accepted axiom. Selye's definition (1982) set the stage for the debate in the literature that was to follow. He described stress in terms of "any demand upon the body, be the effect mental or somatic." A contrasting position has been voiced by Haan (1982) who argues that there is a shared implicit understanding of the meaning of the term *stress,* and therefore an explicit definition is unnecessary. Definitions of stress have ranged from stimulus-based approaches (Holmes & Rahe, 1967) to those defining stress in terms of organismic response (Appley & Trumbull, 1977). A synthesis of these approaches is proposed by Monat and Lazarus (1977) who suggest that stress is a demand that disrupts homeostasis, and thus taxes the individual's adaptive resources.

Automatic or familiar responses are usually considered "adaptive behavior" to problems, whereas effortful activities to master a problem are most commonly referred to as "coping" with stress. White (1974, pp. 48–49) put it succinctly when he stated that "coping refers to adaptation under relatively difficult conditions." Lazarus and Folkman (1984) classify research on coping in two major groupings. One, which relates to definitions of coping in terms of exercising control over adverse environmental conditions, is largely derived from experimental studies with animals. A second body has its roots in psychoanalytic ego psychology and considers coping in terms of realistic thoughts and acts aimed at problem solving, mastery, and the decrease of stress.

Coping, as a response to the disequilibrium of a stressful state, has been viewed as the *successful* reduction of stress (reestablishment of homeostasis), thereby identifying coping behavior as only those actions that produced the desired results. As antecedents and consequences of coping became disentangled, empirical research focused on traits or personality dispositions on the one hand and mental health sequelae on the other (Lieberman, 1969; Reichard, Livson, & Peterson, 1962). Recent years have also seen the development of models that are conceptually recursive and focus on shifting cognitive and behavioral strategies that are employed in dealing with specific stressful or problematic life situations (Green, Wilson, & Lindy, 1985; Lazarus & Folkman, 1984). The growing shift in orientation toward coping as a "process" has resulted in changing emphasis from controlled laboratory studies for coping and stress to the use of naturalistic field studies and retrospective studies of survivors (Figley, 1983; Lazarus & Folkman, 1984).

The very consideration of a process that might exist horizontally as well as vertically through time has expanded the study of stress and coping. Diverse conceptualizations about salient dimensions of coping strategies have been put forth. Billings and Moos (1981) distinguished active behavioral, active cognitive, and avoidance-oriented strategies as the critical components, whereas Pearlin and Schooler (1978) differentiated coping strategies that change the situation, change the meaning of the situation, or control the stress of the situation. Folkman and Lazarus (1980) proposed a bidimensional formulation of coping based on problem- versus emotion-focused dimensions. Kahana, Kahana, and Young (1985) found evidence for a tripartite view of coping distinguishing instrumental, affective, and avoidance strategies.

Two approaches to the issues of stress and coping that are apparent in the literature offer differing views of the relationship between the environment (stressor) and the person (the one who copes). One emphasizes stability and the other emphasizes flexibility or change. McCrae (1984), Billings and Moos (1981), and others have focused on the consistency in coping strategies used by an individual over time and situations. Vaillant (1977) and McCrae (1984) have demonstrated that there is stability in coping traits across similar situations over time. Insufficient evidence, however, is available on the degree to which those preferred strategies are also consistent across a variety of situations.

An alternative approach has been espoused by Lazarus (1980) and his collaborators where the individual and the environment are seen to be in dynamic interaction through the psychological process of appraisal. In this framework, an environmental event is not defined as an objective stressor but implicated as a stressor only when so appraised by the individual (Appley & Trumbull, 1977). Accordingly, Lazarus (1980) distinguishes between potential stresses that are interpreted as (1) harm/loss, (2) threat, or (3) challenge. Harm/loss refers to damage that already occurred; threat refers to harm or loss that is anticipated; and challenge refers to that which is too difficult to attain but is a desirable form of environmental mastery.

As is often the case with divergent views on a common issue, neither position fully explains coping responses to stress, but both must be taken into consideration when attempting to understand the complexity involved. The adaptive strategies marshaled by the person may be seen, on the one hand as rooted in earlier types of adaptation and coping. On the other hand, coping strategies are also likely to represent responses to changing demands of the environment. Thus they may be viewed as having both traitlike and situation-specific components (Kahana & Kahana, 1983).

A major aim of this chapter is to review and analyze prevalent conceptual and empirical approaches to coping as they apply to conditions of extreme stress comprised of man-made disasters and their aftermath. Directions for future research are considered that will add to our understanding of the general dimensions of coping and help provide generalizations about the range and limits of human adaptability.

Development and utilization of a meaningful conceptual framework that incorporates behavioral and social science perspectives is necessary in attempts to understand the long-range effects of trauma on survivors and for understanding the ways survivors adapted to these experiences and to the poststress, conventional aspects of life. It is essential to go beyond the notion that trauma causes long-range irreparable damage (Chodoff, 1986). Accepting the notions advanced in the stress literature that the effect of stress is mediated through psychological processes, social resources, and coping strategies (Kahana & Kahana, 1983; Lazarus, Averil, & Opton, 1970; McGrath, 1970), it is useful to focus on the processes mediating the impact of extreme stress on a full range of outcomes.

Our analysis in this chapter will be limited to wartime conditions, to achieve greater clarity. We will use the context of the Holocaust to illustrate our arguments because of our ongoing research project (Kahana, Harel, Kahana, & Segal, 1987) focusing on Holocaust survivors. Nevertheless, we anticipate that many of our generalizations will extend to the broader area of traumatic stress research.

COPING UNDER CONDITIONS OF EXTREME STRESS

In recent years, coping has been examined under conditions of extreme or traumatic stress, such as natural disasters, combat, and the Holocaust (Figley, 1983; Goldberger & Breznitz, 1982). How applicable are conceptions developed in general stress research for the analysis and understanding of the impact of such extreme conditions? And how can the study of extreme stress help elucidate our understanding of human adaptability and responses to stress? Diverse terms have been used to refer to extremely stressful or traumatic conditions. A review of stress literature revealed at least seven different terms for similar environmental conditions. Words such as *extremity* (Davidson, 1980; DePres, 1976; Garfield, 1979), *extreme stress* (Baider & Sarell, 1984; Benner, Roskies, & Lazarus, 1980; Kahana, Kahana, & Harel, 1985), *massive stress* (Schmolling, 1984), *disaster* (Cleary & Houts, 1984; McCaughey, 1985), and *traumatic event* (Krystal, 1968; Terr, 1979) all refer to stress-provoking conditions that are described as qualitatively different from the normal or predictable stresses of life. They reflect "out-of-the-ordinary" demands on the individual. Porter (1979) and Cleary and Houts (1984), among others, argue that extreme conditions share some important distinguishing characteristics for which traditional models of coping are not particularly useful.

Expositions dealing with stress and coping typically consider stress as a continuum, varying only in degree of mastery required (Lazarus & Folkman, 1984; Wallace, 1956). Other literature, however, focuses on substantive differences between the two sets of conditions (Benner *et al.*, 1980; Torrance, 1965). Although some writers (Lazarus & Folkman, 1984) have delineated formal properties of situations that make them threatening or stressful, such general taxonomies do not always apply to examples of extreme stress, suggesting unique properties in these situations that set them apart from a continuum of "normal" stressors. Based on a careful review of previous work and our own research on survivors of the Holocaust, we have identified five aspects of extreme stress that delineate environmental conditions involving man-made disasters:

1. The total life experience is disrupted. Unlike a single stressful event that takes place against a backdrop of normal psychological and social functioning, these conditions replace the total fabric of normal life with a surrealistic existence, unanchored in familiar elements of reality.
2. The new environment is extremely hostile, threatening, and dangerous.
3. Opportunities to remove or act upon the stressor environment are severely limited.
4. There is no predictable end to the experience.
5. The pain and suffering associated with the experience appear to be meaningless and without rational explanation.

These five characteristics are not suggested as a universal definition. Rather, they are viewed as elements within a distinctive category of environmental conditions. The degree to which these characteristics have a cumulative and interactive effect in determining the intensity of the stress experience has yet to be explored. The literature does suggest to us, however, that all five characteristics tend to be present in most man-made traumatic events, such as war. The focus of our discussion is primarily on wartime conditions, although many of our generalizations apply to a broader range of extreme stress conditions.

These common elements can render environments universally stressful and serve to reduce individual differences in responses. Accordingly, conditions that overwhelm the adaptive capacities of victims may be seen as universal with little room for meaningful subjective differences in appraising the overall situation as stressful (Lifton, 1968).

COPING WITH EXTREME STRESS

Systematic efforts to understand behavior under conditions that tax the limits of human responsiveness require a nomothetic perspective that is enhanced by the development of taxonomies. At present, however, there are no explicit guidelines that even delimit the field of inquiry. There is a common implicit understanding, however, that these circumstances are so disruptive of normal life that they are perceived as extremely stressful by all who experience them. That is to say, individual variation in perception and appraisal in no way diminishes the dominance of the actual environment.

Within that broad context, however, individual variation in response does occur, and much research into conditions of extreme stress has focused on the types of coping strategies employed. In considering traditional conceptualizations of stress, there is an assumption that need gratification is typically within the individual's control. Thus it may be seen as far more functional to change one's undesirable environment in order to obtain gratification than to deny existing problems. In the case of extreme trauma, one cannot make this assumption. Both personal and environmental options in such circumstances are limited; hence, the demarcation between coping and defensive behavior may be blurred (Haan, 1982).

In situations involving ordinary stresses in the average exceptable environment of humans, one can anticipate that individual coping strategies will largely explain variance in outcomes. During extreme trauma, however, less of the variance in outcomes may be a function of personal coping strategies. Some observers have stressed the predominance of chance factors in survival and the fact that victims were totally powerless to influence their fate (Dimsdale, 1974). Others, like Frankl (1963), have emphasized the importance of the way in which victims of extreme stress interpreted the stress and the importance of finding some meaning in their suffering, even if it is beyond their control (Lifton, 1968).

In an attempt to delineate prevalent approaches to understanding coping during events or periods of great trauma and to illustrate the complex issues that must be addressed by research in this area, we will explore, in greater depth, coping by victims of the Holocaust, particularly those interned in concentration camps.

PERSPECTIVES FROM THE HOLOCAUST ON COPING WITH EXTREME STRESS

A review of the literature on coping with the extreme trauma of the Holocaust in the specific context of concentration camps reveals numerous efforts at describing coping under the most inhuman life circumstances (Chodoff, 1970; DePres, 1976; Dimsdale, 1980; Krystal, 1968; Levi, 1961; Wiesel, 1969). Torrance (1965) suggests that distinctive elements in extreme situations are the lack of conventional social structure, the loss of anchor in reality, and the lack of ability to predict or anticipate outcomes. This formulation also has its basis in the description of concentration camp conditions (Bettleheim, 1960) where individuals had little or no ability to anticipate and predict outcomes on a day-to-day basis. Although extensive states of physical degradation, deprivation, lack of food, extreme cold, and prolonged isolation were elements that characterized life in concentration camps and in some prisoner-of-war camps, an additional important factor was the absence of conventional social structure. In concentration camps and in other extreme conditions, conventional modes of behavior were rarely applicable, and the duration of the extreme situation was, in most instances, unpredictable. As a consequence, individuals in such situations were called upon to respond to conditions for which they were unprepared. At the same time, individuals in those circumstances were aware that failure to respond adequately held severe consequences for them, including the constant threat of death.

Levi (1961) eloquently describes the setting of the concentration camp as presenting an ultimate and evil experiment to test human adaptability. He argues that, in normal times and societies, laws and moral principles have a continuing influence on the scope of stress to which human beings might be exposed. These very laws and moral principles allow for meaningful distinctions between the good and the bad, the wise and the foolish, the cowardly and the courageous. In considering the Holocaust, where all principles of civilization were suspended and the average expectable human environment could not be assumed, social scientists cannot be guided by generally held assumptions about the nature of stress, modes of coping, or even basic motives of victims. Thus, although the will to live is generally assumed to be a "given" in considering human adaptation to stress and not subject to investigation, this motivation should not be overlooked with respect to victims of the Holocaust. The orientation to survival must be examined as an important motive, operative under conditions of extreme trauma, which is likely to override in importance other individual differences in the predisposition to respond (Frankl, 1963; Levi, 1961; Wiesel, 1969).

Furthermore, it is important to note, in considering current research on concentration camp survivors, that their memory of the various ways they coped in the Holocaust is limited by their very survival. Data on coping by those who did not succeed at the singular adaptive task of self-preservation and perished are limited to eyewitness accounts by survivors. Such accounts may provide valid data on observed behaviors of those who perished, but they can only offer speculations about cognitive and emotional states of those victims.

Although little systematic research has focused on coping strategies of Holocaust victims and survivors, there are strongly held beliefs and numerous accounts about patterns of coping with such trauma. Consideration of accounts regarding coping by those incarcerated in concentration camps presents a useful reminder of conceptual and operational difficulties in considering the full range of coping with extreme trauma. Table 1 presents a summary of coping strategies described by major researchers and writers who have studied survivors of the Holocaust. For the sake of reducing

Table 1. Literature-Based Accounts of Coping in Concentration Camps

Reference	Accounts of coping
Bettelheim, B. (1943)	Depersonalization, identification with the aggressor
Frankl, V. (1963)	Differential focus on the good, survival for a purpose
Krystal, H. (1968)	Initial shock reaction (depersonalization), imitation of persecutors, "robotization" (numbness), denial
Chodoff, P. (1970)	Regression, identification, denial, isolation of affect, some companionship (friendship), daydreams of revenge, irritable behavior toward other inmates
DesPres, T. (1976)	Will to live, split between self as victim and self as observer, suicide, stealing, smuggling items into the camp, sabotage, giving and sharing, focusing on day-to-day survival
Benner, P., Roskies, E., & Lazarus, R. S. (1980)	Detachment (depesonalization via emotional numbing), attention shift, defense mechanisms: denial, projection, exercising choices
Dimsdale, J. E. (1980)	Differential focus on the good, survival for some purpose, psychological removal, mastery, will to live, hope (active and passive), group affiliation, regressive behavior, null coping: fatalism, anticoping: surrender to stress
Klein, H. (1980)	Creating a "new family" of buddies to share attitudes toward Nazis and to share basic necessities
Eitinger, L. (1983)	Denial, emotional numbing, making some decisions
Schmolling, P. (1984)	Rage, denial, selective perception, emotional detachment, narrowed focus of attention, belief in God, hope for survival, identification with the aggressor (Kapos), development of support groups (friendships)

complexity, accounts also are limited to those of coping in concentration camps.

Bettleheim (1943) was one of the first psychologists to articulate views based on his personal experiences. He notes stages of intellectual withdrawal that characterized inmates of slave labor camps. Early reports of coping tended to isolate specific strategies such as depersonalization (Bettleheim, 1943) or finding meaning in the suffering (Frankl, 1963). The most common strategies described represent forms of cognitive restructuring and a suppression of affective strategies. This is in contrast to the prevalence of instrumental strategies generally reported in accounts dealing with less extreme trauma. The meaning of escape/avoidance coping strategies appear to be altered in the case of victims of extreme war trauma such as the Holocaust. Efforts to escape harm served a highly "instrumental" form of adaptation during this traumatic period. In a less extreme environment, coping by escape or avoidance is generally thought to be maladaptive.

Given the presence of all five conditions of extreme stress noted before, it is not surprising that similar coping strategies have been associated with both physical and psychological survival in prisoner-of-war camps (Nardini, 1952). These include a focus of energies on the present, an ability to retain hope in the face of hardship, a great will to live, a sharp sense of identity and self-respect, and an ability to overcome emotions of hostility and depression.

Reports of coping during the Holocaust generally do not separate the basic drives and motives of victims (i.e., will to live) from cognitive appraisals or maneuvers (i.e., "What could I do? There were guards watching us all the time") or from specific instances of coping behavior (i.e., running away). A perusal of coping techniques reveals considerable overlap from one published report to another. At the same time, it also reveals that there is lack of clarity in units of analysis being discussed. It should be noted that inferred motives and cognitive processes are sometimes confounded with observable behaviors.

Table 2 represents an effort by the present authors to organize modes of coping observed among inmates of concentration camps and described by survivors. It distinguishes motives and orientations to survival from intrapsychic responses (cognitive and emotional) and from observable behaviors.

In the model presented, there is also an effort to distinguish general behavioral orientation in relation to inmates' major reference groups: the persecutors and fellow victims. Furthermore, it is possible to note distinctions between more enduring behavioral coping constellations that may describe characteristic modes of responding by a given inmate (e.g., altruism) from specific actions (e.g., stealing food). Although one cannot make clear connections between specific cognitive maneuvers or cognitive orientations and behavior, it is apparent that certain cognitive appraisals and maneuvers are more likely to lead to given behavioral outcomes than others.

In considering specific concrete coping behaviors in the concentration camp, survivors often indicated that such behaviors were almost reflexive or instinctual ways of coping with imminent stress (e.g., duck the firing squad). Our analyses of accounts of such behaviors suggest that they have often been omitted from survivor accounts of coping because they represented almost universal coping efforts directed at self-preservation among those who had a will to live. The broader behavioral units reported by researchers in this area are more likely to represent conscious efforts at problem-focused coping.

The model presented in Table 2 aims to introduce greater conceptual clarity into the classification of coping with extreme stress. Nevertheless, it is recognized that it still oversimplifies complexities involved in the coping process. In responding to extreme stress, the literature provides lists of coping strategies (DesPres, 1976; Dimsdale, 1974; Nardini, 1952; Rose, 1986; Schmolling, 1984), usually not organized by function or type. Our

Table 2. Elements of Coping: Motives, Intrapsychic Responses, and Coping Behaviors in Concentration Camps

Motivations/ orientations	Intrapsychic responses, cognitive/emotional	Observable coping behavior
No will to live	Acquiescence	Suicide
	Surrender to stress	Null behavior
	Fatalism	
	Emotional numbing	
	Death wish	
	Psychological removal and detachment	
	Denial	
	Regression	
Will to live	Focus on day-to-day survival	Self-preservation behaviors
To bear witness	Hope	Compliance with persecutors
To save self	Split between self as victim and self as spectator	Active compliance
To destroy persecutors	Daydreams of revenge	Passive compliance
To serve God	Differential focus on good	Attempts to negotiate and gain favor of persecutor
	Hope for Messiah	Solicitation of aid from persecutors
		Active identification with aggressor (Kapo)
		Manipulates/outwits system, persecutors
		Feigning insanity/death
		Smuggling
		Feigning compliance
		Stealing
		Bribery
		Escape
		Retaliation/resistance
		Sabotage
		Altruistic behavior
		Shares rations and resources
		Takes risks for others
		Integration/affiliation
		Friendship formation
		Mutual support group
		Creates family of buddies
		Aggression
		Steals from other inmates
		Lashes out against inmates

model attempts to provide a clearer classification scheme for documenting the range of specific coping responses under conditions of extreme stress. In order to appreciate the multidimensional nature of coping, we will now call attention to the added patterning provided by a temporal dimension including interactive or dynamic qualities of the coping process and layering of trauma.

Dynamism has been exemplified in the extreme stress literature on two different dimensions: (1) temporal, and (2) interactional. There appears to be support for considering change over time in coping strategies employed during periods of extreme trauma. A review of recent research suggests that there are at least two experiential phases (Bastiaans, 1982; DesPres, 1976; Krystal, 1968; Rose, 1986) under conditions of extreme stress: an initial reaction period followed by a period of adaptation to the demands of the stress condition. The initial phase, usually of short duration, is characterized by shock or disbelief with attendant coping strategies that protect the individual by blocking out the enormity of the threat. Strategies such as depersonalization, forms of dissociation (Bastiaans, 1982; Krystal, 1968; Lifton, 1968; Rose, 1986) and denial (Schmolling, 1984; Terr, 1979) are such protective defenses. Instrumental or activity strategies are not typically employed during this phase. The second phase appears to allow far more diversity of response as the individual either continues to deny the external demands or begins to engage the environment in a number of specific, perhaps more idiosyncratic ways, such as through emotional numbing (Eitinger, 1983; Krystal, 1968), selective perception, identification with the aggressor (Schmolling, 1984; Rose, 1986), forming friendships (Cleary & Houts, 1984; Chodoff, 1970; Klein, 1980), exercising a will to live (DesPres, 1976; Dimsdale, 1980) and/or other techniques designed to enhance life itself.

DesPres (1976) addresses this temporal issue in coping with the trauma of "extremity." He outlines an initial stage of immobilization followed by integration and recovery into stable selfhood during a second phase. He argues that successful survivors of extremity move from withdrawal to engagement and from passivity to resistance. A similar scheme was proposed by Chodoff (1986) who argues that inmates of concentration camps experienced shock and terror upon arrival, followed by a stage of apathy, and finally evolving into more active efforts at coping and self-preservation. It is noteworthy that most of the coping behaviors represented in Table 2 reflect some form of active engagement. Thus, it is possible that all or most victims went through an initial immobilized phase, but accounts of coping among survivors focus only on the second phase of resolution. One difference between those who "drowned" and those who survived may have been the ability to move beyond the state of collapse or immobilization and marshall their resources toward some form of active mastery. This generalization must, of course, be tempered by the recognition that many of those who have demonstrated such active mastery may have also perished.

The interactional dimensions of coping have been presented in the literature in two different forms: (1) coping as a mediator between a specific situational stressor and an outcome (Kahana, Kahana, & Young, 1985) and (2) coping as a transactional process involving ongoing reassessment of the nature of the situational stressor and one's behavioral response to it

(Lazarus & Folkman, 1984). Despite the differences between them, in both forms, coping is seen as a dynamic response to a specific environmental situation in an effort to reduce the stress from that source.

Piaget's (1937) theoretical framework of assimilation and accommodation may be particularly useful for considering interactional aspects of coping. It is likely that coping with stress represents a regularly changing process with constant feedback to the respondent regarding the efficacy of his or her coping responses. In each response sequence, stressors are reappraised as are the outcomes of given coping responses, and the individual confronting the stress or trauma employs revised or unrevised modes of coping with the continuing stress situation. During the Holocaust, this normal process was strained to the limits as stress was unrelenting and the efficacy of any coping response could at best be minimally successful.

Situations involving extreme trauma pose threats to the individual on multiple levels. Because the context does not permit the usual patterns of meeting one's basic needs, survival issues are a primary concern. In addition, however, the individual must deal with his or her emotional reaction to the new and dangerous situation from which there is no immediate escape activating feelings about self, about loss, and about the threatening conditions of life. Both issues are basic to human existence and both are under assault at the most fundamental level.

In short, under such traumatic conditions, the nature of the demand on the individual appears more pervasive, more central to psychological and physical survival, than is the case in normal life, and nothing in the pretraumatic order of things can be assumed any longer. The individual is faced with extremely stressful specific situations under extremely stressful general life conditions. Such layering of trauma is quite unlike the more typical stresses of normal living, and these extreme conditions allow for no periods of respite from the incessant demand for vigilance.

Strategies of coping with extreme stress must concern both the magnitude and depth of the disruption in the lives of the victims as well as specific stressful demands. Pearlin and Schooler (1978) suggest that coping strategies can be clustered according to three functions they serve: (1) changing the situation, (2) changing the meaning of the situation, and (3) controlling the stress (or negative emotional impact) of the situation. Despite the fact that they were developed for normal life stressors, these categories are suggestive for extreme stress conditions as well. By definition, a victim cannot impact on the nature of the trauma or extreme stress condition. But if one shifts from addressing life conditions at the macrolevel of trauma (e.g. nuclear bomb, Holocaust, guerilla warfare) to specific situations at the microlevel (e.g., hunger, extreme fatigue), some opportunities for limiting or controlling the stress do exist. Coping strategies of selective perception, physical escape, or stealing serve this purpose of minimizing specific aspects of the stress.

Changing the meaning of a situation, usually referred to as "cognitive restructuring," also provides a way of managing in very difficult circumstances. For example, when starvation threatens life, food is often redefined to include things previously inedible, such as grass, tree bark, or insects. Under conditions of forced labor, some jobs come to be viewed as "good" despite the fact that the total context is one of extremely harsh working conditions. Finally, controlling one's emotional reaction to the overwhelming experience is achieved by strategies such as emotional numbing or depersonalization, denial, or isolation of affect.

To the extent that the extremely stressful condition continues for a period of time (such as in combat or in a concentration camp), it appears that coping can take place on the level of more pervasive life conditions as well as in narrowly circumscribed situations (Schmolling, 1984). The human striving for homeostasis extends to a need for the social system and the specific situation in which one is engaged to be orderly and predictable. Schmolling (1984), DesPres (1976), and others have described the searching activities of concentration camp victims for predictable patterns of behavior among those who control the environment. With predictability, there comes some sense of personal control and a reduction in stress (Benner *et al.,* 1980). Schmolling (1984) calls this process "adjustment," which is distinguishable from specific coping strategies of a problem-solving nature.

It should be noted, however, that under conditions of extreme stress, what constitutes the specific stressful situation (or environmental stressor) may become indistinguishable from more general conditions. For example, for a prisoner in the concentration camps, intense hunger was an unending stressor. On one occasion, the response might be to steal potato peelings, at another time to accept a bit of bread from another prisoner, and at yet another time to discuss recipes with others in order to distract oneself from the physical pain. Successful coping actions (that is, obtaining some food) under conditions of such intense deprivation do not reduce the chronic stress, although they may help to preserve life. This is clearly different from coping with normal life events where the efficacy of actions can be more clearly assessed and the trauma is compartmentalized.

SEQUELAE OF EXTREME STRESS

There is general agreement that individuals exposed to situations of extreme stress of trauma suffer diverse short and long-term negative physical and mental health consequences, including, for some, alterations in their basic character structure (Green *et al.,* 1985). Although some research has been concerned with pretraumatic factors interacting with impact of the trauma (Melick, Logue, & Frederick, 1982), the focus of the literature has been on negative psychosocial sequelae of the trauma. Much of the research focusing on the adverse consequences of such trauma has been anchored in the medical and psychiatric literature and is based on populations of survivors seeking assistance for problems that were likely results of their traumatic experiences. The clinical diagnostic category of "post-traumatic stress disorder" (PTSD) defined by the American Psychiatric Association in 1980 is the result of considerable clinical attention to the continued debilitating impact on many who experienced conditions of extreme stress.

Little effort has been directed at understanding the wide range of consequences that are evident within populations of individuals who shared such traumatic episodes. Not all survivors of the concentration camps nor all veterans of the Vietnam War developed PTSD. Even among those whose problems fit that diagnostic category, not all manifested their disorder to the same degree or intensity. This great diversity in the impact of extreme stress has had little attention paid to it among researchers in the field.

Results from our study of more than 300 Holocaust survivors and a comparison group reveal discernible mental health effects on survivors, who were found to portray significantly more mental health symptomatology on the SCL 90 than did controls (Kahana, Kahana, & Harel, 1985). Of special interest, however, is the great overlap in patterns observed between survivors and controls, indicating remarkable intactness among some survivors in spite of the trauma they endured.

Development and utilization of a meaningful conceptual framework that incorporates behavioral and social science perspectives is necessary in attempts to understand the long-range effects of trauma on survivors and for understanding the ways survivors dealt with their stressful experiences and adjusted to the post-stress conventional aspects of life. In seeking a better understanding of sequelae of extreme stress, it may be useful to consider how individual differences in coping affect post-traumatic outcomes. Just as we might expect that trauma would alter an individual's fundamental modes of coping, it is also likely that coping can change the impact of trauma. In addition, consideration of the long-term sequelae of extreme stress in a life-span developmental framework must also acknowledge roles played by the aging process itself in relation to both coping and outcomes.

There appears to be ample documentation for the importance of coping strategies in dealing with stressful conditions. However, to date, there has been little effort to ascertain the role of coping strategies in survivors' attempts to adjust to the conventional aspects of life once the trauma is past. In addition, further work is needed to specify adaptive tasks in the immediate and in the long-term aftermath of the trauma. Our ongoing study of Holocaust survivors (Kahana, Harel, Kahana, & Segal, 1987) represents an important effort in this direction. Based on this research, we have been able to identify adaptive tasks and modes of coping not only during the period of trauma but also in its short- and long-term aftermaths.

CHARACTERISTICS AND RANGE OF POST-TRAUMATIC STRESSORS

The range of stressors as well as relevant categorizations of coping in the aftermath of extreme stress of war situations is presented in Table 3. As indicated, the survivor of extreme trauma is coping with a multiplicity of stressors at any given time, and researchers must be careful in considering the adaptive context and adaptive tasks of the survivor in interpreting his or her coping responses.

Specific aspects of the war or trauma and the survivor's experiences during the traumatic period represent basic and continuous stimuli shaping post-traumatic experiences and coping. For the Holocaust survivor, differential influences may be present for those who spent time in concentration camps or in hiding, whereas the World War II veteran who survived Pearl Harbor may deal with different traces of trauma from the one who participated in the invasion of Normandy.

A second related but distinct stress is represented by the memories of trauma that represent varying degrees of intrusiveness for different survivors (Horowitz, 1986). Our own data indicate that the vast majority of

Table 3. Paradigm for Study of Long-Term Adaptation of Victims of Extreme Trauma

Range of post-traumatic stressors	Coping with stress and resolution of trauma	Outcomes
Diverse aspects of war or traumatic stress	Psychotherapy	Physical health
Continued stress posed by intrusive memories of trauma	Self-disclosure	Mental health/psychiatric symptoms
Post-traumatic life stresses brought on by or related to survivorship	Denial-avoidance of trauma	Social functioning
Life stresses or events unrelated to trauma	Affiliation with other victims	Achievements
Normative developmental tasks creating stress (aging)	Finding meaning in survivorship	Competent coping
	Activism on behalf of other victims	Personality
	Hypervigilance	
	Altruism	
	Efforts to reduce probability of future trauma	
	Differential use of specific coping strategies a. Instrumental b. Escape/avoidance c. Affective coping	

Holocaust survivors interviewed 40 years after the trauma think of their experiences almost daily, have vivid and intrusive memories, and experience frequent dreams involving themes of threat. At the same time, we found important individual differences in intrusiveness, vividness, and frequency of traumatic memories. A third stress factor for survivors of trauma is represented by post-traumatic experiences that may be a direct or indirect consequence of the trauma itself. Thus, for example, Holocaust survivors could generally not return to their country of origin and became immigrants to the United States or to Israel. This immigrant status brought with it new stresses and adaptive tasks (Shuval, 1982). In the case of the Vietnam War veterans, the rejection of their experience by their countrymen became a source of new and enduring trauma (Wilson & Krauss, 1985).

It also must be recognized that survivors had to cope with multiple life events and stressors potentially unrelated to the trauma. Furthermore, they had to face normal developmental tasks of the aging process, such as retirement or widowhood that were likely to pose additional stress. Nevertheless, it is important to note that enduring responses to the original trauma often exaggerate responses to new stressful situations. Moreover, motivational states, perceptual styles, cognitive maneuvers, and coping behaviors that were once appropriate during a great trauma may be repeatedly applied to far more minor stress situations, resulting in negative adaptational outcomes based on responses to old trauma inappropriately applied in a new stress situation.

COPING IN THE AFTERMATH OF TRAUMA

In considering post-traumatic adaptation of survivors of extreme trauma, our data reveal that the enduring response appears to be continued perception of threat in the environment. To a great extent, these persons are confronted by the need to remain vigilant as every new situation is seen as harboring a potential threat. The threat for the survivor is very specific and major; it is not just a threat to competence, status, or happiness. Typically, it is perceived as endangering the psychological survival of self or of loved ones. Such threats may be real but, in objective terms, have extremely low probability of occurrence. Yet to the survivor there may be little distinction between the possible and the probable. If we place survivors' responses in the framework of Selye's (1974) stress paradigm, there is forever the recurrence of "alarm," "mobilization," and, after the threat is over, the inevitable "exhaustion" created by the great effort to cope that often results in "diseases of adaptation."

Thus a major challenge for stress research concerned with post-traumatic adaptation is to focus not only on how survivors confront actual stressful life events but how they might generate, perceive, and cope with "threat" in their environment. Intervention efforts with victims of trauma may be directed not only at the enhancement of coping responses but also at the reappraisal of situations which may pose a threat.

Avoidance and vigilance represent a major thrust in studies of stress and coping (Cohen & Lazarus, 1973). Vigilant individuals tend to be hyperalert to threats in their environment, whereas avoidant ones are likely to deny such threats (Breznitz, 1983). Generally, this tendency toward vigilance or avoidance is considered as a trait (Laux & Vossel, 1982). However, in an interactionist framework, it is possible to view vigilance or avoidance as being in itself a function of dynamic interactions with the environment. For survivors of massive trauma, vigilance or denial may both have been adaptive in the traumatic environment. Yet during the post-traumatic period, such responses may no longer serve a useful function but are difficult to unlearn (Wilson, in press).

The transactional approach, however, also holds hope for change. One goal of therapy would be to replace less effective modes of coping and appraisals with more adaptive ones. Thus, psychotherapy or the healing forces of time may be seen as modifying maladaptive vigilant or avoidant modes of coping in the post-trauma environment. Research based on an interactionist framework also needs to examine the match or appropriateness of the coping response to the adaptive tasks being confronted (Wilson, Smith, & Johnson, 1985).

The post-traumatic healing process may also be profitably considered in a stress-coping paradigm. The person's cognitive maneuvers and behaviors directed at dealing with the enduring stresses and adaptive tasks of post-trauma help clarify adaptational outcomes for survivors.

Positive affect and mental health in the aftermath of trauma have been found to be best predicted by late-life response patterns of self-disclosure, finding meaning in survivorship and altruism (Kahana, Harel, Kahana, & Segal, 1987). The range of relevant coping efforts and approaches to resolution of trauma are outlined in Table 3. They include (1) efforts at interpreting the meaning of trauma, (2) efforts at processing intrusive memories of trauma, (3) efforts at structuring the perceptions of threat, and (4) efforts to diminish inappropriate coping in the poststress situation. Future research in the area of post-traumatic stress should explicitly address coping by survivors not only in relation to old and new life stresses but also in relation to the psychosocial aftermath of the trauma.

ADAPTATIONAL OUTCOMES

In considering post-traumatic outcomes among survivors, the literature has generally focused on physical and mental health problems and in particular on psychiatric symptomatology (Eitinger, 1983; Krystal, 1968). Relatively little attention has been paid to the full range of positive and negative outcomes observable in nonclinical populations of survivors.

If we consider post-traumatic coping of survivors, the use of a life-cycle, developmental perspective also permits us to focus on the positive concomitants of survivorship. Life-cycle theorists anchored in ego psychology, such as Erik Erikson (1963), have called attention to the gradual accumulation of personal coping resources over a person's life. Successful resolution of each developmental crisis, in this view, leads to coping resources that may be mobilized dealing with subsequent crises. Thus it may be anticipated that successful resolution of developmental crises leads to a sense of efficacy and ego integrity in late life (Moos & Billings, 1982; Wilson, 1980).

Utilizing this view, it may be useful for researchers on post-traumatic coping to consider the survivor's mastery of prior extreme trauma as a coping resource that enhances a sense of competence and may lead to the perception of potential stressors as less threatening. Survivors may thus use reality-oriented coping responses that in Haan's (1977) framework involve purpose, choice, flexibility, and adherence to logic. Indeed, there appears to be evidence that Holocaust survivors cope in this competent manner with day-to-day problem situations, especially those that do not involve threat to health or survival.

Research on post-traumatic coping of survivors affords social and behavioral scientists a major opportunity for considering differential effects of stress on enhancing or undermining efficacy of coping. Indeed, extreme stress may selectively do both. Hence, the survivor may be condemned to doing battle with ghosts of the trauma endured, rehearsing them in his or her nightmares, and confronting them time and again in face of a minor illness or slippery roadway. At the same time, he or she may portray both ego strength and competence in his or her job or in navigating through bureaucracies that may render the average person helpless and incompetent.

Accounts of adaptation by Holocaust survivors have often noted compensatory efforts by these individuals to obtain material possessions or to "climb the ladder of success" as a means of making up for losses sustained or for an inner sense of emptiness. Such allegations in our view represent unfortunate examples of blaming the victim. The psychiatric literature frequently offers descriptions of Holocaust survivors as "outwardly successful businessmen who are haunted by dark memories of the concentration camp and fantasies of destruction" (Niederland, 1968). Such individuals may alternatively be viewed as people who, despite "dark memories of the concentration camp" became highly successful and functioning members of society. For the survivor, traditional indexes of ascribed status such as education, occupation, or socioeconomic status must be considered as outcomes of adaptation rather than predisposing antecedent variables. It is for these reasons that researchers may legitimately consider post-traumatic occupational, financial, and personal achievements as valid outcome variables to be considered alongside traditional health and mental health indicators.

DIRECTIONS FOR FUTURE RESEARCH

In considering the directions suggested by previous work on coping with extreme stress, one might usefully employ the "stress" paradigm presented in Table 4 as we begin to address the major challenges of tomorrow. Table 4 summarizes some of the major conceptual, definitional, and measurement issues to be addressed in future research in this area. Most of

Table 4. Issues to Be Addressed in Research on Coping with Extreme Stress

Assessment of stress

Scope of stressor: broad or narrow, modifiability, degree of threat to life, room for appraisal versus universal perception of trauma, secondary stresses created by trauma, intrusiveness of memories of trauma

Context of stress

Time frame
  Pretrauma, trauma, immediate post-trauma, long-term post-trauma
Environment
Culture
History

Motivation/arousal

Will to live, survival as overriding motive, arousal/hyperarousal, interpretation of threat

Coping

Type, range, flexibility, appropriateness, traitlike versus situation-specific, problem versus emotion-focused
Process
  Time, transactional

Coping resources

Ego-strength, physical stamina, social supports, chance factors

Outcomes

Physical health, mental health, personality, coping, achievements, social functioning, adjustment of aging these issues have been implicitly or explicitly addressed in this chapter. Earlier in this chapter the question was raised about the applicability of concepts developed in general stress research for the understanding of extreme stress. Answers to that question are likely to come primarily from future research. Our attempt has been to highlight themes in the literature on coping with extreme stress that appear to point to possible directions for future research.

Issues in Defining Stress

As a first step, we must continue to strive for greater conceptional and definitional clarity to guide our empirical efforts. It is not likely that we can resolve ambiguities in the stress paradigm, nor is it clear that it would be an advantage to arrive at a consensus wherein stress is always discussed in "stimulus" (Holmes & Rahe, 1967) or in "response terms" (Appley & Trumbull, 1977). Nevertheless, it is critical that definitions and limitations of stress, coping, or outcomes always be made clear so that generalization may be limited to the parameters considered in any given research project.

Accordingly, the scope of stress may be defined as related to a broad set of events (e.g., Holocaust or prisoner-of-war camps) or to specific problem situations being confronted in a particular context (e.g., dealing with the problem of hunger). Similarly, in considering post-traumatic stress, the singular or multiple stressors confronted by survivors must be made explicit, and efforts must be made to consider coping in the context of relevant stressors (Elder & Clipp, Chapter 6 in this volume). To the extent possible, subjective definitions of stress should be ascertained separately. Assumptions should not be made by investigators that coping is directed at a specific stress resulting from some aspect of the trauma.

Contextual Issues

In order to fully understand the nature of stress and the appropriateness and potential efficacy of diverse coping efforts to deal with the stress, contextual factors must be taken into account. Adaptive tasks, motivational factors, coping resources, and strategies must be defined and evaluated in the context of pretraumatic, traumatic or post-traumatic periods. Furthermore, generalizations based on research dealing with a given time frame must be applied with great care to another period.

Whether conditions of extreme stress lie along a continuum of stressful life events or represent unique demands on the individual has profound implications for the study of adaptation and coping. If, as we have suggested, extreme stress represents a distinctive set of environmental conditions, we need to have a better understanding of what those parameters are. For example, given coping behavior such as focusing only on day-to-day issues might be understood alternatively as a strategy to adapt to the unpredictable duration of war or to the total absence of familiar elements of pretraumatic reality.

The environmental context must also be addressed, considering coping with extreme stress and its sequelae. Thus, for example, victims of the Holocaust who were confined to the Ghetto, those in concentration camps, those in hiding or with the resistance, were all likely to face different constraints on their coping, and the same strategies were likely to differ in outcomes yielded.

In comparing responses to the Coping Scale by U.S. and Israeli survivors and the respective comparison groups, we gain useful insight about influences of cultural and historical context superimposed on survivorship. Thus it was found that survivorship played a major role in the use of escape-avoidance and of emotional coping responses with survivors in both countries, using more avoidance and emotional strategies than controls. In the case of instrumental coping strategies, however, survivorship did not prove to be an important antecedent, whereas the U.S. versus Israeli cultural/historical background did. Both survivors and controls living in the United States were significantly more likely to employ instrumental coping strategies than were their Israeli counterparts. It was also interesting to note in terms of specific coping items that survivors showed greater risk taking than did controls, whereas U.S. respondents were more likely to turn to religion than were Israelis.

Conceptualizing and Measuring the Coping Process

Methods and approaches to the assessment of coping with extreme trauma are closely linked to conceptual clarity that could be attained in research in this area. Formal research on coping strategies has generally been based on the endorsement of a list of diverse strategies by respondents. Such lists yield a profile of emotion-focused and problem-focused responses that respondents are likely to use in a real or hypothetical problem situation. Although this genre of research has generated some useful findings across diverse problem situations, it also poses much conceptual ambiguity for our understanding of coping responses.

Although conceptualizations of stress and coping generally distinguish actions, feelings, and cognitions in response to stressors, coping scales generally elicit a mixture of these response levels. Researchers working with the survivors of extreme trauma must be particularly concerned with respondents' ability to recall feelings and cognitions of long ago and need to be especially sensitive to their general reluctance to discuss the painful and distressing aspects of their experiences.

The literature on coping strategies generally seeks to identify coping responses that are related to reduction of the adverse effects of stress. It has been recognized (Pearlin, 1975) that the range of coping responses and flexibility of coping strategies may actually play a greater role in affecting positive outcomes than use of specific strategies. Future research on coping among survivors of trauma needs to develop more appropriate measurement strategies for considering this important dimension of the coping response. A particularly useful and challenging area lies in assessing the appropriateness of coping strategies in relation to the demands of the situation. Assessing the persistence of *trauma-specific* strategies in the post-traumatic phase of survivors' life experience would have particularly strong heuristic value, especially if they were found to aid healthy adaptation in life-course development.

Studies of older persons who have undergone experiences of extreme stress also afford unusual opportunities for exploring the universal nature of certain adjustments to the aging process put forth in the gerontological literature. Thus, for example, the life review has been suggested to be a generalized psychological mechanism for older persons, especially as they approach death (Butler, 1974; Marshall, 1980). It may be argued that the meaning of reminiscence and life review would be substantially affected in the case of older persons who underwent extreme psychic trauma during earlier points in their lives. Thus it may be anticipated that reminiscence would not provide the same type of psychological outlet to survivors as it does to less highly stressed groups. This may result in a search for alternative modes of adjustment to late life and even an inability to accept the aging process.

For survivors of extreme stress, normal corollaries of the aging process, increasing dependency, and a need to give up social roles in the areas of work and family may pose especially difficult adaptive tasks. There are certain parallels about the frailty, vulnerability, and dependency of late life that may awaken memories of threats of extermination under the most inhumane of circumstances. To the extent that achievement, engagement, and mastery symbolize survival to these victims, we may anticipate special problems in adapting to retirement, bereavement, illness, or disability. Alternatively, for some survivors, techniques and adaptations developed in the face of traumatic experiences such as the Holocaust may serve as useful coping mechanisms as they confront the aging process.

REFERENCES

Appley, M. H., & Trumbull, R. (1977). On the concept of psychological stress. In A. Monat & R. S. Lazarus (Eds.), *Stress and coping: Anthology* (pp. 58–66). New York: Columbia University Press.

Baider, L., & Sarell, M. (1984). Coping with cancer among Holocaust survivors in Israel: An exploratory study. *Journal of Human Stress, 10,* 3, 121–127.

Bastiaans, J. (1982). Consequences of modern terrorism. In L. Goldberger & S. Breznitz (Eds.), *Handbook of stress* (pp. 664–655). New York: The Free Press.

Benner, P., Roskies, E., & Lazarus, R. S. (1980). Stress and coping under extreme conditions. In J. Dimsdale (Ed.), *Survivors, victims, and perpetrators* (pp. 219–258). Washington, DC: Hemisphere.

Bettleheim, B. (1943). Individual and mass behavior in extreme situations. *Journal of Abnormal Social Psychology, 38,* 417–452.

Bettleheim, B. (1960). *The informed heart: Autonomy in a mass age.* New York: The Free Press.

Billings, A. G., & Moos, R. H. (1981). The role of coping responses and social resources in attenuating the stress of life events. *Journal of Behavioral Medicine, 4,* 2.

Breznitz, S. (Ed.). (1983). *The denial of stress.* New York: International Universities Press, Inc.

Butler, R. N. (1974). Successful aging and the role of the life review. *Journal of American Geriatric Society, 22,* 529–535.

Cannon, W. B. (1939). *The wisdom of the body.* New York: Norton.

Chodoff, P. (1970). Psychological responses to concentration camp survival. In H. Abram (Ed.), *Psychological aspects of stress* (pp. 44–61). Springfield, IL: Thomas.

Chodoff, P. (1986). Survivors of the Nazi Holocaust. In R. H. Moos (Ed.), *Coping with life crisis: An integrated approach* (pp. 407–414). New York: Plenum Press.

Cleary, P. D., & Houts, P. S. (1984). The psychological impact of the Three Mile Island incident. *Journal of Human Stress, 10,* 28–34.

Cohen, F., & Lazarus, R. S. (1973). Active coping processes, dispositions, and recovery from surgery. *Psychosomatic Medicine, 35,* 375–389.

Davidson, S. (1980). Human reciprocity among the Jewish prisoners in the Nazi concentration camps. In *The Nazi concentration camps* (pp. 555–572). Jerusalem: Yad Vashem.

DesPres, T. (1976). *The survivor.* New York: Oxford University Press.

Dimsdale, J. E. (1974). The coping behavior of Nazi concentration camp survivors. *American Journal of Psychiatry, 131,* 792–797.

Dimsdale, J. E. (1980). The coping behavior of Nazi concentration camp survivors. In J. E. Dimsdale (Ed.), *Survivors, victims and perpetrators* (pp. 163–174). Washington, DC: Hemisphere.

Eitinger, L. (1983). Denial in concentration camps: Some personal observations on the positive and negative functions of denial in extreme life situations. In S. Breznitz (Ed.), *The denial of stress* (pp. 199–212). New York: International Universities Press.

Erikson, E. H. (1963). *Childhood and society* (2nd ed.). New York: Norton.

Figley, C. R. (1983). Catastrophes: An overview of family reactions. In C. R. Figley & H. I. McCubbin (Eds.), *Stress and the family* (pp. 3–20). New York: Brunner/Mazel.

Folkman, S., & Lazarus, R. S. (1980). An analysis of coping in a middle-aged community sample. *Journal of Health and Social Behavior, 21,* 219–239.

Frankl, V. (1963). *Man's search for meaning.* New York: Washington Square Press.

Garfield, C. A. (1979). On life in extremity: Psychosocial elements of survival. In C. A. Garfield (Ed.), *Stress and survival: The emotional realities of life-threatening illness* (pp. 3–7). St. Louis: C. Mosby Company.

Goldberger, L., & Breznitz, S. (Eds.). (1982). *Handbook of stress.* New York: Free Press.

Green, B. L., Wilson, J. P., & Lindy, J. D. (1985). Conceptualizing post-traumatic stress disorder: A psychosocial framework. In C. R. Figley (Ed.), *Trauma and its wake: The study and treatment of post-traumatic stress disorder* (pp. 53–69). New York: Brunner/Mazel.

Haan, N. (1977). *Coping and defending: Processes of self-environment organization.* New York: Academic Press.

Haan, N. (1982). The assessment of coping, defense, and stress. In L. Goldberger & S. Breznitz (Eds.), *Handbook of stress: Theoretical and clinical aspects* (pp. 254–269). New York: Free Press.

Holmes, T., & Rahe, R. (1967). The social readjustment rating scale. *Journal of Psychosomatic Research, 11,* 219–225.

Horowitz, M. J. (1986). *Stress response syndromes* (2nd ed.). New York: Jason Aronson.

Kahana, B., & Kahana, E. (1983). Stress reactions. In P. Lewinsohn & L. Teri (Eds.), *Clinical geropsychology* (pp. 139–169). New York: Pergamon Press.

Kahana, B., Kahana, E., & Harel, Z. (1985). *Finding meaning in adversity—Lessons from the Holocaust.* Presentation at Gerontological Society of America Meeting, Chicago.

Kahana, B., Kahana, E., & Young, R. (1985). Social factors in institutional living. In W. Peterson & J. Quadagno (Eds.), *Social bonds in later life: Aging and interdependence* (pp. 389–418). Beverly Hills, CA: Sage.

Kahana, B., Harel, Z., Kahana, E., & Segal, M. (1987). The victim as helper—Prosocial behavior during the Holocaust. *Humbold Journal of Social Relations,* 357–373.

Klein, H. (1980). The survivors' search for meaning and identity. In *The Nazi concentration camps* (pp. 543–553). Jerusalem: Yad Vashem.

Krystal, H. (1968). *Massive psychic trauma.* New York: International Universities Press.

Laux, L., & Vossel, G. (1982). Paradigms in stress research: Laboratory versus field and traits versus processes. In L. Goldberger & S. Breznitz (Eds.), *Handbook of stress* (pp. 203–211). New York: Free Press.

Lazarus, R. S. (1980). The stress and coping paradigm. In L. A. Bond & J. C. Rosen (Eds.), *Competence and coping during adulthood.* New York: Free Press.

Lazarus, R. S., & Folkman, S. (1984). *Stress, appraisal, and coping.* New York: Springer.

Lazarus, R., Averill, J. R., & Opton, E. M., Jr. (1970). Toward a cognitive theory of emotions. In M. Arnold (Ed.), *Feelings and emotions* (pp. 207–232). New York: Academic Press.

Levi, P. (1961). *Survival in Auschwitz: The Nazi assault on humanity* (S. Woolf, trans.). New York: Collier Books.

Lieberman, M. A. (1969). Institutionalization of the aged: Effects of behavior. *Journal of Gerontology, 24,* 330–340.

Lifton, R. (1968). *Death in life: Survivors of Hiroshima.* New York: Random House.

Marshall, V. W. (1980). *A sociology of death and dying.* Belmont, CA: Wadsworth.

McCaughey, B. G. (1985). U.S. Coast Guard collision at sea. *Journal of Human Stress, 11,* 42–46.

McCrae, R. R. (1984). Situational determinants of coping responses: Loss, threat, and challenge. *Journal of Personality and Social Psychology, 46,* 919–928.

McGrath, J. E. (Ed.). (1970). *Social and psychological factors in stress.* New York: Holt, Rinehart & Winston.

Melick, M. E., Logue, J. N., & Frederick, C. J. (1982). Stress and disaster. In L. Goldberger & S. Breznitz (Eds.), *Handbook of stress* (pp. 613–630). New York: Free Press.

Monat, A., & Lazarus, R. S. (Eds.). (1977). *Stress and coping.* New York: Columbia University Press.

Moos, R. H., & Billings, A. G. (1982). Conceptualizing and measuring coping resources and processes. In L. Goldberger & S. Breznitz (Eds.), *Handbook of stress* (pp. 212–230). New York: Free Press.

Nardini, J. (1952). Survival factors in American prisoners of war of the Japanese. *American Journal of Psychiatry, 109,* 241–248.

Niederland, W. (1968). The problems of the survivor: Dynamics of posttraumatic symptomatology. In H. Krystal (Ed.), *Massive psychic trauma* (pp. 8–22). New York: International Universities Press.

Pearlin, L. I. (1975). Status inequality and stress in marriage. *American Sociological Review, 40,* 344–357.

Pearlin, L. I., & Schooler, C. (1978). The structure of coping. In H. L. McCubbin, A. E. Cauble, & J. M. Patterson (Eds.), *Family stress, coping, and social support* (pp. 109–135). Springfield, IL: Thomas.

Piaget, J. (1937). *The construction of reality in the child.* New York: Basic Books.

Porter, J. N. (1979). Social-psychological aspects of the Holocaust. In B. L. Sherwin & S. G. Ament (Eds.), *Encountering the Holocaust: An interdisciplinary survey* (pp. 189–222). Chicago: Impact Press.

Reichard, S., Livson, F., & Peterson, P. C. (1962). *Aging personality: A survey of eighty-seven older men.* New York: Wiley.

Rose, D. S. (1986). Worse than death: Psychological dynamics of rape victims and the need for psychotherapy. *American Journal of Psychiatry, 143,* 817–824.

Schmolling, P. (1984). Human reactions to the Nazi concentration camps: A summing up. *Journal of Human Stress, 10,* 108–120.

Selye, H. (1956). *The stress of life.* New York: McGraw-Hill.

Selye, H. (1974). *Stress without distress.* Philadelphia: Lippincott.

Selye, H. (1982). History and present status of the stress concept. In L. Goldberger & S. Breznitz (Eds.), *Handbook of stress: Theoretical and clinical aspects* (pp. 7–17). New York: Free Press.

Shuval, Y. (1982). Migration and stress. In L. Goldberger & S. Breznitz (Eds.), *Handbook of stress* (pp. 677–694). New York: The Free Press.

Terr, L. (1979). Children of Chowchilla: A study of psychic trauma. *Psychoanalytic Study of the Child, 34,* 552–623.

Torrance, E. P. (1965). *Constructive behavior: Stress, personality and mental health.* Belmont, CA: Wadsworth.

Vaillant, G. E. (1977). *Adaptation to life.* Boston: Little, Brown.

White, R. W. (1974). Strategies of adaptation: An attempt at systematic description. In G. V. Coelho, D. A. Hamburg, & J. E. Adams (Eds.), *Coping and adaptation* (pp. 47–68). New York: Basic Books.

Wiesel, E. (1969). *Night* (S. Rodway, trans.). New York: Avon Books.

Wilson, J. P. (1980). Conflict, stress and growth: The effects of war on psychosocial development among Vietnam Veterans. In C. R. Figley & S. Leventman (Eds.), *Strangers at home: Vietnam Veterans since the war* (pp. 123–166). New York: Praeger.

Wilson, J. P. (in press). Understanding and treating the Vietnam veteran. In F. Ochberg (Ed.), *Post-traumatic therapy.* New York: Brunner/Mazel.

Wilson, J. P., & Krauss, G. (1985). Predicting PTSD among Vietnam veterans. In W. E. Kelly (Ed.), *Post-traumatic stress disorder and the war veteran patient* (pp. 102–147). New York: Brunner/Mazel.

Wilson, J. P., Smith, K., & Johnson, S. (1985). A comparative analysis of PTSD among various survivor groups. In C. R. Figley (Ed.), *Trauma and its wake: The study and treatment of post-traumatic stress disorder* (pp. 142–172). New York: Brunner/Mazel.

4

Diagnosis and Phase-Oriented Treatment of Post-Traumatic Stress Disorder

CHARLES R. MARMAR and MARDI J. HOROWITZ

THE DIAGNOSTIC CRITERIA FOR POST-TRAUMATIC STRESS DISORDER

During the past decade, there has been increasing research and clinical interest in the diagnostic entity of post-traumatic stress disorder. A number of factors have contributed to interest in the phenomenology of traumatic reactions to stress. Publication of the DSM-III criteria for this disorder (American Psychiatric Association Press, 1980), systematic studies of the long-term consequences of exposure to traumatic events in war (Egendorf, Kadushin, Laufer, Rothbart, & Sloan, 1981; Figley, 1978; Laufer, Yager, Frey-Wouters, & Doneallan, 1981; Sonnenberg, Blank, & Talbot, 1985; Wilson, 1987), advances in the understanding and treatment of stress disorders in civilian populations (Horowitz, 1986; Horowitz, Marmar, Weiss, DeWitt, & Rosenbaum, 1984; Marmar, Horowitz, Weiss, Wilner, & Kaltreider, 1988), research on the effects of psychic trauma in children (Frederick, 1984; Terr, 1983), and advances in the measurement of post-traumatic stress disorder (Keane, Malloy, & Fairbank, 1984; Horowitz, Wilner, & Alvarez, 1979; Malloy, Fairbank, & Keane, 1983; Weiss, Horowitz, & Wilner, 1984; Wilson & Krauss, 1985) have stimulated further inquiry.

These clinical and research advances have been influential in the de-

CHARLES R. MARMAR and MARDI J. HOROWITZ • Center for the Study of Neuroses, Department of Psychiatry, Langley Porter Neuropsychiatric Institute, University of California, San Francisco, California 94143.

velopment of revised DSM-III criteria recently published (American Psychiatric Association Press, 1987). Brett, Spitzer, and Williams (1987) have reviewed the major changes in the DSM-III criteria that have been incorporated in the DSM III-R. Revisions include changes in the definition of the stressor, the onset and time course of the disorder, additions to the category of numbing symptoms, replacement of the former miscellaneous symptom category with an autonomic arousal symptom cluster, and elaboration of the unique characteristics of post-traumatic stress disorders in children. The criteria specify the following: a stress event outside the range of usual human experience; persistent reexperiencing of the traumatic event in thought, imagery, and behavior; persistent avoidance of stimuli linked concretely or symbolically with the trauma or numbing of general emotional reactivity; symptoms of increased arousal; and duration of symptomatic disturbance of at least 1 month. All five criteria must be present in order to make the diagnosis.

The DSM-III-R criteria aim to provide a coherent picture of the range of presentations of psychological response to traumatic life events. The goal is to provide efficient criteria for case identification, including the minimization of false-positive and false-negative diagnoses. The criteria assume relative homogeneity of response for different individuals following different kinds of traumatic events at different time points after exposure to the trauma. However, to accommodate individual differences in response, an approach is utilized in which multiple items are given for reexperiencing, avoidant, and arousal criteria. An individual must meet a specified number, but not all, of the items within each criterion in order to qualify for diagnosis of post-traumatic stress disorder.

WAR-RELATED STUDIES OF EXTREME STRESS

Military Combat

Field studies of extreme stress require the occurrence of multiple stressors in a more or less extensive population. War, unfortunately, provides such conditions. Exposure to death, dying, and destruction are common, and people often commit acts of violence and/or witness such acts against others. Surprisingly, psychological stress-response syndromes were not fully recognized until World War II, and recognition was met with considerable resistance. Etiology was often attributed to physical causes because psychological causation implied weakness, cowardice, or lack of patriotism.

The immense number of psychological casualties among combat soldiers, sailors, and airmen in both world wars forced the recognition of a more complex stress-response syndrome. Earlier observations had been made on the long-standing physical consequences of combat, such as DeCosta's description of "soldier's heart" in the American Civil War, but they lacked explicit psychological formulations. In World War I, rather than relating the cardiac symptoms to the strain of combat, the presence of daze, fear, trembling, nightmares, and inability to function were usually attributed to brain damage. Cerebral concussions and the rupture of small blood vessels apparently caused by exploding shells were the accepted etiological mechanisms; hence the term *shell shock* for traumatic war neuroses was common. This organic focus led to concentration on expectable symptoms such as those known to characterize acute and chronic brain syndromes. Earlier, at the end of the nineteenth century, traumatic neuroses after derailments and other train wrecks had been attributed to spinal concussions (Trimble, 1981).

Repeated observations eventually led to the conclusion that physical traumas were not invariably antecedents of combat reactions. Anyone exposed to threat of death and horrendous sights might respond with prolonged symptoms, even if he or she emerged physically unharmed. In certain cases, a single exposure may trigger the reaction. In other cases of combat exposure, multiple stressors simply overwhelmed the persons' coping resources and led to PTSD, even when no physical injury was present.

The large population presenting with characteristic symptomatic responses to traumatic events in World War II stimulated phenomenological reevaluation of the combat-related stress symptomatology (Archibald & Tuddenham, 1965). A good example is the study of combat reactions by Grinker and Spiegel (1945), whose summary of the 19 most common symptoms that persisted long after the soldiers were removed from combat are shown by rank order, according to frequency of occurrence in Table 1. These symptoms are typical of those found in other studies of military combat. After World War II, Lidz (1946), Fairbairn (1952), and Brill and

Table 1. Most Common Signs and Syndrome of Operational Fatigue in Rank Order by Frequency as Found by Grinker and Spiegel (1945)

1. Restlessness	10. Personality change and memory loss
2. Irritability or aggression	11. Tremor
3. Fatigue on arising, lethargy	12. Difficulty concentrating, confusion
4. Difficulty falling asleep	13. Alcoholism
5. Anxiety, subjective	14. Preoccupation with combat
6. Frequent fatigue	15. Decreased appetite
7. Startle reactions	16. Nightmares
8. Feeling of tension	17. Psychosomatic symptoms
(e.g., vomiting, diarrhea)	18. Irrational fears (phobias)
9. Depression	19. Suspiciousness

Beebe (1955) all described nightmares as significant signs of combat neuroses. More recent work by Haley (1974) on patients' reports of atrocities described Vietnam veterans who were depressed, anxious, sad, rageful, and despairing. She saw delayed reactions characterized by denial and leading toward intrusion in the form of sleep disturbances and nightmares.

DeFazio (1975) also pointed to nightmares as a frequent psychological problem for Vietnam veterans. In 1982, Langley reported symptoms of guilt, depression, alienation, irritability, high stress, nightmares, flashbacks, and startle response in a group of Vietnam combat veterans who developed the additional problems of substance abuse and marital, legal, and vocational difficulties. In 1984, Silver and Iacono reported a study of 405 Vietnam veterans that supports the DSM-III's Post-Traumatic Stress Disorder symptoms of intrusions, sleep disturbance, and difficulty concentrating. Similar important findings were also compiled by Figley (1978, 1985; Figley & Leventman, 1982), Kolb (1982, 1983, 1984), and Wilson and Krauss (1985).

The categories of symptoms that Grinker and Spiegel slated for observation and codification may reflect the theory of that time. In his studies of post-traumatic neuroses of World War I veterans, Freud (1955) emphasized nightmares, one form of intrusive and repetitive thought, but had downplayed a similar phenomenon, recurrent unbidden images of frightening scenes that occur in waking thought. Images while awake are a much more common occurrence than Freud believed.

> Now dreams occurring in traumatic neuroses have the characteristic of repeatedly bringing the patient back into the situation of his accident, a situation from which he wakes up in another fright. . . . I am not aware, however, that patients suffering from traumatic neurosis are much more occupied in their waking lives with memories of their accident. Perhaps they are more concerned with not thinking of it. (p. 13)

Wilson and Krauss (1985) made a systematic study of Vietnam veterans with and without post-traumatic stress disorder (see also Wilson, 1980; Hendin & Haas, 1984). Their results indicate that the best predictor of a post-traumatic stress disorder in Vietnam veterans is the extent of combat involvement, subjectively experienced exposure to injury and death, and psychological isolation upon returning home from the war (see also van der Kolk, Blitz, Burr, Sherry, & Hartman, 1984). In a multiple regression analysis of the best predictors of seven post-traumatic symptoms such as intrusive imagery, depression, and problems of anger and rage, Wilson and Krauss found that the variables that account for the greatest proportion of variance of subsequent intrusive imagery were exposure to scenes of injury and/or death and psychological isolation upon return from the war. Psychological isolation, but not injury and death, was the best predictive variable for the other six symptoms of post-traumatic stress disorder. This indicates that the intrusive and repetitive imagery from experiences of violence and death threats is often a specific stress response.

The expression "everyone has his or her own breaking point" evolved from experience with reactions to combat. It suggests that every person, when exposed to great enough stress, may exhibit an acute stress response syndrome. Persons with certain latent neurotic conflicts or predispositions may respond to lower levels of external stress (Hendin, Hass, Singer, Gold, & Trigos, 1983). Persons with a higher stress tolerance will not "break down" until the level of stress reaches greater intensity. Brill (1967) observed that soldiers with preexisting neuroses had a seven-to-eight-times greater chance of psychiatric reactions than did those with more normal predispositional characteristics.

In a lengthy review of the literature, Hocking (1970) verified the hypothesis that individuals adjust differently to varying degrees of stress. However, in his view, exposure to prolonged extreme stress will result in formation of characteristic symptoms in virtually every person exposed to it. He noted that of 303 individuals in military combat during World War II, more than half suffered from subsequent depression, insomnia, nightmares, anxiety, tension, irritability, startle reactions, impairment of memory, and obsession with thoughts of wartime experiences. Significant numbers of men were also observed to deny trauma by channeling their emotional difficulties into psychosomatic symptoms (see also the comprehensive review by Lewis & Engel, 1954).

Despite efforts to distinguish the symptoms and signs of acute and chronic reactions (Kardiner & Spiegel, 1947), extended field studies indicated that stress responses are not necessarily discrete entities; the main difference was the temporal onset or trajectory of the syndrome. Clearly, the phases of symptoms and signs may begin shortly after the stress event, may persist for a long period, or may begin only after a considerable latency period (Archibald, Long, Miller, & Tuddenham, 1962; Archibald & Tuddenham, 1965; Baker & Chapman, 1962; Cobb & Lindemann, 1943; Davis, 1966; Friedman & Linn, 1957; Horowitz, Wilner, Kaltreider, & Alvarez, 1980; Parkes, 1964; Popovic & Petrovic, 1965).

Concentration Camps

Additional evidence regarding the duration and frequency of stress-response syndromes arose from the most deplorable circumstances imaginable. Studies of concentration camp victims indicated that profound and protracted stress may have chronic or permanent effects independent of the predisposition of the prestress personality. This evidence was found in decades of studying survivors of the Nazi concentration camps (Eaton, Sigal, & Weinfeld, 1982). Study after study, as reviewed in two workshops (Krystal, 1968; Krystal & Niederland, 1971), confirm the occurrence of stress response syndromes, persisting for decades, in major proportions of those populations who survived protracted concentration camp experiences. As just one example, 99% of the 226 Norwegian survivors of a Nazi concentration camp in World War II had some psychiatric disturbances when intensively surveyed years after their return to normal life. Of the total population studied, 87% had cognitive disturbances such as poor memory and inability to concentrate, 85% had persistent nervousness and irritability, 60% had sleep disturbances, and 52% had nightmares (Eitinger, 1969). It should be noted that the horror of these concentration camps also meant severe malnutrition and physical maltreatment possibly resulting in brain injury that would ultimately influence observed symptomatology.

In addition to such general stress symptoms as recurrent intrusive memories, concentration camp survivors may have special symptoms and signs due to the protracted duration of their experience and the intensity of their dehumanization at the hands of the Nazis. Such signs as the synecdoche of success, the bleaching away of childhood memories, and specific alterations in the schemata of self and object relationships may distinguish the survivor syndrome of concentration camp victims from stress-response syndromes in general (Furst, 1967; Ostwald & Bittner, 1968; Krystal, 1968; Lifton, 1967).

The effects of being a victim of a concentration camp can lead to changes in personality impacting on patterns of interpersonal relations, including those of parenting. As a result, the children of the victims and subsequent generations may continue to be influenced by the long-term effects of the camp experience (Krystal, 1985). These generations of families thus become carriers of conscious and unconscious values, myths, fantasies, and beliefs as well as actual interpersonal transactive styles that may have been forcibly changed by the violent life experiences of one generation (Danieli, 1982).

To recapitulate, though not negating the influence of prestress personality configurations, findings from large groups of individuals exposed to severe stress indicate that stress-response syndromes are not limited to any subgroup of the exposed populations. There is no doubt, then, that some general stress-response tendencies can be found, even in individuals without preexisting risk factors.

War and concentration camps produce extraordinary visible strain. However, there seem to be phases of response in which denial of intrusive symptoms may predominate. Shatan (1973), in a study of Vietnam veterans 24 months after combat, noted the presence of intrusive symptomatology in the form of insomnia, nightmares, and restlessness that may not have surfaced during combat and demobilization when denial and numbing may have predominated. Horowitz and Solomon (1975, 1978) described the differences between soldiers under great protracted combat stress during World War II and those in Vietnam. Combat soldiers in World War II initially went into a period of denial and numbing, but they did, nonetheless, remain at the front. The stress mounted, and when it exceeded the person's ability to avoid it, intrusive symptoms emerged. In the Vietnam war, repeated rotation to relative safety made it possible for many soldiers to enter and remain in the denial phase during their tour of duty. Other elements, such as the availability of drugs, the lack of group fidelity, and the opposition to the war, contributed to a state of alienation characterized by depersonalization and isolation. Upon return to the United States, denial and numbing may continue during a period of relief and well-being. Ultimately, with the relaxation of defensive coping mechanisms, the veteran might enter the painful phase of intrusive recollection (Egendorf *et al.*, 1981). Shatan (1973) observed that the delay in the manifestation of these symptoms caused the government physicians to assume that the Vietnam War produced fewer psychiatric casualties than is now understood to be the case of high prevalence of PTSD.

In some instances, it may be more useful to think in terms of post-traumatic character disorders, although there is no official inclusion of such a term in the nomenclature (see Parson, Chapter 11 this volume). Wars are often fought by soldiers who are in late adolescence or very early adulthood. Identity is not completely consolidated, and the traumatic experiences of the war become incorporated into self-schemata and concepts of the relationship of self to the world (Wilson, 1980). A confusing war situation, compounded by the domestic unpopularity of the war, led many veterans to become alienated. This situation combined with predisposition before the war, the war itself, and atrocities observed or committed impacted to alter personality while it was being formed and reformed during an important developmental phase. Problems in self-definition, self-coherence, and self-articulation emerged upon return to peacetime society (Wilson, 1987).

Rigid adherence to official diagnostic labels may inhibit individualized case formulations along these lines. Character development occurs throughout adult life, and massive trauma or prolonged strain affects this process. Prolonged denial or intrusion phases may overlay the prewar personality of the individual.

Concentration camp survivors sometimes exhibit such effects. In his studies of these survivors, Chodoff (1970) observed a sequence of reactions to concentration camp life and described this sequence in terms of stages. First was the universal response of shock and terror upon arriving at the camp. This fright reaction was generally followed by a period of apathy and often by a longer period of mourning and depression. Apathy was psychologically protective by providing a kind of emotional hibernation. Lifton (1976) suggested that this kind of depression might, in part, be characterized as a delayed mourning reaction as the victims were unable to engage in a ceremonial mourning for their dead. Gorer (1965) also emphasized the connection between ritual and mourning and the maladaptations that may result if distress is not worked through in a personal and expressive social manner.

Regression was a stage noted in many prisoners of war that was used as an adaptive measure to counter overwhelming pressures. Docility and submissiveness were products of the victims' dependency on their persecutors. Identification with the aggressor was also observed, and irritable behavior was sometimes discharged in petty fights with other prisoners.

The most important defenses utilized by concentration camp survivors during their imprisonment were denial and isolation of affect. Chodoff (1970) named the most distinctive, long-term consequence of Nazi persecution observable over a 30-year period as the "concentration camp syndrome." Invariably present in this syndrome was some degree of anxiety along with irritability, restlessness, apprehensiveness, and startle reactions. Anxiety symptoms were worse at night and were generally accompanied by insomnia and nightmares that were concrete or slightly disguised intrusive repetitions of the traumatic experience.

Lifton pointed out the significance of psychic numbing in the behavior of persons in Nazi camps, stating that anyone faced with such a massive death encounter would experience a cessation of feeling, a desensitization or psychic numbing. An element of this kind of denial was the need to "see nothing," for if it was not "seen," it was not happening. Added to this was the severing of human bonds of identification. "I see you dying, but I'm not related to you in your death." Lifton also described two kinds of subsequent numbing—the apathy of the "walking corpse" and the "know-nothing" who acted as though death did not exist.

A collaborative numbing emerged, an equalizer between the victim and the victimizer. Thus, those persecuted did not exist and the Nazi, the victimizer, was omnipotent but denied the human consequences of his or her actions. Such numbing and denial may be followed, even years later, by a phase of intrusive repetition of ideas and feelings related to the earlier warded-off events. More recently, Lifton has termed this phenomena as *doubling,* in which the person forms a "double" self to cope with the stresses of the death camps (Chapter 1, this volume).

Nuclear Holocaust

Based on interviews with 75 survivors made 17 years after the United States dropped an atomic bomb on Hiroshima, Lifton (1967) described the experience as a permanent encounter with death, consisting of four phases (see also, Lifton, Chapter 1, this volume). First was an overwhelming immersion in death, a "death in life" feeling similar to that of the concentration camp victims. This phase was dominated by elements of extreme helplessness in the face of threatened annihilation and surmounted by an extremely widespread and effective defense mechanism that Lifton called "psychic closing-off," a cessation of feeling within a very short period of time. The unconscious process was described as closing oneself off from death, the controlling fantasy being that "If I feel nothing, then death is not taking place." Thus, it is related to the defense mechanisms of denial and isolation as well as to the behavioral state of apathy and is distinguished by its global quality, a screen of protection against the impact of death in the midst of death and dying. This response to immersion in exposure to death merges with long-term feelings of depression and despair, mingled with feelings of shame and guilt. The shameful fantasy, "I should have saved him or helped him," is interwoven with the guilty fantasy, "I am responsible for his death; I killed him."

The second phase of the Hiroshima encounter with death from the atomic bomb was referred to as the "invisible contamination," in which symptoms of radiation sickness appeared at unpredictable intervals of weeks or months after the bomb had been dropped. There was a fear of epidemic contamination, a sense of individual powerlessness in the face of an invisible agent, and denial of illness when the symptoms did appear.

The third phase occurred after many years with the experience of later radiation effects and was an undercurrent of imagery of an endless chain of potentially lethal impairments that, if not evident that year or 5 years later, would appear in the next generation.

The fourth phase was a lifelong identification with death and dying, which Lifton explained as the survivors' means of maintaining life. Because of the burden of guilt they carry for having survived, the survivors' obeisance before the dead was their best means for justifying and maintaining their own existence and is a continued preoccupation.

Lifton also described the survivors' residual problems, especially those of psychological imagery, that manifested themselves in various ways. He noted a heightened sense of invulnerability; a sense of being among the "elite" who have mastered death and, paradoxically, a sense of vulnerability to death at any time. Years later, many victims carried with them intrusive images of the horror of that day and talked of still seeing images of people walking slowly in the streets with their skin peeling off.

A profound ambivalent pattern emerged of both seeking help and resenting it. Working through this event, Lifton felt, was a reformulation, a way of establishing an inner ideology as a means of dealing with overwhelming feelings and creating a new reality within which the victims could understand and master their experiences and their feelings of shame and guilt. Faced with guilt and resistance to establishing trust in the human order, the survivors of concentration camps, of atomic bombing, and of the Vietnam War may create a new identity, a changed sense of connection with people, as well as develop a new meaning and significance for their life in order to come to terms with the trauma and the world in which they continue to live.

PHASE-ORIENTED MODEL OF STRESS RESPONSE SYNDROMES

Clinical, field, and experimental studies of response to extreme stressors have yielded convergent results. As compared with the pretrauma period, the frequency of two broadly defined states increases following traumatic life events; one is characterized by intrusive experience, the other by denial and numbing. States of intrusion and denial or avoidance do not always occur in a prescribed pattern, because individual differences are seen in the oscillation of these two broad states. However, repeated evaluations of trauma victims over time, conducted at our specialty clinic for the evaluation and treatment of persons with stress-response syndromes following serious life events, reveal a pattern of phasic tendency in these states. At the time of the event, or immediately afterwards, there is frequently an emotional outcry characterized by painful but brief-lived recognition of the salience of the event. This initial period of outcry may be followed by either denial or intrusive states, at times in oscillation with each other. In favorable cases, the intensity and frequency of these states is reduced in a working-through process. Emotion-laden meanings of the event are neither blocked from conscious awareness nor of such intensity as to overwhelm coping capacities. The result is gradual assimilation, mourning of what has been lost, revision of preexisting beliefs, such as views of the self as invulnerable, investment in new plans, and the capacity to form new attachments. Working through may be conceptualized as a psychological metabolism of the impact of the traumatic event such that the person is able to resume work, overcome creative blocks that are common during the adaptational phase, and reinvest in love relationships. This general sequence of normal response is shown on the left side of Table 2.

This framework for the sequential phases of normal response serves to organize pathological variants that may be seen as intensifications of these normal response tendencies. These pathological sequelae are presented in the right column of Table 2. At the time of the event or immediately following, there may be an exaggeration of the outcry phase characterized by panic, overwhelming disorganization, confusional states, or dissociative reactions requiring immediate intervention.

The normal denial phase typically lasts between several weeks and a few months following the event. In a certain proportion of cases, there is a prolonged maladaptive avoidance, which can continue for many months or years after the event, characterized by emotional numbing, withdrawal, a sense of unreality about the event, failure to work through and plan for the

Table 2. Common Poststress Experiences and Their Pathological Intensification

Common routes of response to serious life events	Pathological intensification
Outcry (fear, sadness, anger)	Overwhelmed, dazed, confused Panic, dissociative reactions, reactive psychoses
Denial experiences (numbing and face avoidance)	Maladaptive avoidances (withdrawal, drug or alcohol abuse, counterphobic frenzy, fugue states)
Intrusion experiences (unbidden thoughts and images)	Flooded and impulsive states, despair, impaired work and social functions, compulsive reenactments
Working through (facing reality)	Anxiety and depressive reactions, physiological disruptions
Relative completion of response (going on with life)	Inability to work, create, or feel emotions as a distortion of character

future, blocked mourning, and which may be complicated by the use of drugs, alcohol, or risk-taking behaviors that serve to reenforce numbing and avoidance. Further details of the signs and symptoms of the denial phase are provided in Table 3.

As an example, a woman in her mid-40s whose husband was killed in a mountain-climbing incident, presented for treatment 18 months after the event complaining that she had not cried a single tear since her husband's death. She said that her feelings in general were blunted, as though someone had injected her entire body with an anesthetic agent.

More common than either the immediate overwhelming response at the time of the event, or the prolonged numbing reaction, is the pathological exaggeration of the intrusive phase. Unbidden images, intrusive thoughts, and pangs of emotion contribute to flooded and impulsive states, overwhelming despair, high anxiety, and interference in work and interpersonal functioning. Nightmares, flashbacks, and related symptoms lead to further avoidance rather than gradual assimilation and working through. The symptoms of the intrusive phase are detailed in Table 4. As an example, a woman whose daughter had died of head injuries in an automobile accident, initially coped reasonably well with the event and went through a period of relative denial in which she felt she could function by "going on automatic pilot." She presented for treatment several years after her daughter's death with overwhelming intrusive symptomatology.

Table 3. Symptoms and Signs Related to Denial or Numbing Experiences and Behavior

Daze
Selective inattention
Inability to appreciate significance of stimuli
Amnesia (complete or partial)
Inability to visualize memories
Disavowal of meanings of stimuli
Constriction and inflexibility of thought
Presence of fantasies to counteract reality
A sense of numbness or unreality, including detachment and estrangement
Overcontrolled states of mind, including behavioral avoidances
Sleep disturbances (e.g., too little or too much)
Tension-inhibition responses of the autonomic nervous system, with felt sensations such as bowel symptoms, fatigue, and headache
Frantic overactivity to jam attention with stimuli
Withdrawal from ordinary life activities

When rigid swings from denial to intrusion rather than gradual mastery of the event occur, working through may be blocked for a prolonged period of time. Long-term pathological consequences include increased risk for psychosomatic disorders, inability to plan for the future, creative blocks, and withdrawal from relationships, leading to progressive distortion in character functioning. This may occur in individuals who had good personality development prior to the traumatic events. For example, a Vietnam war veteran who had been president of his high-school class,

Table 4. Symptoms and Signs Related to Instrusive Experience and Behavior

Hypervigilance, including hypersensitivity to associated events
Startle reactions
Illusion or pseudohallucinations, including sensation of recurrence
Insrusive-repetitive thoughts, images, emotions, and behaviors
Overgeneralization of associations
Inability to concentrate on other topics because of preoccupation with event-related themes
Confusion or thought disruption when thinking about event-related themes
Labile or explosive entry into intensely emotional and undermodulated states of mind
Sleep and dream disturbances, including recurrent dreams
Sensations or symptoms of flight or flight readiness (or of exhaustion from chronic arousal), including tremor, nausea, diarrhea, and sweating (adrenergic, noradrenergic, or histaminic arousals)
Search for lost persons or situations, compulsive repetitions

captain of his football team, and popular with his peers presented for treatment 14 years after returning from Vietnam. He had experienced sustained combat experience in which he witnessed death and injury to civilians, to close members of his own fighting unit, and in which his own life was repeatedly in danger. At the time of evaluation, he showed many of the features seen in severe personality disorders, including instability in love relationships, chronic work-identity problems, alcohol abuse, severe marital disturbances, and alienation from his children.

BRIEF THERAPY OF POST-TRAUMATIC STRESS DISORDERS

Our model of normal and pathological phasic response to traumatic life stressors provides an organizational framework for psychotherapeutic intervention. We developed this individual, time-limited dynamic treatment model for delayed, overwhelming, or protracted stress response in civilians following single traumatic events.

Early in the development of the model, we offered a 20-session approach in which patients were seen on a weekly basis. Clinical and research review of these early cases suggested the following patterns: substantial remission occurring in the early sessions, a midtherapy phase during which the focus diffused from stress to character-oriented issues, and risk of dropout prior to termination. After reviewing the work of Mann (1973), Sifneos (1972, 1979), and Malan (1963, 1976), we established a time limit of 12 sessions. This shortened time frame encouraged determined, goal-oriented work on the part of the patient and therapist, provided a structure that tended to counter diffusion of focus, and maximized the therapeutic potential during the termination phase.

The aim of these 12-session treatments is to rapidly engage the patient in a working collaboration, arrive at a mutually agreed upon focus to counter unstable oscillations from denial to intrusion states with tolerable working-through states, and permit further elaboration and mastery of the stress event during the termination phase. The desired outcome is not full resolution and working through during the time frame of the treatment. The aim is to help the patient who has been derailed from a normal psychological recovery process return to an adaptive working through that will continue following termination of the treatment and lead, over time, to mastery of the stress event. The structure of this brief treatment approach is summarized in Table 5.

Initial Exploration of the Stress Event

At the beginning of the treatment, the patient is invited to retell the story of the stress event, including the sequence of events leading up to the event, details of the traumatic experience, and reactions following the event.

Table 5. Sample Twelve-Session Dynamic Therapy for Stress Disorders

Session	Relationship issues	Patient activity	Therapist activity
1	Initial positive feeling for helper	Patient tells story of event	Preliminary focus discussed
2	Lull as sense of pressure is reduced	Event related to previous life experiences	Takes psychiatric history/gives realistic appraisal of his or her syndrome
3	Patient tests therapist for various relationship possibilities	Patient adds associations to indicate expanded meaning of event	Realignment of focus; interpretation of resistances to contemplating stress-related themes
4	Therapeutic alliance deepened	Contemplation of implications of event in the present	Further interpretation of defenses and warded-off contents with linking of latter to stress events and responses
5		Work on themes that have been avoided	Encouragement of active confrontation with feared topics and reengagement in feared activities
6		Contemplation of the future	Time of termination discussed
7–11	Transference reactions interpreted and linked to other configurations	Continued working-through of central conflicts and issues of termination as related to the life event and reactions to it	Clarification and interpretation related to central conflicts and termination; clarification of unfinished issues and recommendations
	Acknowledgment of pending separation		
12	Saying goodbye	Realization of work to be continued on own	Acknowledgment of real gains and summary of future work for patient to do on his or her own
		Telling hopeful plans for the future	

The therapist's interest in hearing about the stress event may be at variance with the patient's expectation that other people will not tolerate hearing the details of the trauma. Where the patient has had this expectation confirmed, as occurs when the patient's important social supports have reacted with shock or denial and withdrawal to the patient's experience, this expectation is intensified. Retelling the event in the presence of an expert healer, who remains calm, understanding, compassionate, and nonjudgmental is itself a therapeutic experience and one that fosters the beginning of a working collaboration.

Establishing the Therapeutic Alliance

In general, the success of short-term psychotherapeutic interventions depends upon the patient's willingness and capacity to engage quickly in the working process. The development of a trusting collaborative relationship may take on special nuances with recently traumatized individuals. Those sensitized by loss, as occurs after the sudden unanticipated death of a family member, may be reluctant to invest emotions in a new tie with the therapist because of a heightened expectation of repetition of the trauma, a concern that may be intensified in a 12-session model. The patient may begin to anticipate the termination phase at the outset of treatment. For the patient who presents in an entrenched denial phase, treatment offers the hope of a safe encounter with warded-off feelings. However, the threat that emotions will escalate to unmanageable proportions, leaving the patient feeling disorganized, or that the therapist would not be able to tolerate the pent-up expression of rage, panic, or searing guilt is ever present.

In all forms of psychotherapy, patients have a tendency to repeat role relationship models that have been internalized following interactions with important figures during sensitive developmental periods. These transference potentials may be intensified following traumatic life events. A woman in her mid-30s, whose husband had been killed in an airplane crash, presented for treatment 8 months following the event with symptoms of intrusive images, nightmares, difficulty concentrating, and hypervigilance. In recounting her husband's death and their relationship, she was intellectual, emotionally remote, and uncertain about the appropriateness of her asking for help with her emotions. When asked about her childhood, she reported that her older sister had severe congenital disabilities, that her parents appeared chronically burdened while caring for her sister, and that both parents became depressed following her sister's death when the patient was age 8. The patient had developed a precocious maturity, attempted to take care of her parents, and felt that she would "push them over the edge" if she asked too much from them. This pattern recreated itself in the early phase of the treatment in her reluctance to make emotional demands of the therapist. Interpretation of her emotional distance, her exaggerated concern that she would overwhelm the therapist with her reactions to her husband's death, and linkage to her childhood worry that she would further burden her already-depleted parents, permitted the patient to risk an exploration of her grief. A more complete presentation of therapeutic strategies for engaging the patient who presents with initial difficulties in the formation of a therapeutic alliance is presented elsewhere (Foreman & Marmar, 1985).

Identification of the Focus

In favorable cases, a mutually agreed-upon focus emerges in the first few sessions of treatment. For individuals with post-traumatic stress disorders, the impact of the traumatic event on the person's self-concept serves as an organizer for the treatment. The patient's conscious concerns most often relate to problematic weak and defective feelings about the self in the aftermath of the trauma. Feelings of fear, vulnerability to repetition of the trauma, sadness over losses, and weakness about not being able to control one's life or one's emotional reactions contribute to feelings of defectiveness about the self. A second set of problematic self-concepts, usually warded off and operating outside of the patient's awareness, concern a view of the self as dangerously powerful and responsible for causing harm to the self or others. Exaggerated feelings of responsibility for the sequence of events related to the trauma are associated with survivor guilt but frequently are not consciously linked to the felt experiences of guilt. The initial focus of treatment centers on the therapist's empathic appreciation of the patient's feelings of vulnerability as well as conscious guilt and exploration of the consciously represented themes. Later, a strategy for managing the patient's defensive avoidance of fantasies of exaggerated responsibility for the event, is developed (Marmar & Freedman, in press).

As an illustration, a man whose wife had been killed as a consequence of a mudslide that destroyed their home presented for treatment with the symptoms of post-traumatic stress disorder. The initial focus was on his feelings of vulnerability, loss, loneliness, and fantasy that he could not survive without his spouse. As treatment evolved, this focus was broadened to include his guilty concern that he was responsible for her death. He felt he should have anticipated this possibility and not purchased this particular home despite the fact that the soil engineer's report had been favorable at the time of the purchase. Only later in treatment, in the course of exploring long-standing ambivalent conflicts with his spouse, was he able to appreciate that his earlier wishes to free himself of this relationship had been magically confused with a view that he had caused her death.

Working Through Thoughts and Feelings Related to the Focus

For the person who has experienced relative failures of control, resulting in intrusive breakthroughs of undermodulated mood states, therapeutic interventions are directed toward helping reestablish a sense of self-regulation. Helpful therapeutic interventions include the provision of support, asking questions or repeating comments, facilitating the patient's effort to compartmentalize and examine in tolerable doses aspects of the experience rather than being flooded, and organizing information through reconstructive interpretations. These efforts help the patient to manage the experience in an orderly sequence, differentiate reality from fantasy-based meanings of the events, and structure time and sequence of the events. Temporary reduction of external demands, duress, and removal of environmental triggers of trauma facilitates mastery of intrusive states. Patients are encouraged to dose their conscious experience of traumatic events, with adaptive use of suppression techniques so that they may carry on with work and interpersonal relationship commitments. The selective use of antianxiety agents, such as low-dose Alprazolam on an as-needed basis, the use of relaxation and desensitization procedures, and adjunct support groups also serve to help modulate the intensity of stress response.

For individuals who present with rigid sustained denial and numbing, techniques are directed at creating a safe environment for the emergence of the warded-off affect-laden meanings of the event. This process begins with the therapist drawing attention to the patient's repetitive avoidance, inviting the patient to explore fantasies of being overwhelmed (should warded-off feelings emerge), and interpretation of the patient's transference concerns that harm would come to the therapist or the patient if she or he were to express the warded-off meanings of the event. The therapist encourages the patient to associate fully to the event, to employ imagery rather than words in recollection and fantasy, to explore emotional aspects of relationships and experiences of the self during the event, and to prime reconstruction of the event in an empathic and evocative resonance to the experience. As presented in Table 5, priorities of technique in relationship to the patient's presenting state are summarized.

The overarching aim of the working-through phase is to move the patient from either a rigidly overcontrolled stance or an intrusively overwhelming emotional state to a tolerable affective encounter with the meanings of the trauma. This achievement is heralded by the patient's growing capacity to contemplate memories of the event, experience emotions, revise distorted meanings, and plan for the future. At the same time that the patient can better tolerate facing the implications of the event, he or she can also, at times, put the event out of mind in order to carry on with roles at work, at home, and in important relationships. The patient learns to dose the intensity and duration of periods of working through, initially in the treatment situation and later on their own.

Termination

In a 12-session treatment plan, termination themes most often emerge in the last few sessions. However, termination reactions may be heralded at the midpoint of treatment as the patient moves from an initial idealized optimistic sense of a hopeful beginning to the realization that the working-through process is a difficult and painful process. Termination represents the loss of a recently acquired meaningful supportive relationship. There is frequently a reactivation of the losses involved in the traumatic event with the anticipation of the loss of the therapist. Transferences that have been successfully managed during the alliance-building and working-through phase may intensify during termination. The patient may feel that treatment is ending because he or she is undeserving of further help, because the therapist is overwhelmed and cannot tolerate the intensity of the patient's reaction to the trauma, or as a punishment for hostile wishes expressed during the treatment. The patient may feel too weak to tolerate the loss of the therapist or too guilty to request further help.

These termination reactions, reminiscent of the epilogue of a play, permit a further working through of incompletely resolved responses to the traumatic life event. Transference reactions stimulated by termination are linked to the focus of treatment. Problematic weak and tenuous self-images, reactivated by the trauma, are often partially resolved during the working-through phase only to reemerge at termination. Linkage of these problematic views of the self to the stress event and when appropriate to early developmental periods facilitate mastery. Disappointments about the therapy can be frankly discussed; anger and sadness can be worked through leading to a more complete mourning of the losses incurred in the trauma. Open exploration of termination themes generally reach their greatest intensity in the ninth, tenth, and eleventh sessions. In the twelfth session, the patient feels less inclined to probe and reopen wounds that are in an early healing stage. There is an opportunity for the patient and therapist to acknowledge the real progress, to share positive feelings, and to anticipate a period of appropriate sadness after termination. The patient is encouraged to view the posttermination phase as a continuing working-through experience that will now take place in the context of the patient's personal reflections, further discussion with family and friends, and in the formation of new relationships.

The reaction of a young female patient to the sudden death of her father illustrates these termination issues. She initially sought help because of feelings of intense sadness, confusion, and blocks in creative initiative following his death. Her conscious concerns were fears of loss of control when entering flooded or dazed states of sadness, associated with weak views of herself as unworthy, having never felt validated by her father's approval of her adult roles and values. Examination of these weak self-images early in treatment in the supportive matrix of the therapeutic alliance led to restabilization, permitting a deeper exploration of her conflictive relationship with her father. She felt her father had betrayed and abandoned her in death but also earlier during her adolescence when he had withdrawn from their relationship. She was struggling with exaggerated feelings of responsibility for her parents' divorce and her father's subsequent intermittent poor health, probably related to a fantasy that she overwhelmed him with her interest in him.

During termination, there was an intensification of her conflicted and somewhat confused self-images. She experienced the termination as a premature interruption in her relationship with her therapist, felt vulnerable, and unprepared to cope without the therapist's supportive interest in her life and validation of her capacities. Further, she struggled with the view that the intensity of her emotions toward the therapist (both disappointment and affection) had driven him away, recapitulating the separations from her father during her adolescence and more recently with his death. The intensification of these transference reactions provided further opportunity for working through her grief and revising the irrational beliefs about herself and her father that activated weak, defective, and destructive self-concepts. Her tendency to either reject appropriate men outright or establish a neurotic repetition in which she attempted to convert her lovers to the idealized father of her adolescence was modulated through insight gained during transference interpretive work in the termination phase. At the end of treatment, she could better accept her realistic disappointments in her father, tolerate her sad feelings about his death, see her role in her parents' unhappy marriage and her father's subsequent health problems more realistically, and feel less guilty and more confident in pursuing her own autonomous choices in love and work.

NUANCES OF TREATMENT FOR PATIENTS OF VARYING PERSONALITY STYLES

The abovementioned treatment principles have general applicability for treatment of individuals following traumatic life events. Further specificity is added when consideration is given to the impact of personality style on the processing of the event. A range of functions are affected by individual differences in character styles, including perception, representation in the visual, lexical, and enactive systems, the capacity to translate images and actions to words, the capacity for association, and problem-solving strategies.

Individuals with an hysterical style represent their experiences in global, impressionistic, and vague terms. Inhibitory mechanisms such as repression and suppression limit access to clear, detailed reconstruction of the traumatic experiences. Attempts to work through meanings are impeded by stereotyping and rapid but often biased conclusions. Therapeutic strategies to counter these impediments include asking for specific details, contributing to the reconstruction of events, provision of verbal labels, clarification, repetition, and support when intense emotional states derail realistic information processing.

Individuals with an obsessional style isolate ideas from emotions, shift from emotion-laden meanings of the traumatic event to detailed, factual reporting of the events, and shift among contradictory views such as the self as victim or victimizer. Repetitive cycles of rumination interfere with working through and resolution. Therapeutic strategies to counter such obstacles in the obsessional individual include linking emotional meanings to factual contents, directing attention to imagery rather than lexical representations, countering switching of topics by holding to a single theme, and interpreting of the patient's resistance to experiencing emotions or making decisions.

Individuals with a narcissistic personality style are prone to panicky states of disorganization and fragmentation following traumatic events. They focus on issues of praise and blame, avoid meanings that would threaten self-esteem and avoid a frank realistic confrontation with the implications of the trauma for their relationships and future plans. The therapeutic counter strategies include attention to tact and timing of interpretations that carry a potential threat to the patient's self-esteem, cautious revisions of grandiose misrepresentations, and support for gradual tolerance of disappointments in the self. In the alliance-building early phase of treatment, the emphasis is on helping the patient to reconsolidate a cohesive sense of self. Once this has been established, the patient can better tolerate a realistic and, at times, self-critical examination of the implications of the trauma.

This review of the nuances of treatment for patients with different personality styles is necessarily brief. Further details, with extended case descriptions are provided in a publication from our group on this topic (Horowitz, Marmar, Krupnick, *et al.*, 1984).

A LONG-TERM AND A MULTIMODAL TREATMENT OF POST-TRAUMATIC STRESS DISORDERS

This brief treatment approach is best suited for relatively well-functioning individuals who have suffered a discrete traumatic event. For individuals who have suffered multiple traumatic events, such as war veterans or for individuals who had serious psychopathology prior to the trauma (for example, those with a history of recurrent affective disorder or severe personality disorder), and for those who present with chronic symptoms many years after the event, brief interventions are usually not appropriate. A range of treatment options should be considered including long-term individual psychotherapy, support groups, alcohol and drug abuse programs, antianxiety and antidepressant medications, marital and family therapy, and, in the most severe cases, inpatient treatment.

REFERENCES

American Psychiatric Association (1980). *Diagnostic and statistical manual of mental disorders* (3rd ed.). Washington, DC: American Psychiatric Association Press.

American Psychiatric Association (1987). *Diagnostic and statistical manual of mental disorders* (3rd ed., rev.). Washington, DC: American Psychiatric Association Press.

Archibald, H. C., & Tuddenham, R. D. (1965). Persistent stress reaction after combat: A 20-year follow-up. *Archives of General Psychiatry, 12,* 475–481.

Archibald, H. C., Long, D. M., Miller, C., & Tuddenham, R. D. (1962). Gross stress reaction in combat—A 15-year follow-up. *American Journal of Psychiatry, 119,* 317–322.

Baker, G. W., & Chapman, D. W. (1962). *Man and society in disaster.* New York: Basic Books.

Brett, E. A., Spitzer, R. L. & Ostroff, R. (1987). The DSM-III-R diagnostic criteria for post-traumatic stress disorder. *American Journal of Psychiatry,*

Brill, N. Q., & Beebe, G. W. (1955). *A follow-up study of war neuroses.* Washington DC: Veterans Administration Medical Monograph.

Brill, N. Q. (1967). Gross stress reactions II: Traumatic war neuroses. In A. M. Freedman & H. J. Kaplan (Eds.), *Comprehensive textbook of psychiatry* (pp. 1031–1035). Baltimore: Williams & Wilkens.

Chodoff, P. (1970). German concentration camp as psychological stress. *Archives of General Psychiatry, 22,* 78–87.

Cobb, S., & Lindemann, E. (1943). Neuropsychiatric observation after the Coconut Grove fire. *Annals of Surgery, 117,* 814–824.

Danieli, Y. (1982). Families of survivors of the Nazi Holocaust: Some short and long term effects. In C. Spielberger, N. Sarason, & N. Milgram (Eds.), *Stress and anxiety* (Vol. 8, pp. 405–423). New York: Hemisphere Publishing.

Davis, D. (1966). *An introduction to psychopathology.* London: Oxford University Press.

DeFazio, V. J. (1975). Vietnam era veteran: Psychological problems. *Journal of Contemporarv Psychotherapy, 7,* 9–15.

Eaton, W. W., Sigal, J. J., & Weinfeld, M. (1982). Impairment in Holocaust survivors after 33 years: Data from an unbiased community sample. *American Journal of Psychiatry, 139,* 773–777.

Egendorf, A., Kadushin, C., Laufer, R., Rothbart, S., & Sloan, L. (1981). *Legacies of Vietnam: Comparative adjustment of veterans and their peers.* Washington, DC: U.S. Government Printing Office.

Eitinger, L. (1969). Psychosomatic problems in concentration camp survivors. *Journal of Psychosomatic Research, 13,* 183–189.

Fairbairn, W. R. (1952). *War neuroses: Their nature and significance.* Boston: Rutledge, Regents, & Paul.

Figley, C. R. (Ed.). (1978). *Stress disorders among Vietnam veterans: Theory, research and treatment.* New York: Brunner/Mazel.

Figley, C. R. (Ed.). (1985). *Trauma and its wake: The study and treatment of post-traumatic stress disorder.* New York: Brunner/Mazel.

Figley, C. R., & Leventman, S. (Eds.). (1982). *Strangers at home: Vietnam veterans since the war.* New York: Praeger.

Foreman, S. A., & Marmar, C. R. (1985). Therapist actions that address initially poor therapeutic alliances in psychotherapy. *American Journal of Psychiatry, 142,* 922–926.

Frederick, C. (1984). Effects of natural vs. human-induced violence upon victims. *Evaluation and change.* Minneapolis Medical Research Foundation, Inc./NIMH, Mental Health Services Development Branch. Special Issue: Services for the Survivor, 71–75.

Freud, S. (1955). *Beyond the pleasure principle* (Standard ed., Vol. 17). London: Hogarth Press.

Friedman, O., & Linn, W. (1957). Some psychiatric notes on the Andrea Doria. *American Journal of Psychiatry, 114,* 426–432.

Furst, S. S. (1967). Psychic trauma: A survey. In S. S. Furst (Ed.), *Psychic trauma* (pp. 3–50). New York: Basic Books.

Gorer, G. (1965). *Death, grief and morners in contemporary Britain.* New York: Doubleday.

Grinker, R. R., & Spiegel, J. P. (1945). *Men under stress.* Philadelphia: Blakiston.

Haley, S. A. (1974). When the patient reports atrocities. *Archives of General Psychiatry, 30,* 191–196.

Hendin, H., & Haas, A. P. (1984). Post-traumatic stress disorders in veterans of early American wars. *Psychohistory Review, 12,* 25–30.

Hendin, H., Haas, A. P., Singer, P., Gold, F., & Trigos, G. O. (1983). The influence of precombat personality on post-traumatic stress disorder. *Comprehensive Psychiatry, 24,* 530–534.

Hocking, T. (1970). Extreme environmental stress and its significance for psychopathology. *American Journal of Psychotherapy, 24,* 4–26.

Horowitz, M. J. (1986). *Stress response syndromes* (2nd ed.). New Jersey: Jason Aronson.

Horowitz, M. J., & Solomon, G. F. (1975). A prediction of stress response syndromes in Vietnam veterans: Observations and suggestions for treatment. *Journal of Social Issues, 314,* 67–80.

Horowitz, M. J., & Solomon, G. F. (1978). A prediction of stress response syndromes in Vietnam veterans. In C. R. Figley (Ed.), *Stress disorders among Vietnam veterans* (pp. 67–80). New York: Brunner/Mazel.

Horowitz, M. J., Wilner, N., & Alvarez, W. (1979). Impact of event scale: A study of subjective stress. *Psychosomatic Medicine, 41,* 3, 209–218.

Horowitz, M. J., Wilner, N., Kaltreider, N., & Alvarez, W. (1980). Signs and symptoms of posttraumatic disorders. *Archives of General Psychiatry, 37,* 85–92.

Horowitz, M. J., Marmar, C., Weiss, D., DeWitt, K., & Rosenbaum, R. (1984). Brief psychotherapy of bereavement reactions. *Archives of General Psychiatry, 41,* 438–448.

Horowitz, M. J., Marmar, C., Krupnick, J., Wilner, N., Kalteider, N., & Wallerstein, R. (1984). *Personality styles and brief psychotherapy.* New York: Basic Books.

Kardiner, A.,& Spiegel, H. (1947). *War stress and neurotic illness.* New York: Paul B. Hoeber, Inc.

Keane, T., Malloy, P., & Fairbank, J. (1984). Empirical development of an MMPI subscale for the assessment of combat-related post-traumatic stress disorder. *Journal of Consulting and Clinical Psychology, 52,* 888–891.

Kolb, L. C. (1982). Healing the wounds of Vietnam. *Hospital and Community Psychiatry, 33,* 877.

Kolb, L. C. (1983). Return of the repressed: Delayed stress reaction to war. *Journal of the American Academy of Psychoanalysis, 11,* 531–545.

Kolb, L. C. (1984). The post-traumatic stress disorders of combat: A subgroup with a conditioned emotional response. *Military Medicine, 149,* 237–243.

Krystal, H. (1968). *Massive psychic trauma.* New York: International Universities Press.

Krystal, H. (1985). Trauma and the stimulus barrier. *Psychoanalytic Inquiry, 5,* Hillsdale, NJ: Analytic Press.

Krystal, H., & Niederland, W. G. (1971). Psychic traumatization. *International Psychiatric Clinics, 8,* 11–28.

Laufer, R. S., Yager, T., Frey-Wouters, E., & Doneallan, J. (1981). Post-war trauma: Social and psychological problems of Vietnam veterans in the aftermath of the Vietnam War. In A. Egendorf, C. Kadushin, R. S. Laufer, G. Rothbart, & L. Sloan (Eds.), *Legacies of Vietnam* (Vol. 3, pp. 19–44). Washington, DC: U.S. Government Printing Office.

Lewis, N. D., & Engel, B. (1954). *Wartime psychiatry*. New York: Oxford University Press.
Lidz, T. (1946). Psychiatric casualties from Guadalcanal: A study of reactions to extreme stress. *Psychiatry, 9,* 193–215.
Lifton, R. J. (1967). *Death in life: Survivors of Hiroshima.* New York: Random House.
Lifton, R. J. (1976). *Life of the self.* New York: Touchstone Books.
Malan, D. H. (1963). *A study of brief psychotherapy.* London: Tavistock.
Malan, D. H. (1976). *Toward the validation of dynamic psychotherapy.* New York: Plenum Press.
Malloy, P., Fairbank, J., & Keane, T. (1983). Validation of a multimethod assessment of post-traumatic stress disorders in Vietnam veterans. *Journal of Consulting and Clinical Psychology, 51,* 488–494.
Mann, J. (1973). *Time limited psychotherapy.* Cambridge, MA: Harvard University Press.
Marmar, C. R., & Freedman, M. (in press). Brief dynamic therapy of post-traumatic stress disorder: Management of narcissistic regression. *Journal of Traumatic Stress.*
Marmar, C. R., Horowitz, M. J., Weiss, D. S., Wilner, N., & Kaltreider, N. (1988). A controlled trial of brief psychotherapy and mutual help group treatment of conjugal bereavement. *American Journal of Psychiatry, 145.*
Ostwald, P., & Bittner, E. (1968). Life adjustment after severe persecution. *American Journal of Psychiatry, 124,* 87–94.
Parkes, C. M. (1964). Recent bereavement as a cause of mental illness. *British Journal of Psychiatry, 110,* 198–204.
Popovic, M., & Petrovic, D. (1965). After the earthquake. *Lancet, 2,* 1169–1171.
Shatan, C. (1973). The grief of soldiers: Vietnam combat veterans' self-help movement. *American Journal of Orthopsychiatry, 43,* 640–653.
Sifneos, P. (1972). *Short-term psychotherapy and emotional crisis.* Cambridge, MA: Harvard University Press.
Sifneos, P. E. (1979). *Short-term psychotherapy: Evaluation and technique.* New York: Plenum Press.
Sonnenberg, S., Blank, A., & Talbott, R. (1985). *War trauma and recovery from stress.* Washington, DC: American Psychiatric Press.
Terr, L. (1983). Chowchilla revisited: The effects of psychic trauma four years after a school-bus kidnapping. *American Journal of Psychiatry, 140,* 1543–1550.
Trimble, M. R. (1981). *Post-traumatic neuroses.* New York: Wiley.
van der Kolk, B., Blitz, R., Burr, W., Sherry, S., & Hartman, E. (1984). Nightmares and trauma: A comparison of nightmares after combat with lifelong nightmares in veterans. *American Journal of Psychiatry, 141,* 187–190.
Weiss, D., Horowitz, M., & Wilner, N. (1984). Stress response rating scale: A clinician's measure. *British Journal of Clinical Psychology, 23,* 202–215.
Wilson, J. P. (1980). Conflict, stress and growth: Effects of war on psychosocial development among Vietnam veterans. In C. R. Figley & S. Leventman (Eds.), *Strangers at home: Vietnam veterans since the war* (pp. 123–166). New York: Praeger.
Wilson, J. P. (1987). Understanding and treating the Vietnam veteran. In F. Ochberg (Ed.), *Post-traumatic therapy.* New York: Brunner/Mazel.
Wilson, J. P., & Krauss, G. E. (1985). Predicting post-traumatic stress syndromes among Vietnam veterans. In P. Kelly (Ed.), *Post-traumatic stress disorder and the war veteran patient.* New York: Brunner/Mazel.

5

Conceptual Issues in Research with Survivors and Illustrations from a Follow-Up Study

BONNIE L. GREEN and MARY C. GRACE

The purpose of the present chapter is twofold. First, we would like to set out some general issues in doing research with survivors of extreme stress events. Initially, we will touch on the subjective narrative as a source of empirical data. We will then propose that there are two different genres of questions that are being asked in trauma research at the present time. The nature of these will be delineated along with more specific subquestions. Next, a set of methodologic considerations that may reduce the generalizability of findings from any particular sample of survivors will be briefly discussed.

After developing these more general issues, we will turn to a consideration of the issues that are particularly salient in studies of survivors who are many years beyond a catastrophic event and in longitudinal studies of extreme stress events. These issues will raise questions about the reliability of retrospective recall about details of the traumatic event, about responses made to the event, and about the integrity of the population sample over time. Finally, we will present data from a recent 14-year follow-up of survivors of a man-made disaster, addressing empirically these specific questions of sample attrition and retrospective recall. Discussion will focus on the implications of these findings for research with other chronic survivor populations.

BONNIE L. GREEN and MARY C. GRACE • Department of Psychiatry, University of Cincinnati College of Medicine, Cincinnati, Ohio 45221.

GENERAL RESEARCH ISSUES

Subject as Informant

As we inquire into the nature and development of responses to extremely stressful life events, we have to make some important choices about how to structure our observations. We want to ask our questions in a way that is respectful of our subject and his or her experience and that will allow a certain flexibility in his or her description of a stressful life event. Yet, we also want to be able to generalize from one subject to another and even from one sample and one population to another. All of these goals are potentially compatible and guide the research efforts in studies of extreme stress.

The subjective narrative, the case history, gives us the flavor of the experience, the sense of an individual story, and how stories and their meaning impact on individual lives. The narrative helps us to identify with the subject, appreciate the meanings that an experience can have for people, and develop hypotheses about the mechanisms involved in the responses we observe. We have also found that subjects' report of the trauma can be therapeutic. Some subjects have never told their stories to someone who can listen empathically and respect their experience. We have learned that the telling of the story is an important way to begin gathering data on a subject for a number of reasons. First, it builds rapport. It establishes the subject as a reporter of his or her own experience who has an important perspective to offer and builds a context for later data that are collected. However, some may argue that this perspective allows collection of better, more complete information, whereas others may argue that it introduces a bias and may not be accurate information. There is probably some evidence to support both perspectives. The danger, of course, is to attempt to use the subjective narrative alone. Subjects will not freely disclose information unless we ask them specific questions. And they will not put their answers, or their stories, in terms that allow direct comparisons to the experiences, thoughts, and feelings of others. This direct comparison is necessary for us to generalize. For purposes of an individual psychotherapy, however, we may be quite interested in the specific idiosyncratic aspects of a particular case. Similarly, for purposes of theory development, and even for the development of therapeutic techniques, we must be concerned with the similarities among cases and with establishing the conditions and parameters for variability across groups of cases. Thus the challenge is to have enough *specificity* to capture the complexity of the phenomena we are studying and to allow unexpected information to emerge, while at the same time providing enough structure and standardization to discover consistencies from one subject, sample, and population to the next. From these we develop generalizations that will inform our theories and our treatment techniques.

We feel that there are two different genres of conceptual questions presently being posed in our field. These questions are being asked by clinicians and researchers as we raise theoretical and clinical questions about extreme stress and provide treatment to those who have been exposed to it. The information that we collect from these different perspectives will give us a more complete picture of responses to stress than either of the perspectives alone.

Nomothetic Principles in Research on Extreme Stress

The first set of questions we are asking attempts to get at *general principles or general rules* that apply to survivors of extreme stress:

1. What is the *nature of the response* to extreme environmental stress, that is, what symptoms does it cause; is there a specific syndrome that we can identify—what is the topology of the response?
2. What is the *longevity of the response?* Do stress responses disappear naturally after a certain time period, or conversely, do they extend indefinitely if left untreated? Or do responses emerge only after a period of elapsed time?
3. What are the *processes involved* in the responses to extreme events—the cognitive, emotional, behavioral, and biological mechanisms by which a certain external event leads to an internal, individual response on the part of the survivor?
4. How does the response *change over time*—are there phases of the response? Does it change form? Are chronic forms different from acute forms?
5. What is the *nature of the recovery process?* What relationship does it have to the original mechanisms of response? How does it proceed over time, treated and untreated?

The preceding questions, then, are those that focus on nomothetic principles, those general notions that tie together the responses of people who have been through a catastrophic event, by focusing on similarities from person to person.

Individual Differences

Another set of questions, however, focuses more on how circumstances alter cases. Such questions, still proceeding at a conceptual level to understand groups of survivors, attend to those categories of constructs that influence the adaptation to extreme stress. A number of models have been proposed to tie together these constructs. Our own group has proposed a conceptual model (Green, Wilson, & Lindy, 1985) of the processing of a catastrophic event that includes the group of variables that are inherent in the questions listed later. The questions address real factors that we are interested in scientifically, independent of the methodological differences. These are described in somewhat more detail elsewhere (Green, 1985). With regard to the impact on the response to extreme events, we would like to know about:

1. *Differences among events.* Events have different characteristics that may affect how they impact on the individual psychologically, as well as similarities, so that we can probably specify some generic elements of extreme situations that may help us define events in more standardized ways. But events have differences that we need to appreciate in order to predict, understand, and treat responses to them.

2. We are also interested in *differences among people within events.* Events happen to different types of people and may influence them differently. People differ on many demographic and personality dimensions, and these characteristics tend to influence how they process a traumatic event. Such variables as coping styles, prior traumatic experiences, and specific vulnerability are important to know in trauma research. Learning about these differences will help us be more precise in our understanding of the particular individual or group that we are working with.

3. *Differences within people across time* are also of scientific interest. Change over time was mentioned as a general question of interest, but it also fits here conceptually for two reasons. Differences in time frame is something that gets addressed too seldom, although it is probably quite important, and there is also some evidence that different experiences lead to different time courses in the life of the stress response. What experiences lead to (a) delayed responses, (b) persistent responses, compared to (c) more acute responses in stress victims are of high interest. People also age, mature, and develop, influencing their perspective and the meaning that they retrospectively assign to events.

4. Finally, *differences in the recovery environment* that facilitate or impede recovery are increasingly being examined. Access to and availability of different types of support systems (both interpersonal and at a group level (Lindy & Grace, 1985)) as well as cultural attitudes toward the traumatic event and the survivor may play significant roles in how survivors and groups of survivors can work through their experiences to a point of psychological mastery. The more we know about these differences, the more we may potentially be of help to them.

Methodological Limitations

In order to obtain answers to our questions about nomothetic principles and individual differences, certain methodological issues need to be addressed that may limit our ability to generalize from our research studies to survivors in general. These issues define the parameters of generalizability of our findings and concern: (1) nature of the sample, (2) defining the traumatized population, (3) the types of data collected, (4) the criteria used to define stress responses, and (5) the timing of the research program. These are discussed next.

1. The first issue has to do with sampling. The *nature of the sample* we choose has much to do with the types of conclusions we draw. Yet the sample we choose *also* determines the type of information we can get. Different types of samples are appropriate for different purposes. Clearly, we would draw different samples for purposes of determining population rates of impairment than we would to determine mechanisms of change in psychotherapy. The issue is not for everyone to ask the same question but to be clear about what goals are being addressed and how the sample studied fits with the question of interest.

2. The second methodological issue has to do with *defining the population* of interest. Although most people are conscientious about describing their sample, they are often lax in trying to define *who they think their sample represents,* or what conclusions about a population or situation might be likely to apply to other populations or situations. Previously, it seems that people either confined themselves to one population of interest, or they assumed that there was generalizability from one type of situation to another. We are presently in a position to address such questions empirically, as will be discussed later in this chapter.

3. *Types of data collected.* As noted earlier, the information collected about a survivor following a catastrophic event may take a variety of forms and come from a variety of perspectives. These modes vary widely and encompass clinical interview data *and* survey data; data collected face-to-face by talking *and* those collected by paper-and-pencil report; data gleaned from open-ended questions *and* those obtained from questions with fixed responses. All of these types and levels of data would yield somewhat different types of information. Although the information would probably not be interchangeable, it hopefully would be complementary.

4. Another issue that complicates research in the area has to do with the *criteria used to define responses to events.* By this category, we wish to encompass two problems. The first has to do with defining a *syndrome:* Is there a group of symptoms that make up a conceptually coherent response? The second relates to the problem of defining the point at which something is clinically significant or problematic. In a clinical setting, the patients will indicate their problems. In more broad-based research, the investigators are charged with defining the point at which what is seen is clinically or conceptually significant. This is not an easy task. Having a diagnosis is helpful but does not take away the judgment calls. What frequency defines a "recurrent" dream, for example, or how much of an

increase or decrease in feelings or behavior is a "yes" along a set of diagnostic criteria? Is adding up responses to a series of self-report items equivalent to making a clinical judgment about the presence of a diagnosis based on a structured interview? Although we are much more likely to see clear-cut cases in a clinical setting, or, alternatively, to have the opportunity to clarify and define because we see people more than once and can explore in depth their problems and symptoms, in the field we have more difficulty. There are clear-cut cases at both ends of the continuum, but there are also those individuals who fall in between, who may be better defined along a meaningful and well-defined continuum. In any event, how each investigator deals with these issues determines to some extent how comparable his or her findings are with those of others.

5. Finally, *timing* issues with regard to when research is done are usually confounded with real differences in response that are attributable to the passage of time and to changes in response over time. Findings among investigators in a particular area may seem difficult to reconcile at times because data may be recollected at very different points relative to the occurrence of the traumatic event. If there are *real* differences over time in how the response looks or what aspects of the event or the recovery environment are more influential, they may be difficult to ascertain because data are not collected at a consistent point in time, or the time frame is not addressed as a parameter in the research program.

All of the preceding points about limits to generalizability are not made to imply that we cannot generalize but rather to express the importance of specifying the parameters of our investigations. We need to take the time to be clear about the purpose of the study, the kind of data that will be generated, and for what purpose it will be useful. We need to specify clearly the design and the population(s) to which we would like to be able to generalize. Multiple approaches to instrumentation need to be used with some rationale of the choice of instruments. Timing issues need to be addressed. If we pay attention to these issues and attempt to be clear about them, trauma researchers do not all need to do the same thing or ask the same questions. Ultimately, we will be able to learn over time how the findings in one area by one group fit together or complement those of another.

SPECIAL ISSUES IN CHRONIC SURVIVOR POPULATIONS

The remainder of this chapter will be devoted to some issues that are especially salient in the study of survivors who are at a relatively distant point from the original traumatic event, as well as in longitudinal studies. We will describe a particular event and present data relating to the questions raised. We are hopeful that the findings are relevant to other types of research as well.

Buffalo Creek Study

The data we will be presenting are based upon a recently completed study of survivors of the Buffalo Creek dam collapse and flood, which occurred in February of 1972. Our department of psychiatry examined 381 adult survivors in depth in 1974 in conjunction with a lawsuit that resulted in compensation for psychological damages. The quantification of the original diagnostic reports, for purposes of reporting the relationship among individual stressors, mediators and psychopathology, was supported by the National Institute of Mental Health (Grant No. R01 MH 26321, G. Gleser, Ph.D., principal investigator), as was the recent 14-year follow-up (Grant No. R01 MH 40401, B. Green, Ph.D., principal investigator). For the latter study, we completed four field trips to the Buffalo Creek valley and one to a neighboring area in West Virginia (to be used as a comparison site) between February and July of 1986. We interviewed, during that time, 215 flood survivors and 50 comparison subjects. Of the 215, 129 were in the original lawsuit.

Access to survivors is clearly an important issue in any study, and traumatized survivors are not a group that are likely to be beating our door down, even to get our help, let alone to be our research subjects. In 1974, we had access to all survivors because they were suing the Pittston Coal Company and were obliged to submit to a diagnostic interview. We were also participating on the side of the plaintiffs. At that time, we were able to show a relationship between the data collected for the two sides of the lawsuit, both in terms of the person's experience, as well as in terms of the symptoms and problems reported, although the *attribution* for the symptoms by the experts sometimes differed as to etiology. Empirically, we were able to demonstrate an association between intensity of symptoms or pathology reported by diagnosticians on both sides of the lawsuit and certain aspects of the flood experience itself, such as life threat, loss or bereavement, and geographic displacement (Gleser, Green, & Winget, 1981; Green & Gleser, 1983).

When we returned this time, we did not have the lawsuit as a mode of entry and were, by definition, now outsiders, although we were from an institution that had been previously supportive. Although people were generally courteous, the litigants were not uniformly open to talking with us again 14 years postflood. Just locating people after 12 years was a challenge. We were helped by the fact that we were working in an Appalachian community where people have strong ties to the land and, once they are adults, they tend not to be highly transient. Thus, we were able to locate or account for over 80% of the original sample, a feat that probably would be next to impossible in an urban setting.

Some people refused to talk with us. They simply wanted to put the flood behind them and were *not* interested in talking about it any more. Other survivors were more ambivalent. They scheduled appointments with us and then canceled or did not show up. We were able to reschedule and complete some of those interviews. In a few cases, friends or family members intervened to deny us access to other survivors (Lindy, 1985; Lindy & Grace, 1985). We also found, in that West Virginia community, that calling on people in person is more effective in eliciting participation than telephone contacts and much more effective than mail contacts. Although not everyone agreed to talk with us, we do have much information on the refusers and cancelers. In most research situations, there are people who volunteer to participate and people who do not, or, even in studies where subjects are selected randomly, there are always refusers. We usually know very little about these people in terms of their experiences or their symptoms or problems. In the present study, we have rather extensive earlier data about the nature of the flood experience and the psychological state of the subjects in 1974, so we are able to address some of the questions of who participates and who does not, in some depth.

Although it is usually the case that original data are available on dropouts from a longitudinal research study, we feel that our own information in this regard is of particular interest because the original group could in no way be considered volunteers. They were ordered to undergo examination as part of the lawsuit. Whether people who participate in *lawsuits* are representative is a separate question, which we can address to some extent with our nonlitigant comparison group. However, of the original adults, it is likely that some would have participated in a research study to explore psychological reactions to extreme stress, and some would not. Therefore, we feel that our contrast between people who participated and refused may have implications for understanding who, of potentially traumatized survivors, might participate in research.

In addition to the preceding question, we were also interested in whether flood experiences or psychopathology contributed in any way to people moving out of the valley or dying. We were able to examine this question as well.

A major issue in the conduct of research about people's responses to catastrophic events has to do with the veracity of the accounts of their experiences and of their responses to the experiences. There are a variety of potential reasons to question the veracity of the accounts. First, people could consciously misrepresent their experiences or responses for purposes of financial or social gain. This is primarily raised in the context of legal proceedings where a person has something to gain by malingering. Alternatively, people may unconsciously or inadvertently distort accounts of events and certainly could distort *their responses* to such events for psychological reasons of which they were unaware. As clinicians, we are interested in such distortions and use them to understand the psychological processes going on within the patient and to track recovery. We are also in a better position to judge the extent and nature of the distortion. With large-scale research, however, the accounts constitute the dependent and independent variables under study, so their reliability and validity are of great importance.

A variety of things might influence the extent to which distortion could be expected to occur. The length of the event would certainly be one potential factor, just in terms of the amount of material to remember. Thus an event like a fire or the dam collapse or a rape is a discrete event. Being interned in a concentration camp or doing a year-long tour of combat duty is not a discrete event but a *series of events.* Part of the difficulty, of course, with those events that extend across time is in our ability to conceptualize them. Describing a prolonged "stressor" in terms of its nature or severity is very difficult because it is hard to know where to focus. Yet as we know, there is evidence that details and aspects of such experiences do have the power to differentiate individuals even years after the events in terms of attitudes, feelings, and behaviors (cf. Gleser *et al.,* 1981; Laufer, Brett, & Gallops, 1985; Lund, Foy, Sipprelle, & Strachan, 1984; Matussek, 1975).

We also have reason to suspect that the context in which events and symptoms are reported and the context of the event itself are important in determining the accuracy of the report. One of the new criteria for post-traumatic stress disorder (PTSD) in DSM-III-R (APA, 1987) is amnesia for a particular aspect or aspects of a traumatic event. We know from clinical work that certain important details in the account of an event are missing at times. We also know that what people report, as well as what they remember, may be in part determined by their own or an anticipated other's judgment of their behaviors. Disclosure of feelings or actions that the survivor thinks will be judged harshly by others, or even more importantly, those he or she judges harshly himself or herself, may be less likely to be reported. For example, it has sometimes been the case in a treatment sample we have studied that behavior originally reported as only indirectly observed turns out to have been engaged in directly. Thus we observe the importance of how the questions are asked and the context in which they are framed. Examples of how this can be handled include the work of Laufer and his colleagues in New York with Vietnam veterans where the questions about participation in atrocities are preceded by a variety of general questions related to war crimes and the types of actions committed by the enemy in order to set up an appropriate context for reporting on one's own behavior.

Although we cannot address directly the validity of the early accounts of details of the flood experience (indirect validity was addressed in the earlier study, Gleser *et al.,* 1981), we *are able to examine the reliability of the retrospective recall* between 2 years and 14 years postflood. We can also examine the extent to which current psychological functioning mediates that recall.

EMPIRICAL FINDINGS

Methods

In both 1974 and 1986, subjects were interviewed using a clinical interview format. In 1974, interviewers were mental health professionals and trainees in the psychiatry department (including psychiatry, psychology, and social work). In 1986, interviewers were usually behavioral science graduate students, with a few exceptions for interviewers with prior experience.

A variety of instruments were used in both studies. In 1974 the diagnostic interviews were rated by research staff on the Psychiatric Evaluation Form (PEF) (Endicott & Spitzer, 1970; Spitzer, Endicott, Mesnikoff, & Cohen, 1968). This instrument includes ratings on 19 subscales and an Overall Severity measure. The subscales were then factor analyzed into Depression, Anxiety and Belligerence. Subjects also filled out a 48-item symptom checklist (Lipman, Rickles, Covi, Derogatis, & Uhlenhuth, 1969). In addition, staff rated the narrative for intensity of life threat during the flood (*initial stress*), extent of loss of possessions, friends, and family members (*bereavement*), and extent of *displacement* (see Gleser *et al.*, 1981, for details; see Table 1)). In 1986, the PEF ratings were made by the interviewers, following a lengthy diagnostic interview (Structured Clinical Interview for DSM-III; Spitzer & Williams, 1986), with a modification of the PTSD section. Subjects filled out the SCL-90 and 12 additional symptoms related to a PTSD diagnosis. As part of the 1986 follow-up, we included several open-ended questions about survivors' flood experiences. Although this was instituted at the second trip to gather stressor information on the nonlitigants, for whom we had limited earlier data, we decided to collect it on the litigants as well and examine empirically the correspondence between the two very different (in time and format) accounts of the same event.

Study Participation

We have grouped the original 381 participants into five categories based on their status in 1986 with regard to follow-up participation (Grace, 1986). Table 2 gives the criteria for inclusion in each of these categories and the numbers of subjects in each. The last category includes a variety of survivors, some of whom were willing to participate but unable to because of schedule conflicts, and some whom we were unable to locate. It is likely that this latter subgroup contains a number of original subjects who moved away. Because this group is so diverse, we need to be cautious about interpreting differences between it and others. However, empirically, the findings from that group most match the group that was known to have left the valley.

Table 1. Stress Scales

Bereavement scores	
Casual acquaintance only	0
Acquaintances and valued possessions	1
Close friends and pets	2
Lateral extended family	3
Family members	4
Displacement scores	
Previous home	0
Different home, same locale	1
Trailer camp in valley	2
Trailer camp near valley	3
Out of valley	4
Initial stress scores	
None—not in flood—no separation	0
Fled with family—plenty of warning or not in flood but separated from family	1
Barely escaped from water and/or concerned for safety of other family members	2
In water below waist or watched own home destroyed or escape temporarily barred	3
In water above waist or witnessing death of others, or fails in attempt to save others or extended exposure to elements	4
Any two items from (4)	5

The main hypothesis with regard to the question of selective attrition was that there would be a significant difference between those who were willing to be followed up versus those who refused and that the previously higher stressed and more impaired survivor would be less willing to complete the follow-up interview. Of additional interest for different conceptual reasons were two other groups: those who had moved away since the flood and those who were deceased.

Table 2. 1986 Follow-Up Status for the Original 1974 Sample

Group	Status	*n*
1	Interviewed in 1986	129
2	Refused to be interviewed	71
3	Moved out of valley	66
4	Deceased	52
5	Uncontacted or unlocatable	63

Demographics. When comparing demographic characteristics of the completers versus the refusers, it was noted that there were no significant differences in *age* between those who completed the follow-up interview and those who refused. Neither was there a significant difference in level of *education* between these two groups. However, a significant difference was noted in the higher proportion of *blacks* from the original sample who participated versus whites.

What is most interesting in the demographic findings is the significant difference in both age and education of the group of survivors who moved away from the valley in the postflood period in that they were younger and better educated than the other groups. This finding suggests a particular mode of coping, that is, *leaving the valley* and the stressful sequelae of the flood, as more likely to have been used by one section of the sample than by the others.

Specific Stressors. Table 3 presents the average of each stressor experience at the time of the flood by follow-up status. Analysis of variance was used to test for significant differences.

The most interesting finding in these data is that those with *higher bereavement* scores were significantly more likely to refuse participation in a follow-up interview than those with low bereavement scores. This finding would support the main hypothesis that the stressor experience is related to follow-up participation. However, this was not the case with the other characteristics of the stressor. Neither the *initial flood experience* itself nor the amount of displacement it caused were significant predictors of follow-up participation. There was a significant difference in *displacement* in that those who were more displaced following the flood and at 2 years were more likely to have moved from the valley at the time of the current follow-up. This is likely related to the environmental reality of not having a house to live in than it is an indicator of psychological status.

Psychopathology. There were no significant differences in clinical (PEF) ratings among the groups. Several differences existed between the

Table 3. Means and Standard Deviations by Follow-Up Status

	Interviewed (n = 129)	Refused (n = 71)	Moved (n = 66)	Deceased (n = 52)	Not contacted (n = 63)
Bereavement	*$\bar{x}$ = 1.89 (.97)	2.22 (1.46)	1.80 (1.52)	2.03 (1.50)	1.77 (1.50)
Displacement	*$\bar{x}$ = 1.50 (1.37)	1.92 (1.46)	2.59 (1.52)	2.04 (1.50)	2.06 (1.50)
Initial stress	$\bar{x}$ = 3.12 (1.20)	3.13 (1.20)	3.18 (1.31)	3.08 (1.41)	3.14 (1.28)

*Difference significant at $p < .05$.

groups on the other measures but these could be attributed to the age difference among the groups. The difference in 1974 Symptom Checklist scores, where participants had higher scores than those who could not be located, disappeared when age was controlled statistically.

Although we found that those who received the highest overall clinical ratings in 1974 are now deceased, this difference was also a function of age. Again, there were no significant differences on any of the psychopathology measures between those who were interviewed and those who refused.

Retrospective Recall

In order to determine the reliability of survivors' recall of their flood experiences over a 12-year period, a number of procedures were required. First, generalizability estimates (a type of interrater reliability that takes into account average rater differences as well as relative ordering of subjects) were obtained on ratings of the 1986 responses to the open-ended question asking for a brief recounting of the survivor's flood experience. A training session was conducted for the two raters involved to discuss the bereavement and initial flood stress scales used to quantify the 1974 data (Table 1). Approximately 20 test cases from the 1986 interviews were rated and reviewed for discrepancies. Following this, each rater scored the 1986 stress information on the 81 litigants for whom we had 1986 data for both bereavement and initial flood stress. Rater generalizability coefficients were .80 for bereavement and .59 for initial flood stress. Next, we looked at the associations between 1974 and 1986 scores. The correlation between 1974 and 1986 ratings of bereavement was quite good, $r = .58$. Average level of bereavement did decrease significantly, however, from 1.84 in 1976 to 1.54 in 1986. Wondering whether this was a result of shifts in nuances, over 12 years, of closeness of acquaintances and friends who died, we did a more gross grouping of the data, dichotomizing losses into acquaintances and friends as contrasted with family members. Although this did not alter the correlation, it did have an effect on the *levels* of bereavement, which showed no change over time with this second grouping.

The reliability of the initial flood stress scales at the two points in time was less notable ($r = .36$). Although this is a significant association, it does indicate some disagreement in the ordering of relative stressfulness of the flood experience at two points in time. There is also a significant decrease in the amount of stress reported, with average scores changing from 3.18 in 1974 to 2.33 in 1986. There are several explanations for these findings. Because the components of the scale are less clear-cut than bereavement (e.g., how much warning is "plenty?"), those data are open to more inferences by raters. This is likely to influence the correspondence across time as well as the interrater reliability. Close scrutiny of a number of cases with discrepancies showed that the 1974 and 1986 reports were compatible rather than contradictory, although aspects of the experience were missing from one or the other of the reports. Because the discrepancy was usually in one direction (i.e., less stress reported in 1986), it seems possible that the intensity of the experience has been modified by the passage of time, and the experience is therefore not as vividly recounted. Suggestions for avoiding this problem are discussed next.

DISCUSSION

Locating the Sample

As noted earlier, one of the interesting questions we had to address upon return to Buffalo Creek 14 years postevent (and 12 years after our first visit) was how many of the original sample we would be able to locate. The fact that we were able to account for nearly 85% of the original sample was very encouraging. It is unclear to what extent these figures would hold in a more urban setting, but they are actually quite similar to another study done in Appalachia that focused on aging survivors of two less destructive floods (Norris, in press). In that study, similar percentages of subjects had died by the time of follow-up (a shorter time period between flood and interview, but the subjects were older in the Norris study). In that study, 14.8% of the subjects had died, compared to 13.6% in our sample. More salient to the present report is the refusal figure. In the Norris study, 17% of the original subjects refused to be interviewed, and 4.3% declined for reasons of poor health. Nineteen percent of our original sample refused the follow-up. The other investigators were more successful locating subjects than we were. Only 3.3% of their original group could not be located, whereas nearly 17% of our subjects, over the longer time period, were uncontactable.

Study Participation

The data that are offered on attrition from our 1974 sample speak primarily to the question of who volunteers for a research project on stress. Conceptually, there would certainly be reason to hypothesize that people who volunteer might be more or less stressed or more or less impaired than people who do not volunteer. We feel that the data we presented can speak to this question because our subjects *had* to participate because of the litigation in 1974 but not in 1986.

As noted in the section on empirical findings, there are indeed differences between people who volunteered to be subjects in 1986 and those who participated in the lawsuit in 1974. Specifically, those subjects with high bereavement, on the average, stayed away from the later study, suggesting some continued pain or discomfort for this group and reluctance to recount the flood experience one more time. With regard to the dimension measuring degree of life threat, the groups were equally stressed at the time of the flood. The stress differences in the 1986 participation groups were not attributable to age even though, as noted, those who had died since 1974 were older on the average and the group who moved away from the valley was younger.

The findings from our study suggest that volunteers are not necessarily a highly select subsample of the population. People who show up to volunteer for a study may have a variety of motives. Concerns that only the sickest people, with a particular perspective, are interested in such studies is certainly not consistent with the findings here. There essentially were no differences on any of the psychopathology measures that were not attributable to age. In our study of survivors of a large supper club fire (Green, Grace, Lindy, Titchener, & Lindy, 1983), we found that dropouts (between the study points of 1 and 2 years) tended to be slightly more impaired than the remainers, a difference that reached significance on the Symptom Checklist. From these two studies, it would seem that there may not be large differences between people who are willing or not willing to participate in a research study about responses to a traumatic event. If there are differences, the nonparticipants may be somewhat more stressed and impaired than the participants, that is, our volunteer samples, if biased, may be a slightly less stressed, more healthy group than the population of interest. That the specific stressor relating to participation was bereavement raises very interesting questions in and of itself. Clearly what aspects of a traumatic experience persist in their effects over time is of high interest to those studying extreme stress. We will be able to address this question in our own sample in future articles from this data set.

Although not especially pertinent to the points being made in the present chapter, we were intrigued by what seemed to be a more common coping mechanism among the younger and more well-educated survivors to move away from the valley. We do know that this is the group that is likely to be transient, especially in areas of high unemployment. However, some young people move and some stay. We did show in our earlier work (Gleser *et al.*, 1981) that women who moved out of the valley were significantly less belligerent than those who stayed. We do have a small sample of people who had left the valley at the time of the follow-up; we are pursuing an additional sample, for whom we have addresses, by mail, to obtain questionnaire data. The relative health or illness of this group is of high interest and salience in our understanding of recovery processes.

Retrospective Recall

The recall information was very interesting in spite of the methodological problems associated with it. How a person describes an experience 15 years after it happened has the potential for not being accurate, as noted earlier. However, the extent to which we trust such information is extremely important because our studies of survivors rely primarily on this reconstructed information as our data source about the survivors' experience. If it is distorted in selected ways, our confidence about what we can say about the relationship between the experience and later responses is decreased. As noted, we did examine this question as somewhat of an afterthought, and the information collected was not as complete as it could have been, or as complete as it was in 1974. Thus, the differences we found between the 1974 and the 1986 reports may be at least partially due to the incompleteness of the data. A particular experience had to be *mentioned* in order to be rated. Rarely would more information lead to a lower score. With regard to bereavement, information about the specific nature of the relationship with those lost was often difficult to categorize. Creating a dichotomy helped, in that, although the distinction between casual acquaintances, acquaintances, and close friends was difficult to make with meager information, the distinction between friend and family was more likely to be consistently made.

The exercise with the stress scores raises a few methodological points that are worthy of note. These have to do both with the conceptualization of stress and its measurement. Even an event as discrete as the Buffalo Creek dam collapse (that is, discrete as contrasted with a prolonged event such as combat duty), contains multiple stressor events within itself. Yet, in this particular instance, we attempted to place them on a logical and meaningful continuum (Gleser *et al.*, 1981). It may not be the case, however, that "lateral extended family" are psychologically closer than "close friends" in all cases (as was assumed for the purposes of scale development). Similarly, the threat, at the hour of the flood, came in a number of forms that had to do with warning, separation from family, contact with the floodwater and sludge, having one's escape barred, trying to rescue someone and failing, and the like. Ordering these or interchanging them also implies assumptions.

Based on our own work with different survivor populations (flood and fire victims, war veterans, etc.) we would suggest that (1) specific aspects or potential aspects of the experience be asked about separately and scaled separately and (2) that each aspect be tested, alone and in combination with the other aspects of the experience, for their prediction of outcome. We followed these procedures in our later work and found them more informative. Although the original work at Buffalo Creek was based on diagnostic reports already completed and therefore could not be quantified beforehand, we were able to break down some of the experiences into smaller units, particularly the types of experiences that occurred in the several weeks following the flood. Although a global rating of how severe these experiences were added little to outcome prediction, some of the separate experiences did predict. For example, having to identify bodies was associated with more long-term psychopathology, whereas cleaning out and restoring one's house was associated with recovery, for the men (Gleser *et al.*, 1981). Asking specific questions addresses the issues of coverage or completeness as well as level of inference and is likely to provide more reliable *and* complete information. For example, Robins *et al.* (1985) did a retrospective recall of early home environment. They compared siblings within the same family and thus obtained individual accounts of whether or not certain things occurred. With regard to the *presence* or *absence* of verifiable facts, the agreement was quite good—about 71%. They found that the people agreed with themselves over time on 76% of the questions. Estimates for *frequency* with which the events occurred were notably lower, whereas agreement on areas where the data were highly inferential, not surprisingly, was low. We are in the process of developing a checklist from the various data sources that taps specific aspects of the stressors separately.

In our study of Vietnam veterans, we reinterviewed veterans, about a third of whom were recruited from clinical referral sources, and asked them to fill out a modification of John Wilson and Gus Krauss's Vietnam Era Stress Inventory Scale. The period of time between the two interviews was approximately 6 months. We got fairly good correspondence between reports of the presence and frequency of certain specific experiences and roles, especially when related experiences were combined into scales. There was no tendency to report experiences as more frequent or less frequent over this short time span.

Examining aspects of the stressor separately also allows for separate hypothesis testing with regard to the impact of various parts of the experience over time. For example, in our Beverly Hills fire study (Green, Grace, & Gleser, 1985), bereavement and life threat decreased in their prediction of psychopathology between 1 and 2 years postfire. On the other hand, injury and time waiting to hear the fate of a loved one (regardless of outcome) maintained their impact, and exposure to dead or charred remains actually was *more* predictive of the longer term outcome.

Thus, for a variety of reasons, we suggest the construction of *a priori* scales or checklists that cover the range of experiences likely to occur to the survivor of a particular event. Relying solely on *a priori* scales, however, should be done only when the experience or type of experience is already well-known by investigators from previous work in an area. In any new area, it is especially important to allow the emergence, in the subject's own words, of stressor experiences that might not be thought of by investigators. This would be an additional advantage of the narrative approach mentioned earlier.

Thus, although we were able to show a reasonable degree of correspondence between ratings of open-ended accounts of aspects of the flood experience made 12 years apart, whenever possible we would recommend constructing scales or items (verbally administered and/or by questionnaire) that cover in a comprehensive way the potential experiences, so that subjects may report on all aspects.

That differences in ratings between 1974 and 1986 tended to be consistently in one direction (i.e., lower in the latter instance) may, as mentioned, be due to incomplete data. We also have the passage of time that may decrease recall. As people recover from, or work through, a traumatic experience, the vividness and emotional intensity of their recall may decline, and aspects of the experience may be left out when the experience is elicited in an open-ended format. Where there are notable shifts, we *can* investigate individual differences that are related to discrepancies. It is possible that people who have recovered more completely from a traumatic event show systematic differences in recall compared to those who continue to be distressed or impaired.

Alternately, discrepancies may be systematically related to certain coping styles. For example, a young lady who was 18 years old at the time of the flood passed out, as did her mother, when the family reached safety on high ground after running from the water. It is not clear whether she initially reported this or her family did, but she was clearly present when it was reported. Reinterviewed in 1986, this young woman's account of her flood experience is relatively accurate compared to the earlier account, except that she did not remember passing out. To the contrary, she asserted, with regard to the experience, that she remembered *every single detail* with great vividness, an unusual assertion. This young woman was also very impaired at follow-up, suggesting an alternative hypothesis: *impairment* may be associated with selected forgetting. We will clearly be interested in the relationship between accuracy, the nature of the person's experience, the present psychological state of the individual, and individual coping styles over time. Examination of these questions is currently underway.

SUMMARY

In summary, we have described some early findings in our work with survivors of the Buffalo Creek dam collapse and flood that occurred in 1972. We feel these findings and the questions and issues associated with them are particularly salient to research investigation involving chronic survivor populations, specifically, who is likely to participate in such studies and the nature of the information they present about their earlier traumatic experiences. Although we have not taken it up here, their memory and recounting of their *responses* over time is also of high interest and will be investigated by us at a later point.

We were encouraged by the findings that we presented. Our investigation of sample attrition between 1974 and 1986 suggested that volunteer participants in studies of extreme stress probably do not represent one end of the continuum of stress or impairment. People who refused to participate when participation became voluntary (at follow-up) were somewhat more bereaved (that is, had suffered more loss during the flood) than their participating counterparts. They were no more or less psychologically or functionally impaired. If there is bias, it is probably in the direction that participants are healthier and less stressed than nonparticipants.

Our data relating recent reports of flood-stressor experiences to earlier, open-ended accounts showed fairly good correspondence. Also, more recent accounts tended to be rated as less stressful. Implications for conceptualization and measurement of stressors were discussed and recommendations made. Individual differences in concordance between the two reports will be examined in the future.

With regard to the general research issues mentioned earlier, the findings that we presented seem to fit best with the section on methodological limitations. Study participation and sample attrition represent the issue of defining the population represented by the research sample in question. The nature of volunteer samples was able to be indirectly addressed by our study. The retrospective recall question, or the reliability of recall, fits with both the issues of types of data collected and findings. The disadvantages of relying solely on open-ended responses were noted in this context. The recall issue is also a substantive one, which we may investigate at a nomothetic level (recall processes over time for people in general) or at the level of individual differences (characteristics of people who show recall discrepancies versus those who do not). Just what aspects of an event are likely to be forgotten is a further nomothetic question of interest, which relates to cognitive/emotional mechanisms in the stress response. An additional question about the conceptualization of stressors and how different aspects, frequencies, and intensities combine to constitute the objective experience was also raised.

REFERENCES

American Psychiatric Association. (1987). *Diagnostic and statistical manual of mental disorders, third edition, revised.* Washington, DC: American Psychiatric Association.

Endicott, J., & Spitzer, R. L. (1978). What! Another psychiatric rating scale? The Psychiatric Evaluation Form. *Journal of Nervous and Mental Disease, 166,* 209–216.

Gleser, G. C., Green, B. L., & Winget, C. N. (1981). *Prolonged psychosocial effects of disaster: A study of Buffalo Creek.* New York: Academic Press.

Grace, M. C. (1986). *Selective attrition in longitudinal research with disaster survivors: A methodological question.* Washington, DC: American Psychological Association.

Green, B. L. (1985). Conceptual and methodological issues in assessing the psychological impact of disaster. In B. J. Sowder (Ed.), *Disasters and mental health: Selected contemporary perspectives* (pp. 179–195). Washington, DC: NIMH, DHHS Publication No. (ADM) 85-1421.

Green, B. L., & Gleser, G. C. (1983). Stress and long-term psychopathology in survivors of the Buffalo Creek disaster. In D. Ricks & B. S. Dohrenwend (Eds.), *Origins of psychopathology: Problems in research and public policy* (pp. 73–90). New York: Cambridge University Press.

Green, B. L., Grace, M. C., Lindy, J. D., Titchener, J. L., & Lindy, J. G. (1983). Levels of functional impairment following a civilian disaster: The Beverly Hills Supper Club fire. *Journal of Consulting and Clinical Psychology, 51,* 573–580.

Green, B. L., Wilson, J. P., & Lindy, J. D. (1985). Conceptualizing post-traumatic stress disorder: A psychosocial framework. In C. R. Figley (Ed.), *Trauma and its wake: The study and treatment of post-traumatic stress disorder* (pp. 53–69). New York: Brunner/Mazel.

Green, B. L., Grace, M. C., & Gleser, G. C. (1985). Identifying survivors at risk: Long-term impairment following the Beverly Hills Supper Club fire. *Journal of Consulting and Clinical Psychology, 53,* 672–678.

Laufer, R. S., Brett, E., & Gallops, M. S. (1985). Dimensions of posttraumatic stress disorder among Vietnam Veterans. *Journal of Nervous and Mental Disease, 173,* 538–545.

Lindy, J. D. (1985). The trauma membrane and other clinical concepts derived from psychotherapeutic work with survivors of natural disasters. *Psychiatric Annals, 15,* 3, 153–160.

Lindy, J. D., & Grace, M. C. (1985). The recovery environment: Continuing stressor versus the healing psychosocial space. In B. J. Sowder (Ed.), *Disasters and mental health: Selected contemporary perspectives* (pp. 137–149). Washington, DC: NIMH, DHHS Publication No. (ADM) 85-1421.

Lipman, R. S., Rickles, K., Covi, L., Derogatis, L. R. & Uhlenhuth, E. H. (1969). Factors of symptom distress. *Archives of General Psychiatry, 21,* 328–338.

Lund, M., Foy, D., Sipprelle, C., & Strachan, A. (1984). *Journal of Clinical Psychology, 40,* 1323–1328.

Matussek, P. (1975). *Internment in concentration camps and its consequences.* New York: Springer-Verlag.

Norris, F. H. (in press). Flood exposure and anxiety in older adults: A prospective study. *Victimology: An International Journal.*

Robins, L., Schoenberg, S., Holmes, S., Ratcliff, K., Benham, A., & Works, J. (1985). Early home environment and retrospective recall. A test for concordance between siblings with and without psychiatric disorders. *American Journal of Orthopsychiatry, 55,* 27–41.

Spitzer, R. L., & Williams, J. B. W. (1986). *Structured clinical interview for DSM-III: Non-patient version.* New York: Biometrics Research.

Spitzer, R. L., Endicott, J., Mesnikoff, A. M., & Cohen, M. S. (1968). *The Psychiatric Evaluation Form.* New York: Biometrics Research.

II

Research

In Part II of the book there are five chapters (Chapters 6–10) that report findings from empirical studies of survivors of wartime stress. The spectrum of research populations in this part includes World War II veterans, prisoners of war, Holocaust survivors, children of Holocaust survivors, and therapists who work with survivors. These chapters address critical issues in the lives of victims of extreme stress such as the long-range impact of combat and war-related stress on mental health and adaptation to aging, the long-range effects of captivity on the lives of former prisoners of war, the moderating effects of postwar experiences and adaptation on the psychological well-being of Holocaust survivors, the evolution of attitudes and relationships between Holocaust survivors and their children, and patterns of countertransference in therapists who work with Holocaust survivors and children of Holocaust survivors.

In Chapter 6, Elder and Clipp report on findings from research that explored the effects of combat experience and comradeship on the psychological health of war veterans. This research is interesting and unique because the study from which the data base was derived was not designed as an exploration of the effects of wartime stress. The data base derived from the archival files of three longitudinal studies at the Institute of Human Development at the University of California, Berkeley, that included men who fought in World War II and Korea and, therefore, offered the authors an opportunity to explore the long-range implications of extreme stress. A survey of the veteran's wartime and military experience was completed during 1985.

The significance of this chapter is underscored by two empirical facts: (1) the older veteran population will number over 9 million by the year 2000 and (2) the lack of empirical evidence on the effects of military service during wartime on health and aging in veteran's lives. Elder and Clipp provide insight into the connection between combat experience, subsequent adaptation to a peacetime society, and the course of aging in the growing population of older veterans. The authors found that heavy combat markedly increased the likelihood of emotional and behavioral problems after leaving the service and that the emotional scars left by combat trauma and the loss of comrades persist in the lives of a good many veterans some 30 years after the war. However, the authors also concluded that combat produced a positive legacy. The acquisition of coping and managerial skills, rewarding memories of experiences with war comrades, and enduring ties with service mates that extend to the present were all viewed as beneficial effects of their combat duty.

The mediating influence that a soldier's precombat coping style and personal resources may have on the process by which combat effects persist or diminish over time is also addressed. The authors found that veterans with more serious problems after the war scored higher on measures of personal vulnerability before the service than did other veterans and, therefore, concluded that veterans who experienced these emotional problems may have been the least equipped to cope with and survive the psychological trauma of combat without some impairment.

In Chapter 7, Hunter provides a historical overview on the status and experiences of prisoners of war and a systematic overview of the psychological effects of imprisonment based on an extensive literature review as well as her own research experience. Her review demonstrates that each captivity or hostage experience was different, depending on the time in history at which the incident occurred, the culture of the captor, the duration and severity of captivity, and the support received from others both while in captivity as well as upon return. Thus the physical residuals of captivity may vary greatly from one POW experience to another. However, she concludes that long-term psychological effects of captivity are more similar for all former prisoners of war.

Hunter asserts that many former captives, but not all, present various degrees of post-traumatic stress disorder (PTSD) in postrelease years, sometimes with a delayed onset. Other conclusions reached include: (1) residuals of captivity may have both psychological and physical manifestations; (2) multiple factors determine the effects of captivity over time; (3) the captor and the captor's culture predict, to a significant extent, both survival and long-term effects of captivity; (4) long and harsh imprisonment appears to solidify basic personality traits; (5) group support and communication with others are critical for coping with effects of captivity; (6) the family to which the former captive returns can be both a stressor and a stress moderator; (7) code of conduct may facilitate coping; (8) coping strategies that are effective immediately following capture or in extreme situations may differ from those that prove effective as imprisonment continues and may prove dysfunctional in the postrelease period; (9) captivity conditions may affect reactions to coercive persuasion or ideological conversion; (10) maturity and committment to a cause or ideology are likely to aid coping with extreme stress; and (11) The "will to survive" is a crucial variable for survival in captivity.

Hunter offers the following insights regarding individuals who have suffered the trauma of prolonged, harsh captivity or hostage experiences: (1) appropriate treatment by knowledgable, empathic caregivers available immediately after release is important for later adjustment; (2) group support from those who have been in a similar situation within prison as well as after release assists in coping; (3) being able to talk about one's feelings of rage, depression, and helplessness benefits not only captives but also their families; (4) flexible homecoming plans are important for reintegration of the former captive into society, and a recognition of the variation in the need for supports of the returning captives is also helpful; (5) the longer the period of captivity and the harsher the treatment during captivity, the longer the period necessary for rehabilitation.

In Chapter 8, Boaz Kahana, Zev Harel, and Eva Kahana report on findings from empirical research on predictors of mental health in three populations of Holocaust survivors: those that were in attendance at the gathering of Holocaust survivors in Washington, DC and two groups of Holocaust survivors, one in the United States and one in Israel. This chapter is significant for two major reasons: (a) the reported research is anchored conceptually in the behavioral and social sciences and (b) the research reports on findings from broad cross-sections of survivor populations.

The authors note that professional perspectives on the effects of the Holocaust in the past have been based almost exclusively on generalizations derived from clinical studies anchored in the medical psychiatirc tradition. Only more recently have studies of Holocaust survivors begun to employ conceptual and methodological approaches anchored in the social and behavioral sciences. This chapter provides converging evidence from three studies of survivor populations concerning the mediating effects of post-stress adaptation and experiences on the long-range effects on extreme stress on psychological well-being in late life. Although there is evidence that documents the negative effects of internment, this chapter substantiates the importance of postinternment factors for the mental health of aging survivors of the Holocaust. More specifically, findings from these studies suggest that adequate health, higher levels of economic and social resources, along with appropriate coping styles and opportunities for self-disclosure, are important determinants of mental health among survivors of extreme stress.

In the authors' view, it is important, therefore, for mental health professionals to acquaint themselves with the empirical evidence from more recent research so as to better understand the experiences of survivors of extreme stress and service their needs. This chapter provides direction for professionals working with stress victims to facilitate and aid survivor's adjustment to the conventional demands of poststress life, including efforts to aid adjustment to aging.

In Chapter 9, Klein-Parker reports findings from an exploratory heuristic-phenomenological study of the common experience of 39 adult children of Holocaust survivors. Participants in this study included 25 women and 14 men, age 24 to 34, who were born within 10 years of their parents' liberation. This study explored retrospectively the evolving nature of the survivor/parent–child relationship from childhood into adulthood.

All children of survivors appeared to have a common awareness of the impact of the Holocaust on their lives. However, the degree of impact varied as did individual histories, life experiences, and family adjustments after the Holocaust. This investigation explored concrete dimensions of the survivor/parent–child relationship over time. Eight dominant interactional patterns of adult children toward their Holocaust-survivor parents, reflective of perceptions, and attitudes and feelings were identified and discussed by the author: (1) perceptions that transactions with parents were intense but superficial; (2) a deep attachment to their parents was felt; (3) shielded parents from painful experiences; (4) perceptions that the Holocaust created barriers in the parent–child relationship; (5) perceptions that parental communications were indirect and ambiguous; (6) a sense of responsibility and guilt in connection with the Holocaust; (7) feelings of uncertainty and conflict aroused by parental expectations; and (8) close identification with the Holocaust experiences of parents.

However, with the passage of time, there was a profound shift in attitude toward parents and a maturational process leading to pride and appreciation. The author found the following maturational changes in dominant attitudes: (a) a resolution process of coming to terms with earlier experiences and a shift toward pride and appreciation; (b) a positive identification with parents and their background; (c) an increasing awareness and consciousness of the Holocaust; (d) a sensitivity and deepening protectiveness toward parents; (e) a recognition of and appreciation for the attributes that enabled parents to survive; and (f) a loving acceptance of parents coupled with a comfortable sense of autonomy from them.

The author concludes that some of the dominant attitudes may be related directly to the Holocaust legacy, whereas other interactional and attitudinal patterns may be more typical of parent–child relationships in families where the children are aware of and sensitive to parental pain.

Mental health professionals who engage in the treatment of adult children of survivors can derive from this chapter an understanding of what it means to have been influenced by parents' Holocaust trauma. Through these data, it is possible to understand the salient aspects of such parent–child relationships and thus approach survivorship with an informed perspective. With better understanding, the therapist can assist the adult child toward a resolution process that entails the working through of conflicts in relation to the self, parents, and the Holocaust legacy.

In Chapter 10, Danieli reports on findings from research on psychotherapists' reactions to victims of the Nazi Holocaust. She notes that Holocaust experiences are frequently avoided in therapy with survivors; survivors and children of survivors have frequently complained of neglect or avoidance of their Holocaust experiences by mental health professionals. In her view, society has a moral obligation to share its members' pain; psychotherapists and researchers have, in addition, a professional obligation to listen, explore, understand, and help.

In this study, Danieli examined the nature and types of emotional responses and problems experienced by psychotherapists in working with this unique group of people. In addition, she compared the "countertransference reactions" of psychotherapists in this sample who were survivors and/or children of survivors themselves with those of therapists who were not themselves victims or children of victims of the Nazi Holocaust.

The identified countertransference themes found in this research included defense, bystander's guilt, rage, shame and related emotions, dread and horror, grief and mourning, murder versus death, victim or liberator, "me too," and sense of bond.

Therapists who were not themselves victims of the Nazi Holocaust reported using various modes of defending themselves against listening to Holocaust experiences such as distancing and hiding behind their professional role to control their distress and felt overwhelmed by their own intense emotional reactions to the survivors' stories. In addition, they reported experiencing themselves as outsiders and, to counteract that experience, made statements such as "we are all survivors." They also expressed attitudes, feelings, and myths disparaging to the survivors both as Holocaust victims and as parents, although viewing the survivors' offspring as the fragile victims. More than their counterparts, they expressed rage and disgust toward survivor parents. As outsiders, they tended to feel contempt, distantly viewing survivors as having gone "like sheep to the slaughter." In comparison, psychotherapists who were survivors or children of survivors expressed a sense of bond, a need or a "mission" to help "their people," and a belief that they themselves would be helped in the process. In addition, they experienced more grief and mourning as well as allowed and encouraged the expression of these emotions by survivors and children of survivors.

Danieli makes clear in this chapter that psychotherapy with Holocaust survivors and children of Holocaust survivors is cognitively and emotionally stressful and that therapists must recognize and deal with their own thoughts and feelings and countertransference reactions. She concludes that whether the therapist is a Holocaust survivor or not, the failure to recognize and deal with countertransference reactions may hinder and ultimately prevent the full stress-recovery process.

The chapters on extreme stress research in this part of the book highlight the importance of psychological, social psychological, social, economic, cultural, political, and other environmental approaches for understanding of the effects that war stress has on the adaptation to poststress challenges and opportunities of survivors. These chapters clearly indicate the need for interdisciplinary conceptual approaches in research on the long-term effects of extreme stress and in studies of late-life adaptation of stress victims.

6

Combat Experience, Comradeship, and Psychological Health

GLEN H. ELDER, JR. and ELIZABETH C. CLIPP

> The impact of the great war has not been fully realized two decades [now four decades] after its termination. The combat fatigue syndrome, which was expected to vanish with the passage of time, has proved to be chronic, if not irreversible.
>
> —Archibald and Tuddenham (1965)

The twentieth century is marked by events of drastic, traumatic change. These include mass immigration and internment, severe economic downturns, as in the Great Depression, famine, and wars. What imprint did these experiences have on the lives of men and women, the young and old? In *Bitter Wounds,* a profoundly moving book on German victims of World War II, Robert Whalen (1984) concludes with an observation that is too obvious and readily ignored: "when wars are over, all the people whose lives have been shattered do not simply return to normal. Everyone involved in a war is in some way a war victim" (p. 15). Many of these victims are also war survivors, now in their later years.

This chapter is about the influence of combat experience in the lives of surviving veterans of World War II and the Korean conflict. Some of these veterans are burdened with symptomatology reflective of their experience,

---

GLEN H. ELDER, JR. • Department of Sociology, University of North Carolina, Chapel Hill, North Carolina 27514. **ELIZABETH C. CLIPP** • Geriatric Research Education and Clinical Center, VA and Duke Medical Centers, Durham, North Carolina 27705.

whereas others have emerged with greater inner strength and adaptive resources. As in the case of life events generally, the effects may be costly and developmental. One particular task in life-course studies is to trace these effects over time by specifying factors that are likely to have negative or positive life consequences (Elder, 1985).

Three specific areas of inquiry are explored. First, we examine the link between combat experience and psychological health in the postwar years and decades later. Next we take up the issue of war comradeship, the loss of friends in war, and the extent to which combat experience is associated with enduring social ties. The third area of inquiry explores veterans' psychological functioning before the war in an effort to clarify the complexities and processes of short- and long-term outcomes.

The data come from the longitudinal archives of the Institute of Human Development, University of California, Berkeley. A total of 202 male members from previous studies of the institute were surveyed during the spring and summer of 1985 on questions pertaining to military service and war experience. These men were born mainly in the 1920s and grew up in the San Francisco Bay Area. Over 60% were members of middle-class families. The chapter centers on the men who served in World War II and the Korean conflict, a total of 149. The veterans are either male subjects or husbands of subjects in the Berkeley Guidance and Growth Studies and in the Oakland Growth Study. Only eight study women served in the military during wartime.

More than half of the men from both wars (62%) were either enlistees or recruits from the Reserve Officer Training Corps. Approximately one-third (35%) were drafted; less than 3% came from the reserves. Most of the sample served in the Army (44%), a quarter in the Navy (27%), and slightly less in the Marines and Air Force (23%). Nearly half of the World War II veterans had entered the war by the end of 1942 and served mainly in the Pacific (58%) and in Europe and Africa (21%). The majority of Korean War veterans entered after 1950 (65%). A significant portion only held U.S. posts (42%). As these assignments suggest, actual participation in combat was higher for the World War II veterans (60%) than for the Korean War men (20%). According to Appel (1966), psychiatric admissions rates in both wars were highest for combat divisions, but they were generally lower for Korean War veterans due to their shorter maximum time (9 months) in combat (Glass, 1957).

By using reports from the end of the life span, we lose information on men who left the same sample through death or other circumstances. Apart from two Oakland women who lost husbands in the war, we have no evidence of war deaths in the sample. Previous analyses (Elder, 1974) have shown that the Oakland men at midlife closely resemble the total sample of males in the adolescent years on family background.

Recent work (Elder, 1986) provides some information on how veterans compare with nonveterans in the sample. The veterans came from the working class and middle class in similar proportions. We find no evidence that emotional distance from parents or clinical health ratings during the adolescent years differentiated boys who eventually entered the service from those who did not. However, one prominent difference appears on four multiple-item indexes measuring elements of a competent self. Veterans ranked below others on adolescent goal orientation, self-inadequacy, submissiveness, and social competence. We consider these differences in our analyses of prewar influences.

SOME LIFE-SPAN IMPLICATIONS OF COMBAT EXPERIENCE

A principle of life-course analysis assumes that the full consequences of human experience, especially extremely traumatic ones, are often expressed across the life span and even into successive generations. Just how these consequences are manifested and the nature of conditions that influence this process are unknown for the most part, especially in relation to the effects of wartime. As large cohorts of American veterans enter the later years, we find that surprisingly little is known about the short-term and enduring influences of their military experience.

The focus of research in this area has not been on post-traumatic stress but on postwar adjustment as described by Brill and Beebe (1955) and Havighurst and associates (1951). However, symptoms that are now part of the post-traumatic stress syndrome have been observed in World War II veterans over a period of 15 to 20 years (Archibald & Tuddenham, 1965) with some of these effects appearing before the service. The evidence on Vietnam veterans is more conclusive (Card, 1983; Egendorf, Kadushin, Laufer, Rothbart, & Sloan, 1981; Green, Wilson, & Lindy, 1985; Harris, 1980; Robins, 1974; Wilson, 1978). All of these studies move beyond stress reactions to a range of issues dealing with personal and situational correlates of wartime experience. Our work fits nicely into this tradition with particular guidance from the life-course perspective.

Matters of Historical Time and Context

Any attempt to investigate the effects of combat must begin with its historical context. World War II ranked well above the Korean War on public support, but even the Korean War seems a popular one when compared to the public's disdain for the Vietnam conflict, especially during its last stages. In our survey, for example, approximately 70% of the veterans of World War II claim they felt appreciated by fellow Americans upon their return to this country and to civilian life. By comparison, only a third of the Korean veterans were so received, as they recall. The percentage drops to less than a quarter for the Vietnam veteran (Wilson, 1978). Some implications of these differences appear in *Legacies of Vietnam* (Egendorf *et al.*, 1981) and the *Forgotten Warrior Study* (Wilson, 1978). War support was strongest before 1968, especially in small-town America. Both of these conditions minimized the negative psychological effects of Vietnam combat.

Other contextual effects such as homecoming and recruit characteristics influence the nature of combat experience. Homecoming experiences address the social aspects of post-traumatic stress disorder (e.g., withdrawal from the external environment). Wilson (1978) notes, for example, that disabled Vietnam veterans reported significantly greater feelings of rejection and less trust and faith in institutions than able veterans. Given the differences in homecoming experiences across various wars, veterans of World War II would seem at lower risk of social stress reactions (i.e., feelings of isolation, alienation) when compared to the veterans of subsequent wars. However, evidence to date suggests that the homecoming impact may be more political than psychological. In three wars with three unique homecoming scenarios, available evidence points to the same relationship between combat and psychosocial outcomes during the postwar years (Laufer, 1986). This suggests that war trauma rather than the type of homecoming is decisive.

Though all veterans have breaking points, their limits for tolerating extreme conditions vary by personal and situational characteristics. Brill and Beebe (1955) found men with more stable preservice personalities less often broke down early and more often only after prolonged combat, and when they did, their illness was less severe than veterans with some degree of preservice impairment. They also found that preservice stability predicted a more rapid recovery. Yet, Wyatt (1945) observed that "the constant and severe pounding went beyond the 'nervous threshold' of a number of veterans who had previously been thought immune to nervous exhaustion . . . this led us to believe that any man could become a nervous exhaustion case if he were exposed to long and severe combat" (cited in Weinberg, 1946, p. 475).

With regard to age, men entered World War II at an older age when compared to men of Vietnam at the time of their induction (Stouffer *et al.*, 1949). As Stouffer shows, young soldiers in World War II were at a higher risk of stress reactions than their older peers. One member of our sample from World War II recalls, "I remember being forced to grow up in a hurry in a relatively unforgiving environment and being thrust into responsibilities of greater importance than would normally be the case for a young 21-year-old just out of college." In addition, the total mobilization of

World War II ensured a relatively uniform proportion of recruits from all socioeconomic strata, whereas Vietnam recruits seldom came from the higher social strata.

The nature of combat experience itself is another source of historical differentiation. An identifiable front line did exist for most of the ground war in the European theater of World War II and for Korea. By contrast, the island warfare of the Pacific had much in common with the extraordinary ambiguity and threat of Vietnam combat. A series of papers by Wilson and Krauss (1982, 1985) and Laufer and associates (1984, 1985) have stressed the analytic value of a multidimensional model of war experience, one that includes aspects of combat and exposure to abusive violence. For example, Laufer and associates (1984) have measured combat exposure using an additive scale of 10 discrete events that the veteran may have experienced, such as the encounter of mines, exposure to fire, ambush experiences, and killing. Prodded by such work, considerable progress has been made by thinking about combat experience in all of its complexity and subtlety. Our work has been influenced by this advance, and we shall use a three-dimensional model of combat—exposure to killing and death either by observation or by action, exposure to combat fire through use of weapon or receiving incoming fire, and duration of time in combat.

This discussion of combat leads to a consideration of psychosocial outcomes and the syndrome known as post-traumatic stress (PTSD) in the Vietnam era and as stress reactions in World War II (Figley, 1985). According to the model of PTSD outlined by the American Psychiatric Association in the third edition of its diagnostic manual, DSM-III defines PTSD as a syndrome with four sets of criteria: (1) exposure to a recognizable stress or trauma; (2) the reexperiencing of trauma through nightmares, flashbacks, or intrusive memories; (3) emotional numbing or withdrawal from the external environment; and (4) changes in personality and adaptive behavior that includes memory impairment, survivor guilt, sleep disturbance and hyperalertness. Two assumptions of the DSM-III definition are that the syndrome is pervasive and that a traumatic experience such as combat will lead to numbing symptom responses and reexperiencing.

Some 15 years after World War II, a former Marine in the institute sample who had four landings in the South Pacific talked about the nightmares that tormented him, the "hollering and screaming in the middle of the night." Ten years later, he observed that "I can close my eyes and feel the water under my arms . . . the fear was awful . . . it took every bit of energy I could summon, every bit of self-control, for me to get out of the landing boat . . . I was so scared I had nightmares for years." When asked in his 50s whether the service made any difference in the kind of person he became, this veteran stressed other differences, especially the ability to survive adversity—"all one needs is the will to survive—and the skill to cooperate with others and to be dependable and self-disciplined." Both symptoms of distress and coping skills are part of our analysis of combat effects.

Perspectives on Combat and Its Enduring Influences

Opinions differ about the enduring effects of combat stress on veterans' psychosocial functioning. From one perspective, combat experience might lead to symptoms of distress only in the immediate postwar period of 2 or 3 years. The short-term view assumes that the intensity and frequency of stress effects are directly related to the proximity of the situation to the original stress event (see Elder, 1974, Chapter 9). Also called the "stress evaporation perspective" (Figley, 1978), this view contends that veterans probably do experience psychological or emotional adjustment difficulties in the civilian life reentry phase but that problems of this kind eventually resolve themselves. The process of stress decay may reflect the mobilization of social support and environmental change that provides a sense of greater personal control and emotional stability. Though a number of studies on Vietnam veterans support the stress evaporation perspective (Borus, 1974; Segal & Segal, 1976; Worthington, 1978), most do not differentiate between levels of combat exposure.

A contrary outcome, "the residual stress perspective" (Figley, 1978), suggests that the psychosocial aftermath of war continues or even intensifies through the postwar years. From this view, veterans do suffer emotional problems in the readjustment phase and often beyond, making life-course adaptation difficult. This outcome is likely if social support is replaced by social rejection when the service men return and by a continuation of this alienation response, as seen in the lives of many Vietnam veterans (Green *et al.*, 1985). Studies supporting the residual stress perspective are substantial in number (for example, Archibald & Tuddenham, 1965; Card, 1983; Struen & Solberg, 1972). Whether retrospective or prospective in design, these works show much consistency between findings on the impact of combat. Some 40 years have passed since the Berkeley and Oakland veterans' military experience. How might we link these two periods (the war years and later life) in terms relevant to emotional health or impairment?

A third account is derived from research on economic stress and its effects across the life span (Elder, Liker, & Jaworski, 1984). This formulation links stress reactions to the characteristics of a particular situation, such as the experience of personal or material loss. Consequently, the reactions are likely to persist if elements of the originating situation persist, as through continuing hard times, or reappear if such elements (i.e., as during retirement) become more pronounced. For example, a sense of vulnerability is likely to increase with aging and the social losses that often occur in later life. These changes heighten the prospect of reexperiencing stress reactions that first emerged from the trauma of severe socioeconomic hardship. This outcome emerged among men and women from the working class after age 60 (Elder *et al.,* 1984). Those who experienced severe and prolonged hardship during the 30s were most likely to be characterized by a sense of helplessness in old age.

Similarly, in their work on nightmares and PTSD, van der Kolk and Ducey (1984) discuss the difficulty associated with diagnosing PTSD in older veterans of retirement age. In many cases, after what may be years of symptom-free living, nightmares about traumatic events in World War II resume when the older individual is faced with the loss of structure once provided by their jobs. In an earlier survey (van der Kolk & Blitz, 1981), about half of the combat veterans from World War II who were of retirement age had a recurrence of nightmares and intrusive recollections. Likewise, Archibald and associates (1962) found that veterans with symptoms of combat fatigue continued to seek treatment in VA hospitals 7 years after World War II ended. Follow-ups extended this pattern over two decades (Archibald & Tuddenham, 1965). In a 3-year study of World War II veterans, Klonoff and associates (1976) reported that psychiatric and physical problems continued for men exposed to intense combat over an extended duration. Though convincing in most respects, the evidence for delayed onset of symptoms runs counter to a reasonable assumption—that time will heal the wounds of war.

Each account (decay, intensification, and resurfacing in old age) has been discussed without regard for the individual differences that men bring to wartime, differences in stamina, resilience, coping, problem solving, and personal stability. All of our work on traumatic change in the 1930s (Elder & associates, 1984), suggests that the pathogenic effects of combat in World War II will be concentrated among men who ranked below average on such personal resources. To use 1940 psychiatric terminology, combat should predict the highest scores on stress reaction scales among men who entered the service with above average scores on the psychoneurotic symptom list. In the second volume of *The American Soldier,* Stouffer and his coauthors conclude that their data "tend to support the interpretation which has frequently been advanced that early combat breakdowns represent the reactions of men who would ordinarily be considered psychogenically predisposed" (1949, p. 453). The present study tests this hypothesis by comparing the effects of combat among men who differed before the service on personal adequacy.

This study of combat influences over the life span is organized around three guiding hypotheses: (1) the intensity of combat experience will be associated with psychological health, both negative and developmental, short and long term; (2) combat experience will be associated with enduring wartime social ties and their loss; and (3) the association with stress reactions will be strongest among the men who ranked below average on coping resources and psychological functioning before entering the service.

We begin with the task of measuring combat experience in a sample of aging veterans from World War II and the Korean War. Using a multidimensional measure, we compare veterans with different levels of experience on psychological functioning both following exit from the service and in later life (after age 55). Indicators include emotional and behavioral problems (e.g., sleep problems, irritability, problem drinking, marital difficulties), enduring stress symptoms, painful memories, guilt, and acquired adaptive skills. The second phase of analysis examines comradeship and wartime social ties in relation to the combat experience. Measures of wounded and lost friends as well as lifelong war relationships are central to this analysis. We then take a closer look at the relationship between postwar emotional problems and long-term effects. Does the emotional health of veterans after the war provide a lead as to why some have long-term difficulties? The final analysis employs preservice psychological assessments to better specify enduring effects. Prewar indicators from adolescents include Q-sort ratings of self-adequacy, self-regulation, introspectiveness, and emotional state.

THE MEASUREMENT OF COMBAT EXPERIENCE

The measurement of combat reflects or should build upon conceptual models of such experience. However, a good many limitations of combat measures stem from undeveloped conceptual formulations. In the past, combat has been measured very simply by a single item that relies upon the judgment of the respondent or interviewer as to what constitutes a combat situation. Summated indexes based on differentially weighted aspects of combat represent a more complex approach. For example, Wilson and Krauss (1985) use several 5-point Likert scales designed to measure the number of combat roles performed and their perceived stressfulness in terms of threat, injury, and death. The 22 items define standard roles in the Vietnam War and provide scores for the total number of roles and how stressful they were thought to be by the veteran. The veterans also reported the duration of each combat role in their tour of duty.

A similar approach is taken by Laufer (1985) who argues that single measures of war stress (e.g., "combat exposure") fail to identify aspects of the experience that may be a source of intrusive memories. He examines three dimensions of war trauma that have been fruitful in the prediction of subseqeunt symptomatology and behavioral problems: (a) exposure to life-threatening situations, (b) exposure to abusive violence, and (c) participation in episodes of abusive violence.

Our approach borrows from the Vietnam studies and takes into account the limits of time and space in our 1985 follow-up of the Oakland and Berkeley men, women, and spouses. We assume that the trauma of combat is associated with major war stressors, in particular exposure to the dying, wounded, and dead, exposure to gunfire, and the duration of combat experience. As one Oakland veteran put it, "combat is the terror of being forced, against one's free will, to kill or be killed." Twenty-two percent of the men claimed to have killed someone in battle, whereas about one-third were exposed to dead and wounded Americans on the battlefield. A fourth of the veterans reported such exposure to enemy casualties. We summed the responses to these items to produce a 3-point scale (Table 1).

The second dimension of combat is exposure to gunfire, either by firing a weapon or by being fired upon. The last dimension is duration of how long a person served in combat. The men who reported being under fire were also likely to have fired their weapon ($r = .75$). Sixty percent of the men reported at least one of the two conditions. We summed responses to the two items to produce a single index (score 0–2). For the duration of combat, we relied upon a single question to form three groups: over 6-months' exposure (score of 2); 1-week to 6-months' exposure (score of 1), and less than a week's exposure (score of 0).

The three dimensions of combat experience are highly intercorrelated (r values above .70), as one would expect, and they are equally predictive of undesirable recollections of their military experience in World War II (an average r of .56). At the end of the military questionnaire, the men were instructed that "life experiences often have some mixture of the good and undesirable." Then they were asked to circle the three most undesirable experiences that happened to them. Less than five percent of the veterans

Table 1. Correlation Coefficients for Interrelations among Combat Indicators for Veterans[a]

		Correlation coefficients for combat indicators					
Combat indicators[b]	% yes	1	2	3	4	5	6
1. Ever fired a weapon	24	—	.71	.72	.69	.68	.63
2. Ever under fire	38		—	.51	.66	.60	.84
3. Ever killed anyone	15			—	.60	.61	.60
4. Exposed to U.S. killed/wounded	22				—	.66	.59
5. Exposed to enemy killed/wounded	19					—	.63
6. Duration of combat	24[c]						—

[a]$N = 140$.
[b]All items except duration of combat are dichotomous.
[c]Percentage more than 6 months.

with no combat selected "memories of death and destruction," whereas this choice was made by over half of the men who ranked high on each combat dimension.

The indicators of combat experience were selected for a measurement model based on LISREL (Joreskog & Sorbom, 1981). We constructed a model of combat experience from the three measures and then used confirmatory factor analysis to ascertain the relative weights of the individual factors and the model's overall fit. The model assumes that the factors do not have correlated errors. All three indicators have standardized factor loadings above .83. Exposure to gunfire is clearly the most prominent dimension of combat experience (.96), followed by exposure to death and the wounded and time in combat (both .84). The model fit is satisfactory, as indicated by a coefficient of determination of .942.

In view of the higher rate of combat among World War II veterans, we carried out the previously mentioned measurement procedures for only these veterans and made comparisons to the total sample. The intercorrelation matrix is very similar to that for the total sample, as reported in Table 1. Lastly, our World War II analyses indicate that the effects of combat on psychological health and social ties are very similar to those reported in this study for veterans of both wars. Indeed, we found no major differences between groups. For all of these reasons and the value of a larger sample, we chose to combine veterans from the two wars.

The model of combat experience is based upon retrospective accounts of combat. To what extent do we have a picture of the way combat was experienced some 4 years ago? This question is not answerable with the evidence at hand, though we were careful to use uncomplicated questions that focused on behavior rather than ones capable of stirring defensive or mnemonic distortions or fantasy (Masson, 1984). One way to approach the issue is to compare low and high combat groups on measures of stress reaction and psychological health. Do the groups differ on such outcomes according to the notion that heavy combat increases the risk of enduring stress reactions?

COMBAT AND PSYCHOLOGICAL FUNCTIONING

Men who reported heavy combat during World War II were also veterans with a high risk of emotional and behavioral problems following the war. This risk diminishes over time, though it remains high in later life. To set up these comparisons, we summed the scores of each component of combat and formed three groups defined by extent of combat. Forty percent of the men were classified as noncombat, 30% were members of the group with light combat (scores of 1–4), and another 30% were in the high-combat category. Table 2 shows each of these groups on reported problems just after leaving the service and after the age of 55 or so.

Table 2. Percentage Influence of Combat Experience on Psychological Functioning

Psychosocial functioning in postwar years (1985 survey)	Percentage of combat experience None (N = 77–81)	Light (N = 30–31)	Heavy (N = 28)	χ^2
Exit from service				
Emotional problems				
One or more of the following: sleep problems, depressed, irritable/anxious, difficulty concentrating, angry	15	19	54	17.74**
Behavioral problems				
One or more of the following: problem drinking, feeling lost, health problems, marital difficulties, problems getting a job	19	19	36	n.s.
Later life, after age 55				
Stress symptoms still present (nightmares, flashbacks, depressed feelings, etc.)	7	3	21	7.26**
Undesirable legacy of service, combat anxiety, bad memories	4	36	68	49.57***
Military experience has been too painful to think about	6	13	43	21.37***
Feel guilty about surviving	16	7	29	5.26*
Acquired adaptive skills				
Learned to cope with adversity, greater self-discipline, learned cooperation/teamwork (at least two of three qualities)	48	74	75	9.82***
Rewarding memories, friends				
Cite at least one	43	45	50	n.s.

*$p < .10$; **$p < .05$; ***$p < .01$.

Reported problems after the war are concentrated among the heavy combat veterans. Consider the experiences of an ex-Marine in the Oakland sample who scored at the top of combat and on stress reactions after the war. He recalled the first time that postwar combat stress led to troubled behavior in his family.

> My father tried to wake me up from a nightmare, and I recall jumping out of bed and knocking him down . . . the minute he touched me, I was up fighting . . . another time at night he couldn't find me . . . I was under the bed with my bayonet, scared to death. . . . I would also sit up in bed and count out loud, just as I did when I was using the tourniquet to keep me from bleeding to

> death. . . . My wife said it drove her crazy, just counting on and on. . . . We were married in 1948 so this stayed with me for a while.

He was still having life-threatening dreams of his battlefield experience at midlife.

A fourth of the heavy combat veterans reported one or more current symptoms of post-traumatic stress, including intrusive memories of traumatic experience. Only three other veterans made such a report. A large number of the veterans regarded bad memories and combat anxiety as the more important undesirable effects of their service time. This complaint applies to a third of the light combat veterans and to three-fourths of the veterans with a history of heavy combat. It is also the heavy combat veterans who were most likely to describe their battlefield experience as too painful to think about. Guilt about survivorship is also concentrated in this group and among men who somehow managed to avoid combat. Wilson (1986) describes how survivor guilt linked with depression may cause the veteran to believe that he has no right to live. In such cases, suicide attempts are often made to resolve survivor guilt and to rejoin dead comrades.

In sum, the heavy combat veterans are individuals who experienced a much higher risk of emotional problems after leaving the service than their comrades with light or no combat. Their postwar period is marked by some combination of anger, anxiety, irritability, sleep disturbance, and depression. In later life (after age 55), this legacy is still pronounced with stress symptoms (flashbacks, nightmares), painful memories, and survivorship guilt.

Consistent with the perspective on stress reduction or decay, the risk of emotional problems after leaving the service is much greater than the long-term risk of stress symptoms. But this decline does not necessarily conflict with the notion that postservice problems actually increase the risk of *enduring* emotional problems for some veterans. This risk could well be nonexistent for veterans who experienced no postwar distress. Indeed, a delayed stress reaction up to later life seems most unlikely from the evidence at hand on these veterans of World War II and the Korean conflict. Unfortunately, we do not have information on delayed stress reactions between service exit and later life.

With such limitations in mind, we explored the hypothesis that stress symptoms in later life are related to the experience of heavy combat through emotional problems after the war or demobilization. Considering the restrictions of sample size, we set up a logistic regression model with three categorical variables: (1) combat versus other, (2) postservice problems or not, and (3) stress symptoms in later life or not. In statistical terms, the hypothesis proposes a significant interaction effect of combat and postwar problems on long-term symptoms. Very briefly, we find strong support for this account. The proposed interaction model fits the data better (chi square = .16, 2 df, probability = .92) than any model of main and/or interaction effects.

Balanced against these indications of enduring stress effects are useful or rewarding outcomes. Among the most frequently mentioned are adaptive skills, such as self-discipline, cooperation or teamwork, and the ability to cope with adversity. These skills are cited by over half of the veterans, regardless of war experience, but they are more frequently mentioned by combat veterans. One of the veterans with 8 months of front-line duty observed that "combat taught me that you can survive if you have the will to survive, but also it is essential that others be able to depend on you . . . you are your brother's keeper." In his later years, another veteran in our sample states, "Navy life made me realize how important it was not to shirk your duty . . . everyone had his job and any letdown could be fatal to the ship and crew." Coupled with the intensity of trauma were rewarding memories and acquired friends. Both negative and positive outcomes were noted by men who looked back to their combat experience. This brings us to a second perspective on combat—its implications for social losses and relationships.

Combat and Comradeship

The extreme personal danger associated with combat includes the high risk of broken attachments. A life-span view of human development recognizes that the distress and anxiety associated with relationship termination is similar from childhood through old age, a process distinguished by the historical embeddedness of the loss event (Lerner & Ryff, 1978). For example, Weinberg noted that among 276 World War II veterans with combat neuroses, many of their stress symptoms were associated with the loss of war comrades. "Some soldiers were so overwhelmed by fierce encounters and by the death of their buddies that they succumbed soon after (1946, p. 467)." Similarly, Weinstein described the nature of modern warfare such that in order to survive in combat, the soldier must "function as part of a group, and his resistance to the trauma of combat will vary with the ability to integrate himself with the group (1947, p. 309)." Emotional problems were accentuated by the disruption of the men's interpersonal relationships in combat situations.

These accounts suggest that groups in life-threatening danger are likely to gain solidarity or cohesiveness. Shared danger enhances the common bond, in part because each man's life is in the hands of his fighting mates. As one Berkeley veteran put it, "the world is so small in combat . . . just men in the foxhole or trench . . . that's all one has." Another veteran noted that "military experience develops an extremely strong sense of belonging." The soldier could go on, could survive, as long as he felt himself to be a member of his primary group—a group bound by expectations and needs of its members (Shils & Janowitz, 1948). An Oakland veteran of three landings in the South Pacific recalled numerous occasions when only the presence of his fighting mates kept him in the action. "I would have bolted if I could." The soldier is empowered by his combat unit, a force greater than himself. Verbal reports by World War II veterans in a 20-year follow-up by Archibald and Tuddenham (1965) also suggest that when these intense, symbiotic relationships are broken, the soldier is left feeling purposeless and alienated from others who have not shared such overwhelming emotions. Loss of comrades in combat may foster survivor guilt and self-blame that perpetuate the symptoms of combat stress.

Many of these corrosive effects are documented in Table 3. Veterans who experienced heavy combat were witness to the destructive power of modern military equipment and the impersonal injury and death of their comrades. "Many of my friends were killed, and some were permanently damaged physically and emotionally," recalls one Berkeley veteran. Half of the heavy combat group lost friends during the war, and a significant portion of the losses occurred through injury (and evacuation) and death. Hendin and Haas's (1984) work with Vietnam veterans suggests that over and above the weapon power, it was the close, personal encounter with killing and the violent death of friends that was most traumatic for the

Table 3. Percentage Service Friendships by Combat Experience

Service relationships (1985 Survey)	Percentage of combat experience			χ^2
	None (N = 78–80)	Light (N = 29–31)	Heavy (N 27–28)	
Friend(s): Events happened				
Prisoner of war	27	36	43	n.s.
MIA/dead	52	52	75	4.91*
Wounded	35	52	79	16.49***
Loss of friend(s) in service	8	23	50	23.85***
Friends from service days (one or more)	33	38	61	6.95**
Contact with service mates (one or more modes of communication, i.e., letter, Christmas card, phone call, visit)	41	48	68	5.88*
Has attended reunion of war buddies	10	13	25	n.s.
Values lifelong friends from service	22	29	36	n.s.

*$p < .10$; **$p < .05$; ***$p < .01$.

combat soldier and the heart of post-traumatic stress disorders. "Many of my friends were killed . . . I also saw young men who lost arms or legs or who were shell shocked . . . it was awful," recalled another Berkeley veteran of World War II.

Balancing the broken attachments of combat are friendships that survived the war and endured over the years. Sixty-one percent of the heavy combat veterans report, after four decades, that they still have one or more friends from the service days. This compares to only a third of the veterans with light or no combat. Deliberate efforts to stay in contact with service mates are also greater for the veterans of heavy combat; 68% preserved these ties through visits, phone calls, or letters, in contrast to less than half of the veterans with light or no combat exposure. A Korean War veteran of heavy combat thought his service experience had many lessons about "deep friendships" and, a World War II veteran saw "the achievement of a greater appreciation of fellowship in subsequent years "as a most valuable personal result of his war experience."

Our results up to this point show the price of heavy combat in terms of emotional problems, both upon exit from the service and in later life. Subsequent analyses indicate that such problems result in part from dissolution of the primary group by injury and death of comrades. The association between emotional problems after the war and loss of friends might be phrased as part of a causal sequence in which such a loss accentuates the effect of combat on emotional well-being. If loss of significant others does account in part for the effect of combat on emotional state, this should be stronger for men with this war experience than among other veterans. The data clearly show this difference. Combat is more strongly correlated with emotional problems for men who suffered a loss than for other men (tau b = .40 versus .22). Another perspective is provided by estimating the probability of emotional problems after the war for men in groups defined by combat and loss of friend(s). Only 13% of the men with no combat exposure or loss of friends experienced problems after the war. This increases slightly to 18% for noncombat veterans who lost a friend and somewhat more for men only in combat (30%). Both the loss of a friend and combat increased the percentage to 41.

Table 4 shows the relationship between service friendships and emotional problems after the war among combat veterans. The basic design for this analysis includes all combat veterans with scores of 2 or more on the combat index and assigns them to one of two groups on emotional status after reentry to civilian life, problematic or not. Problematic refers to men who circled one or more of the following symptoms as a "difficulty" in their reentry to civilian life: sleep problems, poor concentration, irritability and anxiousness, anger and resentment, depression. Ideally, we would have preferred to limit the group comparison to only men with heavy combat experience. However, the sample is not large enough to permit this option.

Table 4. Percentage Service Friendships by Emotional Problems after Service[a]

Service friendships (1985 survey)	Percentage with emotional problems after service: None ($N = 30$)	Some ($N = 20$)	χ^2
Friend(s): Events happened			
Prisoner of war	29	41	n.s.
MIA/dead	53	68	n.s.
Wounded	44	56	n.s.
Loss of friend(s) in service	27	65	5.75**
Friends from service days (one or more)	38	60	n.s.
Contact with service mates (one or more forms of communication, i.e., letter, phone call, visit, etc.)	50	65	n.s.
Reunion with service mates	10	35	3.26*
Values lifelong friends from service	23	45	n.s.

*$p < .10$; **$p < .05$.
[a]Combat veterans in this analysis and in Tables 5 and 6 are defined as men with scores of 2 or more on the combat index.

By including combat variation across the comparison groups on postwar emotional status, we leave open the possibility that some of the difference between groups is merely a reflection of such variation. We investigated this possibility, comparing the groups with and without statistical control of combat experience. In no case did we find a reliable difference between the results.

Note that men with postwar problems experienced more war-related social losses (i.e., friends captured, injured, or killed) than other veterans. Overall, two out of three men with emotional problems lost friends in the war, a significantly higher percentage than veterans who were emotionally stable at exit. In addition to this picture of human loss and separation, the significance of war-linked friendships is greater for men with emotional problems after the war. Overall, the group differences in Table 4 suggest that the emotional damage of war is strongly linked to wartime social losses and to enduring friendships first established in the war.

The loss and enduring social significance of service mates in friendships are clearly central to the experience and psychological consequences of heavy combat. Veterans of heavy combat suffered a greater loss of friends in the war than men who were spared a substantial role in combat, and this social consequence is especially pronounced among the men who were emotionally troubled after leaving the service. Is preoccupation with survivorship guilt a factor in these troubles and in the prospect of enduring emotional wounds? Combat invariably produces feelings of shame and remorse in survivors. The untimely and traumatic death of friends and comrades haunts those who pull through the experience with the unanswerable question, "Why was I spared?" Lifton (1978) describes this question in relation to the veteran's sense of organic balance—the notion of exchanging one life for another. He suggests that death guilt may be the survivor's greatest psychological burden (1978, p. 21). Similarly, in work with survivor guilt and post-traumatic nightmares, Hartmann (1984) found that combat survivors often believed that they, not their buddies, should have died. As one Oakland veteran reports,

> Just before going into the Okinawa Campaign I was made Bn S-4 [staff logistics] . . . the officer who took my place as a forward observer [artillery] was killed on Sugar Loaf Hill. . . . He had been an attorney in Texas and was a very fine Marine. . . . One wonders why him instead of me? . . . Since then I have felt an added responsibility to lead a productive life.

For other men, the burden of survivorship could cause self-blame or even self-destruction.

Before turning to evidence on the psychological burden of survivorship, we should acknowledge an important observation—that postwar emotional problems among combat veterans were indicative of behavioral problems as well, such as heavy drinking, marital discord, and employment troubles (Table 5). In combination, these types of problems depict a host of

Table 5. Percentage Postwar Psychosocial Functioning by Emotional Problems after Civilian Return among Combat Veterans

	Percentage with emotional problems after service		
Postservice psychosocial functioning	None (N = 30)	Some (N = 20)	χ^2
Immediate postwar			
Behavioral problems at exit (one or more)	7	50	10.09***
1985 survey			
Current stress symptoms (one or more)	7	25	n.s.
Military service too painful to think about	14	55	7.62***
Feel guilty about surviving	7	35	4.75**
Felt legacy of service (value life more)	30	60	3.29*
Rewarding memories	33	55	n.s.
Combat anxieties	30	55	n.s.
Misery, discomfort	27	70	7.47***
Bad memories	10	40	4.67**
Death and destruction memories	27	70	7.47***

*$p < .10$; **$p < .05$; ***$p < .01$.

disadvantages for the life course, especially in terms of work and family. By comparison, the initially troubled group of combat veterans seems to have experienced a reasonably successful transition to civilian life and the reestablishment of their civilian pursuits.

The contrasts in Table 5 are especially striking when we consider how the veterans describe themselves and their service experiences in later life, some 40 years after the end of World War II. Over half of the men with postwar problems report feeling that their service experience is too painful to think about. This avoidance extends to not talking about the experience as well. Only 14% of the men without emotional problems after the service reported such feelings. At least some of the painful memories involved the loss of good friends. Over a third of the men with initial problems after the war reported some guilt over their survival. This compares to less than 10% of the combat veterans who did not have reentry problems. Survivorship guilt is linked to emotional wounds at reentry and in later life.

If social bonds in battle made effectiveness and survival more likely, it also made especially vivid a range of memories and emotions, such as the terror and exhileration of combat, the gratitude for life itself, the sustenance of shared humor, and a bitter helplessness in witnessing the sudden death of a companion. Combat veterans with emotional problems after the service were more likely than other men to report both negative and positive legacies of their service experience. The death, destruction, and anxieties of war were especially prominent in their memories and so were the positive memories of good friendship and the belief that life itself became more valuable.

In a powerful account of the Vietnam War, William Broyles (1986, p. 8) concludes that war marks for life the people who are caught up in it. "It visits them in the hour before sleeping; it comes to them bringing grief, pride, shame, and even laughter in the casual moments of everyday life. It never goes away." We find this imprint of combat experience in the lives of a substantial number of men, and it is a legacy of mixed emotions. But a good many veterans in this study display no reliable evidence of a lasting imprint. In their lives, past experience and imprints from wartime service appear to have slipped away, perhaps through the skillful operation of defense mechanisms. Can we find some clues to this difference in long-term effects by returning to the preservice years of these veterans? Does the legacy of combat have something to do with their psychological makeup and competence as adolescents?

PRESERVICE PSYCHOLOGICAL FUNCTIONING

The psychological consequences of combat generally reflect the nature of combat and its interaction with the recruit's dispositional history. We follow this perspective, though much early discussion of stress reactions emphasized either the combat situation or life history. For example, Maskins (1941) attributed neurotic collapse in combat to predisposition, though later he and others (Weinberg, 1946) observed that a substantial number of emotionally stable soldiers also succumbed to the stress of combat. Another study found that nearly a third of the men having breakdowns had no signs of past dysfunction (Hargreaves, 1940). By the end of World War II, the interactional perspective was generally acknowledged by Grinker and Spiegle (1944) as the most compelling model: "No one is immune from war neurosis; anyone no matter how strong or stable may develop a war neurosis under proper circumstances" (cited in Weinberg, 1946, p. 475). In contemporary research, studies (Horowitz, 1986, 1979; Wilson, Smith, & Johnson, 1985) have documented the role of personality processes in moderating the perception, evaluation, and cognitive processing of stress experiences.

Our approach to such individual differences before military service is to draw upon selected 9-point ratings from the California Q-sort (Block, 1971). These ratings were applied to case materials during the adolescence of subjects in the Oakland and Berkeley studies. Four domains of psychological functioning have special relevance to men's response to combat situations and their implications: self-adequacy, emotional state, self-regulation, and excessive self-preoccupation. We measured self-inadequacy with a composite of five related items: satisfaction with life (reflected), being thin-skinned, feeling victimized, brittle, and fearful. Ratings of cheerfulness and moodiness index the emotional state of men prior to the service. Self-regulation refers to impulse control (whether over- or under-controlled) and to judgments of self and others. Guilt feelings arise from demanding judgments of self, whereas moralistic behavior involves harsh judgment of others. Each of these aspects of self-regulation has implications for how men functioned in combat and especially for its consequences. Excessive self-preoccupation entails personal vulnerability to stress through its amplification over time. We shall use ratings of anxiety and tension as expressed in bodily symptoms, introspective, ruminative, and unconventional thinking as indicators of this inward orientation. Introspectiveness connotes a diffuse attention to thoughts and feelings about the self. Hansell and associates (1986) report a greater tendency among introspective adolescents to report symptoms of psychological distress. Introspectiveness also resembles Hartmann's (1984) notion of "thin boundaries" or extreme sensitivity to hurtful actions, an openness and defenselessness. According to Hartmann, men with thin boundaries who experience combat are at risk of postwar nightmares and the post-traumatic stress syndrome.

These preservice data are only available on veterans. This limitation and that of focusing on combat veterans severely restricts possibilities for the analysis. Nevertheless, results from our small sample are thought-provoking and heuristically suggestive. As in prior analyses, Table 6 compares two groups of combat veterans; those who experienced emotional problems after their service and those who did not. Across the Q ratings, combat veterans who ended up with stress reactions after the service were clearly more vulnerable adolescents than other veterans. They scored significantly higher on self-inadequacy, having a somber outlook during adolescence. In group comparisons, they show an excessive preoccupation with self and stronger tendencies toward rumination and introspection. They ranked higher on anxiety and bodily tensions and were more likely to think unconventional thoughts. Last, the veterans with postservice problems were more overcontrolled and less judgmental toward others. Neither group ranked particularly high on guilt feelings.

Another suggestive thread of evidence on predisposing factors comes from records on the childhood sleep disturbances of veterans from the Berkeley Guidance Study. Two types of disturbance were measured with annual interview data from the mothers: *disturbing dreams* or the occurrence of bad dreams at least once a week; and *restless sleep,* being a light sleeper, much tossing and turning nearly every night. These ratings by a clinician were averaged across 3-year periods. Using the data for ages 8 to 10 years (the last period with minimal attrition), we find that three-fourths

Table 6. Mean Scores on Q Measures from Preservice Assessment for Prewar Functioning of Combat Veterans Who Differed on Emotional Problems after Military Service

Q-sort items and indexes, time period, adolescence test	Emotional problems after service: None ($N = 13$)	Some ($N = 9$)	t
Self-inadequacy index	4.7	5.4	1.82**
Emotional state			
Cheerfulness	5.49	3.84	−1.81**
Moodiness	4.74	6.16	1.77**
	($N = 11$)	($N = 9$)	
Self-regulation			
Overcontrolled	4.9	6.2	n.s.
Moralistic	6.4	5.2	1.78**
Feels guilty	5.8	5.6	n.s.
Excessive self-preoccupation			
Anxiety and tension; finds outlet in bodily symptoms	5.2	6.9	−2.62***
Introspective	4.5	5.7	−1.64*
Unconventional thoughts	4.3	5.2	−1.80**
Ruminative	4.6	5.7	−2.02**

*$p < .10$; **$p < .05$; ***$p < .01$.

of the veterans with emotional problems after service experienced nightmares in late childhood. No reliable difference emerged on restless sleep. Eight of the men who served in heavy combat had prior records of sleep disturbances. Of this number, five experienced postservice problems (depression, inability to concentrate, intense anxiety, intrusive memories, nightmares), and four had a childhood history of nightmares (as distinguished from night terrors). The three men who managed to avoid emotional problems after the service showed no evidence of nightmares in late childhood. Again, restless sleep proved to have little predictive significance. Hartmann's thesis on the high risk of a "thin boundary" personality in stressful environments is compatible with these findings.

When we turn to the adult years and Q-sort ratings made at age 50, the general pattern of group differences remains the same, except that the differences are no longer reliable. Only one rating shows the opposite contrast, a greater difference in middle age than in adolescence. Guilt feelings became less salient over time among veterans who had emotional problems after the service but not among the veterans who later experienced problems (adult means, 3.7 for the nonproblem group and 5.4 for the problem group, $p < .01$). This life-span change and contrast are consistent with our findings on survivorship guilt and loss of service mates. A large percentage of the combat veterans who exited from the service with generalized stress reactions reported the loss of service mates during wartime. Their survivorship guilt reflects such loss and no doubt continues to elicit prolonged emotional distress and reverberations issuing from their combat experience.

With a much larger number of cases who were assessed before military service, we could extend our analysis to the interactive effect of preservice characteristics and heavy combat on both proximal and distal aspects of health, psychological and physical. Even without this line of inquiry, it is apparent that individual differences on resourcefulness and vulnerability before combat do influence the likelihood of emotional problems after the service and their persistence into middle age. A ruminative, introspective personality is conducive to the accentuation and perpetuation of trouble over the life span.

But even this personality type does not ensure lasting psychological impairment. Though much continuity is evident from the psychological sequelae of combat, the degree of change is equally impressive. A large number of heavy combat veterans did not experience symptoms of traumatic stress after returning to civilian roles, and a substantial number of those with problems of this sort managed to diminish or put an end to such problems as they aged. Given the large cohorts of World War II veterans in old age, it is important to keep both profiles of the aftermath of war in mind, both the resulting life-span continuities and the turning points and healing experiences that change the course of veterans' lives.

CONCLUSION

Advances in the study of lives over the past decade have shown that cohorts age in different ways according to their interaction with a rapidly changing world. This connection between aging and social change has profound implications for the welfare of American veterans as they approach and enter the last stage of life. Most importantly, it leads us to the premise that veterans will follow a course of aging that differs in notable ways from the aging pattern of nonveterans. The significance of this point is underscored by two empirical facts: the future size of the older veteran population (it will triple in size by the Year 2000) and the lack of empirical evidence on the health and aging implications of military service in men's lives. With the prospect of over 9 million veterans in old age by the end of this century, it is noteworthy that the social science literature does not include a single report of the long-term effects of military service from a prospective longitudinal study.

The present chapter represents a very early stage of inquiry on such problems. Specifically, we have used a longitudinal data archive to investigate the effects of combat experience during World War II and the Korean conflict, as expressed in psychological health or impairment and in the wartime loss of friends and enduring friendships among service mates. The analysis views such effects in terms of the resourcefulness and vulnerability of men before they entered the service. All data come from the archives of the three longitudinal studies at the Institute of Human Development, University of California, Berkeley. The subjects and husbands of subjects are from the Oakland Growth Study (subjects' birth dates, 1920–1921) and the Berkeley Guidance and Growth Studies (subjects' birth dates, 1928–1929). A survey of wartime and military experience was completed during 1985.

Three dimensions of combat experience are part of a single index: exposure to death and dying, exposure to both incoming and outgoing fire, and the duration of combat experience. A measurement model based on these dimensions fits the data very well. For purposes of analysis, we identified three categories of combat severity with the combat measure: no combat, light combat, and heavy combat. A majority of the World War veterans had some combat experience, in comparison to a fourth or less of the Korean War veterans. Despite this difference, the psychosocial effects of combat are very similar in the two samples. For this reason and the value of a larger sample, we chose to combine the two groups of veterans.

Heavy combat, in particular, markedly increases the likelihood of emotional and behavioral problems after leaving the service. Emotional problems refer to sleep difficulties, depressed feelings, inability to concentrate, intense anger, irritability, tension, and anxiety. Problem drinking, difficulties getting a job, marital discord, and feeling disconnected or lost were defined as behavioral problems. Thirty years later or so, the emotional risk of heavy combat remains. These men are significantly more likely to report undesirable memories, the feeling that the war experiences are too painful to think about, and guilt about their survival in the midst of so much suffering and death. They are also more inclined than other men to report the loss of friends. But combat also produced a positive legacy, the development of coping and managerial skills, rewarding memories of experiences with war comrades, and enduring ties with service mates that extend to the present through reunions, letters, phone calls, and visits.

Combat trauma persists in the lives of a good many veterans, and we find that social losses in wartime are correlated with the enduring costs of combat. Men with emotional problems after the war were most likely to report the loss of friends during wartime. For a number of these men, the bonds of war and combat continue up to the present. Combat veterans with emotional wounds after the war are most likely to claim that they have friends from the service days, that they contact them by letter, phone call, or visit, and that they have attended reunions of their service mates. These are the veterans who are most likely to say that they value lifelong friendships from the service.

Social bonds support and protect in traumatic situations, but they also entail heavy costs when valued mates and friends are lost in battle. Emotional problems after the war among combat veterans were most likely when such losses occurred. Among combat veterans, such postservice problems were predictive of enduring stress symptoms at age 55 or older, along with persistent guilt feelings about survival, the pain of thinking about military experiences, and both negative and positive memories of war.

The proximal effects of combat raise two issues that we have just begun to address. Men bring varying experiences and qualities to combat situations, and the influence of this situation is certain to vary according to these individual differences. The second issue concerns the process by which proximal effects persist or diminish over time. According to Q-sort ratings on the adolescent behavior of the veterans, the men who had problems after the service scored higher on measures of vulnerability to stress in adolescence, when compared to the problem-free veterans. Yet both groups experienced combat. In brief, veterans with problems after the war ranked higher on self-inadequacy, moodiness, and self-preoccupation, as in ruminative behavior, introspectiveness, and anxiety and tension. We may be looking at a group of men with substantial capacity for reflection, a reflection that makes combat experience more traumatic than it would be otherwise.

Many tasks remain in this early phase of research on wartime experiences in the life course and aging. These include an investigation of the process by which memories of combat trauma fade or are otherwise overcome through a healing experience. Symptoms of emotional distress after the war were highly predictive of long-term problems, but why is this so? What are the mechanisms by which early troubles are resolved and fragmented lives are made whole? The major challenge of life-course research is to explicate the processes of continuity and change in the course of aging.

ACKNOWLEDGMENTS

This chapter is based on a program of research on social change in the life course. We acknowledge with gratitude support from the National Institute of Mental Health through Grant MH-37809 (Glen H. Elder, Jr., principal investigator) and a Senior Scientist Award (MH00567) to the first author. We are indebted to the Institute of Human Development (University of California, Berkeley) for permission to use archival data from its files and to the Geriatric Research, Education and Clinical Center at the Durham VA for its support of our work on military service in aging and health. We would also like to thank Robert Laufer and John Wilson for their helpful comments on earlier drafts of this chapter.

REFERENCES

Appel, J. W. (1966). Neuropsychiatry. In R. S. Anderson, A. J. Glass, & R. J. Bernucci (Eds.), *Neuropsychiatry in World War II* (Vol. 1, pp. 373–415). Washington, DC: U.S. Government Printing Office.

Archibald, H. C., & Tuddenham, R. D. (1965). Persistent stress reaction after combat: A 20-year follow-up. *Archives of General Psychiatry, 12,* 475–481.

Archibald, H. C., Long, D. M., Miller, C., & Tuddenham, R. D. (1962). Gross stress reaction in combat: A 15-year follow-up. *American Journal of Psychiatry, 119,* 317–322.

Block, J. (1971). *Lives through time.* Berkeley, CA: Bancroft Books.

Borus, J. F. (1974). Incidence of maladjustment in Vietnam returnees. *Archives of General Psychiatry, 30,* 554–557.

Brill, N. R., & Beebe, G. W. (1955). *A follow-up study of war neuroses.* Washington, DC: Veterans Administration Medical Monograph.

Broyles, W. (1986). *Brothers in arms: A journey from war to peace.* New York: Knopf.

Card, J. J. (1983). *Lives after Vietnam: The personal impact of military service.* Lexington, MA: Lexington Press.

Egendorf, A., Kadushin, D., Laufer, R. S., Rothbart, G., & Sloan, L. (1981). *Legacies of Vietnam: Comparative adjustment of veterans and their peers.* Washington, DC: U.S. Government Printing Office.

Elder, Jr., G. H. (1974). *Children of the Great Depression.* Chicago: University of Chicago Press.

Elder, Jr., G. H. (Ed.). (1985). *Life-course dynamics: Trajectories and transitions 1968–1980.* New York: Cornell University Press.

Elder, Jr., G. H. (1986). Military times and turning points in men's lives. *Developmental Psychology, 22*(2), 3–17.

Elder, Jr., G. H., Liker, J. K., & Jaworski, B. J. (1984). Hardship in lives: Depression influences from the 1930's to old age in postwar America. In K. McCluskey & H. Reese (Eds.), *Developmental psychology: Historical and generational effects* (pp. 161–201). New York: Academic Press.

Figley, C. R. (1978). Psychosocial adjustment among Vietnam veterans: An overview of the research. In C. R. Figley (Ed.), *Stress disorders among Vietnam veterans: Theory, research, and treatment* (pp. 57–70). New York: Brunner/Mazel.

Figley, C. R. (Ed.). (1985). *Trauma and its wake: The study and treatment of post-traumatic stress disorder.* New York: Brunner/Mazel.

Fligstein, N. D. (1980). Who served in the military: 1940–1973. *Armed Forces and Society, 6,* 297.

Glass, A. J. (1957, April). *World War II: A discussion.* Paper presented at the symposium, Prevention and Social Psychiatry, Walter Reed Army Institute of Research, Walter Reed Army Medical Center. Available through the U.S. Government Printing Office, Washington, DC, 185–197.

Green, B. L., Wilson, J. P., & Lindy, J. D. (1985). Conceptualizing post-traumatic stress: A psychosocial framework. In C. R. Figley (Ed.), *Trauma and its wake: The study and treatment of post-traumatic stress disorder* (pp. 53–69). New York: Brunner/Mazel.

Hansell, S., Mechanic, D., & Brondolo, E. (1986). Introspectiveness and adolescent development. *Journal of Adolescence and Youth, 15,* 115–132.

Hargreaves, G. R. (1940). The differential diagnosis of the psychoneurosis of war. In E. Miller (Ed.), *The neurosis of war* (pp. 57–79). New York: Macmillan.

Harris, L. (1980). *Myths and realities: A study of attitudes toward Vietnam-era veterans.* Washington, DC: U.S. Government printing Office.

Hartmann, E. (1984). *The nightmare: The psychology and biology of terrifying dreams.* New York: Basic Books.

Havighurst, R. J., Baughman, J. W., Burgess, E. W., & Eaton, W. H. (1951). *The American veteran back home.* New York: Longsman & Green.

Hendin, H., & Haas, A. P. (1984). Posttraumatic stress disorders in veterans of early American wars. *The Psychohistory Review, 12,* 25–30.

Horowitz, M. J. (1979). Psychological response to serious life events. In V. Hamilton & D. M. Warburton (Eds.), *Human stress and cognition* (pp. 115–132). New York: Wiley.

Horowitz, M. J. (1986). *Stress response syndromes* (2dn ed.). New York: Jason Aronson.

Joreskog, K. G., & Sorbom, D. (1981). *LISREL: User's guide.* Chicago: International Educational Resources.

Klonoff, H., McDougall, G., Clark, C., Kramer, P., & Hogan, J. (1976). The neuropsychological, psychiatric and physical effects of prolonged and severe stress: 30 years later. *Journal of Nervous and Mental Disease, 163,* 246–252.

Laufer, R. S. (1985). War, trauma and human development: Vietnam. In S. Sonnenberg, A. Blank, & J. Talbot (Eds.), *The trauma of war: Stress and recovery in Vietnam veterans* (pp. 52–71). Washington, DC: American Psychiatric Press.

Laufer, R. S., Gallops, M. S., & Frey-Wouters, E. (1984). War stress and trauma: The Vietnam veteran experience. *Journal and Health and Social Behavior, 25,* 65–85.

Lerner, R. M., & Ryff, C. D. (1978). Implementation of the life-span view of human development: The sample case of attachment. In P. B. Baltes & O. G. Brain, Jr. (Eds.), *Life-span development and behavior* (Vol. I, pp. 1–44). New York: Academic Press.

Lifton, R. J. (1978). Advocacy and corruption in the healing profession. In C. R. Figley (Ed.), *Stress disorder among Vietnam veterans: Theory, research, and treatment* (pp. 209–230). New York: Brunner/Mazel.

Maskins, M. (1941). Psychodynamic aspects of the war neuroses: A survey of the literature. *Psychiatry, 4*(1), 97–115.

Masson, J. (1984). *The assault on truth.* New York: Farrar, Strauss & Giroux.

Robins, L. N. (1974). *The Vietnam drug user returns.* Special Action Office Monograph, Series a, No. 2. Washington, DC: U.S. Government Printing Office.

Segal, D. R. & Segal, M. W. (1976). The impact of military service on trust in government, international attitudes and social status. In. N. L. Goldman & D. R. Segal (Eds.), *The social psychology of military service* (pp. 114–139). Beverly Hills, CA: Sage Press.

Shils, E. A., & Janowitz, M. (1948). Cohesion and disintegration in the Wehrmacht in World War II. *Public Opinion Quarterly, Summer,* 280–315.

Stouffer, S. A. *et al.* (1949). *The American Soldier* (Vol. 1 and Vol. 2). Princeton, NJ: Princeton University Press.

Stuen, M. R., & Solberg, K. B. (1972). The Vietnam veteran: Characteristics and needs. In L. J. Sherman & E. M. Caffey (Eds.), *The Vietnam veteran in contemporary society* (pp. 106–112). Washington, DC: Veterans Administration.

van der Kolk, B. A., & Blitz, A. (1981). Characteristics of nightmares among veterans with combat experience. *Sleep Research, 10,* 179.

van der Kolk, B. A., & Ducey, C. (1984). Clinical implications of the Rorschach in post-traumatic stress disorder. In B. A. van der Kolk (Ed.), *Post-traumatic stress disorder: Psychological and biological sequelae* (pp. 30–42). Washington, DC: American Psychiatric Press.

Weinberg, S. K. (1946). The combat neuroses. *American Journal of Sociology, 51,* 465–487.

Weinstein, E. (1947). The function of interpersonal relations in the neurosis of combat. *Psychiatry, 10,* 37–314.

Whalen, R. W. (1984). *Bitter wounds: German victims of the Great War, 1914–1939.* Ithaca, NY: Cornell University Press.

Wilson, J. P. (1978). *Forgotten warrior project.* A partial and preliminary report submitted to the Disabled American Veterans Association.

Wilson, J. P. (1986). Understanding and treating the Vietnam veteran. In F. Ochberg (Ed.), *Post-traumatic therapy.* New York: Brunner/Mazel.

Wilson, J. P., & Krauss, G. E. (1982). *Predicting post-traumatic stress syndromes among Vietnam veterans.* Paper Presentation at the 25th Neuropsychiatric Institute, Coatsville, PA.

Wilson, J. P., & Krauss, G. E. (1985). Predicting post-traumatic stress syndromes among Vietnam veterans. In W. Kelly (Ed.), *Post-traumatic stress disorder and the war veteran patient* (pp. 102–147). New York: Brunner/Mazel.

Wilson, J. P., Smith, W. K., & Johnson, S. K. (1985). A comparative analysis of PTSD among various survivor groups. In C. R. Figley (Ed.), *Trauma and its wake: The study and treatment of post-traumatic stress disorder* (pp. 142–172). New York: Brunner/Mazel.

Worthington, E. R. (1978). Demographic and pre-service variables as predictors of post-military service adjustment. In C. R. Figley (Ed.), *Stress disorders among Vietnam veterans* (pp. 173–187). New York: Brunner/Mazel.

7

The Psychological Effects of Being a Prisoner of War

EDNA J. HUNTER

> My room was almost totally black. The window was covered by a sheet of steel with small holes drilled in it, just enough to let light in. That sheet of steel got awfully damned hot, . . . it just about killed me. . . . I started thinking . . . we are going to have a tough time if we are here for any length of time, because the problem is going to be a psychological problem.
>
> —Returned POW, 1974

More individuals have experienced a prisoner of war or hostage situation than most people realize. There were over 130,000 American service personnel captured during World War II alone; over 7,000 were taken POW during the Korean War; and nearly 600 returned from Vietnam to U.S. control during Operation Homecoming in the spring of 1973. The men held in Southeast Asia during the Vietnam conflict were held longer (almost 9 years for some) than the POWs of World War II (4 years), Korea (3 years), those held during the *Pueblo* incident (11 months), or more recently by Iran (approximately 1 year).

Research shows that each captivity or hostage experience is different, depending upon the time in history at which the incident occurred, the culture of the captor, the duration of captivity, its harshness, and the support received from others, both while in captivity as well as upon return. Thus the physical residuals of captivity may vary greatly from one POW

EDNA J. HUNTER • Hunter Publications, P.O. Box 81391, San Diego, California 92138-1391.

experience to another. In contrast, long-term *psychological* effects are perhaps more similar for all captivities.

There are other aspects that determine the long-term physiological or psychological effects on former captives. These factors include the captives' innate predispositions or temperaments, commitment to whatever ideology or task placed them in jeopardy initially, maturity, personal value systems, and satisfaction with family relationships during the precapture period. Where families have not coped well during the captivity period and have become dysfunctional, additional stresses are there to face captives when they return home.

LOOKING BACK THROUGH HISTORY

Historically, both military and civilian prisoner populations have been cruelly exploited, with little value placed on their lives (Segal, Hunter, & Segal, 1976). Rules for the treatment of prisoners of war as well as for the conduct of captives have evolved over time. In ancient times, wars had but one purpose—complete annihilation of the enemy. Thus, the vanquished could expect only death or slavery—not eventual reunion with their families when the hostilities ended. From ancient times to the beginning of the Middle Ages, treatment of prisoners of war has varied from country to country, depending upon philosophical ideals and the beliefs of those in the locale of capture. With the fall of the Roman Empire in the Middle Ages, Europe experienced violent anarchy, and brutality was common. Lowly foot troops were shown no mercy. They were expendable, although noblemen were sometimes ransomed (Mowery, Hutchins, & Rowland, 1975).

With the Renaissance, European civilization became more structured and more complex, and conflicts were again characterized by a variety of practices in the treatment of POWs. Extreme brutality was the rule during the religious fanaticism of the Thirty Years War. A turning point in the treatment of POWs came at the conclusion of that war. In 1648, under the Treaty of Westphalia, prisoners were actually released without ransom. Thus a marked change in attitudes toward war prisoners had begun to develop during the late Middle Ages.

The first Geneva Conference took place in 1863, along with the formation of what was to be known as the International Red Cross. A second Geneva Conference was held the following year. Between the years 1581 and 1864, as many as 291 international agreements were made in efforts to provide maximum protection for human life during war. Perhaps because of these efforts, World War I could be called the "brightest chapter" in U.S. POW treatment (Mowery *et al.,* 1975).

In 1929, representatives of 46 nations met to correct some of the faults of earlier conventions that had become apparent during World War I. Thirty-three nations signed the provisions of the 1929 convention. Thus, when World War II began, there finally existed a legally binding convention with regard to treatment of POWs that all who signed were supposed to observe. Although ratification of the Geneva Conventions does not prevent acts of inhumane treatment any more than laws prevent crimes, they did create legal obligations, and their existence was a source of moral and ultimately political pressure on a detaining power to accord humane treatment.

The Conventions specified precisely who was to be considered a POW. Also, the agreement prohibited punishment as a public enemy and prohibited any revenge in the form of inflicting suffering or disgrace, cruel imprisonment, want of food, by mutilation, death, or any other barbarity. If prisoners escaped and were recaptured, they were not to be punished for their escape, except by stricter confinement. Also, every wounded enemy captured was to be medically treated according to the ability of the captor's medical staff.

The 1929 Geneva Conventions were adopted to rectify the faults of the earlier Hague Conventions; and, still later, the 1949 Conventions sought to do the same thing in light of World War II. When World War II began, Russia had not signed the existing Geneva agreement, and Japan had not ratified it. Nonetheless, Japan announced her intention to observe the Geneva Conventions. However, the Germans flatly denied the 1949 Convention requirements applied to the Russians and acted accordingly. Many Soviet prisoners were branded, others subjected to medical experiments, and still others died after being shot with poisoned bullets during research testing (Mowery *et al.,* 1975)

During World War II, approximately 11% of all British and American POWs died in captivity, most of them from malnutrition or deliberate neglect. Some 45% of the Germans imprisoned in Soviet camps and 60% of the Russians captured by the Germans also did not return from their ordeals. Despite Japan's stated intentions of observing the obligations of the Geneva Conventions, the treatment of U.S. POWs during World War II presented stark proof that Japan failed to do so. Long-term effects of Japanese captivity provide evidence of the inhumane treatment of POWs held there. On the other hand, the Germans *did* attempt to live up to requirements laid down by the Geneva Conventions insofar as American POWs were concerned. Their treatment of Jews and political internees within their concentration camps was another story entirely.

When the conflict with Korea began, none of the early participants in that war were parties to the 1949 Geneva Conventions, although a number of countries who contributed troops to the Unified Command had ratified them. There is no record to indicate the Chinese Communist regime or the commander of its "volunteers" explicitly tried to abide by the conventions.

Neither was there any assumption by the United Nations that the Geneva Conventions were in effect as a matter of law with respect to the Korean War during the 1950s.

During the Vietnam War (1964–1973), the United States and North Vietnam were both parties to the Conventions. Although this fact did not ensure compliance, the partial restraint shown by North Vietnam in the treatment of prisoners was perhaps influenced by that fact. Nonetheless, as an example of how captivity experiences can vary even within the same war and at different points of time during that war, it should be noted that men captured and detained in North Vietnam underwent an experience quite different from the experience of those captured in the South. Moreover, men captured prior to 1969 had a much more stressful experience than those who became POWs subsequent to October 1969, a point in time when the treatment of the prisoners took a definite turn for the better. If the men had been released in 1969, some would have weighed only about 90 pounds and would have resembled the survivors of Corregidor after World War II captivity.

Why this change in treatment occurred is unclear and subject to pure speculation. Perhaps the Vietnamese were responding to the families' efforts to call worldwide attention to the ill treatment the men were receiving at the hands of the Vietnamese. Still another explanation may be the death of Ho Chi Minh at about that point in time. Or, it may have been that the Vietnamese recognized the war was winding down and saw the captives as "bargaining chips" for peace, who were worth more if fattened prior to negotiations.

The POWs held in South Vietnam generally suffered less torture and brutality and fewer interrogations and indoctrinations than those captured in the North. On the other hand, they suffered severe physical deprivation and harbored realistic concerns about basic personal survival. In contrast, those in the North reported borderline diets and living conditions, severe initial physical torture, and intermittent psychological mistreatment for interrogation and propaganda purposes. American POWs held in Vietnam discovered very soon after capture that literal adherence to the U.S. Military Code of Conduct instituted after the Korean conflict was impossible. Almost all the men who returned in 1973 reported they had been made to do or say something they did not think they could be forced to do or say; they would die first! One returned POW entitled the chronicle of his years in Vietnam, *They Wouldn't Let Us Die* (Rowan, 1973). Failing to live up to the code was a basis for future guilt for some of these men.

In July of 1966, North Vietnam insisted these men were war criminals, not POWs, and threatened them with war crimes trials and possible execution. Unable to obtain information through normal interrogation, the Vietnamese began a program of severe torture. The "lenient and humane" treatment of the Vietnam captor was anything but lenient and humane.

French prisoners of war had suffered much the same treatment during their detention in Vietnam during the 1950s (Hunter, 1978). Moreover, over a decade after presumedly all American POWs were released at the end of hostilities in 1973, a question still remains in the minds of many POW/MIA families—whether all POWs were actually released. Live sightings of American captives continue to bubble to the surface, causing heart-wrenching anguish among family members. History tells us that French POWs were returned 16 long years after the fall of Dien Bien Phu. History gives hope to some families who have little hope left after 20 years of waiting.

Just as one cannot speak of one Vietnam POW experience, neither can one speak of the World War II POW experience because those POWs held by Germany suffered fewer long-term effects than those captives held by the Japanese because of the differing treatment to which they were subjected (Beebe, 1975; Cohen & Cooper, 1954; Nefzger, 1970a, b). Considering the increasing number of terroristic kidnappings in the "hotspots" of the world today, it becomes apparent there is no *one* POW experience and no universal complex of long-term effects. Each experience is unique to some extent, and prisoners' reactions to this stressor are even more idiosyncratic.

Nonetheless, threads of commonality are woven through all captivity experiences, including the Nazi Holocaust of World War II concentration camps where captives faced extremity of a degree not known to many wartime POWs in recent times (Segal *et al.*, 1976). The purpose of this chapter is not to chronicle treatment of POWs *per se* but rather to look at those common psychological residuals of captivity, regardless of war or time in history, that persist to impact the psychosocial adjustment of former captives and their families while they adjust to freedom and struggle for family reintegration. Although the focus of this chapter is on the *psychological* residuals of captivity, discriminating between psychological and physiological etiologies may be presumptuous.

The stress associated with physical torture has many psychological effects, and vice versa. For example, during the Vietnam war, American POWs were recipients of a concerted campaign of torture, terror, and deprivation of food, medical treatment, and sleep. The most prevalent form of torture was a technique known as "the ropes." Although there were many variations of this torture, it usually took the form of tying the elbows behind the back and tightening them until they touched or arching the back with a rope stretched from the feet to the throat.

Other tortures included chains and manacles placed on legs and ankles with a heavy iron bar; cuffs of a ratchet type that were tightened until the metal bit into the flesh, sometimes down to the bone; aggravation of injuries received at ejection from the plane, such as twisting a broken leg; forced self-mistreatment, such as forced kneeling on a concrete floor or on a small stick or forced standing at attention for hours, or forced sitting on a low stool with ankles shackled and tied together with arms behind the back, hour after hour. Certainly such torture resulted in physiological effects; the *fear* of further torture resulted in psychological effects. The POWs returned from Vietnam presented much evidence of torture. Over 40% of the 1973 returnees had peripheral nerve injuries resulting from use of "the ropes." Harsh treatments such as these have long-term *psychological* as well as physical aftereffects.

The degree of stress caused specifically by psychological tortures is a difficult-to-quantify variable. A fascinating but frightening observation is that individuals in extreme situations sometimes appear to suddenly give up, curl up in the fetal position, and die. This phenomenon was reported for POWs held both in Korea and Vietnam. Within the Holocaust camps, it was referred to as the "Musselman" stage. Such a reaction is frightening because we observe what extreme stress can do to a person very quickly. On the other hand, it is fascinating because it often makes no sense in terms of the relative lack of danger to the captive at that particular time compared to what had gone before or the type of behavior being manifested, for example, the refusal to eat while starving (Richlin, 1977).

Other critical variables that must be considered in any study of captives are how the stress is perceived and how the individual coped—or failed to cope. These variables must all be taken into account when we try to determine the price POWs have paid or may pay in the future in terms of physical and psychological health. Nor can we ignore the fact that any time we study ex-POWs, we are looking only at *survivors.*

A CAPTIVE'S RESPONSE TO BEING CAPTURED

During those first 12 to 24 hours following capture, captives or hostages typically experience a total shock and trauma almost impossible to describe to another person. They are knocked totally off balance by the suddenness, the helplessness, and the aura of power that surround them. There follows an immediate and overwhelming fear of death accompanied by deep concern as to what the effect will be upon their families. At that point, extremely strong survival instincts take over. They try to memorize where they are being taken, usually without success. They experiment with methods for just getting through the moment to bring themselves under control emotionally. They are dismayed by their inability to think clearly. Instinctively, they may find themselves deciding to cooperate as completely as possible with the captor to prevent their own whimsical or capricious death. They usually try hard not to antagonize their captor in any way (Miller, 1974).

After 24 to 48 hours, the captive begins to calm down. The ever-present danger of death persists, but now, along with it, are the hope that they will survive and a growing resignation to the circumstances. Captives usually try to kill time by slowing down their activities or by trying to sleep, a difficult task during the first few days after capture. At this time they may begin to reassess their value systems and the circumstances that led them into the predicament. They also worry about their families' reactions. They may find themselves experiencing physical symptoms, ranging from headaches to excessive urination. By now they are exhausted to the point where it undermines confidence and self-control. They try to fight off the severe depression that envelops them, accompanied by feelings of helplessness and abandonment.

If they are held 48 hours or longer and no orchestrated program of torture begins, a remarkable adjustment and adaptation to the situation begins. Captives find themselves devising means of keeping their minds off the situation. They find themselves immersing themselves in the minute events of daily living. They structure their strictured environment. While engrossed in trivial activities, they find they cannot dwell on the misery and hopelessness of the situation. They also try not to think of their families too much; it is too painful.

Even so, the overwhelming fear of death is ever present. At this point in time, there may be drastic shifts in personal values and their outlook toward life in general. There is a beginning of what may well become a permanent shift in values. Life, and freedom itself, take on an importance they never before had. As time goes by, victims often find, much to their surprise, that no matter how harrowing the experience, they may harbor only minimal ill will, if any, toward their captors. In some instances, the captors themselves may also have developed positive feelings toward the captive. In psychodynamic terms, these phenomena are called *transference* and *countertransference.*

Therein lies the basis for one of the early psychological residuals following captivity—"the Stockholm Syndrome." The Stockholm Syndrome first received widespread public attention through media coverage of a bank robbery in Stockholm in 1974. When the robbery attempt miscarried, the robber retreated with hostages to the bank vault where he barricaded himself and attempted to barter the hostages' lives for a series of demands. To the astonishment of the authorities, police spike microphones tapped into the vault revealed considerable affection for the robber. The captives subsequently went to the defense of the very person who had threatened their lives. This identical process had been mentioned much earlier in the research literature on "brainwashing" (Biderman, 1957).

The Stockholm Syndrome appears to require compassionate treatment alternating with threats of death or injury for the hostage–captor bond to occur. Where torture and other inhumane methods are consistently employed, captives find resistance to captor demands easier, and their animosities toward the captor more readily maintained. Thus, most

POWs held in Southeast Asia during the Vietnam conflict had little difficulty maintaining ill feelings toward their captor because of the harsh treatment to which they were subjected throughout the captivity period.

A CLUSTER OF CAPTIVITY RESIDUALS: WHAT SHOULD IT BE CALLED?

For more than half a century, there has been a growing recognition that the extraordinary stresses of incarceration are related to heightened vulnerability to both physical and psychological problems over time. In reviewing these long-term effects, Segal (1974) pointed out the dichotomy drawn between physical and psychological phenomena is often an arbitrary one. Contemporary concepts of human behavior are based increasingly on the awareness that earlier distinctions between body and mind are of little practical relevance. By way of example, one might take a given psychological stressor, such as the ever-present threat of death, which may result either in psychological or physical symptomatology, for example, anxiety or hypertension, or both. Similarly, physical stressors such as hunger or beatings may result not only in physical complaints in later years, such as weakness and weight loss, but also in psychological problems such as depression and apathy. Some investigators have focused on physical trauma; for others the chronicity of symptoms over time was thought to be more dependent on psychological than on organic factors (Segal, 1974).

At an International Conference on Later Effects of Imprisonment and Deportation, held in The Hague in 1961, an examination was made of the delayed pathology that had emerged in ex-prisoners of war after 5, 10, or even 20 years. A broad range of postcaptivity health problems emerged: pulmonary disorders such as tuberculosis, chronic bronchitis and emphysema; cardiovascular disorders, including functional cardiac disturbances; arteriosclerosis; digestive disorders; chronic rheumatism; lesions of the central and peripheral nervous systems; and premature aging, including deficits in memory and attention and chronic fatigue. Many of the deficits found in ex-POWs were thought to be attributable to the poor diet received during internment.

In a follow-up of U.S. ex-captives of World War II and Korea (Beebe, 1975), observations pointed to lingering, irrational irritability, acute startle reaction, repetitive nightmares, and lacerating guilt in former captives. The same held true for New Zealand and Canadian POWs held by Japan (Kral, Pazder, & Wigdor, 1968). Indeed, research suggests that any person who had spent 3 or more years as a POW in the Far East during World War II presented these characteristic residuals of captivity (Segal, Hunter, & Segal, 1976).

The role of predisposition in causing later effects has been a matter of debate. Mattusek (1971), in examining survivors of the World War II Nazi Holocaust, pointed to individual and family adjustment in the preinternment period as predictors of latter adjustment. Many years later, research at the San Diego Center for Prisoner of War Research (Hunter, 1982, 1983, 1985; Hunter & Plag, 1977) on captivity in Vietnam corroborated Mattusek's observations. Vietnam-era ex-POWs who had evidenced precapture morbidity were found four times as likely to receive psychiatric diagnoses at the time of homecoming (O'Connell, 1975).

Cohen and Cooper (1954) found that ex-POWs interned in Japanese-conquered territory during World War II experienced a mortality rate during the first 2 years following liberation 2.2 times greater than veterans of comparable age and service. The rate diminished over time but remained high for the next 4 years. However, American and Canadian World War II POWs held in Europe showed no such trend (Segal *et al.*, 1976). In a study of mortality rates of U.S. Army veterans taken captive during World War II and also during the Korean War (together with control groups), Nefzger (1970a, b) found that captives of an Asian captor were 40% more likely to die during the early years subsequent to release than other American males of the same age, who had not been taken POW.

CHANGING LABELS FOR THE RESIDUALS OF CAPTIVITY

As early as Post-World War I, it had been noted that returned French POWs presented a cluster of symptoms that was designated "nostalgic psychoses," so-called because the primary characteristic appeared to be anxiety focused on their uprooting and separation from family. The French literature also makes reference to "reaction states of liberation" that often took the form of melancholia or manic "fits" and referred to them as "mania of return." Other French ex-POWs were described as demonstrating "asthenic states of captivity" (Juillet & Moutin, 1969).

More recently, various designations used for this cluster of symptoms (primarily, anxiety masked by an underlying depression) have been called "postincarceration late injury," "concentration camp syndrome," or "KZ Syndrome" (Eitinger, 1961; Hermann, 1973); "concentration camp neurosis" (Bensheim, 1960); and "survivor syndrome" (Niederland, 1968).

POST-TRAUMATIC STRESS DISORDER (PTSD)

With the development of the *Diagnostic and Statistical Manual of Mental Disorders,* third edition (DSM-III) by the American Psychiatric Association (1980), this cluster of symptomatology related to postcaptivity effects now falls under the category of Post-Traumatic Stress Disorder (PTSD). According to DSM-III, the criteria for assigning the PTSD designation are set forth next.

First, a recognizable stressor must exist that would evoke significant symptoms of stress in almost everyone. There must be a reexperiencing of the trauma, which would include at least one of the following symptoms: recurrent and intrusive recollections of the event; recurrent dreams of the event; or sudden acting or feeling as if the traumatic event were reoccurring because of an association with an environmental or ideational stimulus. Next, there is a numbing of responsiveness to or reduced involvement with the external world beginning some time after the trauma. Either the person has a markedly diminished interest in one or more significant activities, or shows feelings of detachment or estrangement from others, or presents constricted affect. Finally, to be categorized as a person who manifests PTSD, at least two of the following symptoms must currently be present that had not been present prior to the trauma:

1. Hyperalertness or exaggerated startle response
2. Sleep disturbance
3. Guilt about surviving when others did not, or about behavior required for survival
4. Memory impairment or trouble concentrating
5. Avoidance of activities that arouse recollection of the traumatic event
6. Intensification of symptoms by exposure to events that symbolize or resemble the traumatic event (American Psychiatric Association, 1980, p. 238)

Scores of former POWs from all wars meet these criteria. They demonstrate the residuals of captivity; they suffer from PTSD, as defined by DSM-III.

LESSONS LEARNED ABOUT PSYCHOLOGICAL RESIDUALS OF CAPTIVITY

Reviewing the literature and research results dealing with the long-term effects of captivity or hostage-taking experiences, the conclusion can be made that many former captives, but not all, present PTSD in the postrelease years, sometimes with a delayed onset. Other statements can be made based on knowledge gleaned from past investigations, and are presented next:

1. Residuals of captivity may have both psychological and physical aspects, which cannot be easily separated etiologically, and the psychological residuals appear more long-lasting in relation to current functioning

than the physiological ones. Also, there may be delayed onset of symptomatology not present immediately after the trauma.

2. There is no "one" captivity experience; multiple factors enter into the equation to determine the effects over time on the captive.

3. Although precapture personality or family adjustment has been shown related to later psychological and social adjustment, investigators are in fair agreement that POWs of an Asian captor who have spent 3 or more years in prison invariably show latter effects. Thus, to some extent, it is the captor and the captor's culture that predict both survival and long-term effects for the captive.

4. Rather than a complete change in personality, a long, harsh imprisonment appears merely to solidify basic personality traits. For example, the tolerant person becomes more tolerant, the intolerant one more intolerant, and the patriotic person becomes even more patriotic.

5. Group support and communication with others in similar situations, both for captives and families of captives, are critical variables in coping. Group support may also alleviate survivor guilt in the postrelease era.

6. The family to which the former captive returns can be both a stressor and a stress alleviator.

7. Although a "code of conduct" cannot be strictly adhered to in an extreme situation, having such a code, either laid out for one (e.g., the Military Code of Conduct) or imposed by one's own set of values or religion, acts as a moral guideline and facilitates coping.

8. Coping strategies that are effective immediately following capture or in extreme situations may differ from those that prove effective as imprisonment continues. These same coping mechanisms may actually become *dysfunctional* in the postrelease period; for example, the psychological numbing, blunted affect, and mechanisms of denial that typically accompany the event of capture and may be functional at that time but not later on.

9. To some degree, captives themselves determine the treatment received from the captor. However, unrelenting harsh treatment may make it easier for the captive to resist attempts at coercive persuasion or ideological conversion.

10. Based on investigations of POW/hostage and concentration camp survivors, the older, more mature captives, who were strongly committed to a cause or ideology were more likely to cope more adequately with the extreme stresses of the prison environment.

11. The manifestations of prolonged, extreme stress of captivity are described by the criteria for PTSD as outlined in DSM-III (American Psychiatric Association, 1980).

12. The "will to survive" is a key variable in survival, and the seemingly conscious decision to survive the ordeal occurs within a matter of days or weeks after capture. Without that will, captives have been observed to curl

up and die within a very brief period of time. Nonetheless, most individuals in extreme conditions find they can cope with much more stress than they had originally thought they ever could. It is probably the person who early in life developed a positive outlook, who can see alternatives in outcome in almost any situation no matter how bleak, and who continues on in spite of the odds against him, who makes it through. In other words, it is the one with a strong internal "locus of control" who appears invulnerable and who becomes the survivor. On the other side of the coin, the person with an external locus of control (e.g., believes what happens to him lies outside his control completely and is due solely to "luck" or "fate") is more likely to become the victim of "give-up-itis" or "Musselman" syndrome.

IMPLICATIONS FOR TREATMENT

The lessons learned enumerated before lead to a number of implications for treatment of individuals who have suffered the trauma of prolonged, harsh captivity or hostage experiences.

1. Appropriate treatment by knowledgeable, empathic caregivers immediately after release is important for later adjustment. Those who first deal with the returning captive must be aware of phenomena such as the Stockholm Syndrome and survival guilt.

2. Within the prison environment, "buddies" are extremely important. Camaraderie, with a code or "chain of command" for guidance, assists the captive in coping with the stresses of captivity.

3. Any person who is "at risk" of becoming a captive could benefit from pretraining, such as "survival" training, knowledge concerning the potential captor's culture, and an understanding of the Stockholm Syndrome and the possibility of survivor guilt. Recognizing the importance of communication while in captivity and learning the "tap" code prior to capture can prove beneficial for the captive. In other words, "stress inoculation" is effective in preventing some of the residuals of prolonged, extreme stress such as captivity or hostage experiences.

4. Findings from studies of captives highlight the importance of early childhood training and the development of a sense of identity, high self-esteem, religious or spiritual beliefs, and internal locus of control.

5. Just knowing that individuals can cope with much more stress than they ever dream they can helps with survival in extreme situations.

6. Group support within prison as well as after release from those who are or have been in a similar situation assists in coping. Being able to talk about one's feelings of rage, depression, and helplessness benefits not only captives but also the families who wait for their loved ones' release.

7. Flexible homecoming plans are important. There should be a recog-

nition of the wide variation in the need for various supports of the returning captives. One should not assume all ex-POWs require the same treatment, and not all families have the same needs.

8. The longer the period of captivity and the harsher the treatment during captivity, the longer the period necessary for rehabilitation. Many families of the Vietnam POWs estimated it took 1 year of adjustment for every year of captivity; others found they were still "adjusting" 10 years later (Hunter, 1980, 1983).

Echoes from the concentration camp experience during World War II and from men who survived up to almost 9 years imprisonment in Hanoi four decades later, point to benefits as well as scars from the trauma behind stone walls and barbed wire. Quoting Nietzsche, Viktor Frankl (1959), survivor of the Holocaust, stated, "He who has the *why* to live can bear with almost any *how*."

In 1973, on that first Sunday of freedom at March Air Force Base in the Philippines, American POWs, released from Hanoi a few hours earlier, requested and conducted their own church service. Humbly, one ex-POW, who had been held six long years in captivity, offered a prayer:

> Few men have the opportunity to be born again . . . to be able to stand in freedom again . . . to see the sun shining on the flowers, the trees, and the grass . . . to see clouds rolling past the hills in the distance . . . to hear birds sing . . . and more than that, to be able to share love with our families and friends again. (Returned POW, personal communication, 1973)

One must wonder—does this outpouring of gratitude and happiness continue as the former captive adjusts to freedom? His own strengths, his coping skills, and his will to survive delivered him from imprisonment. Compassionate, caring individuals in the environment to which he returns will undoubtedly moderate the impact of the captivity experience during future years. No former captive will ever forget the experience, for it has made an indelible imprint upon the future. Whether that imprint is perceived as a blemish or a rare patina is determined, to a large extent, by the one on whom it has fallen.

REFERENCES

American Psychiatric Association. (1980). *Diagnostic and statitical manual of mental disorders* (3rd ed.). Washington, DC: American Psychiatric Association.

Beebe, G. (1975). Follow-up studies of World War II and Korean war prisoners: II. Mortality, disability, and maladjustments. *American Journal of Epidemiology, 101,* 400–422.

Bensheim, H. (1960). Die KZ-Neurose rassisch Verfolgter. *Nervenarzt, 31,* 472.

Biderman, A. (1957). Communist attempts to elicit false confessions from Air Force prisoners of war. *Bulletin of the New York Academy of Medicine, 33*(9), 616–625.

Cohen, B., & Cooper, M. (1954). *A follow-up study of World War II prisoners of war.* Washington, DC: Veterans Administration Medical Monograph.

Eitinger, L. (1961). Pathology of the concentration camp syndrome. *Archives of General Psychiatry, 5,* 371–379.

Frankl, V. (1959). *Man's search for meaning: An introduction to logotherapy.* Boston: Beacon Press.

Hermann, J. (1973). *Canadians who were prisoners of war in Europe during World War II.* Report to the Canadian Minister of Veterans Affairs, Ottawa.

Hunter, E. (1978). The Vietnam POW veteran: Immediate and long-term effects of captivity. In C. Figley (Ed.), *Stress disorders among Vietnam veterans: Theory, research, and treatment* (pp. 188–206). New York: Brunner/Mazel.

Hunter, E. (1980). *Lessons learned from the Vietnam POW/MIA studies, mobilization I: The Iranian crisis.* Unpublished paper prepared for the Emergency Meeting of the Task Force on Families of Catastrophe, sponsored by the Family Research Institute, Purdue University, West Lafayette, Indiana.

Hunter, E. (1982). Families under the flag: A review of military family literature. New York: Praeger.

Hunter, E. (1983). Captivity: The family in waiting. In C. Figley & H. McCubbin (Eds.), *Stress and the family: Coping with catastrophe* (Vol. II, pp. 166–184). New York: Brunner/Mazel.

Hunter, E. (1985). Treating the military captive's family. In F. Kaslow & R. Ridenour (Eds.), *The military family: Dynamics and treatment* (pp. 167–196). New York: Guilford Press.

Hunter, E., & Plag, J. (1977). The longitudinal studies of prisoners of war and their families: An overview. In E. Hunter (Ed.), *Prolonged separation: The prisoner of war and his family* (pp. 1–7). San Diego: Center for POW Studies (NHRC Report no. 77-26).

Juillet, P., & Moutin, P. (1969). *Psychiatrie Militaire.* Paris: Masson.

Kral, V., Pazder, L., & Wigdor, B. (1968). Long-term effects of a prolonged stress experience. *Canadian Psychiatric Association Journal 12,* 175–181.

Mattusek, P. (1975). *Internment in concentration camp and its consequences.* New York: Springer.

Miller, W. (1974). *POW's.* Unpublished report. San Diego: Center for POW Studies.

Mowery, E., Hutchins, C., & Rowland, B. (1975). *The historical management of POWs: A synopsis of the 1968 U.S. Army Provost Marshal General's study entitled, "A review of the United States policy on treatment of prisoners of war."* San Diego: Center for POW Studies, unpublished report.

Nefzger, M. D. (1970a). Follow-up studies of World War II and Korean war prisoners: Study plan and mortality findings. *American Journal of Epidemiology, 91*(2), 123–138.

Nefzger, M. (1970b). Readjustment problems of returned prisoners of war. *Medical Service Digest, 24,* 17–19.

Niederland, W. G. (1968). Clinical observations of the survivor syndrome. In H. Krystal (Ed.), *Massive psychic trauma.* New York: International Universities Press.

O'Connell, P. (1975). Trends in psychological adjustment: Observations made during successive psychiatric follow-up interviews of returned Navy-Marine Corps POWs. In R. Spaulding (Ed.), *Proceedings of the Third Annual Joint Medical Meeting Concerning POW/MIA matters* (pp. 16–22). San Diego, CA: Center for POW Studies.

Richlin, M. (1977). Positive and negative residuals of prolonged stress. In E. Hunter (Ed.), *Prolonged separation: The prisoner of war and his family* (pp. 19–28). San Diego: Center for Prisoner of War Studies.

Rowan, S. (1973). *They wouldn't let us die: The prisoners of war tell their story.* New York: Jonathan David.

Segal, J. (1974). *Long-term psychological and physical effects of the POW experience: A review of the literature.* San Diego, CA: Center for Prisoner of War Studies.

Segal, J., Hunter, E.. & Segal, Z. (1976). Universal consequences of captivity: Stress reactions among divergent populations of prisoners of war and their families. *International Social Sciences Journal, 28,* 593–609.

8

Predictors of Psychological Well-Being among Survivors of the Holocaust

BOAZ KAHANA, ZEV HAREL, and EVA KAHANA

INTRODUCTION

In this chapter, findings from empirical research on predictors of mental health in three populations of Holocaust survivors are reviewed and discussed. Earlier perspectives on the effects of the Holocaust have been based almost exclusively on generalizations derived from clinical studies anchored in the medical psychiatric tradition. More recent views on the long-range effects of the Holocaust have begun to rely on findings from more systematic studies of Holocaust survivors that employed conceptual approaches anchored in the social and behavioral sciences. This chapter provides converging evidence from three studies of survivor populations concerning the effects of extreme stress on psychological well-being in late life. It substantiates the importance of poststress factors for the mental health of aging survivors of the Holocaust. More specifically, findings from these studies suggest that adequate health, higher levels of economic resources and social resources, along with type of coping and self-disclosure are important determinants of mental health among survivors of extreme stress. It is important, therefore, that mental health professionals acquaint

BOAZ KAHANA • Department of Psychology, Cleveland State University, Cleveland, Ohio 44115. **ZEV HAREL** • Center on Applied Gerontological Research, Department of Social Service, Cleveland State University, Cleveland, Ohio 44115. **EVA KAHANA** • Elderly Care Research Center, Department of Sociology, Case Western Reserve University, Cleveland, Ohio 44106.

themselves with the empirical evidence from more recent research so as to better understand the experiences and service needs of survivors of extreme stress.

THE EFFECTS OF THE HOLOCAUST ON SURVIVORS

Generalizations based on the clinical, psychiatric, and medical literature underscore the presence of pathological consequences of the Holocaust not only among survivors but also among children of survivors. As a consequence of these effects, survivors and their children are viewed as emotionally and socially impaired. However, more recently, there have been a number of studies in which behavioral and social science perspectives and methodologies were employed to ascertain the long-range effects of the Holocaust on survivors and on their children. The review of findings from such studies reveals that the medical psychiatric perspective derived conclusions from observations of persons seeking psychiatric help and those applying for restitution from Germany. More recent studies of survivors and children of survivors raise serious questions about the validity of the generalizations based on the psychiatric literature. In one of these studies, Matussek (1975) evaluated a group of 245 survivors approximately 15 years after confinement. Contrary to Krystal (1968) and Chodoff (1966), Matussek concluded that there were no concentration camp syndromes identifiable among participants in his research.

In a comparative study of survivors of the Holocaust with a random sample of household heads in a Montreal community, Eaton, Sigal, and Weinfeld (1982) found that there appeared to be varying long-term stressful consequences from the Holocaust. For those who survived, the long-term consequences for physical illness seemed to be slight, whereas the long-term psychiatric consequences were associated with perceived potential for ethnic persecution.

Based on his ongoing research, the late S. Davidson (1981) underscored the remarkable adaptive and reintegrative capacities of survivors, their creation of healthy families, and their significant social achievements. He stated that the presence of traumatization symptoms does not preclude good social and family functioning. He advised against generalizations applied to the large heterogeneous population of survivors and their families.

Shanan and Shahar (1983) studied the personality functioning of Jewish Holocaust survivors, aged 46 to 65, during the midlife transition in Israel. They found no significant differences between concentration camp survivors and those who had lived underground on any of the personality variables included in their study. The few significant differences between the Holocaust survivors and the Israeli group were on measures of coping behavior. Contrary to expectations, Holocaust survivors tended to be more task-oriented, to cope more actively, and expressed more favorable attitudes toward family, friends, and work.

A review of more recent research that employed behavioral and social science perspectives and methodologies suggests that earlier Holocaust studies conducted within the medical-psychiatric frame of reference have serious theoretical and methodological limitations. Harel (1983), in a review of the earlier Holocaust literature, found that most of the studies drew exclusively on the psychiatric literature and almost completely neglected behavioral and social science perspectives. The result is a serious gap in the informational and analytical content of these studies. Second, attempts have been made in most of these studies to draw theoretical inferences that were not warranted by observations and/or research data.

DesPres (1976), in a general review of issues related to survival, points to the limitations of the Holocaust literature and questions the utility of psychoanalytic models for the explanation of behavior in concentration camps. Furthermore, he questions the efficacy and wisdom of applying psychoanalytic models with their excessive reliance on unconscious processes to provide explanation of the effects that the Holocaust experience had on survivors. He also suggests the need to consider the objective realities of the environmental situation in concentration camps and the environmental and social conditions in which Holocaust survivors lived in subsequent years.

Solkoff (1981), following a critical evaluation of earlier studies of children of Holocaust survivors, questions the wisdom of relying on assertions about the intergenerational effects of persecution that have been derived from poorly designed studies. Methodologically, Solkoff finds that both the clinical and experimental research in this area are problem-laden. He believes that investigators and clinicians often follow personal hunches and look to the survivor population for evidence to substantiate their private hypotheses. Samples are haphazardly selected, and control groups are nonexistent or poorly described. Solkoff states that one must guard against vast theoretical leaps from inadequately gathered and reported data.

There is also a recognition in the professional literature that earlier-practice assumptions based on the medical-psychiatric literature may have been exaggerated. Rustin (1980) warns against the temptation to view all survivors of the Holocaust and their children as one homogeneous group. The particular circumstances of each individual and his or her family must be examined if helpful therapy is to result. Feuerstein (1980) also cautions against the trend, present in the psychological literature on the Holocaust, to view survivors as a homogeneous group. He stresses the value of studying the Holocaust and its "victims" and warns against the danger of trivializing or diminishing the overall immense importance and dimensions of the Holocaust itself. Kinsler (1984) advocates that there is a need for a better understanding of possible difficulties resulting from massive trauma. Krell (1984) asserts that the successful adaptation of survivor families has not as yet received sufficient attention in the professional literature.

More recent research indicates that, although some Holocaust survivors have been scarred to various degrees by their experiences, there is also evidence that a percentage of the survivors not only adjusted well as individuals but also made substantial contributions to collective communal efforts in their new environments. Similarly, although there is evidence indicating that children of survivors sought professional help, there is also considerable evidence that indicates that children of survivors have adjusted well personally and enjoy healthy family relationships (Solkoff, 1981).

A potentially dangerous implication of the earlier psychiatric literature and research on survivors of the Holocaust and their children has been the tendency to blame the victim either blatantly or in subtle ways. The focus has not been on understanding the experiences of survivors and the effects of their experiences. Instead, the tendency has been to generate a list of psychopathological manifestations present in survivors and in their children. There have been also assertions that some of the damage is nontreatable. This form of labeling, in turn, may have been used to justify the conclusion by some mental health professionals that stress victims may not benefit from interventions.

The conclusions about the long-range effects of the Holocaust, derived from the psychiatric literature, may have added an unintended burden on survivors and their children by labeling them as emotionally and socially impaired. Professionals concerned with the well-being and service needs of survivors will do well to acquaint themselves with findings from more recent cross-sectional studies and from studies that also report the concern and perspectives of survivors.

Presented in this chapter are data on predictors of psychosocial well-being measured by affective states and morale among three groups of Holocaust survivors. The first study included 275 survivors of the Holocaust who attended the 1983 Washington, DC, Gathering of American Holocaust Survivors. The second study included a cross-section of Holocaust survivors in a midwestern city in the United States. The third study included a cross-section of survivors of the Holocaust in Israel. A unique feature of this study is that the authors employed a behavioral and social science conceptual and methodological approach.

In the literature on the psychological aftermath of the Holocaust, survivors have been depicted to suffer from chronic, progressive, and irreversible forms of psychopathology that are assumed to be unaffected by post-Holocaust experiences (Shanan & Shahar, 1983). One goal of these studies was to examine the validity of this general assumption by considering the differential importance of sociodemographic status, wartime experiences, and postwar adaptation as they impacted on the affective states of survivors. The studies represented efforts to learn about the social and psychological characteristics of a broader cross-section of survivors. In contrast to much of the earlier work, the study of those who attended the Gathering of Holocaust Survivors in Washington focused on indications of positive and negative aspects of mental health in the lives of survivors. As most of the survivors are approaching old age, 40 years after the Holocaust, the investigators raised questions about the perceived impact of survivorship on adjustments to aging. The investigators were also concerned with the perceived impact of the Holocaust experiences on survivors because recent research (Giordano, 1976) has pointed to the important implications of group identity for mental health following stressful situations.

More recent literature and research on mental health predictors among survivors, even though still limited, point to three variable groups that are likely to affect the long-term adaptation and well-being among extreme stress victims. These variable groups include: (1) stress factors (nature and duration of stress experiences); (2) current sociodemographic and socioeconomic status and health; and (3) the current modes of coping with conventional life and survivorship experiences.

More recently, DesPres (1976) has argued for the value of greater consideration of the objective realities as well as the environmental and social conditions in which survivors lived during the Holocaust and in subsequent years. Harel (1983), in a review of Holocaust literature, found that situational factors during the Holocaust, such as mode of survival, duration of time in camps, and the nature of the camp experiences played important roles in psychological sequelae among survivors. Coping strategies used during the trauma of the Holocaust have also been considered as factors that may influence long-term adaptation. Dimsdale (1974) called attention to coping mechanisms used by survivors such as "differential focus on the good," "group affiliation," and "hope," as significant means of dealing with and mastering the extreme psychological trauma of the war years. Bettleheim (1943) focused on the intellectual withdrawal as a useful adaptive mechanism, whereas Frankl (1969) stressed the importance of the victim's interpretation of the stress and the value of finding meaning in survivorship.

Although research has thus far not focused on the potential influence of post-Holocaust adaptation patterns in mitigating negative consequences of stress, there are compelling arguments for considering ongoing adaptive efforts. After liberation, survivors were confronted by societal indifference, avoidance, and denial of their experiences (Danieli, 1981). As the conspiracy of silence regarding the Holocaust has lifted, the survivors' ability to disclose and speak about wartime experiences may be seen as an important determinant of mental health. Inability or lack of opportunity to verbalize suffering has been cited as contributing to negative psychological sequelae among survivors (Hoppe, 1971). Furthermore, the inability to verbalize traumatic events has been seen as a specific antecedent of lack of affect (Krystal, 1968). There have been suggestions advanced that factors associated with adaptation to aging may exacerbate the symptoms experienced by survivors (Danieli, 1981). Abandonment and isolation among some aged may be seen as similar to feelings of being abandoned during the Holocaust. On the other hand, it has been argued by developmental theorists that successful adult development is closely related to one's recall and utilization of the past for current adaptation (Peskin 1981).

NATIONAL GATHERING OF HOLOCAUST SURVIVORS STUDY

The Gathering of Holocaust Survivors in Washington, DC, in 1983 provided the opportunity for a study of survivors who were in attendance at this meeting. Questionnaires were returned by 275 respondents (132 males and 143 females). Respondents' ages ranged from 43 to 85 years, and the average age was 61. The vast majority of respondents (76%) arrived in the United States within the 6-year period of 1946 to 1951. Respondent residences prior to 1939 included 12 European countries, with a high percentage of respondents from Poland (57%), followed by lower percentages from Czechoslovakia (13%), Germany (9%), Hungary (8%), and still smaller percentages from Greece, Sweden, Romania, Belgium, and Holland. Respondents' current residences included 24 U.S. states with a high percentage of respondents from New York (21%) and California (17%). Four percent of respondents reported Canadian residences.

Only 10% of the present sample indicated that they had received regular counseling or psychotherapy (an additional 13% received some counseling). Thus it is noteworthy that the present study is based on a broad range of survivors who may be quite different in terms of psychosocial and mental health characteristics from patient populations typically considered in earlier studies of Holocaust survivors. Furthermore, only 40% of respondents reported that they were members of survivor groups or organizations, further underscoring the fact that the present study extended the pool of survivors studied.

A brief questionnaire was specifically developed for this study. The questionnaire was easy to understand so that it could be readily completed by respondents with possibly limited test-taking skills. The survey covered basic sociodemographic (sex, age, marital status, and religious affiliation) and socioeconomic status (level of education and occupation) as well as aspects of mental and physical health. Mental health indicators were drawn from the Affect-Balance Scale (Bradburn, 1959). This 10-item scale of psychological well-being is based on positive and negative affect items (e.g., "pleased about having accomplished something" vs. "depressed or unhappy"). It has reported Cronbach alphas in the high 60s. (Sauer & Warland, 1982). Cronbach's alpha coefficient derived from the present sample for this measure was .72.

Additional measures addressed Holocaust experiences. Several items measured the effect of wartime experiences on current emotional and physical well-being and degrees of current preoccupation with the Holocaust (e.g., "how often do you think of your Holocaust experiences?"). Other items assessed the effect of the Holocaust experiences on aging (e.g., "do you feel that your experiences as a survivor made it easier or more difficult to cope with problems of getting older?"). Items were included that measured degrees of self-disclosure about experiences with friends and family members. Degree of mental health service utilization was assessed by inquiring about professional counseling sought by survivors.

Items that covered information about survivors' experiences during the Holocaust included (a) length of time in hiding, in ghettos, in work camps, in concentration camps, or with resistance groups; (b) loss of family members; (c) applications for reparations from Germany; and (d) memberships in survivor organizations.

RESULTS

A review of demographic characteristics of the respondents reveal that the vast majority of survivors were married (73%) with an additional 9% reporting being widowed. A low percentage of respondents (8%) report to have been divorced, with only 3% currently divorced and 5% remarried from divorce. These data suggest that survivors have maintained more traditional marriage and divorce rates. The reported divorce rate is substantially lower than rates for cohorts in the general population. The great majority of survivors (71%) reported being currently married to other survivors. The data also suggest a tendency toward small families among survivors, indicating that their ordeal during the Holocaust may have lead them to opt for smaller families.

A high percentage of survivors (57%) reported their religious affiliation as Conservative followed by lower percentages reporting their affiliation as Orthodox (23%), Reform (11%), and unaffiliated (8%). The high percentage of respondents indicating orthodox and conservative religious affiliation (79%) may reflect the importance of continued Jewish religious traditions among those who experienced the extreme trauma of the Holocaust. This finding is especially interesting as it contradicts notions that extreme psychic trauma undermine strict religious affiliation and adherence.

Educational level of respondents ranged from 2 to 20 years with a high percentage having completed less than 12 years of schooling (47%) followed by lower percentages of respondents completing 12 years (24%), 13 to 16 years (20%), and more than 16 years (10%).

Physical and Mental Health of Survivors

About one-half of respondents reported their health to be either good or excellent (52%) with lesser percentages reporting their health to be fair (41%) or poor (7%). These data are likely to provide somewhat conservative estimates of health problems as questionnaires were distributed to survivors who were well enough to travel to the national conference. The combined percentage of respondents reporting fair to poor health (48%) is lower than the percentage for aged cohorts in the U.S. population. A very high percentage of survivors reported that Holocaust experiences had negatively affected their physical health (89%) with 31% reporting that their Holocaust experiences negatively affected their health a great deal.

Nearly all of the respondents reported that their Holocaust experiences negatively affected their emotional well-being (92%), and a combined 61% reported thinking about their Holocaust experiences either daily or several times a week. Despite these high percentages, indicating negative mental and physical sequelae associated with extreme trauma, a high percentage of respondents reported that they had not received any professional counseling (77%).

Forty-five percent of respondents indicated that their Holocaust experiences made coping with problems of getting older more or much more difficult with lower percentages of respondents indicating no difference (29%) or that their Holocaust experiences made current coping easier or much easier (26%).

Predictors of Well-Being

A review of findings from the correlational analysis revealed varied patterns in the relative importance of the sociodemographic and socioeconomic status, the stress experience, and the current coping and adaptational factors on the positive affect, negative affect, and affect balance. The findings indicate that lower age, higher number of children, and religious affiliation had a significant positive association with both positive affect and with affect balance. Educational attainment was also significantly associated with positive affect. None of the sociodemographic measures were found to have a significant association with negative affect. Self-rated good health was found to have a significant positive association with positive affect, whereas poor health was found to be significantly associated with negative affect. These findings are in line with findings from gerontological research that indicate that better health, lower age, and higher educational attainment are significantly associated with higher morale (psychological well-being) among the aged (Larson, 1978; see Table 1).

Somewhat surprisingly, none of the wartime stress experiences were found to have a significant association with either one of the three measures of affect among Holocaust survivors. Of the wartime experiences, wartime resources (being with one or more people) and languages spoken were found to have a significant association with positive affect indicating the possible buffering role of personal and social resources in time of

Table 1. Correlates of Affect for Survivors of the Holocaust in the United States ("National Gathering" Sample)

	Correlates of affect		
Variables	Positive affect	Negative affect	Affect balance
Age	−0.24**	−0.08	−0.18**
Sex	−0.05	0.01	−0.00
Marital status	0.07	−0.00	0.05
Number of children	0.10*	−0.01	0.13*
Religious affiliation	0.11*	0.07	0.11*
Highest grade in school	0.15**	−0.04	0.05
Work done most of life	0.07	−0.04	0.08
Current health	0.20**	−0.16**	0.10
Months in hiding	−0.01	0.05	−0.07
Months in ghetto	0.02	0.07	0.05
Months in work camps	0.04	0.07	0.03
Months in concentration camps	0.01	−0.01	0.02
Months in resistance	0.06	−0.09	−0.04
Losses	−0.03	0.05	−0.06
Was alone during war	−0.01	−0.02	0.04
Wartime resources	0.12*	−0.01	0.09
Languages spoken	0.11*	−0.03	0.06
Disclosure	0.37**	0.09	0.14**
Spouse a holocaust survivor	0.21**	0.08	0.15**
Survivorship helped aging	−0.31**	0.27**	−0.07
Holocaust affected physical health	−0.16**	0.14**	0.01
Holocaust affected emotional health	−0.04	0.29**	0.17**
Think of Holocaust experience	−0.03	0.15**	0.05
Hours of counseling	−0.05	0.33**	0.03
Belong to survivor organization	−0.05	0.07	−0.02
Concern for children	0.20**	0.19**	0.15**
Perception of age group	−0.22**	0.15**	−0.07
Locus of control	0.31**	0.04	0.14**
Altruism	0.35**	0.08	0.21**

*$p < .05$; **$p < .01$.

stress. It is important to note, however, that almost all survivors perceive their Holocaust experiences to have had a lasting negative effect on their mental health.

Contrary to expressions in the general media and in some of the professional literature, our findings reveal that survivors shared their Holocaust experiences extensively with spouses, children, other family members, friends, and co-workers. Furthermore, our findings indicate that sharing of wartime experiences is positively associated with more positive affect. Positive affect is also significantly associated with having a spouse who is a survivor of the Holocaust and a perception that survivorship was a positive factor in facilitating adjustment to aging. Along with these findings, there is also an indication that survivors who report that the Holocaust affected their physical health to a lesser extent are more likely to exhibit positive affect. Interestingly, altruism, internal locus of control, younger age identification, and concern for children were found to have highly significant associations with positive affect.

Correlates of negative affect emerged as distinctively different from the factors that were associated with positive affect. Measures that had a significant association with negative affect included extent of counseling received, a perception that the Holocaust adversely affected their mental health, and a perception that the Holocaust experiences made adjustment to aging more difficult. Other significant, though more modest, associations were found between negative affect and a perception that the Holocaust adversely affected physical health, frequent thoughts about the Holocaust, concern for children, and age identification with an older age group. Review of the bivariate associations appears to indicate that, in a number of instances, the association with positive and negative affect cancel each other out, as represented in the correlates of affect balance. Significant sociodemographic correlates positively associated with affect balance were age, number of children, and religious affiliation. Neither one of the wartime stress variables was significantly associated with affect balance. Other variables that had a significant bivariate positive association with affect balance included disclosure, having a survivor spouse, a perception that the Holocaust affected their mental health, concern for children, internal locus of control, and altruism.

In multivariate analyses on the predictive importance of individual measures from the three groups of variables included in this research, reported elsewhere, only a small number maintained their significance (Kahana, Kahana & Harel, in press). Only four measures—self-disclosure, altruism, having a survivor spouse, and the perception that survivorship helps the adjustment to aging (in order of significance)—were found to be significantly associated with positive affect. These findings indicate that, among survivors, positive affect is most strongly and significantly associated with post-Holocaust adaptations and life experiences such as sharing of Holocaust experiences, altruism, a perception that survivorship aids the adjustment to aging, and a spouse who is a survivor of the Holocaust.

The exploration of the predictors of negative affect in a multivariate analysis yielded findings different from those found in the prediction of positive affect. Of the measures included, only counseling received and the perception that the Holocaust negatively affected survivor's adjustment to aging were found to be significant. These findings indicate that negative affect is most significantly associated with Holocaust-related counseling and a perception that the Holocaust affected one's mental health and makes adjustment to aging more difficult.

In the multivariate analyses, the smallest variance accounted for was found in affect balance, and only two measures were significant—fewer losses during wartime and the perception that the Holocaust did not significantly affect survivors' mental health. Interestingly, among this sample of survivors, affect balance proved to be a less useful mental health indicator than either positive or negative affect. It appears that the associations with positive and negative indications of mental health cancel each other out. Thus it may be more appropriate to consider the relative importance of positive affect and negative affect separately rather than in combination in studies of Holocaust survivors.

The second and third studies explored predictors of psychological well-being among survivors of the Holocaust in the United States and Israel. These studies offer the opportunity to examine predictors of psychological well-being among a cross-section of Holocaust survivors not only in the United States but also in Israel. The authors employed a behavioral and social science orientation in considering sequelae of massive psychic trauma as compared to earlier studies based primarily on psychodynamic approaches. One of the primary objectives of this research was to examine the relative and differential importance of sociodemographic status and postwar adaptation as they impact on the psychological well-being of survivors. This research represents one of the few systematic efforts to understand the importance of social and psychological factors in the lives of survivors.

More recent literature and research on mental health predictors among survivors, even though still limited, point toward three variable groups that are likely to affect the long-term adaptation and well-being among extreme stress victims. These variable groups include stress factors (nature and duration of stress experiences), current sociodemographic and socioeconomic status and health, and the current modes of coping with conventional life and survivorship experiences.

Although, to date, research has not focused on the potential influence of post-Holocaust adaptation patterns in mitigating negative consequences of stress, there are compelling arguments for considering ongoing adaptive efforts. The broad questions of human adaptation and adjustment have long been central to theoretical formulations dealing with personality, social behavior, and mental health. Social and behavioral scientists have long been intrigued by the human capacity to endure and rebound from extreme stress. Reliance on conceptual approaches that incorporate behavioral and social science perspectives is necessary in attempts to understand the long-range effects of trauma on survivors and for understanding the ways in which survivors adjusted to the demands and challenges in the postwar years. It is essential to go beyond the notion that trauma causes long-range irreparable damage. It is important to explore not only the pathological consequences and scars caused by the Holocaust but also to ascertain the factors that are likely to reduce these adverse consequences and aid the psychosocial adjustment of survivors.

Post-Traumatic Adjustment of Survivors

In considering post-traumatic adaptation of survivors of extreme trauma, including their adjustment to aging, it is important to use variables employed in gerontological research along with variables that are significant for the understanding of the special experiences of survivors. Therefore, this study employed sociodemographic, socioeconomic status, and health variables, along with social and psychological measures that may be salient to the experiences of survivors in the postwar years.

Sociodemographic variables in this research included age, sex, marital status, country of origin, work background, perceived income adequacy, and education before and after World War II. Health measures reported here included self-rated health, health measures from the OARS instrument (Blazer, 1978), and an inventory of illnesses. Of the sociodemographic variables, it was expected that being married and perceived income adequacy would be associated with higher psychological well-being in both groups. Similarly, it was expected that psychological well-being would also be associated with better health (Larson, 1978). To ascertain recent stressful experiences and concerns in the lives of the respondents, several measures frequently employed in gerontological research were employed: (1) Antonovsky's Life Crisis History and (2) the impact of life changes based on the Elderly Care Research Center (ECRC) Recent Life Event Scale. Reliability testing of these measures yielded alpha coefficients in the high 60s. Two measures of social concern were also employed in this research, a Social Concern Scale and a Concern for Children Scale. The Social Concern measure was subjected to a factor analysis and yielded two constructs—one reflected concern over a safe future and one reflected concern about economic security. The reliability testing of these measures yielded alpha coefficients ranging from the low 70s to the low 80s. Another measure, concern about raising of children, yielded alpha coefficients in the high 80s. It was expected that survivors would have high rates of stressful life events and a high degree of concern for the future. This is based on the assumption that survivors not only experienced more stress but are also likely to have a greater need to remain vigilant because every new stress situation may be seen as a potential threat. These concerns may be perceived by survivors as endangering the national, social, and psychological survival of self and others. Survivors are likely to perceive the probability of the recurrence of dangers that they have experienced or observed.

A measure of Jewish identification was also included in this research. When subjected to a factor analysis, the Jewish Identification Scale yielded three components; one reflected primarily issues related to identification with Jewish values and practices (alpha coefficients in the high 70s); the second reflected concerns about Israel (alpha coefficients in the 60s), and one item concerned with the Arab Israeli conflict.

Several personality measures were also included in this research. These are Wrightsman's Locus of Control and the Framingham's Scale, which are measures of personality style. Wrightsman's Locus of Control measure, when subjected to factor analysis, yielded two components: one more directly reflecting perceived locus of control and a second one indicating not being resigned to fate. The reliability testing of these measures yielded alpha coefficients ranging from the high 50s to the low 70s. The Framingham Scale is divided into two factors, referred to here as First Factor (hard driving, pressed for time, bossy, need to excel, eating quickly) and Second Factor (very pressed, work stays with me, work is demanding, uncertain how well I am doing). Reliability testing yielded alpha coefficients in the mid-60s for the First Factor and in the high 70s for the Second Factor on the Framingham Scale.

A measure of coping, the Elderly Care Research Center Coping Scale, was also included in this research. The ECRC Coping Scale was subjected to a factor analysis that yielded three constructs: instrumental coping, emotional coping, and escapist coping. Subjecting these measures to reliability testing yielded alpha coefficients ranging from the high 60s to high 70s.

Several measures of communication concerning everyday matters, important matters, concerns about sex, and finances were included in this research. The communication targets included spouse, children, grandchildren, other family members, friends, and co-workers. Reliability testing of communication with target groups yielded alpha coefficients from the low 60s to the high 70s. For the purposes of this chapter, findings from the two studies on predictors of psychological well-being (measured by morale) among survivors in Israel and the United States are presented. It was expected that similar patterns would emerge in the prediction of psychological well-being among survivors in both countries because of the universal nature of the importance of conventional predictors of psychological well-being among the aged, including aged survivors of the Holocaust.

HOLOCAUST SURVIVORS IN THE UNITED STATES

Participants in the U.S. research included a group of 168 survivors of the Holocaust who immigrated to the United States between the end of World War II and 1965. They ranged in age from 45 to 90, with an average age of 63. Women (56%) outnumbered men (44%). The overwhelming majority of the respondents were married (82%), and a significant percentage were widowed (17%). Interestingly, only a negligent fraction was never married (1%) or divorced (1%). The majority was from Poland (56%). Significant percentages were from Czechoslovakia (16%) and Hungary (12%). Other repondents were from Germany (6%), Romania (4%), Russia (3%), Austria (2%), and France (1%).

Respondents represented a diverse occupational background. These included self-employed small businessmen (23%), housewives (25%), clerical and service jobs (12%), skilled occupations (11%), management (3%), supervisors (1%), and professionals (1%). Others indicated that they were unskilled workers (4%), and a significant number did not indicate an occupational group (10%). The percentage of respondents who perceived their income to be adequate was rather high (66%); others viewed their income to be just enough (14%) or inadequate (21%). Regarding educational attainment, more than one-half of the respondents did not complete high school prior to World War II; 39% had a high-school education, 7% had some college education, and less than 1% reported some post college education. Survivors in the U.S. acquired additional education in the post war years (see Table 2).

As reported elsewhere (Kahana, Harel, & Kahana, 1986), survivors were found to have lower mental health and morale than members of the comparison group of similar sociodemographic and sociocultural background who have not endured the Holocaust.

In a correlational analysis, among survivors, higher morale was found to be associated with better health, higher income adequacy, and higher education. Men, compared with women, were also found to have higher morale. These data confirm the importance of health, economic status, and education as correlates of morale, a finding similar to findings from cross-sectional studies on predictors of well-being among the general aged population. Occupational status was not significantly associated with morale, which is somewhat surprising. Four variables, reflecting on crises and concerns, were significantly associated with morale. Higher morale was associated with a lesser concern for security, lesser concern for the future, lower scores on Antonovsky's Life Crises Inventory, and lower scores on the Elderly Care Research Center Recent Life Events Scale. Concern for children was not significantly associated with higher morale.

No significant association emerged between morale and the Jewish identification measures. Thus the data indicate that in the United States

Table 2. Means and Standard Deviations of Demographic and Summary Measures for Survivors of the Holocaust in the United States and Israel

	U.S. sample		Israel sample	
Variables	Mean	*SD*	Mean	*SD*
Sociodemographic				
Age	62.62	9.04	65.08	6.91
Sex (M = 1; F = 2)	1.56	0.51	1.53	0.50
Socioeconomic				
Work background	7.56	14.23	5.07	1.78
Income adequacy	3.65	1.22	2.12	0.68
Education before war	8.87	5.18	9.26	3.70
Education after war	4.22	8.39	4.76	5.74
Health				
Self-rated health	2.49	0.79	2.80	0.82
Illness severity	5.93	4.82	4.43	4.78
Crisis and concerns				
Antonovsky Life Crises	5.77	2.49	5.38	3.00
Recent life events	6.19	4.36	5.61	5.85
Concerns for future	8.31	2.65	15.57	3.67
Concerns for security	6.23	2.91	10.49	3.91
Worry about children	17.19	6.40	17.51	6.79
Jewish identification	12.85	3.20	13.47	4.55
Israel identification	2.19	1.05	2.60	0.87
Arab–Israel conflict	1.36	0.64	1.51	0.73
Personality				
Wrightsman locus of control	2.17	0.95	1.54	1.07
Wrightsman not resigned	1.35	1.15	1.21	1.14
First Factor Framingham	11.29	3.75	14.69	3.80
Second Factor Framingham	1.75	1.49	1.51	1.42
Coping				
Instrumental coping	21.23	4.51	17.41	4.62
Emotional coping	15.70	4.19	10.34	3.78
Escapist coping	12.95	4.83	15.81	4.99
Communication				
Communication with spouse	12.45	6.76	9.94	5.20
Communication with children	10.25	4.01	11.10	4.60
Communication with grandchildren	2.85	2.94	6.21	3.55
Communication with family	6.46	3.96	6.05	2.89
Communication with friends	5.80	2.73	6.07	2.77
Communication with co-worker	5.80	2.73	5.12	3.05
Psychological well-being				
Lawton Morale Scale	8.17	3.03	9.32	3.91

strong Jewish identification was not significantly correlated with higher morale.

Two personality measures were positively associated with higher morale: locus of control (i.e., not being resigned to fate) and higher scores on the second Framingham Scale factor, which is reflective of high energy level and hard work.

Table 3. Correlates of Morale for Survivors of the Holocaust in the United States and Israel

Variables	U.S. survivors	Israel survivors
Sociodemographic		
Age	−.04	−.17
Sex	−.21*	−.17
Marital status	.12	.33*
Socioeconomic		
Work background	.05	.11
Income adequacy	.33**	.20*
Education before war	.19*	.06
Education after war	.11	.12
Health		
Self-rated health	.27**	.35**
Illness severity	−.42**	−.26**
Crisis and concerns		
Antonovsky Life Crisis	−.43**	−.24*
Recent life events	−.20*	−.17
Concern for future	.25*	−.19*
Concern for security	.33**	−.13
Worry about children	−.02	−.01
Jewish Identification Scale	.11	.11
Identification with Israel	−.02	−.03
Stake in Arab–Israel conflict	−.01	.07
Personality		
Wrightsman locus of control	.08	.15
Wrightsman not resigned	.25**	.37*
First Factor Framingham	.13	.17
Second Factor Framingham	.33**	.07
Coping		
Instrumental coping	.23*	.14
Emotional coping	−.33**	−.33*
Escapist coping	−.30**	−.16
Communication		
Communication with spouse	.15	.31**
Communication with children	.12	.24*
Communication with grandchildren	.01	.09
Communication with family	−.12	.20*
Communication with friends	−.07	.07
Communication with co-workers	.13	.30**

$*p < .05$; $**p < .01$.

On the coping measures, as expected, higher levels of instrumental coping had a positive association with morale, whereas higher levels of emotional coping and escapist coping were associated with lower morale.

Somewhat surprisingly, although most of the communication measures had a positive correlation, none were significantly associated with higher morale (see Table 3).

A two-stage multiple regression analysis, reported elsewhere (Kahana, Harel & Kahana, 1986), was performed. First, all predictor variables were entered into the regression equation to ascertain the total explained variance. Second, variables that were not significant in the prediction of morale were excluded via a stepwise multiple regression procedure. In the stepwise multiple regression analysis, four variables were significant and accounted for 38% explained variance in morale among survivors. These included Antonovsky's Life Crises Investory, illness severity, and two coping measures (higher use of instrumental coping and lower use of emotional coping).

HOLOCAUST SURVIVORS IN ISRAEL

Respondents in this research included a group of 175 survivors of the Holocaust who immigrated to Israel after World War II. Respondents ranged in age from 55 to 90, with an average age of 65. Fifty-two percent of respondents were women. The overwhelming majority of the respondents were married (77%), and a significant percentage (21%) was widowed. Interestingly, only a small fraction had never been married (1%), divorced, or separated (2%). The majority was from Poland or Russia (56%). Significant percentages were from Romania (16%), Germany, and Austria (11%). Other respondents were Hungarian (6%), Czechoslovakia (3%), from the Balkan Peninsula (3%), Belgium and Holland (1%), and other countries (3%).

Respondents represented a diverse occupational background. These included clerical and service jobs (18%), skilled occupations (18%), housewives (13%), management (11%), supervisors (10%), unskilled workers (16%), and self-employed or professionals (2%). The percentage of respondents in Israel who perceived their income to be adequate was rather small (4%), and a low fraction viewed their income to be just enough (14%). The overwhelming majority of the respondents viewed their income to be not quite adequate (70%) or not at all adequate (11%). Regarding educational attainment, approximafely two-thirds of the respondents did not complete high school prior to World War II, 21% had a high-school education, 11% had some college education, and less than 5% reported some postcollege education. However, survivors in Israel acquired an average of 5 years of additional education in the postwar years (see Table 2).

As reported elsewhere (Harel, Kahana, & Kahana, 1988), survivors were found to have lower morale than members of the comparison group of similar sociodemographic and socio-cultural background who had not endured the Holocaust.

In a correlational analysis, among survivors, higher morale was found to be associated with being married, with better health, and with higher perceived income. Among members of the comparison group, marital status and the two measures of health were also positively and significantly correlated with morale. These data confirm the importance of health, economic status, marital status, and education as correlates of morale, a finding similar to cross-sectional studies on predictors of well-being among the general aged population. Occupational status and educational attainment were not significantly associated with morale, which is somewhat surprising. Of the crises and concern variables, worry about children was not positively associated with morale. Lower scores on the Elderly Care Research Center Recent Life Events Scale were minimally but not significantly associated with higher morale. Less concern for the future was significantly associated with higher morale. Higher morale was also associated with lower prevalence of life crises (see Table 3).

There was no significant association found between morale and the Jewish identification measures. All personality measures were positively associated with morale, though the association ranged from a minimal nonsignificant association to significant associations.

On the coping measures, as expected, higher levels of instrumental coping had a positive association with morale, whereas higher levels of emotional coping and escapist coping were associated with lower morale. Of these, however, only the association between emotional coping and morale was significant.

Of the communication measures, higher levels of communication with spouse and children were significantly associated with higher morale. Communication with other family members and with co-workers were also positively associated with morale. A more positive attitude toward aging was also found to be significantly associated with morale (see Table 3).

A two-stage multiple regression analysis, reported elsewhere (Harel, Kahana, & Kahana, 1988) was performed. First, all predictor variables were entered into the regression equation to ascertain the total explained variance. Second, variables that were not significant in the prediction of morale were excluded via a stepwise multiple regression procedure. In the stepwise multiple regression analysis, nine measures accounted for 52% explained variance in morale among survivors. These included two communication measures (with co-workers and family); two coping measures (lesser use of emotional coping and higher use of instrumental coping); fewer life crises and fewer concerns regarding the future; better health; being married and not being resigned to fate (higher internal locus of control).

CONCLUSIONS

The three studies included a broad cross-section of survivors of the Holocaust living in the United States, Canada, and Israel and focused on stress-related mental and physical health indicators as well as on reports of coping with problems of aging and with the effects of Holocaust experiences.

Findings of this study underscore the importance of recognizing that Holocaust survivors are not a homogeneous group and that their diversity provides important clues about the complex nature of post-traumatic adaptation. Although there is considerable evidence to indicate that some Holocaust survivors have been scarred to varying degrees by their experiences, there is also considerable evidence to indicate that a large percentage of the survivors adjusted well as individuals and have become productive citizens in their new environments.

Consideration of a broad cross-section of U.S. survivors allowed the investigators to go beyond previous perspectives on illness and pathology that characterized studies of patient populations and that comprised samples of most earlier studies. It is important to recognize, based on findings from this study, that aging survivors of the Holocaust share many characteristics with older adults in the general population. Hence, conventional predictions of social and psychological well-being in late life (Larson, 1978), found in this study, need to be included in future research.

Our data indicate that positive affect as an indicator of mental health 40 years after the Holocaust is less affected by stress experiences than the literature has indicated. However, the manner of coping with memories of the trauma and losses and the meaning found and attached to survivorship do play an important role in current mental health. Specifically, findings from this research underscore the potential value of sharing and disclosing traumatic experiences with willing and interested parties. Individuals married to survivors had greater opportunities to share their experiences. Furthermore, those able to talk to other family members and friends consistently portrayed more positive affect than those unable to do so. These results are congruent with observations in the mental health literature about the self-healing value of sharing stressful life experiences with others. Our data also indicate the importance of altruism for mental health. Those persons with higher altruistic tendencies and practices were found to have higher positive affect, indicating the importance of investing one's energies and resources toward improving the well-being of others.

Our data regarding predictors of negative affect revealed that survivors who feel adversely affected by the Holocaust and who sought mental health services for their problems, indeed, are more likely to have poorer mental health. These findings underscore the importance of differentiating persons who sought mental health services from those who did not seek assistance in evaluations of post-traumatic reactions.

Findings from the cross-sectional studies of the U.S. and Israeli survivor populations clearly indicate that, in the bivariate associations, the conventional sociodemographic predictors of morale, being married, better health, and adequate income are equally important in the prediction of morale among survivors as these variables are in studies of aged who have not been exposed to the stresses of the Holocaust. These data contribute, therefore, converging evidence to the increasing body of gerontological literature regarding the universal importance of better health and functional status, adequate economic resources, and marriage for better psychological well-being in advanced years of life (Larson, 1978).

Review of the findings on the crises and concern variables in this research clearly indicates the importance of concern for the future in Israel and that the greater the concern the lower the psychological well-being. Because life in Israel reflects an ongoing state of danger, it may not be surprising to find that constant concern for the future may lead to lower morale. In this regard, it is important to underscore that both survivor groups in these studies arrived in the United States and Israel from European countries where they observed and experienced anti-Semitism and threats on Jewish life. In this context, the continued threat to survival by the surrounding Arab countries affect the psychological well-being of aging members of the Israeli society. In addition, these data indicate that the psychological well-being of survivors is significantly affected by more frequent life crises and critical life events.

There is a clear indication in these data that personality style and coping style are also significant predictors of psychological well-being. Most significant of the findings in this area appear to be the indications that reliance on emotional coping is conducive to lower psychological well-being, whereas instrumental coping contributes toward a higher level of psychological well-being among members of both survivors groups.

There is also a clear indication in these data that the availability of social support and communication with members of one's primary group (i.e., spouse, children, and other family members) and friends are indeed important contributors toward higher levels of psychological well-being in both groups.

These data confirm the utility of employing conceptual approaches anchored in the behavioral and social sciences for the study of mental health among survivors of the Holocaust and possibly among other survivor populations of extreme stress. The data from this study clearly indicate that current states of psychological well-being among survivors are affected by recent states of health and functional status, cumulative life experiences, coping and adaptation and social support in ways similar to those found in cross-sectional studies of other populations of older persons (Larson, 1978).

These findings have, therefore, important implications. First, traumatic stress victims who seek professional services are indeed in need of the assistance they seek. Every effort should, therefore, be made to make available the services that stress victims need and seek. At the same time, it is also important to underscore that, to the extent that seeking counseling serves as the most significant predictor of mental health symptomatology, results of studies conducted exclusively with those seeking mental health services cannot be generalized to the entire survivor population.

REFERENCES

Bettlheim, B. (1943). Individual and mass behavior in extreme situations. *Journal of Abnormal and Social Psychology, 38,* 417–452.

Blazer, D. (1978). The Durham survey: Description and application. In *Multidimensional functional assessment—the OARS methodology: A manual* (2nd ed., pp. 75–88). Durham, NC: Duke University Center for the Study of Aging and Human Development.

Bradburn, N. M. (1969). *The structure of psychological well-being.* Chicago: Aldine.

Chodoff, P. (1966). Effects of extreme coercive and oppressive forces: Brainwashing and concentration camps. In S. Arieti (Ed.), *American handbook of psychiatry* (Vol. III, pp. 384–405). New York: Basic Books.

Danieli, Y. (1981). The aging survivor of the Holocaust. *Journal of Geriatric Psychiatry, 14*(2), 191–210.

Davidson, S. (1981). Clinical and psychotherapeutic experience with survivors and their families. *The Family Physician, 10,* 2, 313–321.

DesPres, T. (1976). *The survivor: An anatomy of life in the death camps.* New York: Oxford University Press.

Dimsdale, J. E. (1974). The coping behavior of Nazi concentration camp survivors. *American Journal of Psychiatry, 131,* 792–797.

Eaton, W. W., Sigal, J. J., & Weinfeld, M. (1982). Impairment in Holocaust survivors after 33 years: Data from an unbiased community sample. *American Journal of Psychiatry, 139*(6), 773–777.

Feuerstein, C. W. (1980). Working with the Holocaust victims psychologically: Some vital cautions. *Journal of Contemporary Psychotherapy, 11*(1), 70–77.

Frankl, V. (1969). *The will to meaning.* New York: New American Library.

Giordano, J. (1976). Group identity and mental health. *International Journal of Mental Health, 5*(2), 3–147.

Harel, Z. (1983). Coping with stress and adaptation: The impact of the Holocaust on survivors. *Society and Welfare, 5,* 221–30.

Harel, Z., Kahana, B., & Kahana, E. (1988). Predictors of psychological well-being among Holocaust survivors and immigrants in Israel. *Journal of Traumatic Stress Studies.*

Hoppe, K. (1971). The aftermath of Nazi persecution reflected in recent psychiatric literature. *International Psychiatry Clinic, 8,* 169–204.

Kahana, B., Harel, Z., & Kahana, E. (1986). Growing old in the aftermath of extreme trauma. Annual Meeting of Gerontological Society. *Gerontologist, 26,* 90.

Kahana, B., Kahana, E., & Harel, Z. (in press). Predictors of psychological well-being among Holocaust survivors. *Journal of Traumatic Stress Studies.*

Kinsler, F. (1984). *Surviving and overcoming trauma.* Paper presented at National Conference of Christians and Jews, Los Angeles.

Krell, R. (1984). Holocaust survivors and their children: Comments on psychiatric consequences and psychiatric terminology. *Comprehensive Psychiatry, 25*(5), 521–28.

Krystal, H. (1968). Studies of concentration camp survivors. In H. Krystal (Ed.), *Massive psychic trauma* (pp. 23–40). New York: International Universities Press.

Larson, R. (1978). Thirty years of research on the subjective well-being of older Americans. *Journal of Gerontology, 40,* 109–129.

Matussek, P. (1975). *Internment in concentration camp and its consequences.* New York: Springer.

Peskin, H. (1981). Observations on the first international conference on children of Holocaust survivors. *Family Process, 20*(4), 391–394.

Rustin, S. L. (1980). The legacy is loss. *Journal of Contemporary Psychotherapy, 11*(1), 32–43.

Sauer, W. J., & Warland, R. (1982). Morale and life satisfaction. In D. J. Mangen & W. A. Peterson (Eds.), *Clinical and social psychology* (pp. 195–228). Minneapolis: University of Minnesota.

Shanan, J., & Shahar, O. (1983). Cognitive and personality functioning of Jewish Holocaust survivors during the midlife transition (46–65) in Israel. *Archiv für Psychologie, 135,* 275–294.

Solkoff, N. (1981). Children of survivors of the Nazi Holocaust: A critical review of the literature. *American Journal of Orthopsychiatry, 51,* 29–42.

9

Dominant Attitudes of Adult Children of Holocaust Survivors toward Their Parents

FRAN KLEIN-PARKER

INTRODUCTION

Reported here are the results of a heuristic-phenomenological study exploring the experience of adult children of Holocaust survivors. Participants in this study included 25 women and 14 men, age 24 to 34, who were born within 10 years of their parents' liberation. Of the 39 participants, 34 had two survivor parents, whereas the other 5 had a parent who escaped to Russia or Israel for the duration of the Holocaust.

This study began as a personal search motivated by a need to understand the impact of my parents' Holocaust ordeal on my relationship with them and attitudes toward them. It explored the evolving nature of the survivor/parent–child relationship from childhood into adulthood.

As the research progressed, the variables of country of origin, duration of parental incarceration, parental experiences, parental pre-Holocaust personalities, and resettlement experiences revealed many differences. Whether the parents were in latency, adolescence, young adulthood, or later adulthood, and whether they had lost a first family during the Holocaust effected their personalities and subsequently effected the relationship they had with their children. The country or continent in which each parent lived after the Holocaust (Israel, United States, South America, Canada, or Europe) also made a difference.

FRAN KLEIN-PARKER • Comprehensive Psychiatric Services at Southfield, Southfield, Michigan 48076.

Not all survivors were in concentration camps—some were hiding in the woods; others were resistance fighters; some were passing as Christians or hiding in the homes of Christians; some survivors escaped to other countries like Russia or Israel; some survivors were in labor camps. There variables contributed to the survivors' adjustment and adaptation during and after the Holocaust and consequently affected their children.

The Holocaust began for the survivors when the Nazis infiltrated their respective cities/villages. Persecutions lasted from 6 months (Hungary) to 6 years (Poland) depending on parents' homeland and individual circumstances. The countries of origin for parents of the research participants' included 21 from Poland, 12 from Czechoslovakia, 2 from Hungary, 1 from Transylvania, 1 from Lithuania, and two with 1 parent from Poland and the other from Czechoslovakia. Most of the participants' parents married someone from their own country, usually from different cities or villages.

Nineteen of the participants were born in the United States, and 20 of the participants had a different experience, having been born in Europe and immigrating to the United States between the ages of 1 ½ to 10. Birth order differed among participants. There were 21 firstborns, 12 secondborns, 1 third-born, and 5 "only" children (a different experience in itself). In most of the families, there were two offspring, unlike the average larger European family of six children. This phenomenon may be a function of several factors: (1) American families typically had fewer children than European families did, and survivors may have chosen to follow that model; (2) survivors were typically older at the time of marriage than the general population that may have influenced the length of childbearing years; (3) parenthood may have been overwhelming for the survivors; and (4) survivors may have viewed the world as an unsafe place to raise children.

All children of survivors appeared to have a common awareness of the impact of the Holocaust on their lives. The degree of impact varied as did individual histories, life experiences, and family adjustments after the Holocaust. This investigation explored concrete dimensions of the survivor/parent–child relationship over time to present a full portrayal of the experience, depicting the dominant attitudes adult children express toward parents.

THE HOLOCAUST LITERATURE

Much of the early research on children of Holocaust survivors indicated the transmission of psychopathology from survivor to their offspring. Survivors were depicted by psychiatrists as suffering from a "survivor syndrome" that consisted of chronic depressive states, anxiety, psychosomatic complaints, and psychological numbness. However, this literature did not consider that the rebellion typical of adolescence and young adulthood (developmentally a time of turmoil) as well as the climate of rebellion and change in the 1960s could have conceivably affected attitudes and behaviors of the second generation of Holocaust survivors.

More recent literature is unequivocal in its interpretation of the degree of psychopathology observed in Holocaust survivors and their children. Clinicians such as Niederland (1965), Russell (1974), Krystal (1968), Dimsdale, (1980), Kestenberg (1972), Barocas and Barocas (1979), and Sigal, Silver, Rakoff, and Ellin (1973) reported the presence of psychopathology in survivors and/or their children. In contrast, Rustin (1980), Trachtenberg and Davis (1978), Fogelman and Savran (1979), Wittenberg, (1978), Pilcz (1979), Danieli (1979), and Aleksandrowicz (1973) reported that children of survivors were well-adjusted. The study of Leon and associates (1981) also indicated no significant differences in psychopathology between children of survivors and control groups.

The differences in the earlier literature may be attributable to clinical studies generalizing from a select sample of survivors and their children to all survivors and their offspring. Solkoff (1981), in his review of the literature, noted theoretical and methodological deficiencies in studies of survivors and children of survivors. Often the population studied was in treatment with the professionals who wrote about their general impressions of them. Another methodological problem may involve issues of secondary gain as survivors who saw these psychiatrists did so in order to obtain restitution from the German government and may have exaggerated their difficulties. Therefore, these studies may have overestimated the prevalence and intensity of symptoms present in survivors. The medical psychiatric literature also failed to consider countertransference issues. Kestenberg (1972) found that psychoanalysts failed to consider the possibility of a link between symptomatology observed in children of survivors and parents' past history of persecution. There are assertions that treatment with survivors may invoke anxiety or guilt in the therapist. Axelrod, Schnipper, and Rau (1980) reported that countertransference problems in treating survivors and their offspring were frequent, severe, and persistent. Often issues related to the Holocaust were not raised by the family therapist. Rakoff (1971) stated that he experienced the nightmares of the survivors he was treating and gave up his research efforts (see also Dimsdale, 1980). In view of these noted countertransference issues, it appears that clinicians found it difficult to face the painful issues presented by survivors and instead attached a pathological diagnostic label to post-traumatic stress phenomena.

More recent reports of Epstein (1979), Fogelman and Savran (1979), Rustin (1980), Trachtenberg and Davis (1978), Danieli (1979), Pilcz (1979), Prince (1975), Bergman and Jucovy (1982), and others addressed the fact that children of survivors differ in attitudes, adjustment, and self-esteem. Unlike most of the earlier clinical studies, these researchers were sensitive in not portraying all survivors and their children as a generalized problematic population. Since the mid-1970s, the number of studies of adult children of survivors has been growing. Adult children of survivors are now expressing anger for themselves and their parents for the diagnostic labeling of both generations based on select groups who manifested symptoms of psychopathology.

Israeli researchers (Gay, 1972; Aleksandrowicz, 1973; Klein, 1971) reported that Israeli survivors reared healthy families, in part, because they had worked through the bereavement process mourning for their losses. They found the survivors' children had similar attitudes and adjustment to other Israeli children of the same age and socioeconomic groups. However, they did note some differences such as survivor parents' overindulging and overprotecting their children and their children's greater attachment to them. More recently, psychoanalysts recognize that survivors and their families had inherent strengths and may have been healthier than previously reported (Klein, 1971; Krell, 1984). Psychoanalysts Bergman and Jucovy (1982, p. 11) underscore that pathology does not occur in all survivors: In recovery, many survivors have shown an unusual degree of psychic strength and resiliency and have adapted to the renewal of their lives with great vitality. (It is likely that people who survived had great psychic strength to begin with). Many have achieved remarkable success and, perhaps because of their need for continuity and compensatory life-affirming attitudes, have inspired their children to be energetic and dedicated to responsibility and service.

Several investigators have recognized that what was related to parents' survivor status may have been in reality a function of being refugees of Eastern European Jewish backgrounds. Each survivor's experiences may have been unique in personal meaning as well as in the details of particular circumstances (Solkoff, 1981). The survivor's precaptivity personality characteristics correlated with their adaptation during and after the Holocaust and in turn affected the development and adaptation of their children. The comradeship that survivors had in camps is now being noted by researchers as contributing to the adaptation to postliberation life (Matussek, 1971). Bergman and Jucovy (1982) noted that many survivors rehabilitated themselves and raised children who made excellent adjustments.

Bergman and Jucovy (1982) recognized a wide variation of conflicts and symptoms in children of Holocaust survivors that would be difficult to differentiate from other groups of children. They also noted a balance between unusual ego strength and psychopathology, asserting that both developed out of the stress imposed by being born under the shadow of the Holocaust.

A common theme discovered in children of survivors is a "survival complex" that has been transmitted to them by their parents (Bergman & Jucovy 1982). Issues of survival have been evident in most, if not all, developmental phases. Many of these features have been described as "expressions of strength." By transmitting the qualities of their own survival, parents have taught their children how to survive. On the other hand, some children of survivors have *unconsciously* incorporated the Holocaust experiences of their parents into their own lives. In either case, when preoccupied with parental suffering, there is a tendency on their part to repeat the suffering of their parents.

Today researchers are recognizing the need for the children as well as their survivor parents to come to terms with the Holocaust through developing a realistic perspective of what happened (Danieli, 1981) and integrating it into their present lives. Prince (1975) feels that children of survivors universally want to pass on knowledge of the Holocaust not only to the world but also, most importantly, to their own offspring in order to preserve the past, alert their children to the dangers of the world, and fulfill a desire for their children to know and understand them better as parents.

Bergman and Jucovy (1982) identify three ways of reacting to the Holocaust: (1) live as if the Holocaust is still a current reality; (2) try to repress the memories of the Holocaust: or (3) attempt to sublimate through writing and speaking about the Holocaust, to keep its memory alive. This third group characterized many of the participants in this research as well as other children of survivors. International and national conferences have drawn survivors and their children together to remember the Holocaust and work through the bereavement and memories associated with it. Both survivors and children of survivors are active in promoting Holocaust education to the community at large through lectures, programs, discussions, and projects. The pursuit of knowledge about the Holocaust by the second-generation survivors is an attempt to impose meaning and order on the present (Prince, 1975) and appears to contribute to their adjustment and overall sense of well-being. This sublimation and integration has been observed to occur in the participants through the process of maturation.

FINDINGS

In this study, a "dominant attitude" is viewed as a core disposition, mood, or state of mind common in children of Holocaust survivors. Special focus is placed on the parent–child relationship. Dominant attitudes include perceptions. feelings, and convictions. For ease of presentation, these attitudes are discussed in three separate sections. However, this is not to imply that they are mutually exclusive. On the contrary, they are interdependent and interactional in nature.

The emphasis in the first section is on the adult child's perceptions of the nature, extent, and characteristics of the relationship with his or her parents. The emphasis in the second section is on the adult child's feelings toward his or her parents and his or her perceptions of parents' feelings toward him or her. These two sections reflect the adult child's description of his or her present perception of past feelings and relationship with parents while growing up and into adulthood. The third section describes how these dominant attitudes and perceptions have evolved and changed over time from childhood to the present.

DOMINANT ATTITUDES CONCERNING PERCEPTIONS OF THE PARENT–CHILD RELATIONSHIP

Adult Children's Interactions with Parents

Respondents described their relationship with their parents as characterized by a paradox of intensity coupled with superficiality. Lack of depth was reported in the latency years and carried into adulthood. The superficiality grew out of children's sensitivity to the parents' past and a consequent desire to shield parents from experiencing additional pain. Failure to broach the critical topic of the Holocaust kept the relationship safe but on superficial grounds.

Participants in this research reported that parents were opinionated, consistently gave advice, and attempted to direct their lives. These patterns heightened the need to maintain a cursory relationship in order to avoid conflicts. A common statement was "I feel I can deal with both my parents better if we keep our conversations superficial." The following excerpt is illustrative:

> When my parents asked how things were, I said everything was fine. It was a superficial relationship. I didn't want to upset them, and if I upset them it would upset me because I would feel personally responsible. I didn't share things unless I absolutely had to. In fact, I didn't share about my divorce until is was almost complete. I have difficulty telling them things I know they won't like. I don't want to invite that kind of problem. . . . I would like to have a close relationship with them, but I realize the limits. I have very consciously put the distance between us.

The majority of research participants stated that the main topics of conversation with their fathers were business affairs, money matters, and politics, especially with reference to Israel. Without exception, the Jewish participants indicated that their fathers were well-informed about world affairs and especially enjoyed talking about Israel. Conversations with mothers revolved around food, clothing, and survivor network gossip. Because these were the main topics of conversation at home, many participants made special efforts to develop an interest in these areas but missed opportunities for more openness:

> I wished my mother was more open and could talk more. It seems like the only time my parents and I get into deep conversations is when it involves business. For a great part of my life I worked at getting to know business. It was the only thing we had in common to talk about. My father only likes to talk about business, money, and politics. I have never asked them about their problems other than business. I know after the war they had nothing, no true possessions which must have made them feel worthless which is the reason for their preoccupation with money.

Research participants related to their parents in terms of what they thought their parents wanted. They discussed parents' concerns and interests, primarily revolving around family survival and security.

The Adult Children's Deep Attachment to Their Parents

Despite a seemingly casual relationship, a deep bond and sensitivity between parent and child had developed. Research participants believed that parents loved them so much that they could not tolerate anything going wrong in their children's lives. The following is illustrative:

> I was talking pretty openly, and at one point while I was talking I broke down and cried—something I haven't done in front of my parents in years. My father's reaction was that he could not take it and had to walk out of the room, and he said something to the effect of don't get emotional. The truth of the matter is that it pained him so much to see me like that, that he could not tolerate it. I recognized that it is because he loves me and because he hurts for me so much that he had to leave the room.

Many respondents expressed a desire to be open and intimate with their parents but realized the limits of their parents' tolerance. They were very protective of their parents and experienced great difficulty when parents were upset. A common expression was to perceive that "they deserve a break; things should be easier for them now; they have had more than their share of suffering." The degree of attachment to parents varied with the individual's sensitivity. One woman who teaches Sunday School saw a presentation on the Holocaust. Identifying immediately with her parents, she remarked, "I couldn't wait to get home to call my mother. I wanted to make her feel good today. I had the need to be close to her."

The spiritual connection between parent and child is felt by all participants. Many expressed "a strong attachment and a real fear of their parents' death." Some participants were more verbal than others in expressing their intense feelings, as illustrated:

> Sometimes I feel my whole world revolves around my parents. I think to myself, my God, if anything ever happened to my father, first of all my mother would go to pieces because she is so dependent and I am, too. I always know my dad will be there if I need him. I try to prepare myself for the inevitable separation that will take place at some time.

Participants' lives were intertwined with their parents. Many participants conversed daily with their parents and met with them regularly. One participant stated, "I feel a void when my parents are out of town." Nearly all had formed close relationships.

In this research, deep attachment to parents was manifested in a protective attitude. Participants were extremely sensitive to their parents' well-being. Parents were also perceived to be deeply attached to them.

Shielding Parents from Painful Experiences

All participants stated that they shielded their parents from painful situations and rarely shared their own problems or concerns. They believed that their parents would be overwhelmed if they appeared distraught in any way. Participants stated that they work hard not to inflict disappointment or to discomfort their parents. They knew well their parents' way of responding that consisted of attempts to make things better immediately by offering suggestions and minimizing or denying their concerns. Participants reported that parents could not tolerate their distress. An example follows:

> I used to share with my mother, but she would become so overwhelmed and suffered more than I did when I had a problem that it became more of a burden on me. If I cried, it was like she would assume my pain. Every time I had a problem and I went to her, I felt worse. I felt like I had to calm her down even though I was upset myself.

Participants recognized their parents' tendency to show only the bright side of things to avoid enduring more darkness in their lives. In return, participants felt a pressure to "put on a happy face" in the presence of their parents:

> My mother never allowed me to express real feelings. I should be happy and feel good all the time. My mother would say, "look how happy you could be. You have so much to look forward to. It could be worse." If I feel unhappy about something, she doesn't let it be. She wants to deny some of my upset feelings. She accentuates the positive . . . sometimes I get down and say it's going to be a crummy year [with regards to husband's business], and my parents immediately rally to the cause. They always say, "don't worry, you're so lucky. You have two beautiful children and a wonderful house. So you will

> have one less *shmata* [Yiddish word for *rags*]." They always give me this pep talk and remind me of what I have.

This dominant attitude reflected the "lifeline" that participants in this study perceived between themselves and their parents. Parents were experienced as living so much for their children that they considered their children's distress to be their own. Research participants indicated that the same phenomenon occurred within themselves; their parents' pain literally became their own. Their parents' painful past had penetrated the core of their being. Although, with the passage of time, the heaviness lifted, there was always an unyielding sadness:

> The scar is there forever for their life and mine. My life was full of day-to-day pain. I think my parents have had an internal flame of pain inside of them. I have always had that pain. It has lessened. I think the reason I always appear to be so happy is because I think that's the way I should be. I try very hard to be happy, so it kind of rubs off on me. I think of my pain as very normal. I think I am very together.

Further aspects of this dominant attitude are its subtle elusiveness and pretension. These elements are evident in the participants' statements regarding secrets, sharing of negative experiences only after they had been handled, being on guard with parents, and the pervasive dictum, "Don't rock the boat." One participant described family guardedness in the following statement: "I am frustrated around my father and that upsets me because I don't have a normal relationship. I can't just be. When I am with him, there is not a freedom. I have to watch everything I say." The home atmosphere was permeated with attitudes that encouraged concealing feelings. To spare their parents worry, participants in this study would not relate critical events, activities, or plans. Parents also participated in this ensconcement by not disclosing their personal histories or current illnesses. One participant's father had been ill in a hospital in Florida for 4 days, and her mother did not let her or her brother know about it until he was out and doing well.

Another element of concealment was manifested by maintaining family secrets. One woman shared, "My mother's attitude is keep all evil from your children." The adult children recognized parents' protective intentions, but most respondents felt that they had a right to know their family's history and background. When participants discovered secrets on their own, from old pictures or from outside sources, they often felt hurt and angry that they had been cut off from family roots. The following is illustrative of this pattern:

> It seems like I always knew about the Holocaust. My parents did not tell me much about it, not until I confronted them [angrily] at a later age. My father

would not discuss his prior life because he had another family. My mother wouldn't discuss it because she had a sister. My mother's sister was my father's wife. I discovered old pictures and put it all together.

Once the secrets were discovered, they became "unmentionable" taboos outside the nuclear family. In fact, respondents felt that they had to conceal from extended family and friends not only the secrets but also all other problems. This was expressed by one participant in the edict: "Keep your mouth shut, don't talk outside the home." On one level, withholding of family secrets trivialized the relationship between child and parent and kept it shallow. The result was that the adult children had an unclear picture of their parents' lives before the Holocaust. A common statement from respondents was "I know nothing about my parents." Many respondents learned about the Holocaust through books rather than firsthand. However, in spite of the failure to communicate on deep and honest emotional levels and in spite of the need to confine conversations to safe and often trivial subjects, a deep spiritual connection developed between parent and child that somehow transcended all else.

Perceiving the Holocaust Experience in the Parent–Child Relationship

The respondents were deeply affected by their parents Holocaust experience. They believed their parents' world had been constricted and that their parents were out of touch with everyday experiences. Respondents viewed their parents as being emotionally unavailable to them in their formative years because of the lingering aftereffect of the Holocaust. One participant related:

My parents' Holocaust experience made me feel cheated, that I was not able to have parents who could be there, in the sense like many of my [American] friends' parents. I think most of my friends were much more open with their parents about what was going on in their lives.

Participants felt that they could not go to their parents for emotional support because they were growing up in America and that automatically meant the good life. According to the participants, their complaints seemed trivial compared to the trauma and radical uprooting their parents had endured. The following is illustrative:

My parents always discount whatever we were upset about. It is nothing compared to what they have been through. They would say, "You have four beautiful children, a house, a car, you grew up in America, your husband is nice to you, what are you complaining about?"

Respondents felt their own scope of experience and "being in the world" was radically different from their parents' and resulted in a disturbing disparity, particularly during the adolescent years. They perceived their parents as not understanding the depth of their emotions or the meaning of their psychic pain. The only form of pain their parents seemed to understand was their own emotional discomfort as it related to the horrors of the Holocaust or direct physical pain. The following is illustrative: "When I try to talk to my parents, they don't understand so I somaticize it, like I have a headache and that they understand, the physical. They can't understand the emotional."

Others indicated that their parents could not relate to expressions of emotions; there was a void, a lack of depth in communication. The following excerpt is representative:

> My parents can't relate to feelings and emotions like love and affection. Even though I have an affectionate relationship with them, there is that coldness, a feeling of not really wanting to be involved. I feel that there is something missing, a lack of depth of emotions in the family. I feel it in myself.

Some persons described their parents as emotionally "dulled" and recognized the same emotional dullness in themselves, as a result of their upbringing. Many participants believed that their parents had learned to deny their emotions in order to survive and that they conveyed the same message to their children. One participant remarked:

> When I show emotions, my father's response has been, you have to be strong, you get yourself together. He had become stoic as a result of the Holocaust. It is difficult for him to show my sister and me any affection.

The consequence was a diminution of emotions and interference in the development of intimacy. Although there were undertones of much love and caring, love was expressed through material objects rather than verbal communication. Respondents recall that when they were moody as children, their mothers indulged them with some trinket to appease them. In order to dress their children properly, parents literally had walked around in *shmatas* (Yiddish for *rags*). Consequently, many adult children recalled feelings of shame and embarrassment with peers because their parents looked so different.

As adults, many participants have recognized that the material gifts acquired in childhood represented the love of their parents that they were unable to express spontaneously, as depicted next:

> My mother deprives herself. Before the camp, according to my aunt, she was very indulged and spoiled. She demanded the best of everything. I just got it

> but never asked for it. Mother gave a lot materially but not emotionally. I was not confortable going to her. We never had an affectionate home. I think her way of showing me she loved me was indulging me materially. I don't think she is able to show me any other way.

After the Holocaust, respondents' parents were uprooted from their homes in Eastern Europe due to the Communist annexation. This was perceived as yet another trauma that their parents had to endure. Nearly all participants commented that their parents' immigrant appearance, lack of spontaneity, and Old World perspective added additional burdens to the relationship. They described feelings of loneliness in growing up with parents who were alien to the American culture. As a result, the children turned inward and became introspective and analytical in handling their own lives. They stated that they were envious of the typical American families portrayed on television ("Donna Reed" and "Father Knows Best") and of their friends' families who were more open and able to generate good times. Many participants as children experienced these differences as objectionable and attributed them to their parents' immigrant status. They felt that their parents did not relate well to their needs and did not understand the contemporary world in which they were growing up. The following excerpt is illustrative:

> My parents lacked social skills. They were like my friends' grandparents, even though agewise they were contemporaries with my friends' parents. As a child I resented that they were greenhorns [immigrants], and I wished for American parents like my friends'.

Summing up the adult children's perception of the Holocaust experience as creating barriers between survivor and child, the major themes were feelings of isolation in not being able to communicate in emotional language during the early years; not being understood in the affective realm; lack of parental empathy with child; emotional distance in parent–child relationship; being given material advantages as substitutes for genuine parental love; and the loneliness of growing up with parents who were immigrants from a different culture and world, who were in the United States only because of the Holocaust.

Adult Children's View of Parental Communications as Indirect and Ambiguous

As a group, the respondents stated that their parents did not directly express their feelings. Parents conveyed expectations and disappointments in subtle ways while communicating pride in their children through a third party. Disappointments were communicated through stories about how children of relatives or friends were bringing joy to their parents. Respondents felt they were set up by parents to compete with friends' and relatives' children in order to enhance their parents' self-esteem. Parents relied on their children to act as mediators, therapists, or social workers in ameliorating conflicts and tensions at home.

It was indicated that, in the survivor network, the parents would boast about their children's accomplishments. Thus, pressure was placed on the child to accomplish great things for his or her parents' sake. Rivalry among survivors created a competitive attitude among their children, a source of discomfort for most of the participants. Consequently, now many intentionally avoid competitive situations. Nearly all expressed the feeling that their parents were keeping up with other survivors and that was their major basis for judging life. One participant remarked: "I think I have always had to pay for my parents being greeners [immigrants]. They [survivors] begrudge things, and it is always something. If you married the King of Siam, they would find something wrong with him."

Parents compare their children to others' children implying, "We wish you were doing as so and so's child is," thus implying, "you are not quite good enough and you are a disappointment to us."

Many individuals felt threatened by the expectations imposed on them at an early age. Some children focused strongly on attaining status for their parents, whereas others did not. These comparisons created rivalry among cousins as well as children of their parents' close friends who were part of the "extended family." The rivalry promoted dissonance among them and interfered with family intimacy. An example:

> I was always set up to compete with my cousin closer in age. It was always K. is ambitious and she's going to make something of her life. This made me feel like I could never be as good as K., and I became antagonistic toward her.

Though the adult child may have felt that he or she did not quite measure up, parents boasted about and exaggerated his or her accomplishments to friends and relatives. The parents, however, did not let their children know the extent of *naches* (proud pleasure) they were deriving from them. All respondents stated that they wished their parents were able to communicate affection or dissatisfaction directly to them. The following is illustrative:

> I think my activity in the Jewish community was a need I had to fulfill. I think my father was very proud of me, however, he never said it to me outwardly. He had a problem saying it and he always had a problem discussing his feelings about me, but I knew he was proud when other people came to him and said I heard your daughter speak at such and such. It's funny because other people always tell me how much my father loves me and I am always in shock.

According to the majority of participants, their parents approached third parties to learn about their children's lives. As one respondent remarked: "My father noticed my sister's moodiness and became concerned. He could not go to her himself; he asked me to find out what was wrong and to make her feel better."

In summary, adult children viewed parental communications as indirect and ambiguous. They described frustration and sadness related to their parents' indirect expression of their fondness and their pride or dissatisfaction toward their children. They feel set up to compete, manipulated into rescuing, and urged to mediate or intervene for their parents.

DOMINANT ATTITUDES PERTAINING TO ADULT CHILDREN'S FEELINGS TOWARD PARENTS AND PERCEPTIONS OF PARENTS' FEELINGS ABOUT THEM

Adult Children's Sense of Responsibility and Guilt in Connection with the Holocaust

Respondents felt an obligation to undo the traumatic past of their parents. They felt it was up to them to bring joy, pride, and pleasure into their parents' lives. This obligation to make parents happier through their own lives was described by all participants. Accepting this responsibility meant following the "life plan" that participants perceived their parents had envisioned for them.

All participants were aware of their parents' painful past and wanted their lives to be better in America. They felt indebted to their parents whose suffering and determination to survive made it possible for them to "make it" and attain status for their parents among survivor friends. The adult children described feelings of constant pressure to fulfill goals that parents had set for them.

Other pressures felt were in reference to marriage and having children and obtaining an education in order to "be something." Until these goals were achieved, the majority of participants stated that their parents appeared discontented and unsettled, adding a constant strain on the relationship. The following is illustrative:

> I feel like I am making it up to them for suffering. I am being just what they want, but I am not doing anything I wouldn't do anyway. I have a nice house, I have children, I am happy, and they are a part of our life.

Some persons felt guilt feelings related to the Holocaust. Guilt was intensified when the parent suffered silently or was difficult to please. Guilt was also intensified when the adult children did not live up to their parents' expectations and when they became aware of how much better their lives were than their parents. The following is illustrative:

> If there was no Holocaust, I don't think I would feel so guilty. I would not feel so overprotective of them in not wanting to see them hurt, in not wanting to see them struggle. When you know that your parents have been through that hell, you just want to see them have it better—success, happiness and not have to see them have to struggle any more. . . . My mom never talks about anything so I have really been sheltered in that respect. My dad talked about it. How it had affected me is it made me feel real guilty. I feel indebted to them. I wish I could do something to please them. Feeling guilty is a constant feeling. It is always eating at me.

Feelings of guilt pervaded many aspects of some respondents' world, reflected in the following way, "I feel guilty about what I should be doing and what I am doing. I feel guilty when something has happened and someone feels bad."

Nearly all of the respondents recalled that as children they sensed that their parents could not handle the demands of parenthood. Their parents were viewed as nervous and easily overwhelmed by the needs of their children. One respondent stated, "My parents were threatened and overwhelmed by their history and the responsibilities of parenthood."

Many persons reported that the oldest child assumed the responsibility for smoothing the transition from European to American life. However, if the eldest was a behavior problem, then the second-born took over this role. This child was extremely sensitive to the traumata of his or her parents' uprooting, generated by the Holocaust. He or she wrote or interpreted letters, made telephone calls, and maintained checking accounts to ease the transition for parents. One person stated, "I think I turned myself into a sacrificial lamb. I was so busy being a good daughter that I didn't see what it was doing to me."

Those who assumed this role took life very seriously, giving up the carefree life of childhood. The following is illustrative:

> I always thought in the American Jewish family the children were able to laugh and have a good time. They were able to be free, to be able to go out and play in the street and have fun. I always had to worry. I always worried whether my parents were okay. Was my mother worried about me, was I going to do the right thing for her, was I going to come in late, and was she going to be worried that someone kidnapped me? I never had an easy time. I remember as a child always worrying. I felt I had to take care of my parents. I think she looked up to me as being a mature person and someone she could count on even though she didn't want to count on me. I felt children around me had much more freedom, a carefree attitude. Life was carefree and fun where I don't feel I had that. I was more burdened in feeling responsible for

> my parents. I was very mature. I was never a child, able to play and have fun. I took life very seriously as a child.

Many respondents censored their parents' viewing anything involving the Holocaust. Many felt very protective of parents and could not tolerate seeing them hurt in any way. When the film, "Holocaust," was aired on television in April 1977, some respondents insisted that their parents not watch it, whereas others called their parents daily to make sure they were okay. Respondents stated that they were more upset by documentaries, movies, and photographs of the Holocaust than were their parents.

For some participants, another feature was a sense of powerlessness. They felt a need to turn back time and erase the painful memories of their parents' past. In processing the Holocaust for themselves, respondents assumed the responsibility of making parents' lives more meaningful through theirs, reflected in the following way: "I had to think I could do something about it, or I don't think I could have taken it. It was such a horrible thing to accept."

Adult children's fantasy of being able to undo the Holocaust made it easier for them to handle their parents' trauma. Coming to terms with one's powerlessness meant facing the painful remnants of the Holocaust in both their lives and their parents. This realization has also relieved some of the burden of guilt and responsibility and has helped participants in this research to rechannel energy into their own lives.

In summary, respondents' responsibility and guilt regarding the Holocaust include the pressure to compensate parents with *naches* (happiness) for their suffering through accomplishment; a desire to protect and care for parents; a deep sadness and pain awakened by Holocaust memories; and feelings of powerlessness to undo the Holocaust for their parents.

Adult Children's Feelings of Uncertainty and Conflict Aroused by Parental Expectations

All participants indicated that life plans and goals were imposed on them. This often meant not listening to one's own inner callings. The common concern was: "What is for me? What is for them? Where do I draw the line to establish my own identity?" Autonomy had to be developed silently and indirectly, a delicate balance between finding oneself while not alienating one's parents.

The issue of freedom of choice in living one's own life was a lifelong challenge. The pressures of "shoulds," opinions, judgments, and expectations inevitably influenced respondents' lives. Many mechanically followed their parents' plans for them without realizing the consequences. Once an awareness emerged, they experienced confusion and conflict. The conflict endured in the relationship with parents until the adult child felt satisfied with the direction his or her life was taking. In the words of a respondent:

> Our parents did not have a normal separation from their own parents. I know my mother could not separate from me and allow me to go off to be my own person because she never had the experience of normal separation from her parents and that's where the grabbing on, "you have to do this," "should do this," comes from. They can't see us as independent adults. My mother still tries to control and tell me what to do. She wants to live my life with me for my own good.

Tensions and conflicts lessened as adult children met some of their parents' expectations. Most of the participants indicated that they were still sensitive to parental approval. Many respondents now recognize that high expectations grew out of their parents' hope for a better life for their children. Parents were perceived as not being able to accept their children's individuality and desire to live as separate adults. This is exemplified as follows:

> I think my father wants to see a carbon copy of himself, and if I feel differently from something than he does, he just can't understand why I can't see it the same way he does. Fundamentally we are very much the same type of person. On the one hand, they call me up for advice; on the other hand, my father resents the fact that I have something (education) that he lacks. I understand his frustration for he feels he could have been something other than he is.

Many participants felt angry that their parents were intrusive and controlling. However, there was guilt in feeling anger toward parents who had been through so much horror. The following statement illustrates the anger/guilt response of one participant:

> My life-style was very much laid out for me. I could never deviate from anything they wanted for me because I would feel guilty. I did everything and I hated doing it. I may have enjoyed it had I chosen it for myself, but I never felt they were my choices initially. I think we all did it [she and siblings] out of obligation and guilt. . . . I used to be very passive. The first part of my life I felt guilty because I wasn't happy and angry for not being in charge of my own life. Now that I have changed things that makes me happy, feeling that I am in control of my own life.

In summary, the characteristics of the dominant attitude pertaining to feelings of uncertainty and conflict regarding parental expectations were perception of parents as attempting to impose their choices onto their children; awareness of being only conditionally accepted when veering from parental expectation; recognition that parents are living vicariously through their children; experiencing parents as overprotective, demanding, and intrusive; and mixed feelings of anger and guilt in attempting to establish an independent life.

The Adult Children's Close Identification with Their Parents' Holocaust Experience

Just as the parents were seen as over identifying with the lives of their children, respondents also experienced an "overidentification" with their parents. They felt that they, too, have been through the Holocaust. They internalized their parents' fears, worries, anxieties, and dreads.

Holocaust imagery is pervasive in the respondents' lives, in their dreams, and in their conscious thoughts. Many of the respondents stated that they experienced the same nightmares as their parents. A common dream depicted scenes of being on cattle trains as they were transported to the camps. Vivid imagery of the Holocaust terrors was reported over and over again. As stated by a respondent:

> I have a lot of American friends who have lots of conflicts with their parents somewhat similar to mine. The only difference is this feeling of overidentification. I think it's the feeling that I sustain all the losses they had, it's that I feel the same way as them. It's almost as if I have gone through the war and also the feeling that something terrible is going to happen. That when everything is good, the bomb is going to drop and something is going to be taken away from me.

The question, "Did I survive the Holocaust with my parents?", produces a profound and searing feeling. The aftermath of the Holocaust has penetrated the core of the respondents' being to the extent that some feel that it would almost have been easier to be the survivor. Children have experienced their own vulnerability in identifying with their parents.

Early home environments transmitted the legacy of the Holocaust. Many respondents recalled that as children they were fearful of parents being captured again and of Hitler trying to destroy them also. The Holocaust has become part of the identity of children of survivors. The adult children recognized that their parents imparted attitudes of fear and dread. Parents were reluctant to plan ahead; they distrusted the world at large and were overly cautious about safety and security. Many respondents lived with the constant fearsome question, "Could there be another Holocaust?"

CHANGES IN DOMINANT ATTITUDES AS ADULT CHILDREN MATURE

The Resolution Process

A majority of the participants reported that in adulthood they had moved toward a reconciliation with their parents and had come to terms with themselves. However, those who had not progressed toward substantial maturity were unable to achieve this resolution.

Maturing participants have been able to work through their anger and guilt. They accepted their identities as children of Holocaust survivors. This acceptance occurred through the adult child's own individual resolution process. For many, this entailed imagining themselves in their parents' places having survived a Holocaust while their loved ones did not and having to start all over with newly established families in a foreign country. One participant expressed: "I feel that in coming to terms with them, I an more my own person than ever before. I accept them now. I accept the fact that my mother could not have done things differently."

As participants married and had their own families, they grew closer to their parents and were more understanding of their early parenting. They discovered for themselves the demands and responsibilities of parenthood. They became aware of the challenge of their parents in raising them with little money, no family support system, and a limited knowledge of the English language and American culture. Maturation and life experiences have enhanced their resolution process. This has enabled them to have more insight into how overwhelming parenthood must have been for their parents without any support system. The following excerpt exemplifies coming to terms with one's roots and background:

> Today I like the fact that they are not average American people and that they have a history that I feel proud of. I see them as incredibly strong to endure such a trauma and to adjust to a new life in a new culture.

Some participants have come to terms with their parents' history by immersing themselves in Holocaust-related issues, activities, and organizations or Jewish political causes dealing with oppression, anti-Semitism, and the plight of Russian Jewry. Others either have gone into psychotherapy or have practiced self-therapy through writing journals of prose, poetry, and self-reflections in order to more fully understand the impact and after effects of the Holocaust on the family. Some have expressed themselves through the arts (painting, photography, and other art forms).

Maturational Changes of the Eight Dominant Attitudes

Many participants remarked at the beginning of the interview that they would be talking about two different sets of parents: the parents of yesterday who were burdened with the painful memories of the Holocaust and the adjustment to a new culture, and the parents of today who have assimilated themselves to a certain extent in the new culture and are now letting go of painful memories.

With the maturation of the participants, the eight dominant attitudes continue to be prevalent in their lives but are modified. The quality of the relationship and their feelings about themselves, parents, and their roots have changed significantly. A discussion of the transition of each dominant attitude follows.

1. The parent–child relationship continues to be intense and at times somewhat superficial. However, the nature of the relationship has become more personal. Maturing participants are sharing more with their parents but still with care and hesitancy as reflected in the following statement:

> I have learned that it is not that simple to share with them. So what I am trying to do basically is test the waters little by little and hope to come to the point where I am really sharing with them. I am beginning to share elements of my personal life with them.

2. The deep attachment between parent and child is still prevalent. The change is in the feeling of contentment with the interdependent relationship that many participants have established with their parents. One participant expressed the change in the following way:

> A lot has changed in me. Before I used to feel I had to love them, respect them, give them my time. Now I feel I want to. While I was growing up, I so wanted Donna Reed for my mother. Now I realize and understand the effect of the Holocaust on my mother. I truly love them both and feel the emotional bond in a more mature way.

3. The need to shield parents from painful experiences by covering up or concealing true feelings has diminished. Nevertheless, the protective quality of the relationship has become more intensified. A common attitude in adulthood is: "I want to shield them from any kind of harshness in their lives now. I am feeling this more intensely as I get older." What has changed is that participants are now probing for more and more information about their parents' past lives and the family history instead of preserving the silence. Some participants have revealed that their parents have been responsive and somewhat eager to share. In most cases, one parent was more willing than the other to disclose his or her life. Many participants have also felt a need to have their parents know them on a deeper level. One participant stated:

> One time I got very upset, and that was the first time I talked to her about anything very personal. I just wanted to feel there was someone interested and concerned about me. She gave me the emotional support that I needed.

4. The barrier that participants had attributed to their parents' Holocaust experience and resulting immigrant status has progressively dwin-

dled. Parents are no longer viewed as limited and totally out of touch with their children's lives. Most of the participants' attitudes have shifted from shame to pride in parents, their European heritage, and roots (as illustrated in the section on resolution process). One participant explained:

> I have learned that even though they did not have book-learning knowledge, they are wise people. I respect their judgment now. Many of my contemporaries' parents have not grown as much as mine. That's why I am so proud of them. I feel very special and unique because of my background. It has given me a good understanding of people and compassion for those who are less fortunate. I am open and proud to let those whom I meet know that I am a child of Holocaust survivors.

5. The communication between survivor/parent and child still possesses indirect and ambiguous characteristics. However, maturing participants are now pointing out to their parents their understood meanings of the indirect messages. They are asking parents to be more direct and are assisting them in this approach. One participant told his parents, "I need you to tell me you are proud of me instead of bragging to someone else." There are some participants who feel secure and accepting and have unquestioningly accepted this indirect mode of communication.

6. The individuals who have reached a reconciliation with themselves and their parents seem to transcended much of the guilt and responsibility in connection with the Holocaust. However, the responsibility is felt in a different way. The obligations of the past no longer hinder the relationship. As the participants have matured, they report that their sensitivity to their parents' well-being has increased. The feelings of protectiveness have deepened. Problems of parents concerning retirement or other major decisions dealing with their welfare become paramount issues in the lives of children. The following is illustrative:

> I feel very sorry for my father. I feel a tremendous pain for him that I will never get over. As I get older now, I feel it even more but in a mature way. Before I felt it with a lot of guilt, but I don't feel the guilt any more. I just feel more protective of him as I get older.

7. The conflicts and uncertainty that had been aroused by parental expectations are not as intense. Maturing participants feel at ease with their own life choices. They have developed a comfortable sense of autonomy and their parents have adapted to their children's needs. The values imposed by their parents that many of the participants rebelled against as children are now increasingly similar to their own values. As one participant related: "I think a lot of the things my parents geared me toward were a benefit even though I hadn't recognized them then." Another participant expressed:

> The strange thing is the older I get, I come more and more to respect and accept my father's ways. If you would have told me that 10 years ago, I would have said: "Gee, I am the farthest thing from him."

8. The only dominant attitude that has not changed in adulthood is the identification with parent's Holocaust experience. With the increase in sensitivity toward parents, adult children appear to feel a greater sensitivity and vulnerability about their own lives. Participants have an intellectual understanding of the fears, insecurities, and dreads, but these feelings are held in check and do not interfere with their daily functioning.

The relationships between survivor parents and their children has not been static but has evolved and matured. The dominant attitudes have changed in intensity and emphasis. The dominant attitude that had once been a focal issue may now be peripheral or viewed more positively.

In examining the dominant attitudes as a whole, the most salient feature of the change is the shift from guilt and shame to pride and appreciation. During childhood and adolescence, the children were embarrassed by their parents' bitter history and lack of assimilation. They wished for a typical American family with roots. As participants came to terms with their own roots, they reached a positive understanding and a prideful relationship with their parents. The following excerpt reflects the changing relationship:

> When I was younger, I was ashamed of my father for being crude. I was very hostile. As I've gotten older, I've come to understand my father was miserable because he had not made the right choices. Instead of hostility, I feel compassion. Now my parents are the envy of all my friends. They are so caring, kind, warm, and they are very giving.

The childish wish to be an average American is no longer a hope of the majority of the participants. Without exception, Jewish participants feel a proud identification with the country of Israel. One woman expressed feeling like a "wandering Jew," the remnants of the Holocaust in her life. She fulfilled her need for identity and belonging in Israel, as did her parents. A strong Jewish identity was evident in all the Jewish participants, regardless of whether or not they observed the Jewish traditions. An example follows:

> While I was growing up, I wanted the typical American family roots. I wanted to be able to say that I have three generations going back somewhere. I don't even know the names of my ancestors. My father doesn't remember the name of his grandmother. If it had not been for the Holocaust, I know I wouldn't have the strong need for belonging and identity which I now find in Israel. I have a strong need for roots. My psychological home is Israel.

Through a positive identification with parents, there is an increasing recognition and admiration for parents' attributes that enabled them to survive. The dominant response describes parents as being resourceful, having common sense and practicality, and being incredibly strong. Many participants feel that their parents' durability, resourcefulness, strong will, determination, ambition, and an ability to fight have been transmitted to them, enhancing their own ability to survive and overcome adversity. The strength that their parents derived from their suffering and struggles is reported by the adult children as having been internalized by themselves. The recognition of parents' positive attributes is illustrated, as follows:

> I truly believe the only reason they survived is because most of their life was very hard. They knew how to fight against hardships and struggled all their lives to get ahead and had anti-Semitism all around them. They were real fighters. My mother and father survived mentally. My father knew he was going to overcome it, and he was not going to give up. They both had the will to live. He survived because of the struggles he had to overcome as a young person which made him even stronger. I have had many hardships that I have gone through, and I could only overcome them through my mental attitude. My parents' experiences have definitely given me a lot.

On the whole, the participants are more appreciative of their parents because of what they have learned from their examples. One woman commented: "I learned to be appreciative of life from my parents. I appreciate everything I get or even have."

The shift from shame and guilt to pride and appreciation occurred more readily for those participants whose parents were open to discuss the positive and heroic aspects of their past lives. Parents explained that prior to the Holocaust, they had a good upbringing, a good self-image, and self-confidence. They demonstrated the benefits of these early positive experiences by their resiliency and adjustment to life after the Holocaust. Regardless of their parents' adjustment to life after the Holocaust, most of the participants have become wiser from their own experiences. Maturity has enabled them to take pride in their parents who chose to fight for life rather than give up and submit to the calling of death.

Summing up the maturational changes of the eight dominant attitudes, the major characteristics were a resolution process of coming to terms with earlier experiences and a the shift toward pride and appreciation; a positive identification with parents and their background; an increasing awareness and consciousness of the Holocaust; a sensitivity and deepening protectiveness toward parents; a recognition and appreciation for the attributes that enabled parents to survive; and a loving acceptance of parents coupled with a comfortable sense of autonomy from them.

CONCLUDING COMMENTS AND IMPLICATIONS

Findings of this study revealed five dominant attitudes that pertained to the relationships of the adult children to their parents: (1) perceived transactions with parents, which were intense but superficial; (2) deep attachment to their parents; (3) shielding of parents from painful experiences; (4) perceptions that the Holocaust created barriers in the parent–child relationship and; (5) perceptions that parental communications were indirect and ambiguous. Three additional dominant attitudes reflected the feelings of the adult children: (1) a sense of responsibility and guilt in connection with the Holocaust; (2) feelings of uncertainty and conflict aroused by parental expectations and; (3) close identification with the Holocaust experiences of their parents. However, with the passage of time, there was a profound shift in attitudes toward parents and a maturational process leading to pride and appreciation.

Certain characteristics of the eight dominant attitudes relate directly to the Holocaust legacy. Other features are characteristic of typical parent–child relationships, particularly families where the children are aware of and sensitive to parental pain. However, the degree and intensity of the Holocaust survivor/parent–child relationship differentiates this relationship from most other parent–child relationships. The differences among adult children of survivors are attributable to their unique family histories, their birth order, and their sensitivity to their parents' traumata.

This study of dominant attitudes offers adult children of survivors and their parents a description and understanding of these attitudes and the subsequent influence on their relationships. It adds a more conscious understanding to these intensely felt relationships.

Mental health professionals who engage in the treatment of adult children of survivors can derive from these dominant attitudes an understanding of the poignancy of having been influenced by parents' Holocaust trauma. Through this data, it is possible to gain insight into essential aspects of such parent–child relationships and thus approach survivorship with an informed perspective. With this understanding, the therapist can better assist the adult child toward his or her own resolution process that entails the working through of his or her conflicts in relation to the self, parents, and the Holocaust legacy.

The therapist must assist the adult child of survivors to make the necessary connection between the impact of the Holocaust and his or her undesirable thoughts, feelings, and behavior. Only in this way can these feelings be understood and dissipated. A participant related that once she connected the Holocaust to brutal imagery that had plagued her, it stopped. I recommend that care and consideration of what the adult child and therapist both can handle guide any treatment approach.

This study demonstrates the power of transcendence. Life exists in spite of the Holocaust. Determination and the will to survive and grow can offset the destructive influence of the Holocaust on the second generation. These results offer new hope and new dreams to the children of survivors who, by their very existence, remind humanity of the horrors of war and the destructiveness of irrational power and prejudice. This study has enriched my own understanding and increased my ability to value the relationship between the parent and adult child. It has heightened immeasurably my faith in the human spirit to overcome and endure.

The positive dimensions of the transmission of the survivor instinct to the second generation require further exploration. A consideration for future research would be studies of children of other survivor groups such as Hiroshima and Nagasaki, Buffalo Creek, Vietnam, and non-Jewish Holocaust survivors. I believe that research of such catastrophes would provide significant comparative data to determine if a generalized phenomenon exists unique to children born after a parental trauma.

REFERENCES

Aleksandrowicz, D. (1973). Children of concentration camp survivors. In E. J. Anthony & C. Koupernik (Eds.), *The child in his family: The impact of disease and death* (Vol. 2, pp. 385–394). New York: Wiley.

Axelrod, S., Schnipper, O. C., & Rau, J. H. (1980). Hospitalized offspring of Holocaust survivors. *Bulletin of the Menninger Clinic, 44*(10), 1–14.

Barocas, H. A., & Barocas, C. B. (1979). Wounds of the fathers: The next generation of Holocaust victims. *International Review of Psychoanalysis, 6,* 331–340.

Bergman, M. S., & Jucovy, M. E. (Eds.). (1982). *Generations of the Holocaust.* New York: Basic Books.

Danieli, Y. (1979). *Children of Holocaust survivors.* Paper presented at the meeting of the National Jewish Conference Center.

Danieli, Y. (1981). Families of survivors of the Nazi Holocaust: Some short and some long term effects. In Milgram, N. (Ed.), *Psychological stress and adjustment in time of war and peace* (pp. 405–421). New York: McGraw Hill/Hemisphere.

Dimsdale, J. E. (Ed.). (1980). *Survivors, victims and perpetrators.* New York: Hemisphere Publishing Corporation.

Epstein, H. (1979). Children of the Holocaust—are the traumas of the parents visited on the children? *The National Jewish Monthly, April,* 14–21.

Fogelman, E., & Savran, B. (1979). Therapeutic group for children of Holocaust survivors. *International Journal of Group Psychotherapy, 29*(2), 211–235.

Gay, M. (1972). Children of ex-concentration camp inmates. In L. Miller (Ed.), *Mental health in rapid social change* (pp. 337–338). Jerusalem: Jerusalem Academic Press.

Kestenberg, J. S. (1972). Psychoanalytic contributions to the problems of children of survivors from Nazi persecution. *Israel Annals of Psychiatry and Related Discipline, 10*(4), 311–323.

Klein, H. (9171). Families of Holocaust survivors in the Kibbutz: Psychological studies. In H. Krystal & W. Niederland (Eds.), *Psychic traumatization: Aftereffects in individuals and communities* (pp. 67–93). New York: Little, Brown.

Krell, R. (1984). Holocaust survivors and their children: Comments on psychiatric consequences and psychiatric terminology. *Comprehensive Psychiatry, 25*(5), 521–528.

Krystal, H. (Ed.). (1968). *Massive psychic trauma.* New York: International Universities Press.

Leon, G., Bethcher, J., Kleinman, M., Goldberg, A., & Almagot, M. (1981). Survivors of the Holocaust and their children: Current status and adjustment. *Journal of Personality and Social Psychology, 41,* 503–516.

Matussek, P. (1975). *Internment in concentration camp and its consequences.* New York: Springer.

Niederland, W. G. (1965). Psychiatric disorders among persecution victims: A contribution to the understanding of concentration camp pathology and its aftereffects. *Journal of Nervous and Mental Diseases, 139,* 458–474.

Pilcz, M. (1979). Understanding the survivor family: An acknowledgement of the positive dimensions of the Holocaust legacy. In L. Y. Steinitz & D. M. Szonyi (Eds.), *Living after the Holocaust: Reflections by the post-war generation in America* (rev. ed., pp. 157–167). New York: Block Publishing Co.

Prince, R. M. (1975). *Prehistorical themes in the lives of young adult children of concentration camp survivors.* Ann Arbor, MI: University Microfilms.

Russell, A. (1974). Late psycho-social consequences in concentration camp survivor families. *American Journal of Orthopsychiatry, 44*(4), 611–619.

Rustin, S. (1980). The legacy of loss. *Journal of Contemporary Psychotherapy, 11*(1), 32–43.

Sigal, J. J., Silver, D., Rakoff, V., & Ellin, B. (1973). Some second generation effects of survival of the Nazi persecution. *American Journal of Orthopsychiatry, 43*(3), 320–327.

Solkoff, N. (1981). Children of survivors of the Nazi Holocaust: A critical review of the literature. *American Journal of Orthopsychiatry, 51*(1), 29–41.

Trachtenberg, M., & Davis, M. (1978). Breaking silence: Serving children of Holocaust survivors. *Journal of Jewish Communal Service 54,* 293–302.

Wittenberg, C. K. (1978). Children of Nazi victims seen as “marked” by stress. *Psychiatric News,* August 4, pp. 34–38.

10

Confronting the Unimaginable

Psychotherapists' Reactions to Victims of the Nazi Holocaust

YAEL DANIELI

INTRODUCTION

> As a witness the survivor is both sought and shunned; the desire to hear his truth is countered by the need to ignore him. . . . Too close a knowledge of vulnerability, of evil, of human insufficiency, is felt to be ruinous. . . . The ostracism of outsiders, or bearers of bad news, as we feel compelled to defend a comforting view of life, we tend to deny the survivor's voice. We join in a "conspiracy of silence." (DesPres, 1976, pp. 41–42)

In *The Road Back for the D.P.'s: Healing the Psychological Scars of Nazism* (1948), Paul Friedman expressed his astonishment that the first plan for the rehabilitation of Europe's surviving Jews overlooked entirely their need for psychological assistance.

To recreate in these thousands of people the ability to live free and mature lives, he said it was necessary to establish "a sound program of mental hygiene," ranging from availability of intensive psychiatric treatment for selected individuals to structures for the rapid integration of the survivors into the economic and social life of their countries. Friedman saw that to achieve this reintegration into human society after their experiences "on its outermost edges—the concentration camps," the survivors must be

Some of the material presented in this chapter appeared previously in "Psychotherapists' Participation in the Conspiracy of Silence about the Holocaust" by Y. Danieli, 1984, *Psychoanalytic Psychology, 1*(1), pp. 23–42. Copyright 1984 by Lawrence Erlbaum Associates. Reprinted by permission.

YAEL DANIELI • Group Project for Holocaust Survivors and Their Children, 345 East 80th Street, New York, New York 10021.

surrounded by people who understood and loved them and empathized with their difficulties. "The only road back to psychological health," he stated, was to make the survivors remember the *facts* of their victimization in an atmosphere of love and understanding that would bolster their weakened confidence and carry them through the first stages of the inevitable shock.

Despite the fact that the need was recognized and the call for help clearly stated by Friedman and others by 1948 and despite the vast literature on the long-term effects of the Holocaust published in the following decades, any attempt to develop a structured program for helping survivors of the Nazi Holocaust and their children to reintegrate into society was abortive. In truth, after liberation, as during the war, the survivors were victims of a pervasive societal reaction comprised of indifference, avoidance, repression, and denial of their experiences. Shunned, abandoned, and betrayed by society, the survivor could share the most horrifying and painful period of their lives and their immense losses only with their children, with fellow survivors, or even worse, with no one. The most pervasive consequence of the conspiracy of silence for survivors and their children has been a profound sense of isolation, loneliness, and alienation that exacerbated their mistrust of humanity and made their task of mourning and integration impossible.

Elsewhere I have described some of the negative and obtuse societal attitudes and reactions and some of the survivor's fears that contributed to the long-term *conspiracy of silence* between Holocaust survivors and society (Danieli, 1981a,b). Also discussed[1] were the harmful effects upon the survivors' families and upon their subsequent integration into the postwar society, which further impeded the possibility of intrapsychic integration and healing.

The phrase *conspiracy of silence* has also been used to describe the typical interaction of Holocaust survivors and their children with psychotherapists when Holocaust experiences were mentioned or recounted (for example, see Barocas & Barocas, 1979; Krystal & Niederland, 1968; Tanay, 1968,). Originally, Niederland (1964) described the phenomenon as "the tendency to gloss over [which] appears to be widespread in both doctors and patients—likely enhanced in the latter by denial and guilt, and in the former by anxiety at being brought face to face with the stark horror of the patient's experience" (p. 461). In 1968, he added, "Insofar as it cannot be true, a kind of tacit agreement is reached between the patient and doctor—an agreement to gloss over, and thereby ignore the potentially traumatic data" in a "flight from horror" on the part of the psychotherapist (1968, pp. 62–63).

[1]A review of this literature and an up-to-date bibliography can be found in Wanderman, 1979; Bergman & Jucovy, 1982; Danieli, 1981b, e, 1985; and Steinberg, 1986.

Workers in psychiatric facilities have noted that they usually find only one sentence at most in the patients' history devoted to the topic: "The patient is a concentration camp survivor . . . his or her parents are Holocaust survivors," or worse, ". . . came from Europe . . . Poland." Psychotherapists and researchers who have interviewed survivors and their children and have worked with them after they have been seen by other therapists have repeatedly observed that Holocaust experiences were almost totally avoided in previous therapy. In addition, survivors and their children have frequently complained of neglect or avoidance of their Holocaust experiences by mental health professionals. This professional avoidance is amply documented in the clinical literature that often contains the authors' reports of an extreme "countertransference reaction." The term *countertransference* is used herein as it has been commonly used to describe therapists' own emotional reactions and difficulties experienced when working with this traumatized population. A comprehensive review of the literature on the "countertransference reactions" reported by reparation examiners, psychotherapists, and researchers working with Holocaust survivors and their children can be found in Danieli (1981e). However, it must be recognized that whereas society has a moral obligation to share its members' pain, psychotherapists and researchers have, in addition, a professional contractual obligation. When they fail to listen and understand, they participate in the conspiracy of silence and may inflict further trauma on the survivor (Rappaport, 1968) or "the second injury to victims" (Symonds, 1980).

Many survivors suffer amnesia for their lives before the Holocaust, whereas others idealize their pre-World War II life and continue to live psychologically in that time period, being unable to recall their war experiences. The therapist is thus confronted with discontinuity and disruption on all levels in the order of living—uprootedness, loss of families, communities, homes and countries, and values. Recreating a sense of rootedness and continuity and meaningfully integrating the Holocaust into their lives are major struggles for survivors and their children. When psychotherapists focus only on certain periods in the patients' lives to the exclusion of others, they may hinder the recovery process and perpetuate their sense of disruption and discontinuity.

THE "CONSPIRACY OF SILENCE" BETWEEN PSYCHOTHERAPISTS AND PATIENTS

Although several major "countertransference themes" have appeared in the literature, they are based almost entirely on anecdotal comments, confessional self-reports, and impressionistic statements and observations. The most striking phenomenon encountered in reviewing the professional

Table 1. Countertransference Themes

Major themes and subthemes	Frequency (N = 61)
Defense	54
Numbing	36
Denial	37
Avoidance	40
Distancing	30
Clinging to professional role	40
Reduction to method, theory	17
Guilt	49
Guilt expressed	42
Guilt inferred	24
Rage	47
Rage At Nazis	29
Rage at being seen as a Nazi and fear of survivor's rage	15
Rage at the survivor and fear of one's own rage	26
Identification with the aggressor and sadism	16
Rage at colleagues for avoiding the Holocaust	14
Rage at survivor as parent	13
Rage at child of survivor's treatment of parents	8
Shame and related emotions	45
Shame—fourth, ethical blow to humanity's narcissism	32
Shame—contempt of survivors viewed as having gone like "sheep to the slaughter"	22
Fear of contagion	2
Viewing the survivor as immoral	10
Pity toward the survivors	10
Disgust	9
Dread and horror	46
Grief and mourning	44
Reference to murder	8
Reference to death	5
Inability to contain intense emotions	45
Victim/liberator	43
Viewing the survivor as fragile victim	27
Viewing the child of survivor as fragile victim	9
Therapist as liberator–savior	27
Liberator inferred, e.g., rage at negative therapeutic reaction	17
Viewing the survivor as hero	37
Privileged voyeurism	23
Jealousy of survivor or child of survivor having "special status"	7
"Me too," e.g., "we are all survivors"	16
Viewing the Holocaust as unique	10
Sense of bond	15

Table 1. ***(Continued)***

Major themes and subthemes	Frequency (N = 61)
Feeling like an outsider	7
Self-help for the therapist	9
Conflict over maintaining professional authority	7
Recognizing the Holocaust as reality	12
Need for more knowledge and experience	16
Need for integration	4
Attention and attitudes toward Jewish identity	32
Parent–child relationship	32
Therapist adopting role of child to compensate the survivor	4
Therapist adopting role of parent to compensate child of survivor	4
Liberate child of survivor from parents	6
Liberate survivor parent from child	3
Overidentification with survivor parent	11
Overidentification with child of survivor	22

literature about the Holocaust is that most of the writers seem to feel compelled to share their emotional and/or moral reactions to their subject matter. The near universality of this phenomenon is unique when contrasted with other scientific writings. Furthermore, these same authors approach the Holocaust quantitatively different than they do other subjects. Although not surprising when we consider the topic, this feature attests to the intensity of reaction and involvement that the Holocaust commands in the mental health professionals who otherwise hold "neutrality" and "objectivity" as their primary values. Notably absent in the Holocaust literature are systematic analyses or empirical data on this important topic.

In this chapter, I will discuss some of the major findings of a study, which systematically examined the nature of the emotional responses and other problems experienced by psychotherapists in working with this unique group of patients. Next, a comparison between the "countertransference reactions" of psychotherapists in this sample who were survivors and children of survivors (SCS Group) with those of therapists who were not themselves victims or children of victims of the Nazi Holocaust (NVH Group) will be reviewed and discussed.

Participants in this study were 61 psychotherapists, 40 women and 21 men, with 4 to 40 years of experience. Within this group, 28 were social workers, 23 were psychologists, and 10 were psychiatrists. Fifty had completed postgraduate training and all but 1 had undergone psychoanalysis or psychoanalytic psychotherapy. A survivor in this study is defined as one who was in Nazi Occupied Europe and subjected to Nazi persecution sometime after 1938 until 1945. Of the 56 Jewish (8 Israeli) participants, 10 were themselves Holocaust survivors, and 8 were postwar children of survivors. The latter comprised the SCS group mentioned before.

The participants in this study were recruited for interviewing by announcements at professional conferences, through contact with colleagues known to be working with survivors and their family members, and through contact with the Group Project for Holocaust Survivors and Their Children (see Danieli, 1981c). They responded with great eagerness and astonishing candor. The open-ended interviews ranged from one to three meetings, of an hour to 6 hours each, and were sometimes completed via telephone conversations or by mail. The atmosphere of the interviews tended to be intense and serious. Many of the participants were deeply involved in the process and expressed themselves with much emotion. *All participants stated that their reported reactions in working with survivors or children of survivors of the Nazi Holocaust were unique to this popolulation.*

In the content analysis of the "countertransference themes," I relied most heavily upon the existing literature and the participants' self-observations. Forty-nine "countertransference themes" were generated from the interviews. These themes and the number of therapists in the study who mentioned each theme at least once are outlined in Table 1. Independent interrater reliability for the 40 themes across the 60 participants ranged from .94 to 1.00.

COUNTERTRANSFERENCE THEMES

Defense

The various modes of defense against listening to Holocaust experiences and against therapists' inability to contain their intense emotional reactions comprised the most frequent "countertransference phenomena" repeatedly reported by psychotherapists and researchers in working with survivors and their children. Some therapists reacted to feeling overwhelmed by numbing themselves. Others reacted with disbelief and accused their patients of exaggerating. Therapists reported a variety of avoidance reactions: They kept "forgetting," "turning off," "tuning out," and "getting bored with the same story repeated over and over again." Many used distancing. They listened to the stories as though they were "science fiction stories" or "as if it happened 5,000 years ago." Others became very abstract, "professional," and intellectual, frequently lecturing the patient. An extreme "cutting-the-Holocaust-out" behavior on the part of psychotherapists was to refer the children of survivors to therapists in the group project "to take care of the Holocaust part" while continuing to see them "for the rest of their personality problems."

Some psychotherapists defended themselves by *overreliance on available methods, theories, theoretical jargon, and prescribed roles.* They used theoretical rationalizations such as: "Let's talk about the here and now. The past is gone . . . there is no sense in complaining. . . . You are in the United States now." Some stated that "the children were born and raised in America; they behave just like typical American Jews. This is just a variant of narcissism." At other times, they may have focused exclusively on the survivor's pre-Holocaust childhood. The latter is especially true of classical psychoanalysts. For example, Zetzel (1970), states: "External events, no matter how overwhelming, precipitate a neurosis only when they touch on specific unconscious conflicts." This avoidance rendered such therapists unable to consider Holocaust traumata as etiologically significant and often central to the understanding of their patients' psychodynamics. In many cases, this omission led to a misinterpreted etiology, one that circumscribed the therapists' understanding—and therefore their therapeutic activity—to their familiar psychodynamic orientation.

In supervision, a therapist described a patient, Mr. S., whose presenting problem was compulsive showering and scrubbing, which resulted in severe damage to his skin. The therapist worked under the assumption that Mr. S.'s symptomatology was a manifestation of an anal fixation and kept probing into his childhood. An old intake report stated: "In Auschwitz Mr. S. worked for 10–12 hours a day" without mention of the nature of his work. Following the supervisor's suggestion to explore the nature of the patient's "work detail," the therapist learned that Mr. S. removed corpses from the crematorium. This information served as a breakthrough for both therapist and patient and resulted in a dramatic reduction of the symptom. Whereas all psychological phenomena are overdetermined, it seems clear that the dramatic result here was related to reviewing the patient's Holocaust experience.

A similar example of theoretical reduction and avoidance was naming the following Holocaust-derived dream imagery reported by a survivors' offspring as "pregenital sadism." The dream contained pits full of hundreds of corpses . . . mutilated bodies against barbed wire . . . a baby blown to pieces while thrown up into the air . . . a skeleton crying for food."

The distortion caused by insufficient understanding of the meaning and function of the experience of "survivor's guilt" is one of the most poignant instances of how extraordinary human experience exposes the limits of traditional psychological theories of conventional life. The pervasiveness of bystander's guilt among psychotherapists and researchers described later may account for their overuse, stereotypic attribution, and reductionistic misinterpretation of concepts such as "survivors' guilt" as described by Niederland (1961, 1965) and by Krystal and Niederland (1968) as a major feature of the survivors' experiences whose central meanings and functions psychotherapists may miss by responding in the ways described here (Danieli, 1988a).

Bystander's Guilt

The most common of the affective reactions therapists reported in their work with survivors and their children is bystander's guilt: "I feel an immense sense of guilt because I led a happy and protected childhood while these people have suffered so much."

Therapists who felt guilty were much more fearful of hurting the patient and used guilt to explain their avoidance of asking questions. Merely asking a question, they feared, would hurt the patient "who has suffered so much already." Some therapists who felt guilty were also afraid that survivors were fragile, that they would fall apart, overlooking the fact that these were people who had not only survived but also had rebuilt families and lives despite immense losses and traumatic experiences. Therapists also tended to attribute fragility to survivors' offspring. Such therapists tended to do too much for survivors and their children to the point of patronizing them and not respecting their strengths.

Guilt often resulted in the therapist's inability to set reasonable limits; not wanting to hear stories or adopting a masochistic position in relation to the survivor. In some instances, the survivors or their offspring were allowed to call at any time of day or night.

Therapists also felt guilty in reaction to their own rage at these individuals. Some therapists stopped exploring the patient's problems when they saw tears in their eyes despite the fact that tears are a perfectly appropriate reaction. Researchers reported feeling guilty for using survivors as subjects and then trying to put such human suffering into a "cold," objective scientific design. Some therapists feared that demonstrating the long-term negative effects of the Holocaust was tantamount to giving Hitler a posthumous victory. In contrast, others feared that demonstrating these individuals' strengths was equivalent to saying that because people could adapt, "it couldn't have been such a terrible experience, and it is almost synonymous with forgiving the Nazis."

Elsewhere (Danieli, 1981a,b) I have proposed that survivor guilt, in part, serves as a defense against the total helplessness and passivity experienced during the Holocaust. The bystander guilt of therapists also appears as a defense when they experience their helplessness to undo the long-term consequences of the Holocaust for their patients. The pervasiveness of bystander's guilt among psychotherapists may account for their tendency to overuse stereotypic attribution and reductionistic misinterpretation of concepts such as "identification with the aggressor" (Bettelheim, 1943) and "survivor guilt" (Niederland, 1961, 1964). The pervasiveness and the misuse in application of the concept of "survivor guilt" in the treatment of survivors led Carmelly (1975) to divide it into two categories, passive and active. *Passive guilt,* the one actually meant by Niederland (1964) when he coined the term *survivor guilt,* is experienced by those who survived "merely because they happened to be alive at the time of liberation" (Carmelly, 1975, p. 140) as "I was spared the fate of those who were murdered." *Active guilt* stems from having committed immoral acts and/or knowingly having chosen not to help when one could possible have done so. Asserting that "the greatest majority of concentration camp survivors are 'passive guilt carriers,'" Carmelly (1975) notes that

> therapists have interpreted hostile, aggressive and depressive symptoms [of survivors] as a direct result of unrelieved active guilt feelings . . . [out of their] mistaken belief that any survivor must have committed immoral acts. . . . As a result of the focus on the relief of active guilt feelings (which do not exist in reality), these patients have not been helped to relate constructively to their present life. Instead . . . they developed distorted guilt feelings . . . [and their] already painful life might become more drastically painful. (pp. 143–145)

Rage

Rage, with its variety of objects, is the most intense and one of the most difficult affective reaction experienced by therapists in working with survivors and their children. They often reported that they became enraged listening to Holocaust stories and were overwhelmed by the intensity of their own reactions.

Nazi Germany created a reality far worse than any fantasy normally available to the human psyche. But the Nazis are not present as targets for bystander's rage, and thus the survivors or their offspring may become the symbol of the Holocaust in its totality, available for the displacement of these feelings. Survivors remind therapists of their own anger and destructiveness. Some therapists accused victims of bringing the Holocaust upon themselves. This appears to be a rationalization of their displaced anger.

Other clinicians were seriously distressed by the conflict between feeling angry toward survivors and the meaning they attributed to their anger. "How can I get angry with this person who has already suffered by abuse of the Nazis? That makes me a Nazi." This tendency to identify with the aggressor also contributed to the therapists' fear of further harming their patients and could lead to a cycle of rage and guilt. This pattern seemed to be intensified by compliant and sometimes masochistic behavior of survivors with regard to authorities in general and doctors in particular. As previously noted, guilt often rendered the therapist unable to set limits that then, led to conscious or unconscious resentment when patients became more demanding.

During the war, being separated meant total and permanent loss. When separation issues are addressed, especially in family therapy, therapists are often confronted with the family's perception of them as Nazis. When therapists overidentify with the child's rebellious rage against parental clinging, they "victimize" the parents. The latter behavior may be further abetted by the general tendency among mental health professionals to blame parents for their children's problems. Some therapists called survivor parents "Nazis" when they described parents' interactions with their offspring. When they overidentified with the parent's anxiety and hurt at the child's attempt at separation, they tended to inhibit the child's normal anger by "lecturing" the child to "understand" the parents who "have suffered enough." This dilemma may induce helpless rage in therapists who often reported experiencing murderous feelings toward "these parents" or "these children."

Therapists resorted to counterrage in three major instances: (1) in response to being viewed by survivors or their offspring as Nazis; (2) when survivors did not live up to expectations to rise above hate and prejudice (e.g., "I hate all Germans"); or (3) when they became terrified of the extent of rage they anticipated in survivors.

Therapists' inability to cope effectively with the rage they experienced toward survivors and their children led some to reject them or to shorten their therapy. They often justified their actions with reference to "patient's resistance," which again appears to be a rationalization. Some therapists personally sought further psychotherapy primarily to work through issues surrounding (re)awakened intense rage and related imagery.

Shame and Related Emotions

Two criteria were used to categorize affective reactions related to shame. First, all have the common elements of humiliation and degradation. Second, all assume projective identification of the listener with the protagonist in Holocaust stories. One aspect of shame is derived from therapists' fantasies of what the survivor must have done in order to survive. Shame was also related to the therapist's *disgust.* Disgust and loathing frequently impelled the therapist to prohibit survivors and their offspring from telling these stories.

Shame was often related to the therapists' acceptance of the myth describing the behavior of the victims during the Holocaust as *going like sheep to the slaughter.* This myth not only implies that they could have fought and that they should have been prepared for the Holocaust but also assumes that Holocaust victims had somewhere to go if they chose to escape. As historical evidence clearly indicates, there was no place to escape to because other countries failed to help or outright aided the Nazis. Therapists who accepted this myth tended to feel contemptuous toward and condemn survivors for having been victims and, as such, weak, vulnerable, and abused. The process usually began with shame and contempt, and when therapists could no longer tolerate their shame, they became enraged. Therapists who indignantly expressed their contempt and rage consequently victimized their patients.

Perhaps the deepest aspect of shame is what I have called the *fourth narcissistic blow*. Freud (1917) speculated about the reasons people rejected and avoided psychoanalysis, stating that Copernicus gave the first (cosmological) blow to humanity's naive self-love or narcissism, when humankind learned that it was not the center of the universe. Darwin gave the second (biological) blow, when he said that humanity's separation from and superiority to the animal kingdom is questionable. Freud claimed that he gave the third (psychological) blow, by showing that "the ego is not even master in its own house" and that, indeed, we have limits to our consciousness. I believe that Nazi Germany gave humanity the fourth (*ethical*) blow, by shattering our naive belief that the world we live in is a just place in which human life is of value, to be protected and respected.

A country that was considered the most civilized and cultured in the Western World committed the greatest evils that humans have inflicted on humans and thereby challenged the structure of morality, dignity, and human rights, as well as the values that define civilization. Not only therapists, but all of us, in various degrees of awareness, share this sense of shame. Indeed, this fourth narcissistic blow may have caused many in society to avoid confronting the Holocaust by refusing to listen to survivors and their offspring who bear witness to the experience and its consequences.

Although all four "blows" forced confrontation with essential truths about human existence, the ethical blow distinguishes itself by massively exposing the potential boundlessness of human evil and ugliness. Unless humanity is willing to integrate this historical narcissistic blow, the pessimistic prophecies stated by Freud (1930) in *Civilization and Its Discontents* may be fulfilled.

Dread and Horror

Another reaction that occurs frequently among psychotherapists is dread and horror. "I dread being drawn into a vortex of such blackness that I may never find clarity and may never recover my own stability so that I may be helpful to this patient." Therapists felt traumatized as if attacked by their own emotions and fantasies. They also reported horror in reaction to cathartic experiences that survivors tend to relive with much vividness and intensity. Those therapists who attempted to control their own reaction were often drained by these sessions. A few found themselves sharing the nightmares of the survivors they were treating.

One therapist reported experiencing herself "tuning out to the point of fainting" in reaction to her patient's telling her about her own baby being smashed against a wall in front of her eyes and about other children clinging to their parents' bodies in mass graves. This therapist stated that she was "afraid to share this horror with [her] supervisor."

Dread and horror were also reactions to the sense of total passivity and helplessness conveyed in Holocaust stories, which often led the therapists to prevent the recounting of any Holocaust experiences by using the various evasive and defensive maneuvers described earlier.

Grief and Mourning

Therapists also reported experiencing deep sorrow and grief during and after sessions with survivors and their offspring, especially when losses and suffering were recounted. Some found themselves tearful or actually cried at those times. One therapist reported "becoming progressively crushed to the ground . . . with endless, bottomless sadness" when constructing a family tree in an interview with a child of survivors. Having done his "homework," the patient reported when, where, and how each of the 72 family members had perished, leaving only 2 survivors, his mother and father, whose children were killed before their parents' eyes after being torn from their arms.

Some therapists attempted to avoid listening to pain and suffering by asking such questions as, "How did you survive?" instead of "What happened to you?" or "What did you go through during the war?" Others spoke of "sinking into despair" and fearing to be "engulfed by anguish."

The anguish they experienced is related to the impossibility of adequately mourning so massive a catastrophe as the Holocaust. "How can one ever mourn all of this?" Most, if not all, survivors not only view the destruction of their lives, their families and communities, but also 6 million anonymous, graveless losses and the total loss of meaning as their rightful context for mourning.

Therapists who were unable to contain these powerful, intensely painful—yet appropriate—feelings in themselves and in their patients became intolerant or immobilized. They were, therefore, unable to provide a "holding environment" (Winnicot, 1965) in which survivors and/or their offspring could begin to grieve and mourn personal losses, a necessary healing process for them and their families (Danieli, 1988b).

Murder versus Death

Two related phenomena, albeit more specific, are therapists' use of the words *death* and *dead* as contrasted with *(mass) murder* and *murdered* to describe the fate of the victims and/or the deeds of the perpetrators of the

Holocaust. Some of the participants in this study who have worked with survivors of the Nazi Holocaust and with the elderly and/or the terminally ill (some of whom were also survivors) have used these words to differentiate between their reaction to personal "normal death" and to the evils of mass murder and its anonymity in the Holocaust.

Therapists who work with members of survivors' families encounter individuals whom the Holocaust deprived of the normal cycle of the generations and ages. The Holocaust also robbed them, and still does, of natural, individual death (Danieli, 1981d; Eitinger, 1980) and normal mourning. The use of the word *death* to describe the fate of the survivor's relatives, friends, and communities appears to be a defense against acknowledging murder as possibly the most crucial reality of the Holocaust.

Victim/Liberator

Therapists may view survivors as either victims or heroes. When they view survivors as *victims,* they are seen as fragile, helpless martyrs. This image generates bystander's guilt, rage, and shame in the therapist. Ramifications of these countertransference reactions have already been considered in previous sections.

In the context of viewing the survivor as a victim, therapists reported another response that I have labeled *therapist as liberator/savior.* When therapists perceived the survivor as if still living in the camps, passive and helpless, they became "annoyed and impatient" and felt the need to liberate them. This need stemmed from the therapist's intolerance for the patient's survivor guilt, resulting in negative therapeutic reactions. Therapists reported feeling frustrated, angry, and unable to bear the patient's persistent suffering. As stated in previous sections, therapists generalized their view of the survivors to their offspring. When they viewed the child of a survivor as a victim, they tended to respond to the offspring as they did to the parents. Some t therapists, however, viewed the offspring as victimized by their parents. These therapists attempted to rescue the children from their survivor parents, compete with their survivor parents, and/or compensate for parental deprivation.

Viewing the Survivor as Hero

When therapists view survivors as heroes, they see them as superhumanly strong, capable, heroic figures to be worshipped and admired. Some therapists were awed by the courage, hope, and sheer determination reflected in Holocaust accounts. A sense of awe led some therapists to glorify the survivors, to conceive of them as special people who, having experienced ultimate evil and destruction, have found the essential truths and meanings of life. Some researchers looked for "superior methods of coping" in them. This, in addition to the historical distortion involved in such a view, also implies derogatory attitudes toward the 6 million dead. The main pitfall in overestimating the strengths of survivors in therapy is the therapist's resulting insensitivity to the pain and suffering and the problems in living, which brought the survivor to therapy.

The idealization of both victims and heroes may humble therapists and lead them to view problems and concerns in their own lives as trivial when compared to the survivors'. Such attitudes may result in envious and competitive feelings toward survivors and in feeling excluded or like an outsider.

Some therapists who were not themselves Holocaust survivors or children of survivors reported feeling envious of the moral stature that has accrued to survivors because of their sufferings. Much like survivors' offspring, they reported feeling inferior to survivors because they believed they would never have survived the situations described by their patients. Some therapists reported envying the fact that survivor's offspring are by definition members of a special group with its own identity, and they condemned the offspring for using their parents' suffering to claim this special status. They stated a preference for working with offspring of only one survivor/parent, assuming that they will share a better cultural rapport: "They are more American."

Most therapists generally preferred working with *heroes* to working with *victims*. One therapist reported wishing to hear heroic stories and "turning off" when his patients "kept complaining." Most therapists also stated that they would rather lead offspring groups than groups of survivors because "hearing the stories second hand is easier."

Privileged Voyeurism

Privileged voyeurism, in contrast to the "countertransference reactions" described previously, tends to lead therapists and researchers to dwell excessively on the Holocaust. Indeed, some professionals reported feeling privileged to work with survivors. One therapist reported feeling "excitement, glamour, and an extra quality of titillation." Therapists' sadism appears to be a major factor in many such reactions. Another therapist chose to treat survivors as a way to learn and understand his family's history and behavior. These therapists tended to become totally engrossed with the Holocaust and asked numerous questions, many of which may not have been relevant to the particular survivor's war experiences. Because of their zeal, they sometimes totally ignored their patient's present life situation, including their experiences following liberation. Similarly, they tended to neglect the patient's prewar history. A major danger of privileged voyeurism is to neglect the survivor or child of survivors as a whole person.

"Me Too"

A somewhat related reaction among psychotherapists and researchers is what I call the *me-too* reaction, also stated as "We are all survivors." Although this global attitude may stem from a sincere attempt on the therapist's part to empathize with his or her patient, I believe it poses a real danger of blurring distinctions among various kinds of survival experiences, under various conditions and degrees of trauma. Therapists who are not survivors or children of survivors of the Nazi Holocaust have claimed "I am a survivor myself" after having initially felt they "had no right being here. I hadn't shared their experience."

Many therapists who are survivors and/or children of survivors used similarity of experience in the service of empathy and understanding, which they reported to be helpful to their patients. However, it was sometimes used in the service of defense or was otherwise problematic. For example, the me-too reaction that assumed sameness of experience sometimes took the form, on the part of some of these therapists, of foreclosing remarks such as, "I know what you mean, I am a survivor [or, a child of survivors], too."

The defensive me-too response on the part of either group of psychotherapists may interact with the patient's own fears that sharing their traumata would lead to reliving them. As such, this "countertransference reaction" acts to perpetuate the conspiracy of silence, rather than to aid the patient's exploration of his or her own particular experiences. It ignores the uniqueness of both the Holocaust and the particular meaning and consequences these have for the survivor and/or for the survivor's child (see also Danieli, 1981a, b; Edelstein, 1980; Furst, 1978).

Sense of Bond

Therapists who are survivors and/or children of survivors were uniformly convinced that they were better able to understand and help survivors and their offspring because of their shared complex history and unique experiences, culture, language(s), and customs. For example, "I was there. . . . Nobody [who wasn't there] could really know what hunger was really like. Nobody knows what it's like to emerge out of hell to only find out that every single person you know had perished from the face of the earth." Some acknowledged that "partly, I also wanted to help myself with my own issues and I knew my peers, my 'cousins,' are the right people to do it with."

This sense of kinship and "connectedness" was often related to these therapists' stated need to reestablish their own (extended) families and sense of community. Sharing Carmelly's (1975) belief that "'professional neutrality and detachment' cannot be helpful in counseling [survivors]" (p. 143), some participants in this study expressed conflict over maintaining professional roles and authority in working with "their people." Elsewhere (Danieli, 1981b) I have pointed out that in addition to self-assertion, "assuming authority was also frightening because it was associated with the possibility of abusing one's power (and acting like a Nazi) or of becoming ineffectual and inconsistent (like their parents)" (p. 143). This proved to be an additional component of the conflict for therapists who are children of survivors.

Attention and Attitudes toward Jewish Identity

Several factors determine whether therapists encourage or even permit their patients to raise and explore unavoidable concerns about the meanings of being Jewish after the Holocaust and the establishment of the State of Israel. The first is whether therapists believe that cultural, political, and religious issues belong in therapy or in psychology in general. The second is their conscious and unconscious attitudes toward these issues in their own lives.

Some participants in this study judged their patients as "ethnocentric" for claiming that the Holocaust was a uniquely Jewish phenomenon. Others were clearly perturbed by the cultural self-hate, inferiority, and shame expressed by their patients. These therapists needed survivors and children of survivors not only to be proud of their heritage and cultural identity but also to (re)establish continuity with and belongingness to the whole Jewish history and culture, rather than define their identity and their relationship with the postwar world solely in response to the Holocaust.

COMPARISONS BETWEEN SCS AND NVH GROUPS

Earlier I referred to the comparison in the study between the "countertransference reactions" of psychotherapists in this sample who were survivors and children of survivors (SCS group) and those of therapists who were not themselves victims or children of survivors of the Nazi Holocaust (NVH group). Because space limitations do not permit a full report, I will briefly present the major differences. The full report of this data can be found in Danieli 1981e.

In comparison to psychotherapists who were survivors and children of survivors, those therapists who were not themselves victims or children of victims of the Nazi Holocaust reported using various modes of defending themselves against listening to Holocaust experiences recounted by their patients and being overwhelmed by their intense emotional reactions to them. In addition, they reported experiencing themselves as outsiders and, to counteract that experience, made statements such as "we are all survivors." They also expressed attitudes, feelings, and myths disparaging to the survivors both as Holocaust victims and as parents while viewing the survivors' offspring as the fragile victims. Furthermore, therapists in the NVH group showed a pattern similar to the one previously described in working with the survivor population in general, with the exception of expressing jealousy at viewing children of survivors as being "special." That is, more than the psychotherapists who were themselves victims or children of victims, they reported ways of defending themselves against Holocaust material and their emotional reactions to it, particularly by distancing and clinging to their professional role. More than their counterparts, they expressed rage at survivor parents and disgust. Experiencing themselves as outsiders, they tended to feel pity and contempt, and to view the survivors as having gone "like sheep to the slaughter."

In comparison to the psychotherapists in the NVH group, psychotherapists in the SCS group expressed a sense of bond, a need, or a "mission" to help "their people," and a belief that they themselves will be helped in the process. The latter may be related to the therapists' feeling more conflict over maintaining their professional authority. They insisted on the need for integrating the Holocaust into the totality of their patients' lives. In addition, both patient and therapist experienced more grief and mourning. Also, more than their counterparts, they often used the words *murder* and *murdered* to describe the deeds of the perpetrators and the fate of the victims of the Holocaust. Psychotherapists in the SCS group also demonstrated essentially the same pattern of responses when relating to children of survivors as they reported while working with the survivor population as a whole.

The differences between the SCS and the NVH groups were tested and found to be independent of both the length of experience of the therapists and the therapists' gender.

IMPLICATIONS FOR TRAINING

Traditional training generally does not prepare professionals to deal with *massive trauma* and its long-term effects (see also Wallerstein, 1983). One psychotherapist stated, "I think the biggest problem is not having any guidelines to deal with the Holocaust. The fear is of going into uncharted territory where your only guide is your patient, and yet you are in the role of the expert."

Knowledge about the Holocaust greatly increases the therapist's ability to help survivors and their offspring. Although information cannot undo unconscious reactions, it does provide a frame of reference that helps the therapist know what to look for and what types of questions to ask. Knowledge of pre-Holocaust background is also important. This may include (1) the characteristics and dynamics of the survivor's family of origin in pre-World War II European Jewish life in its heterogeneity and (2) demographic factors such as the age, education, occupation, marital and social status of the survivor at the outset of the Holocaust—to cite but a few. These are of particular significance in understanding the survivors' families' post-Holocaust adjustment and helps reestablish continuity.

Familiarity with the growing body of literature on the long-term psychological sequelae of the Holocaust on its survivors and their offspring helps in the same fashion. Nonetheless, mental health professionals should guard against the simple grouping of individuals as "survivors," who are expected to exhibit the same "survivor syndrome" (Krystal & Niederland, 1968) and the expectation that children of survivors will manifest a single transmitted "child-of-survivor syndrome" (e.g. Phillips, 1978). Indeed, the *heterogeneity* of the responses to the Holocaust and post-Holocaust life experiences in families of survivors that I have demonstrated (Danieli, 1981a) and that Rich (1982) substantiated empirically suggests the need to match appropriate intervention to particular forms of reaction if optimal therapeutic or preventive benefits are to be obtained.

The reader may note that many of the examples given here are reactions to patients' Holocaust *stories* rather than to their behavior. The unusual uniformity of psychotherapists' reactions suggest that they are in response to the Holocaust—the one fact that all the otherwise different patients have in common. Because the Holocaust seems to be the source of these reactions, I suggest that it is appropriate to name them *countertransference reactions to the Holocaust* rather than to the patients themselves. The themes that have been described among psychotherapists and researchers were also observed among other groups such as lawyers and judges, in their interactions with survivors and their children. As stated previously, I believe that these feelings and attitudes may have contributed, at least in part, to the long-term conspiracy of silence between Holocaust survivors and society. I hope that increased awareness of the countertransference reactions revealed in this study and of the different patterns of their frequency in the NVH and SCS groups will assist therapists and investigators to contain and use them preventively and therapeutically.

Although the previously discussed cluster of reactions was reported by professionals working with survivors of the Holocaust and their offspring, I believe that similar reactions may occur to other victim/survivor populations who may suffer similar consequences. Lindy (1987) has already revised and adapted these countertransference categories to compare and contrast responses from therapists of Vietnam veterans with post-traumatic stress disorder. I hope that professionals working with other victim/survivors will further investigate the applications and implications of these findings to their populations.

REFERENCES

American Psychiatric Association. (1980). *Diagnostic and statistical manual of mental disorders* (3rd ed.). Washington, DC: Author.

Barocas, H. A., & Barocas, C. B. (1979). Wounds of the fathers: The next generation of Holocaust victims. *International Review of Psycho-Analysis, 6,* 1–10.

Bergman, M. S., & Jucovy, M. E. (Eds.). (1982). *Generations of the Holocaust.* New York: Basic Books.

Bettelheim, B. (1943). Individual and mass behavior in extreme situations. *Journal of Abnormal and Social Psychology, 38,* 417–452.

Carmelly, F. (1975). Guilt feelings in concentration camp survivors. Comments of a "survivor." *Journal of Jewish Communal Service, 2,* 139–144.

Danieli, Y. (1981a). Differing adaptational styles in families of survivors of the Nazi Holocaust: Some implications for treatment. *Children Today, 10,* 5, 6–10, 34–35.

Danieli, Y. (1981b). Families of survivors of the Nazi Holocaust: Some short- and long-term effects. In C. D. Spielberger, I. G. Sarason, & N. Milgram (Eds.), *Stress and anxiety* (Vol. 8). New York, McGraw-Hill/Hemisphere.

Danieli, Y. (1981c). The group project for Holocaust survivors and their children. *Children Today, 10* (5), 11–33.

Danieli, Y. (1981d). On the achievement of integration in aging survivors of the Nazi Holocaust. *Journal of Geriatric Psychiatry, 14* (2), 191–210.

Danieli, Y. (1981e). Therapists' difficulties in treating survivors of the Nazi Holocaust and their children. (Doctoral dissertation, New York University). University Microfilms International, #949-904.)

Danieli, Y. (1985). The treatment and prevention of long-term effects and intergenerational transmission of victimization: A lesson from Holocaust Survivors and their children. In C. R. Figley (Ed.), *Trauma and its wake.* New York: Brunner/Mazel.

Danieli, Y. (1988a). Treating survivors and children of survivors of the Nazi Holocaust. In F. M. Ochberg (Ed.), *Victims of violence and post-traumatic therapy.* New York: Brunner/Mazel.

Danieli, Y. (1988b). Mourning in survivors and children of survivors of the Nazi Holocaust: The role of group and community modalities. In D. Dietrich & P. Shabad (Eds.), *The Problem of loss and mourning: Psychoanalytic perspectives.* New York: International Universities Press.

DesPres, T. (1976). *The survivor: An anatomy of life in the death camps.* New York: Oxford University Press.

Edelstein, E. L. (1980). The concentration camp syndrome and its late sequlae. In J. E. Dimsdale (Ed.), *Survivors, victims, and perpetrators: Essays on the Nazi Holocaust.* New York: Hemisphere.

Eitinger, L. (1980). The concentration camp syndrome and its late sequelae. In J. E. Dimsdale (Ed.), *Survivors, victims, and perpetrators: Essays on the Nazi Holocaust.* New York: Hemisphere, 1980.

Freud, S. (1917). A difficulty in the path of psychoanalysis. In J. Strachey (Ed. and Trans.), *The standard edition of the complete psychological works of Sigmund Freud* (Vol. 17). London: Hogarth Press.

Freud, S. (1930). Civilization and its discontents. In J. Strachey (Ed. and Trans.), *The standard edition of the complete psychological works of Sigmund Freud* (Vol. 21). London: Hogarth Press.

Furst, S. S. (1978). The stimulus barrier and the pathogenicity of trauma. *International Journal of Psycho-Analysis, 59,* 345–352.

Friedman, P. (1948, December). The road back for the DP's: Healing the psychological scars of Nazism. *Commentary, 6*(6), 502–510.

Krystal, H. & Niederland, W. G. (1968). Clinical observations on the survivor syndrome. In H. Krystal (Ed.), *Massive psychic trauma.* New York: International Universities Press.
Lindy, J. D. (1987). *Vietman: A Case Book.* New York: Bruner/Mazel.
Niederland, W. G. (1961). The problem of the survivor: Some remarks on the psychiatric evaluation of emotional disorders in survivors of Nazi persecution. *Journal of the Hillside Hospital, 10* (3–4), 233–247.
Niederland, W. G. (1964). Psychiatric disorders among persecution victims: A contribution to the understanding of concentration camp pathology and its aftereffects. *Journal of Nervous and Mental Diseases, 139,* 458–474.
Niederland, W. G. (1968). An interpretation of the psychological stresses and defenses in concentration-camp life and the late aftereffects. In H. Krystal (Ed.), *Massive psychic trauma.* New York: International Universities Press.
Phillips, R. D. (1978). Impact of Nazi Holocaust on children of survivors. *American Journal of Psychotherapy, 32,* 370–378.
Rappaport, E. A. (1968). Beyond traumatic neurosis: A psychoanalytic study of late reactions to the concentration camp trauma. *International Journal of Psychoanalysis, 49,* 719–731.
Rich, M. S. (1982). *Children of Holocaust survivors: A concurrent validity study of a survivor family typology.* Unpublished doctoral dissertation, California School of Professional Psychology, Berkeley.
Steinberg, A. J. (1986). *Separation-individuation issues among children of Holocaust survivors.* Unpublished doctoral dissertation, Ferkauf Graduate School of Psychology, Yeshiva University.
Symonds, M. (1980). The "second injury" to victims. *Evaluation and Change, Special Issue,* 36–38.
Tanay, E. (1968). Initiation of psychotherapy with survivors of Nazi persecution. In H. Krystal (Ed.), *Massive psychic trauma.* New York: International Universities Press.
Wanderman, E. (1979). *Separation problems, depressive experiences and conception of parents in children of concentration camp survivors.* Unpublished doctoral dissertation, New York University.
Wallerstein, R. S. (1973). Psychoanalytic perspective on the problem of reality. *Journal of the American Psychoanalytic Association, 31*(1), 5–33.
Wiesel, E. (1970). *Legends of our time.* New York: Avon Books.
Winnicot, D. W. (1965). *The maturational processes and the facilitating environment.* London: Hogarth Press.
Zetzel, E. R. (1970). *The capacity for emotional growth.* New York: International Universities Press.

III

Treatment

Part III of the book is concerned with the assessment, diagnosis, and treatment of the spectrum of mental disorders and problems of adjustment that are typically found in individuals who have been immersed in extreme stress experiences. Although there are very clear differences between traumatic events (e.g., concentration camps and guerilla warfare), situations of extreme stress contain multiple stressor experiences that place extraordinary demands on those who are forced to cope with them. The psychological effects of these experiences are usually prolonged and generally produce significant changes in individual identity, values, world view, and personality functioning. And although it is the case that not all survivors are debilitated by these unusually stressful life events, many do need various forms of emotional and social support, and some require individual and group psychotherapy. But what are the forms of therapies and healing for victims of extreme stress? What set of assumptions underlies the various treatment approaches to psychotherapy and counseling with traumatized persons? Do existing conceptual approaches to psychotherapy apply to those who survive massive psychic trauma? In what way does culture affect the recovery process?

These and related questions are addressed in the six chapters contained in Part III of this book. Within these chapters, the authors grapple with difficult problems of identifying the special needs commonly faced by humans who struggle, often heroically, to overcome the distressing legacy of their experiences. Moreover, the distress of the survivor is often shared in empathic ways by the therapist who has the responsibility to listen in nonjudgmental ways about some of the most cruel, hideous, and tortuous experiences that man has inflicted on his fellow man. The severity of the experiences related by the patient often creates unique problems of countertransference in the therapist (see Danieli, Chapter 10). As noted by all of the authors in Part III, helping traumatized persons is difficult work that demands flexibility, multimodal treatment approaches, conceptual clarity, patience, and a knowledge of what happened to the person during the trauma. Part III reports on clinical and therapeutic techniques useful in work with Vietnam War veterans, Holocaust survivors, Cambodian refugees who survived the Asian Holocaust of the Khmer Rouge regime, and Native American war veterans. This section of the book is rich in information and will provide practioners with a wealth of insight as to the processes and problems of working with survivors of war-related extreme stress experiences. On the other hand, it is important to acknowledge that many of the conceptual and theoretical approaches to treatment have yet to be tested empirically. Clearly, our knowledge of effective post-traumatic therapy is in its infancy, something that survivors often seem to know implicitly.

In Chapter 11, Erwin Parson discusses the concept of post-traumatic self-disorder (PTsfD) as the core psychic injury to Vietnam veterans. In an adaptation of Kohut's self-theory, Parson argues that extreme stress can lead to dysadaptation and the fragmentation of the self-structure. He defines the fragmented self as "one in which adult ambitions, ideals, introspection, self-caring skills, empathy, and effective tension management are diminished or virtually absent." Parson further argues that just as inadequate empathy or mirroring by parents at critical stages of ego development can lead to narcissistic injury and self-disorders, so did the failure of collective-societal empathy lead to fragmentation and post-traumatic *self*-disorder in Vietnam veterans. He writes, "The problems of Vietnam veterans may be seen as a post-traumatic self-disorder due to aggravation of the grandiose self and empathetic failure that would lead to a cohesive self. Withdrawal, isolation, and angry attacks against authority are responses to narcissistic injury." Stated differently, the absence of a positive and supportive healing environment after the war set the stage for a high prevalence of PTsfD among Vietnam veterans who were typically 19 years old in combat and in a critical stage of identity development.

To heal the wounds of war, Parson has developed an eclectic approach to treatment that has five phases: (1) clinical-psychohistorical, (2) regulation and control, (3) consolidation, (4) trauma work, and (5) reintegration. Parson discusses each stage thoroughly as the veteran progresses in developing mature goals and ambitions that result from the repair work of therapy that overcomes the scaring produced by the war. Similar to Danieli's work on countertransference problems in working with Holocaust survivors, Parson details many different types of countertransference problems that can block progress in treatment.

In Chapter 12, Ehrlich reviews and discusses what, in her view, are critical issues in psychotherapy with Holocaust survivors. She suggests that treatment issues in the psychotherapy of Holocaust survivors for the future need to be based upon a continuum of underlying issues including Holocaust experiences, adjustment through the intervening years, and the aging process. In her view, therefore, treatment modalities and worker roles need to be based on issues of survivorship and include a critical understanding of defining elements of the aging process, the integration of these issues within the boundaries of a societal perspective for the survivor in late life, and an integration of the survivor's Holocaust experiences with 40 years of adaptations. Incorporating this passage of time dictates that clinical services for Holocaust survivors and families should be provided within the boundaries of general practice and gerontological perspectives. Ehrlich advocates the need to recognize the heterogeneity that characterizes the Holocaust survivor population. Therefore, she suggests that a variety of treatment approaches are needed in therapeutic interventions in order to meet the diverse needs of survivors of the Holocaust.

The following are some of the suggested guidelines for refining clinical roles in work with the aged survivor: (1) investment in developing knowledge of the history and experiences of the Holocaust and prewar environment; (2) learning from the client about his or her unique and shared experiences during the Holocaust; (3) understanding the heterogeneity of the survivors and individualizing their needs and services; (4) being aware of the total countertransference reaction to both person and issues; (5) empathetic and sensitive listening to what the client cannot or is anxious about disclosing; (6) being open to experience in order to understand the depth of the Holocaust experience; (7) refraining from assuming the enforcer/authority role—that is, understand the hesitancy of the survivor to establish new and trusting relationships, being patient for change; (8) being able to accept anger, frustration, and intense demands; (9) being nonjudgmental—respecting each person's history and coping styles; (10) exploring individuality in the grieving process; and (11) refrain from overpowering, rescuing, or victimizing the client and aid him or her in problem solving.

The sensitivity and professional principles recommended by Ehrlich are likely to facilitate work not only with Holocaust survivors but also with survivors of other wartime stress experiences.

In Chapter 13, J. D. Kinzie discusses the psychiatric effects of the Asian Holocaust of the Khmer Rouge in Cambodia. Between 1975–1980, nearly 3 million Cambodians were killed by the Communist regime that has been termed autogenocide. The revolution largely destroyed the culture of the country through forced labor, starvation, and mass executions and produced thousands of refugees who fled to the United States after the Vietnamese ended the genocide in 1980.

In 1978, the Oregon Health Science Center in Portland, Oregon, established the Indochinese Refugee Center that to date has seen over 500 patients. Of these, 85 Cambodian refugees were evaluated. In this chapter, Kinzie presents a detailed analysis of 13 adult patients and a group of 46 adolescent Cambodians from a local high school who were studied closely.

To begin, Kinzie notes that all of the refugees had suffered massive amounts of trauma. All patients had family members who had disappeared or who were executed or starved to death. Moreover, all had also witnessed indiscriminate killing and were subject to family separation and evacuation. It is of little surprise, then, that adult patients were severely depressed and strongly avoided talking about their experiences. The majority of the patients had a dual diagnosis of post-traumatic stress disorder (PTSD) and a major depression. However, after 1 year of treatment five patients improved and no longer met the DSM-III criteria for diagnosis of PTSD. On the other hand, their avoidance tendencies were less affected by treatment, and themes of shame and guilt were universal.

The adolescent patients had also been exposed to massive trauma including assault by their captors. Ninety percent of the adolescents had symptoms of PTSD, and all were especially vulnerable to increased pressures and stresses in life. Kinzie found that their symptoms of intrusion waxed and waned over time and became more florid when subjected to hassles in living. Themes of abandonment were prevalent as were tendencies to somatize conflict. Of all the Indochinese patients seen at the clinic, the Cambodian refugees demonstrated more severe symptomology that was similar to that reported in the literature for Nazi Holocaust Survivors.

Kinzie and his colleagues found that treatment for this population of traumatized refugees was extremely difficult and required a long-term approach and medication to establish a therapeutic alliance and achieve reasonable goals. Additionally, Kinzie indicated that the Cambodians in treatment had practical needs of social and economic support fulfilled in order to lay a secure foundation for psychotherapy.

In Chapter 14, Williams discusses the diagnosis and treatment of survivor guilt. Based on his extensive work at the Post-Trauma Treatment Center in Colorado, Williams proposes that "those who do not improve with PTSD have not resolved their survivor guilt." Williams presents a conceptual model of reactions to trauma that includes the dynamics of survivor guilt. Similar to Marmar and Horowitz (see Chapter 4), he proposes a three-phase model that includes shock, impact, and recovery phases. In the first phase, the victim experiences confusion, denial, immobilization, and disorganization. In Phase 2, the trauma impacts on the individual and results in symptoms of anger, anxiety, tension, and intrusive imagery. During this phase, survivor guilt may take the form of asking "what if" or "maybe" as a type of self-questioning behavior. In the recovery phase, the person works through various aspects of the trauma, including survivor guilt that generally has two forms: (1) "why me?" and (2) guilt over behavior during the trauma, typically a *failed enactment* (see Lifton, Chapter 1 in this volume).

At the end of the chapter, Williams discusses a variety of treatment techniques that include the following: issues of responsibility, cognitive restructuring, clergy referral, empty chair reversal, symbolic memorials, and others. For clinicians working with patients who have unresolved survivor guilt, this chapter will be a valuable guide to assist in treatment.

In Chapter 15, Silver and Wilson discuss Native American perspectives of recovery from war trauma. They begin by reviewing the diverse ways in which different tribes view war. Among the more fascinating perspectives is that some tribes consider warfare to be an aberration of the normal, harmonious balance of a peaceful and natural universe. Thus, when men go to battle, they must prepare to enter a "warrior state" in order to kill the enemy as quickly as possible so as to restore balance to nature. However, because the warrior mentality is a different and altered psychological state, many tribes have sophisticated rituals to return the warrior to a normal state of being. These rituals are often quite elaborate and occur on a periodic basis under the guidance of medicine persons. The authors report in some detail on several of these rituals including the Red Feather Ceremony, the Lakota Sweat Lodge, The Gourd Dance, and Ceremonial Dancing and Honoring.

The authors explore the social-psychological significance of these fascinating rituals and assert that they serve a number of functions for healing and recovery from war trauma. These include (1) establishing continuity between the individual and the culture; (2) psychological catharsis to purge distressing affect; (3) recognition, acceptance, and appreciation for serving in the military; (4) opportunities to obtain special status within the tribe by accepting responsibilities to be a leader; and (5) achieving a coherent sense of ego identity that is part of a larger group identity. This chapter underscores the importance of sociocultural forces in aiding the recovery and reintegration of survivors of war stress.

In Chapter 16, Atkinson, Reaves, and Maxwell discuss complicated postcombat disorders in Vietnam veterans. The central purpose of this chapter is to illustrate the complexities of in-patient care of difficult cases at Veterans Administration (VA) hospitals. The authors suggest that the VA has the responsibility to properly assess and treat Vietnam veterans with postcombat problems of adjustment. However, they note that throughout the VA system across the United States, approximately 14 in-patient PTSD units exist and that not all VA medical facilities are responsive to the special and often intense needs of Vietnam veterans. The authors contend that a multidisciplinary program with multiple alternatives is a unique way to rehabilitate dysfunctional combat veterans. To accomplish this treatment objective, the authors carefully review the major components of such a program that includes the following: (1) multiple assessment procedures (i.e., psychological testing, structured interviews, review of war experiences, etc.); (2) careful screening for factitous disorders and concurrent diagnoses; (3) coordination with outreach counseling centers, VA mental hygiene out-patient clinics and substance abuse programs; and (4) evaluation for admission to in-patient units and emergency units. Because Vietnam veterans with postcombat problems of adjustment often present very complex cases for treatment, Atkinson and his colleauges argue that the coordinated multiple alternatives treatment approach stands the greatest chance of succeeding because it can monitor in sensitive ways the patients progress in recovery. However, as noted by several of the authors in Part III, treatment of Vietnam veterans with complicated cases poses special challenges to the individual therapists and the VA health care system. Countertransference reactions are easily provoked by this group of angry, depressed, and rejected war veterans.

As a collected set of chapters, Part III notes general similarities in approaches to treatment as well as important idiosyncratic needs of traumatized persons. All of the authors clearly indicate that working with traumatized individuals is challenging, difficult, and emotionally taxing. And yet their research and clinical efforts point to a growing body of knowledge about the stress recovery process in a rapidly growing field of traumatic stress studies. Finally, it must be kept in perspective that models of treating persons with post-traumatic stress are only as useful as they aid the recovery process. As it has been noticed in other areas of stress and coping (e.g., bereavement and irrevocable loss), there is a potential danger to our collective clinical efforts if we uncritically accept or reify an approach to post-traumatic therapy because it meets with our preconceived beliefs about what the survivor should be doing next in the treatment process. If nothing else, work with survivors has taught us that there are many patterns of coping with trauma. Some persons transform and quietly triumph over their personal trauma and distress. Others spend the rest of their lives searching for answers. In between these extremes of coping lies a vast, uncharted area for future research on what it means to be a survivor.

11

Post-Traumatic Self Disorders (PTsfD)

Theoretical and Practical Considerations in Psychotherapy of Vietnam War Veterans

ERWIN RANDOLPH PARSON

INTRODUCTION

People who have endured extreme stress suffer a profound rupture in the very fabric of the self. The manifestations of this rupture go far beyond mere symptomatic expressions; they go deep to the core of the self, tearing asunder and cutting through its biological and psychic integrity. In tandem with this self-rupturing is the shattering of the survivor's object world, which Terrence DesPres (1976) observed in survivors of the Holocaust. He observed that many had lost faith in the capacity of human beings for goodness. Similarly, Lifton (1980) describes the severed connectivity between self and others among survivors in his concept of the "broken connection."

The concept of extreme or cataclysmic stress denotes a supraordinated level of psychotoxic impact, originating primarily in some extraordinary external event that overtaxes the self's capacity for regulated accommodation and assimilation (Piaget, 1954). Any definition of extreme stress must encompass several person–stressor characteristics: the survivor's personality organization, the nature of the postcatastrophe environment, as well as the subsequent psychological responses, such as intrusion, numbing, and their various derivatives (Green, Wilson, & Lindy, 1985).

ERWIN RANDOLPH PARSON • Parson Associates, Inc., P.O. Box 14015, Albany, New York, 12084.

The focus of this chapter is on psychotherapy of veterans suffering the psychological aftermath of extreme war stress. Conceptual formulations of the effects of extreme stress upon the veteran's personality organization and a system of intervention will be presented. Additionally, a multitechnical, multiphasic, broad-spectrum psychotherapy model is described in detail. A clinical case study will highlight and integrate the various theoretical, clinical, and psychodynamic elements pertaining to the treatment of Vietnam veterans with extreme stress.

WAR STRESS REACTIONS AND PSYCHOPATHOLOGY

War has been waged by mankind for thousands of years. Herodotus (born c. 484 B.C.) was probably the first chronicler of war between the Greeks and the Persians and describes the case of a valiant soldier becoming blind with no apparent physical or organic cause.

During the Civil War (1861–1865), psychological breakdowns on the battlefield were widespread. The military historian, John Fortescue (1922) states that "numbers of men went out of their minds in the old campaigns as they still do (p. 9)." Men succumbing to battle stress on the field were dubbed as malingerers, nostalgics, and as cowards lacking in military discipline with a predisposition to react pathologically under stress. In this war it was the neurologists who treated combatants with psychological reactions.

World War I brought increased clinical awareness of the psychological effects of war, the need for social policy (Parson, 1987), and the rudimentary beginnings of conceptual formulations were established. Because of the popular belief that

> protracted military barrages and exploding shells . . . caused a variety of post-traumatic symptoms thought to result from physiological damage, medical officials used the term "shell shock" to describe the after effects of fighting on the soldier's mind. (Brende & Parson, 1985, p. 66)

Like Freud, Abraham Kardiner (1941) clinically observed World War I returnees from which his formulations on "traumatic neurosis" evolved. Believing that traumatopathology could originate in the event itself, Kardiner was ostensibly the first psychoanalyst to depart from the assumption of a predisposition on etiology. He maintained that traumatopathology was not necessarily rooted in childhood. Emphasizing the ego's failure in adaptation, he noted a tendency in war veterans to fixate on the traumatic episode, manifesting traumatic dreams, irritability, exaggerated startle reactions, aggressive, explosive outbursts, ego contraction, and "shrunken inner resources." He also observed a pronounced pathophysiological syndrome in these veterans that he referred to as a "physioneurosis."

Physicians and military psychologists were more alert to psychological casualties incident to fighting in combat during World War II than in past wars. By 1944, over 1 million soldiers had been relieved from military service for psychological reasons, despite the systematic preservice psychosocial screening (aimed at excluding men with predispositional vulnerabilities). Headed by Dr. William Menninger, a commission of civilian psychiatrists set out to study this phenomenon. The germ *combat exhaustion* was subsequently coined to describe a variety of symptoms found in combatants to include fear, mental and physical fatigue, loneliness, anger, helplessness, guilt over their performance, sleep disturbance, irritability, hypersensitivity, withdrawal, depression, and confusion. The utter complexity of manifest symptomatology in these veterans, and the absence of useful psychological models at the time, resulted in an only tentative statement from the commission. The statement, according to Kormos (1978), concludes on what war stress was not:

> This picture of psychological disorganization does not correspond, either in its moderate or its extreme form, to any recognized or established psychiatric syndrome . . . it certainly is not merely a state of exhaustion . . . it certainly is not a neurosis in the ordinary sense . . . it certainly cannot be adequately described as anxiety or fear . . . it comes closer to a situational psychosis than anything else but its subsequent clinical course is quite different. (p. 5)

As veterans of World War II and the Korean War assimilated into the mainstream of American society, combat-related stress pathology was soon forgotten. Kardiner (1959) observed that "neurosis incidental to war alternates between being the urgent topic of the times and being completely and utterly neglected" (p. 245). Freud (1955) also had expressed a similar conviction after World War I, when, after having convinced officials of the Central Powers to establish and fund local centers for research and treatment of war neuroses, he was later dismayed to discover a dwindling of interest in the subject when the war ended. And Kardiner (1959) was also mindful that most clinicians do not believe that war experiences have long-term psychological effects on those who fought in combat. He states: "No one exposed to war experiences comes away without some of the symptoms of the traumatic syndrome, however temporary they may be" (p. 243).

The Vietnam War and its aftermath produced a climate of renewed interest, even zeal, in the study and treatment of war stress reactions and disorders. Certainly the inclusion of the nosology, "post-traumatic stress disorder" (PTSD) in the DSM-III (APA, 1980) was a major factor in fueling current clinical and research interests in this area, in addition to the growing collective tolerance for and integration of Vietnam by this nation. Essentially, PTSD is a conglomeration of reactions and symptoms related to psychic *reanimation* of psychoinvasive imagery and painful memory, affect, and action directly related to the original traumatic experience(s). Additionally, it includes symptoms of numbing, emotional constriction, and chronic hyperarousal of the autonomic nervous system.

CONCEPTUAL FORMULATIONS ON THE SELF

Kohut's Theory: Its Implications for Understanding Post-Traumatic Self-Disorder (PTsfD)

Extreme psychological stress often leads to pervasive impairments in a variety of systems, processes, and functions of the self and its relationship to its environment. I have referred to the resultant pathological forms as a state of dysadaptation.[1]

Before explaining the concept of "post-traumatic self-disorder," I will introduce Heinz Kohut's (1971, 1977) self-theory.[2] The psychology of the self is a newer theory in psychoanalysis and represents an important conceptual and technical shift in paradigm from traditional psychoanalytic emphasis on instinct and defense to the centrality of the self. Whereas Kohut's (1971) earlier formulations conceived the self as a structural unit of the personality that was subservient to the ego, his later view (Kohut, 1977) enthroned the self as the organizing center of the personality. In Kohut's self-theory, the ideal developmental achievement is a psychological structure Kohut calls the *cohesive self*.

[1]The term *dysadaptation* describes the *faltering* struggle of the organism to regain equilibrium after trauma. I believe the term can offer some conceptual clarity to the often misunderstood concept of *adaptation*. There seems to be a reciprocal relationship between extreme stress and adaptation, in that extreme stress always forces the organism into renewed struggles in regaining equilibrium. Thus, extreme stress responses, which significantly affect psychosocial behavior, are indications that adaptation has failed.

My own belief is that underlying the concept of trauma is the notion of failure in adaptation. Whether adaptation is regained depends upon a variety of person- and situation-specific variables, as well as on the cohesiveness of the recovery environment (Green, Wilson, & Lindy, 1985). In my experience, extremely traumatic events subvert habitual modes of adaptation, spawning new, but primitivized forms of inner-outer equilibrium. These primitive, less-than-adequate forms of *self–environment balance* often feature an admixture of healthy and pathogenic forces and structures that coexist in the survivor's personality. In most cases of extreme stress I have seen over the years, the resulting rigidity of psychological structures undercuts healthy adaptation in veterans and others suffering from traumatopsychic experiences.

My understanding of the concept of *adaptation* emerges from Heinz Hartmann's ego psychology. In *Ego Psychology and the Problem of Adaptation,* Hartmann (1939) defined adaptation as "primarily a reciprocal relationship between the organism and its environment" (p. 24). Developing the concept further, he explained that this reciprocal relationship consists of the capacity of the organism to modify itself as well as to act on the environment. He referred to the former capacity as *autoplastic* activity and the latter as *alloplastic* behavior. Thus, in extreme trauma, the self may lose its plasticity, becoming less effective in performing its essential tasks for healthy adaptation. Hence, psychotherapy of *dysadaptational forms* must focus on progressively reestablishing the patient's healthy coping by a variety of therapeutic interventions that will be discussed in this chapter.

[2]It is noteworthy that other theories of the self have been formulated by other theoreticians. For example, Horney, Adler, Lifton, Erikson, Modell, and others (Decker, 1985; Wylie, 1968).

According to this perspective, the basic design of the nuclear self consists of native potential and two parallel structures, the *grandiose self* and the *idealized parental image,* each representing the young child's biopsychological needs in relation to care-giving persons. The grandiose self represents the child's natural tendency to exhibitionism and expansive grandiosity, whereas the idealized parental image is linked to the child's desire for merger with omnipotent and perfect parents. These two tendencies produce two types of transference reactions in psychotherapy and psychoanalysis: the *mirror transference* and the *idealizing transference.*

The actualization during development of these two basic self-tendencies of the infantile nuclear self require the active participation of the *self-object,* a person experienced by the infant as an extension of the self. In the absence of a self-object, these two structures will fail to develop into adult self-generated patterns of initiative (ambition) and inner-directed guidance (ideals). It is through the parents' pride and delight in relation to the infant's exhibitionism and other grandiose self expressions (mirroring self-object) that later result in adult ambitions. Also, providing the parents (especially the father) make themselves available for idealization and merger, the infantile self develops adult ideals. Ambition and ideals, once attained, lead to the capacity for introspection and empathy (basic capacities of the cohesive self).

For Kohut, the centrality of human relationships traverses all phases of the life cycle. No human being ever outgrows the need for human contact, relationship, and respect. And, no veteran of any war can continue post-war adjustment successfully—that is, achieving patterns of ambition, ideals, and values—in the absence of individual, familial and national collective sanctioning and mirroring (see Figure 1).

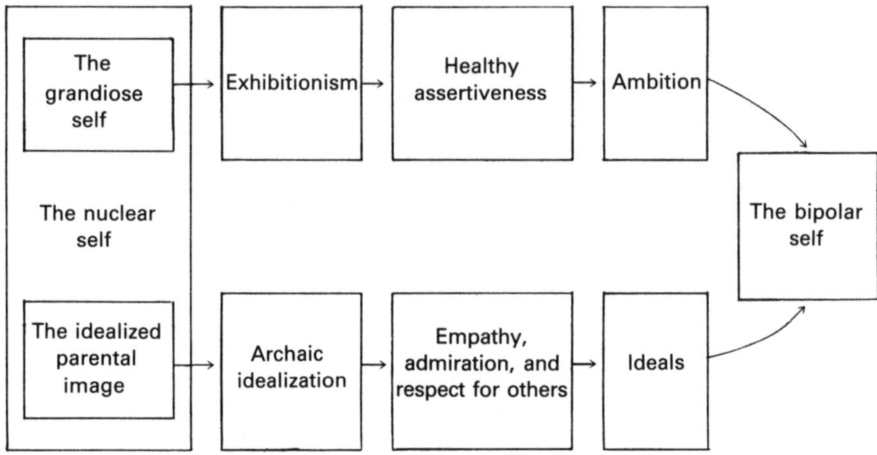

FIGURE 1. Progressive development of the bipolar self.

The Disorders of the Self

In contrast to the Freudian view of psychopathology as the ego's failure to regulate instincts. Kohut believes that psychopathology is a *response* to a disruption of normal narcissistic development. Generally, narcissism is conceived by him as a normal process in the course of development. Disorders of the self, conceived as narcissistic disorders, occur when parents have chronically or traumatically failed to mirror and/or are unavailable for idealization. Thus when parents create prolonged frustration in meeting the child's self-needs, a narcissistic imbalance ensues that produces a pathological state of the self Kohut calls *fragmentation.* He also makes a distinction between narcissistic personality disorders, on the one hand, and borderline and psychotic conditions, on the other. He maintains that persons with narcissistic personality disorders have a cohesive self, albeit fragmentation-prone, whereas in the borderline and psychotic personality structures a cohesive self either failed to develop or had become regressively enfeebled. A fragmented self is one in which adult ambitions ideals, introspection, self-caring skills, empathy and effective tension-management are diminished or virtually absent. Clearly, when we think of the severity of war trauma, it is possible that such events could lead to a fragmented self in adolescence or adulthood if collective "healing mirroring" and/or "healing idealizing" are absent afterward.

POST-TRAUMATIC SELF DISORDERS

Dual Traumatic Matrix as Etiology

The term *post-traumatic self disorders* (PTsfD) has been coined here to describe the utter pervasiveness of disturbances in the organization of the self in response to *psychological traumatization.* The PTsfD concept incorporates Kohut's concept of "self disorders" but extends the concept to accommodate the classical signs and symptoms of traumatic neurosis (Freud, Ferenczi, Simmel, & Jones, 1921; Grinker & Spiegel, 1945; Kardiner, 1941) *and* the psychological effects of national rejection and collective empathic failure in relation to Vietnam veterans upon their return home to the United States (Brende & Parson, 1985, 1987; Figley, 1978; Haley, 1985; Parson, 1982).

The pathogenicity of post-traumatic self disorder originates in what I refer to as the "dual traumatic matrix." The dual traumatic matrix consists of two components: (1) the *Vietnam traumatic stress* (VnTS) and (2) the *sanctuarial traumatic stress* (SaTS). In this context, the *self* can be conceived as *structure* and *experience* that contains the *self-representations* (crystallized ideas and affects concerning oneself with conscious, unconscious, and experiential components); *object representations* (crystallized ideas and affects concerning oneself in relation to others with conscious, unconscious, and experiential components); the *tripartite structures* (id, ego, and superego), as well as the *ego ideal.* Thus, post-traumatic self-disorders can be viewed as narcissistic injury to the self, adversely affecting psychological, biological social, phenomenological, and cultural aspects of the personality (Parson, 1985a; see Table 1).

The Vietnam Traumatic Stress Dimension

Over a decade ago, Horowitz and Solomon (1975) predicted that a significant number of veterans from the Vietnam War would succumb to *delayed* traumatic stress syndromes. Three years earlier, Chaim Shatan (1972), a New York City psychoanalyst, had brought to public awareness the persisting readjustment problems of Vietnam veterans. Many years later, several clinical and empirical studies were subsequently published (Brende & Bendict, 1980; Caplan, 1970; Figley, 1978, 1979; Fox, 1974; Haley, 1974; Lindy 1987; Parson, 1980; Shatan, 1972, 1973, 1974; Smith, 1980; Van Putten & Emory, 1973; Wilson, 1977, 1978, 1980). These studies delineated the various psychological and social problems of Vietnam veterans after the war. Without exception, these reports pointed to a causal link beween Vietnam combat and subsequent emotional problems *and* the problematic nature of the homecoming experience. Though war stress and its relationship to later problems have historically been known to be correlated, less than a decade ago this "revelation" was a breakthrough to many!

John Wilson's (1977, 1978, 1980) empirical investigations have contributed immensely to our understanding of the relationship of specific war-zone stressors to long-term psychopathology in Vietnam veterans. More recently, Wilson and Krauss (1985) studied the relationship between combat roles, nature of specific stressors in combat, degree of soldiers' investment in fighting and surviving, the homecoming experience, *and* post-traumatic stress disorder (PTSD). They found the number of combat roles (e.g., being a medic in combat, being part of a river patrol or on a gunboat, performing LRRP, combat photography, etc.), the number of weeks in combat, and the veteran's subjective appraisal of stress inherent in these roles are all significantly correlated with post-traumatic stress disorder. Among their many other findings was a robust correlation between the stressor factor, "exposure to injury/death", and the severity of PTSD.

Laufer, Brett, and Gallops (1985) have also contributed to a clarification of the role of specific combat stressors and post-traumatic stress symp-

Table 1. The Dual Traumatic Matrix of Post-Traumatic Self-Disorders (PTsfD): Conditions and Symptoms

Vietnam traumatic stress
Intrusive, recurrent floods of memory, ideas, images, affects, and behaviors
Psychic numbing and related splitting defenses
Somatic and biochemical disturbances
Paranoid defenses and dysadaptations
Intense fears and inhibitions over the "return of the dissociated"
Cognitive impariments and amnesias
Ritualistic, "automatized" idiosyncratic behaviors traceable to Vietnam precursors
Initial identity disruption
Parenting anxieties traceable to Vietnam
Sexual dysfunctions and disorders of desire
Depression and chronic grief states
Chronic death anxiety and death obsession
Sanctuarial traumatic stress
Absence of purpose in life
Low ambition and disturbed will and aspirations
Countertender tendency (intimacy avoidance)
Lack of cohesive set of human ideals, goals, and values
Narcissistic vulnerability and narcissistic rage
Tendency to utilize aggression-borne defenses to "repair" narcissistic hurt, betrayal, and abandonment
Pansuspicious orientation to world
Profound self-doubting and ruminative indecisiveness
Panphobic orientation to life (fear of living, dying, and achieving and enjoying success)
Intense fear and rage toward people
Tendency to devaluation of self and others
Postwar shame
Postwar guilt syndromes
Impoverished capacity to regulate affects, drives, and impulses due to "missing" and precariously organized defensive structure
Chronic "fragmenting" anxieties
Advanced forms of developmental arrests, identity disruption, and fragmentation
Pervasive fears of authority dominance and control
Profound feelings of betrayal and institutional neglect

tomatology. In their work, they trichotomized war stressors: combat, witnessing abusive violence (atrocities), and participating in abusive violence. They found that each of these stressors resulted in different types of post-traumatic "adaptation" (denial vs. intrusion). Building on the seminal research listed before, post-traumatic self-disorders' central symptoms are listed in Table 1.

The Sanctuarial Traumatic Stress Dimension

In addition to the previously mentioned effects of war stress on the Vietnam returnee is sanctuarial stress experienced during the return home from the war. The term *sanctuarial* denotes qualities pertaining to a specific place reserved to provide safety, succorance, and protection for those in need of relief from inner or outer torment or oppression. Few words in the English language can communicate the utter shattering of the "sacred" and long-implied covenant between a government and its veterans with greater force and impact. When one expects to be accorded sanctuary because of a moral contract and that contract is unilaterally broken and violated, the individual often feels betrayed, abandoned, confused, and devastated.

When Vietnam veterans returned, most expected their country to value and uphold the mutual covenant. Instead, veterans were subjected to scorn, ridicule, derision, hostile name calling, and institutional neglect, all within a climate that denied opportunities for personal growth and career well-being. Perhaps the greatest collective injustice was to deny Vietnam veterans the opportunity to heal after the war. Historically, healing rituals involving flags, parades, and postwar ceremonies and sanctions were an integral part of the warrior's readjustment and integration back into society. As Schwartz (1984) notes, "Civilizations in the past have respected the psychic crisis that combat inflicts on its soldiers." He goes on to state that "the fears, fantasies, and guilt of battle have been integrated into collective cultural mythology which acts as a collective seconding process for the overwhelmed soldier" (p. 253). However, for Vietnam veterans, it appeared that, as a society, the needed healing rituals never materialized.

America and the Self–Object Function

Kohut's concept of the self-object can be extended from the individual developmental context to a national collective one. Similar to developing persons, Vietnam veterans have depended on their country to reflect back (and thereby confirm) deep inner pride over a job well done and in surviving where others died, acquiring esoteric knowledge of life and death, and mirroring the need for recognition of sacrifice and a place to heal. America's empathic failure toward Vietnam veterans may have aggravated the grandiose self and undermined the protective power of the idealized parental image. Some behavioral and attitudinal problems observed in many Vietnam veterans probably stem from the utter devastation of these two component structures of the self, producing a state of fragmentation—*post-traumatic self disorder.*

Grandiose self-disturbances are seen in veterans' habitual search for a mirror to confirm their sense of entitlement, as many arrogantly fight the "system." Elsewhere, I have highlighted this narcissistic sense of entitlement seen in a number of traumatic self-disordered veterans who in their own way are seeking some sort of self-cohesion through *narcissistic reparative demands.* These demands are unconsciously . . . motivated to "repair" the insult-induced damage to the self" (Parson, 1984a, p. 31). It is as if these veterans had a deeply recorded unconscious message to America and the world: "*you* have deprived me, shamed me, devastated me, coerced me to do everything *you* wanted me to do in Vietnam. Yes, *you* royally screwed me, and really fucked me around. Now, *you* take care of *my* needs, *all* of them without question. After all, I am entitled!" Many Vietnam veterans with immature or archaic grandiosity often manifest a tenuous, fragile self-structure that they appear "driven" to protect and "defend" against anyone, at any time. Additionally, these veterans also show a profound sense of worthlessness, incompetence, low ambition, and fragile self-esteem.

Self-disturbances in the area of the idealized parental image sector produce an aimless wandering life-style (Lipkin, Blank, Parson, & Smith, 1982), emptiness, depressions, strong dependency, separation anxieties, and a constant search for powerful people and institutions that they hope can protect them from their deeply felt inner fragmentation, narcissistic injuries, and rage. For some, this search eventuates in pathological fixations to Veterans Administration Medical Centers (Parson, 1986a) and to vet centers in the form of institutional transferences (as exemplified in the "take over" of the Queens vet center in late 1984 by severely disturbed veterans). Unlike most persons with narcissistic disturbances who are able to *merge* with powerful persons and institutions in an unconscious effort to bolster self-esteem and achieve some sense of cohesion, Vietnam veterans with post-traumatic self-disorders are often unable to achieve this merger satisfactorily. In part, this is because of the suspicious and panphobic defenses these veterans utilize, defenses that make it almost impossible for them to attain self-cohesion through merger. Consequently, they may seek cohesion through a regressive and narcissistic retreat into isolation and schizoidal detachment.

Withdrawal into isolation is a response to narcissistic injury. For some Vietnam veterans, "being called 'baby killer,' 'drug-crazed psychopathic killer' and 'loser' struck at the narcissistic levels of the self" (Parson, 1984b, p. 13). I believe that the profound depth of narcissistic wounding in Vietnam veterans (i.e., the sanctuarial traumatic stress) is as centrally involved in long-term, life course problems as are the psychic aftereffects of combat stress. It is the Vietnam veteran's vulnerability to "rewoundings" and to narcissistically mortifying experiences with people that makes therapy especially difficult. As a consequence, sanctuarial traumatic stress may result in conditions summarized in Table 1.

Further, Wilson and Krauss's (1985) work has also shed light on the nature of what I have called "sanctuarial traumatic stress." They found the best predictor variable of PTSD and its various factor-analytically described dimensions—depression, physical symptoms, stigmatization/alienation, sensation seeking, anger, intrusive imagery, and intimacy conflicts—was the homecoming variable they call "psychological isolation." This variable represents a psychological condition in which:

> The veteran feels trapped in the trauma and unable to talk about it with significant others. Consequently, the veteran may have lost a sense of communality because psychological isolation meant that the network of bonding, support, trust and mutuality with the larger corpus of society was no longer functional. (p. 141)

I submit that psychological isolation is a complex human response to severe narcissistic injury. Not only was there no cohesive *restorative-containing environment,* which is critical for any psychic reparation after war, but the environment was hostile and narcissistically injurious. *Narcissistic stress* creates its own brand of recovery dynamics after war. Vietnam veterans had to create their own inner worlds that would be capable of providing the shielding functions, the containing and facilitating opportunities to aid self-cohesion that the social structure failed to provide. Thus, post-traumatic disorders of the self were generated by a "dual traumatic situation" (or a "dually traumatic" situation), involving both Vietnam combat and narcissistic stress (of having been blamed and hostilely rejected by one's own country). The point of view here is that combat trauma produces a specific configuration of symptoms referred to as post-traumatic stress syndrome or PTSD. However, when it comes to post-traumatic narcissistic stress in Vietnam veterans, another symptom configuration emerges synergistically with PTSD. These symptoms are: feelings of dejection, low self-esteem, and isolation, fantasies of retaliation, sense of being used and abused, sense of being a pawn, paranoid ideation and affect (inner terror), avoidance of crowds, stigmatization, self-consciousness as a Vietnam veteran, feelings of alienation, distrust of people and of authority persons and symbols (Parson, 1988), pervasive hypersensitivity to phoniness, deceit, lies and injustice, and purposeful distantiation (Wilson, 1986). These constitute conditions of the self. To a large degree, this view implies that were it not for sanctuarial traumatic stress, the previously mentioned narcissistic symptoms and conditions might have been less salient in Vietnam veterans than they are today (see Figure 2).

It is my view that of the few clinicians working today with Vietnam veterans, fewer still pay attention to the vicissitudes and psychic impact of the homecoming experience, despite tacit acknowledgment that immediate postwar experiences are important to the understanding and psychotherapy of traumatized Vienam veterans. There are many Vietnam veterans who do not have PTSD but who do suffer an existential malaise, narcissistic hurt and rage, as well as a profound state of meaninglessness (Parson, 1986). In business settings, I have observed highly successful Viet-

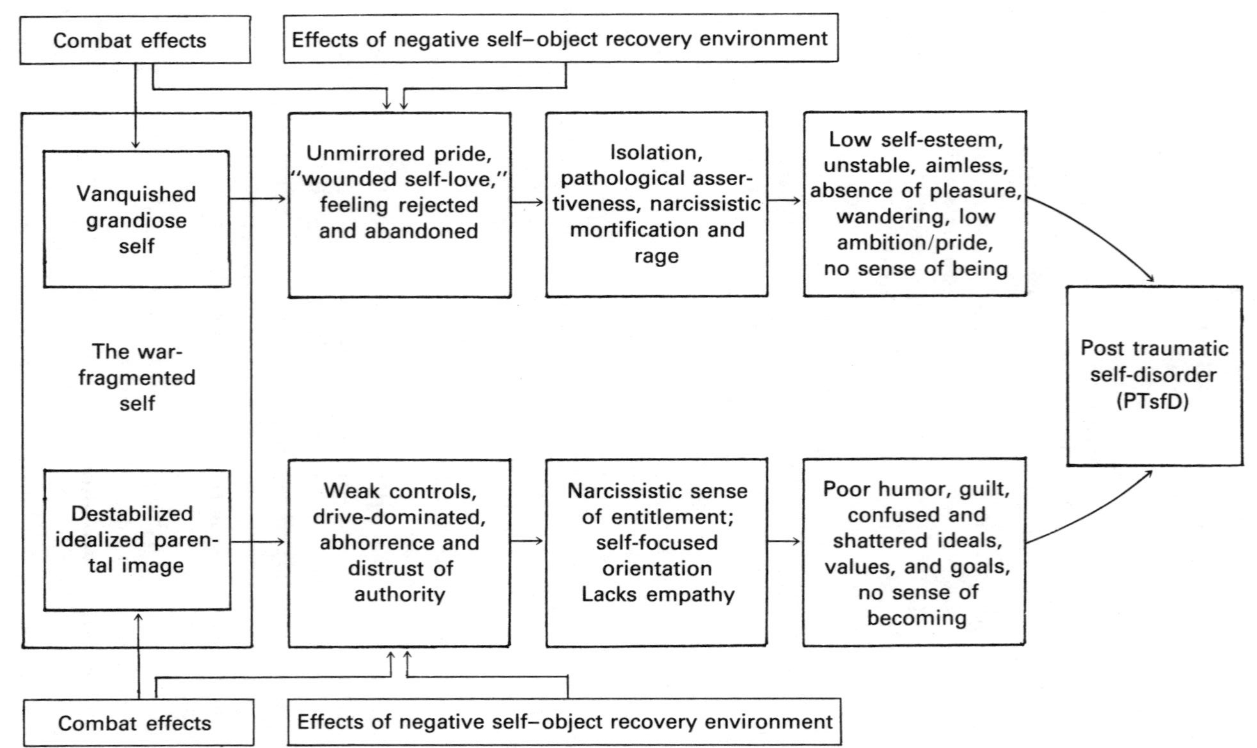

FIGURE 2. Dual traumatic matrix in development of post-traumatic self-disorders (PTsfD).

nam veterans (e.g., in the Wall Street financial district of New York City) express strong emotions when they recount the details of their homecoming. As they speak, their demeanor and countenance abruptly change: from a controlled businessman's polished exterior to an outward manifestation of inner crumbling of defenses, as strong emotions swell up inside them, and troubling, vengeful tears appear, which they reflexively attempt to control and disavow. All of them appear scarred by their negative homecoming. Narcissistic wounds go far deeper than stress-related symptomatology stemming from the war itself; they affect the self-as-a-whole. Thus, any useful psychotherapy must address directly the nature of these narcissistic wounds to the self.

CASE STUDY

Joe D. is a 38-year-old Vietnam combat veteran who experienced extreme stress in the Vietnam war during the Tet offensive in 1968. He was referred to me by a colleague who believed that the veteran patient needed a psychotherapeutic experience that would address lingering war-related psychopathology. Joe's presenting complaints were pervasive, affecting every sphere of his life: his mental, somatic, interpersonal, social, ethnocultural, and vocational aspects of his self. He had worked for an automobile sales and repair company for 16 years. He had progressively moved up the ladder from a mechanic to the president of the company. He had enjoyed the prestige, power and control afforded him by the position. However, less than a year prior to my treatment with him, his life had progressively declined. Joe lost interest in his job and "settled" for a much lower position in the organization. In his own words, "I had to give up the presidency of the company. I was losing it and couldn't take the stress anymore." His delayed post-traumatic self-psychological decline was also evidenced in his self-imposed isolation, increased irritability, and traumatic dreaming, as well as the profound sense that "the bottom was falling out of my life." As as previously outgoing and gregarious member of the social and professional community, he was now isolated, benumbed, and guilty (overperceived failures in life).

During the initial session, Joe also spoke of his profound shame and guilt over his Vietnam combat experience, for which he was mostly amnesic. He was unable to recall the exact date of his overseas travel to Vietnam, the dates of his various tragic losses and ambushes he survived, and the exact day he lost his left eye and ear as a result of vicious exploding projectiles (shrapnel). This was his third wounding, his most serious, and he was taken out of the field. During the course of the inquiry at the second session, it was clear that the patient was either unable or unwilling to remember the details of his combat experience because of the threat of emotional flooding and attendant high levels of anxiety. Thus, many questions were answered with "I don't know"; "I don't remember"; or "I can't think of that now." His paranoid hyperalertness and basic distrust were manifested in his refusal to sit in a comfortable reclinable soft chair in my office. He chose instead, after the second session, to sit "on the high seat; I want to be ready." My immediate impulse was to ask him what he had meant by this statement, but I was convinced such inquiry would have been responded to by a statement such as "I don't know why, I just don't know. I don't see what that has to do with my problems."

Realizing that Joe had avoided the entire subject of Vietnam, due to what appeared to be massive resistance to getting in touch with powerful feelings about the war and that he had passionately avoided going to the Vietnam Veterans Memorial in Washington, DC, in 1982, I decided to limit my clinical inquiry to early life experiences (before the war) and to his homecoming experience in 1969.

Joe was 17½ years old when he went to Vietnam. Today he is 36, married for the second time, with three children, one from his first marriage and two from his current one. He was born in Brooklyn and grew up in Manhattan in an intact family environment, with both parents present and hard-working. Joe felt loved and respected by his parents and excelled in sports in grade school and in high school. Except for a few skirmishes with friends during his grade-school and early high-school years, Joe's younger years were uneventful, in terms of youthful delinquency, trouble in school, or problems with the criminal justice system. He had volunteered for the U.S. Army. He wanted to be proud of himself as his father and uncle were proud of their service during World War II. He was patriotic and found it difficult to comprehend the popular antiwar sentiments on the campuses. The general clinical impression was that Joe had a cohesive self-structure prior to the war and that much of his current distress and recent *post-traumatic regression* in love, work, recreation, and general motivational functioning was probably due to his war and homecoming experiences.

As the sessions progressed, it was became increasingly clear that Joe was extremely anxiety-ridden, impulse-driven, shame-oppressed, and guilt-burdened. He later reported to have struck his wife while he was dreaming about Vietnam and had hit her a number of times in the past year. Conflict between them was mounting: She felt unloved by him and wanted a divorce. Now that he was no longer the president of the company, he was in financial difficulties—hopelessly mired in debts and excessive pressures from creditors. He has a daughter with spina bifida and a son who is learning disabled. The more overwhelmed he felt from his daily struggles, the more traumatic symptoms, irritability, rage, and helplessness abounded in his life. Though sturdily built, articulate, and of at least above average intelligence, Joe lacked interest, ambition, and enthusiasm for most things in his life. It was only after months of treatment that the patient was able to give bits and pieces of his Vietnam history, but yet in an incomplete way. He was still amnesic for a number of specific details of his war experience.

Joe arrived in South Vietnam in January of 1968. He was assigned to an Army unit that fought in the most heated battles during Tet. His unit had taken heavy casualties and deaths. He was among the few surviving members of his unit to leave Khe Sanh after the battles there. Joe fought as a "grunt" in 9 of 12 major operations during this period. Among the major battles in which he participated were Operation Kentucky 5, Operation Pegasus, Operation Scotland II, Operation Scotland II/C, Operation Napoleon Saline, and others (verified by military record). He fought primarily in Quang Tri Province and in Da Nang, Quang Nam Province. Many of the most painful experiences of Joe's "stress career" in Vietnam (Laufer *et al.*, 1985) were difficult for him to talk about. Others he was unable to recall due to cognitive impairment in memory related to significant repressive psychic barriers and dissociation.

As the months passed by and the treatment progressed, Joe seemed better able to remember, work through, and integrate some of his Vietnam trauma. He finally recalled his first kill. As he put it, "It was not that my first initiation to Nam was in a massacre, but that, after it was all over I found an 11-year-old Vietnamese boy. I said, 'Oh, no, he's just a kid.' His entire left side of his face was gone." Another stressor was when Tim, his high-school buddy, was killed. It was during the siege of Khe Sanh. After a particular battle, with the Viet Cong and the NVA (North Vietnamese troops), Joe had looked frantically for his buddy. They had both been on this particular mission. He found him with a wound in his head. He attempted to pull his friend into a less wooded area so he could care for him. As he pulled the body, only the uppermost half of his dead friend was moving. He was shocked at the gruesome and grotesque sight of his close friend.

> I was sick for days. I couldn't do much of anything. But I had to keep on fighting. I had to keep my feelings inside. I couldn't let it get to me. I had to be strong, for him and for the other guys in that unit who were still alive.

After his fourth month in Vietnam, Joe became a platoon leader. He had served earlier as a pointman and felt pride in guiding his men "in the right direction—out of trouble." As a leader, he felt responsible for his men and gave his "job 2,000%." Though wounded a few times in the past, he had managed to "keep on going, doing my job as best as I can." In the overall, Joe had experienced extreme stress—in killing a number of VC and NVA troops, a number of civilians—women, children, the aged; he had lost his closest buddy and three other close friends in combat; he both witnessed and participated in abusive violence (or atrocities); he was wounded a total of five times; and he lost most of his platoon just prior to his being hit the last time. This last time, he was hit in his left eye and left ear, which were "violently removed from my head." This happened in the tenth month of his Vietnam tour. Joe expressed shame for not having been "good enough" to complete his 1-year tour. Upon his evacuation to a hospital in Saigon, a member of his company had taken his place and was killed 3 weeks after Joe's evacuation from the field.

Joe still has very little recall for this period of his life. He recollects being sent to Japan and then to Walter Reed Army Hospital in Washington, DC, for further surgery. The excruciating pain from his eye wound kept him in continual inner turmoil, anxiety, and hyperarousal. After several months, Joe was told that his eye could not be saved. It was removed and later replaced by an artificial one. Today, he suffers excruciating head and neck pain: There are still a few shrapnel remnants in his head. As time went on, Joe's rage built up to a high crescendo. He would ask, "Why did this happen to me? I was just a kid. What did I know? I should've never been there; all of us should've not been there. What a waste!"

Describing his homecoming experience, he expressed his anger at being denied a "normal homecoming." When I asked him what he meant, he indicated that even though most returning Vietnam veterans' homecoming "was patently fucked up," at least they were able to walk off the airplanes "on their own steam." He said, "I was really cheated, fucked, really!" Many members of his family and friends from his community in Brooklyn came to visit him while at Walter Reed. However, when he came home:

> Even my father and uncle, those great heroes of the Second World War, yeah, the big one, they started treating me coldly. I couldn't understand why they treated me this way. I was hurt and felt like really hurting them. One day I confronted my father and asked him why he didn't even want to look me straight in the eye. I asked him why he was so ashamed of me. I had served my country as he had. He started to yell at me, saying, "Don't compare my service with yours. I won the war; you lost the war. How can you compare us?" I said, "Pa, I gave a lot; I was a good soldier, just what you wanted me to be. Look at my face, my ear, I don't have an eye. I gave a lot, Pa, a lot!" My mother was silent, too. Three friends I used to hang out with came by and we went out with a bunch of girls. The evening started very good: We were all having fun, the girls were great. We had a few drinks [I started drinking in Vietnam after my first firefight and ever since]. I got pretty loaded; so were the others. Then, the real bullshit started. Nick, one of my friends, started asking me what it was like killing so many people. He said he heard I was well decorated and cynically quipped that no one gets all the medals I got without doing a lot of killing for them.
>
> My rage started to build up. The girl I was with got scared and ran out the door. I started throwing things around the joint, breaking up furniture like a raving maniac. The cops came and took me in. This kind of outburst of violence happened three times. Then the word was out: Joe is a looney-tune, crazy, a shell, and very dangerous. Stay away from him.

Deep inside, Joe was constantly reminded of his losses—his eye, his ear, his family, his friends who were killed in Vietnam, and those he had lost after being back home. He felt alone, destitute. For most of the 3 years immediately following his discharge from service, Joe lived in virtual isolation.

> I thought it was best that way. No one bothered me and I didn't have to get so angry to feel I wanted to kill someone. I just got those urges to kill, kill when I got angry. Another thing that made me want to hurt people was when I sought a job, and I was turned down because I was a Vietnam vet. I remember the deep insult I felt. Many told me I had no experience. And I knew well I had the experience. I just felt exploited—no one cared about what I had done for my country. So I didn't care. I started not giving a fuck.

Toward the end of Joe's first 3 years after coming home, a cousin called him and offered him a job as a mechanic. He said he had heard he was looking for work, and as the shop's head mechanic and supervisor, he had become aware that one of the mechanics was retiring. Joe had not worked on cars for about 5 years and was not sure he wanted to return "to being a grease monkey again," but he took the job. He met his first wife, and his life began to stabilize. Though he was a good provider for his family, his wife finally asked him for a divorce after 10 years of marriage. "She said I was cold, irritable, uncommunicative, self-centered, and that I never let her into my life."

"THE REPAIRWORK": PSYCHOTHERAPY OF POST-TRAUMATIC SELF DISORDERS IN VETERANS

The pervasive power of the *dual traumatic matrix* has been referred to as the *ruinous experience of the self* (Parson, 1984a). Like extreme stress survivors of the Holocaust who were noted by Krystal (1984) to have suffered "human emotional damages," veterans with extreme stress have also been damaged by their combat and homecoming experiences. The concept of *repairwork* emanates from a conceptual position that extreme stress survivors are in need of a psychotherapeutic *reparative* experience. Viewed from this perspective, psychotherapy is a process of repairing damaged aspects of the self.

Diversiform Model for Treating PTsfD

The model of psychotherapy presented in this chapter is "diversiform" in that it focuses on the relationship between and among divergent theoretical schools of psychotherapies. The model is hence transtheoretical and goal-directed—to meeting patients' needs as comprehensively and as rationally as possible. Thus the diversiform model of treatment utilizes a variety of theoretical and technical orientations in order to meet the patient's needs in a systematic and rational manner. The treatment of survivors with extreme stress often requires such a system of treatment to achieve self-cohesion through integration of the trauma.

If there is one population whose psychotherapeutic care cannot be adequately met by a single theory and technique, it is the survivors of traumatic experiences. The diversiform model seeks to reduce rigid boundaries that separate major psychotherapy models and to create a utilitarian or pragmatic blending of models that work for the patient.

Persons suffering from extreme psychological stress symptomatology seek psychotherapeutic assistance for a broad spectrum of problems that originate in the traumatic experience itself or are exacerbated by the trauma. Experience with traumatized patient populations has shown that patients' needs change during the course of the treatment. These changes often lay the foundation for developmentally more challenging therapeutic acquisitions as intrapsychic structure matures. The trauma model of psychotherapy begins by dealing with the primitive defenses, stormy affectivity, and relative devastated cognitive controls of the patient in the acute distress phase. It then progresses through to the elevation of self-esteem and self-awareness, to building a cohesive self. From the self-psychological perspective, the patient in acute inner chaos precipitated by external or internal triggering events is essentially in a state of self-fragmentation.

Phases of Repairwork

In order to achieve the ultimate objective of a cohesive self, the psychotherapy must be geared to providing the patient with opportunities for regulated control over inner affective storms. It is only when these acute states of the self are brought under self-psychological control that movement can be made toward reparation (or integration). To do so requires five phases:

1. The clinical-psychohistorical inquiry
2. Regulation and control
3. Consolidation
4. The *traumawork*
5. The reintegration-cohesion phase

Phase 1: Clinical-Psychohistorical Inquiry

Phase 1 is an important stage in the self-reparative process in that it represents a systematic compilation of vital, indispensable data pertaining to the survivor's psychobiography. It seeks to make "meaningful connections" (Jaspers, 1963) between and among persons, events, things, emotional states, and cognitions experienced by the veteran at conscious, preconscious, and unconscious levels of awareness, historically and currently. Consider the following case illustration.

In the case of Joe D., for example, during the fifth interview I said to him, "Joe, I'd like you to tell me the first thing that comes to mind you think most other people would find unusual, strange, or even bizarre." He then conveyed one of his idiosyncratic behaviors, which originated in Vietnam: "I don't drink water; I haven't since I came home." I then queried, "What happened in Vietnam from which you *learned* to avoid water? Tell me all about it." His water-drinking phobia began in Vietnam after his company had killed over one dozen VC who had attacked the compound at night. The next morning, to the company's consternation, only two bodies were found. As the taste of the drinking water became more and more bitter and putrid over many weeks, dead bodies were found in the well. The VC had thrown the bodies in the well to demoralize American troops by deceptively contriving a scenario of failure for the Americans who depended on the body count to measure success. This meaningful connection between Joe's water avoidance and the specific precursor experience was useful throughout his treatment, as were others. Later, at advanced phases of the treatment, Joe dreamt he was in a swift descent into a "strange" well. He would awaken with strong pangs of anxiety just prior to entering the well headfirst. During one session I said to him, "I wonder what's in *that* well." The patient had had this recurrent dream since he returned home from Vietnam. Cognitive and affective connections were made to the elements of the dream and to the decomposing VC bodies in the well. Joe achieved some relief from his unconscious terror of dead VCs and of being poisoned. This was one of several *meaningful* connections—the main objective of Phase 1.

These kinds of linkages make it possible for the clinician to understand vital metaphors to be later "exploited" to enhance the treatment. For example, this dream and its actual Vietnam referents and attendant affect became an unconscious metaphor for the therapist's forcing him to drink the bitter, "stinking," perhaps even putrid, waters of psychotherapy of which he was afraid. The Phase 1 inquiry, then, involves the veteran's trihistorical experience (childhood history, Vietnam history, and homecoming history) and the presenting problems.

Perhaps the most critical aspect of Phase 1 inquiry is the systematic, step-by-step chronological ordering of the veteran's entire Vietnam history, emphasizing and highlighting specific traumatic experiences and events. In highlighting these experiences the clinician, in great detail, focuses on specific *persons* (superiors, peers, men, women, children, the aged—both dead and alive); specific *dates, time* of day or night, the month or season of the year the events occurred, and the degree of manifest distress and anxiety in the veteran as he recollects specific stressors of the Vietnam experience. The clinician pays attention, moreover, to the specific experiences around which blocking, suppression, denial, and general affective intensities emerge. Noting the specific experiences that have been "forgotten" by amnesias is useful to the treatment as a whole. Also, the cultural and psychodynamic meaning of being white (WASP, Italian, Jewish, etc.), black, Hispanic, American Indian, or Asian Pacific Islander has been identified as important in understanding the veteran's experiences more fully (Parson, in Ransom, 1983; Parson, 1984b,c,g; Penk *et al.*, 1985; Readjustment Counseling Service, 1984; Wilson, 1986).

In my clinical experience with Vietnam veterans and other survivors of traumatic experiences, I have been struck by the utter pervasiveness of survivors' tendency to repeat dimensions of original traumatic experiences in virtually *all* spheres of their lives. Much of the clinical literature on PTSD in Vietnam veterans tends to focus on dramatic repetitive or reliving tendencies, as in the mental phenomena such as "flashback" (dissociative states), traumatic dreaming, night terror, and other ideational, affective, and physiological reenactments. What is neither discussed nor appreciated to any extent, it seems, is the multiplicity of nondramatic ways repetitive phenomena are replayed. Thus, the detailed information gleaned on the traumatic history is imperative in understanding the survivor's "reenactment probabilities" in human relationships with the wife or partner, children, boss, or subordinates and in the transference. Some veterans have strong emotional identifications with Vietnam victims and aggressors. Such knowledge empowers the treatment with forecasting or "prediction potential" as to who the therapist is likely to become from time to time in the transference and countertransference (Parson, 1985f).

In summary, the Phase 1 Inquiry aims at a comprehensive, detailed cataloging of the veteran's childhood experiences, the Vietnam history, and the homecoming dynamics, as well as symptoms and coping capabilities. Throughout the inquiry, the clinician elicits information in the context of "third-ear" listening and sensitivity (Reik, 1949). Psychological testing is geared toward understanding the veteran's unconscious motivations, fantasies, and characterological defenses, level of cognitive and intellectual skills (to be utilized in treatment), and screening for neuropsychological problems. For clinical guides to acquiring military history, Vietnam history (with attendant combat roles, nature, and toxicity of stressors, etc.), and homecoming experiences, the reader is directed to the following works (Brende & Parson, 1985; Figley, 1978; Laufer *et al.,* 1985; Lindy, 1987; Scurfield, 1985; Scurfield & Blank, 1985; Wilson & Krauss, 1985; Wilson, 1986).

Phase 2: Regulation and Control/Therapist's Psychological Stability

In Phase 2 of the treatment, the therapist assumes a stable, warm, disciplined, knowledgeable, and idealizable posture. Moreover, the therapist must be adequately prepared for the work of becoming *transexperientially competent* (Parson, 1985b). Competence here refers to more than cognitive knowledge about Vietnam veterans and clinical experience in the ordinary sense. The therapist is expected to be a "container" for the veteran's drive-dominated inner world of heightened arousal and affective turmoil.

Increasing maturation and control in the veteran comes *primarily* through the veteran–therapist emotional relationship. Through the basic therapeutic attitude referred to as the "empathic-support context" (Parson, 1986b), the therapist empathically and affectively connects with the patient, while monitoring his or her internal reactions, and uses these reactions, as appropriate, in the service of the patient's ultimate recovery. Because of the profound vulnerabilities many Vietnam combat veterans bring with them to the treatment situation, they tend to require a *powerful, foolproof container* in the person of the therapist to help regulate their persecutory anxieties from war experiences and aid integration. In this state, these veterans desire the "perfect container" and are emotionally "oblivious" to the fact that the most they can realistically expect is the optimal functioning of the "imperfect container" (Saretsky, 1981). Though no therapist can provide perfect containing for the patient, there is still much therapists can do to enhance self-reparation and cohesion in traumatized patients.

Countertransference in Relation to Vietnam Veterans

The need for therapists to prepare themselves adequately for conducting psychotherapy with traumatized patients, especially Vietnam veterans with their deep narcissistic wounds and rage, is seldom addressed in the clinical literature. Notable exceptions are Haley (1978, 1985), Lindy (1987), Margolin (1984), and Parson (1985c). Haley (1978) discusses three reasons for countertransference reactions that have critical implications for therapists' internal stability, an important variable in treating Vietnam veterans. These are

1. Confrontation with one's own personal vulnerability to catastrophe
2. The challenge to one's moral attitudes about aggression and killing
3. The fear of the intensity of the countertransference and the transference

Speaking of therapists' countertransference reactions to treating Vietnam veterans, Margolin (1984) notes that some therapists

> view Vietnam veterans as victims, others as villains. Some believe that they are both, others that they are neither. I have seen trained psychotherapists recoil in fear when a Vietnam veteran whom they have never met enters their presence, and others who would too eagerly welcome that stranger with open arms. There are some who insist that there is no such entity as "post-traumatic stress disorder," that the effect of combat was simply to unleash pre-existing pathology. They will speak eruditely of borderline and narcissistic conditions, paying due homage to Kernberg and Kohut, while dismissing the encroachment into psychic structure of life-and-death trauma. . . . Others, viewing these veterans as a constellation of symptoms, are prepared to treat these, symptom by symptom, with an armamentarium of specialized techniques, much in the way I have seen orthopedic surgeons examine a limb, oblivious . . . that it is attached to a small child. (p. 3)

Thus, to provide appropriate containing and empathic self–object functions for the Vietnam War veteran, therapists must become aware of personal feelings about the Vietnam War, its veterans, the personal impact of the social change of the 1960s, their military service or avoidance of it, antiwar activism during this time, and a good personal understanding of reasons for working clinically with Vietnam veterans. Table 2 shows the various common types of countertransference entanglements that therapists need to recognize and work through if they are to provide effective psychotherapy with these men and women.

Guilt is a powerful motivator of behavior. Therapists who feel guilty about Vietnam and its veterans may make unconscious "reparations" for their "sinful" conduct in "avoiding" service in Vietnam, or, for those who

Table 2. Types of Countertransference Reactions Common to Psychotherapy with Veterans

Countertransferential neutrality. Therapists with this kind of difficulty attempt to maintain psychoanalytic technical neutrality (or blank screen posturing) with the veteran. They are often terrified of engaging the veteran in a true mutuality and are unable to listen to the veteran's repertoire of Vietnam experiences. They may thus tend to explore pre-Vietnam experiences in the hope of finding some justification for the therapy.

Countertransferential avoidance. Therapists with this difficulty avoid thinking and talking about Vietnam, especially with a Vietnam veteran. The therapist may or may not have been in Vietnam. If the treatment progresses beyond a few initial sessions, both therapist and veteran may unconsciously collude to avoid Vietnam, its symbols, and its mutual impact.

Countertransferential enmeshment. Therapists with this problem are those who did not go to Vietnam or may have been against the war but are now insatiable in wanting to know and hear Vietnam veterans' "war stories." Enmeshment is also a problem for combat veteran therapists whose Vietnam experiences are yet unresolved. Their lack of self-awareness undermines their capacity to use their self in behalf of fellow combat veterans. Enmeshment is also seen in therapists who desire to save the veteran from his nightmares, from himself, and from society—a need to finally set things right for the Vietnam veteran. Often, such messianic zeal is related to guilt from some specific source or another (see Table 3); this type of problem poses a formidable threat to the therapy.

have served in Vietnam, not having been wounded and suffered enough. These therapists often have problems in regulating and controlling their self-esteem and self-boundaries in relation to their veteran patients. Thus, such therapists may be unable to help their veteran patients gain self-control over their ego boundaries. Table 3 features the various sources of guilt therapists struggle with or succumb to in treating Vietnam veterans. Unless these and other countertransferential blockages are recognized and controlled, the therapist becomes an ineffectual "leaky container" unable to provide the patient holding capacity and "transmuting internalizations" (Kohut, 1977) that these patients require to grow. These kinds of internalizations are defined as the bit-by-bit acquisition of new psychic structure during psychotherapy (Ornstein, 1979).

Some may wonder why so much of this aspect of the chapter is being spent on discussing therapists' variables, especially countertransference, as opposed to an exclusive focus on patient variables. The point here is that therapists who work or desire to work clinically with Vietnam veterans or any other survivor group need to sharpen their "personal instrumentation." This will assist them in achieving the "containing facilitative capacity" that veterans with internal instability and self-fragmentation require.

Psychotherapy with Vietnam veterans sooner or later is confronted with issues pertaining to authority conflicts, especially the veteran's idiosyncratic perspectives about leadership. Vietnam veterans suffering the psychic impact of extreme stress maintain an "either-or" position when it comes to conceptualizing types of leadership (Parson, 1988). Many of their esoteric and highly idiosyncratic beliefs emanate from specific Vietnam precursors. For example, many veterans' personal leadership in the war resulted in the death or serious wounding of men in their charge. Other veterans speak of being seriously wounded and witnessing their buddies killed in what they believe to have been the result of poor strategy, judgment, or greed on the part of a superior. Many veterans today believe their leaders in Vietnam abused their power and led them down the road to shattered values, ambition, and ideals. This is why it is critical for the therapist to establish and maintain a consistent *positive, idealizing transference.* With such ideal-hunger in these veterans, experiences show that engagement and treatment is virtually impossible in the absence of idealizability on the part of the therapist.

These Vietnam veteran patients unconsciously dichotomize leadership into types: (1) safe leadership and (2) dangerous leadership. The first type of leader is regarded as "good and competent," whereas the latter is "bad and—not just incompetent—dangerous". The good leader is one who cares about his troops' welfare, puts their needs above his own while leading them courageously and selflessly from one battle to another. This type of leader brings his men back to the safety of the compound with a minimum of casualties and fatalities. Then there are the leaders to be avoided at any cost because they are dangerous and cannot be trusted. In psychotherapy, the therapist is viewed as a leader and is evaluated by the veteran in this "good-bad" formula of extremes (with no shades in between) whether the therapist is comfortable with this or not. Some practitioners respond countertransferentially to veterans' burning, avid search for the "truth" regarding their therapists' motives and competency in treating Vietnam veterans. Unconsciously, the psychotherapeutic enterprise is

Table 3. Classification of Countertransferential Guilt

Indebtedness guilt. Guilt over not going to Vietnam, no military service.

Homecoming guilt. Guilt over contributing to the negative experience at the homecoming of a relative or friend, through insensitive verbal, gestural, intonational, intentional, or behavioral indications.

Kindred guilt. Guilt over death of relative or close friend.

Deception/avoidance guilt. Guilt over resisting service in Vietnam by "failing" induction physical examination or going to Canada or to some other place to escape service.

Omission guilt. Guilt over not going to Vietnam—with military service.

Participation guilt. Guilt over "staying" in the "rear" in a support combat role only.

Survivor guilt. Guilt over being alive now when others have died in the war.

Masochistic guilt. Guilt over not having been wounded in combat or over not having been wounded severely enough (like the "real" combat heroes).

Normative/expectable guilt. Guilt over killing enemy soldiers in combat.

Civilian mishap guilt. Guilt over killing innocent children, women, aged, and infirm Vietnamese.

Savagery guilt. Guilt over acts of atrocity in the war, to include eyewitnessing.

viewed as "the mission." They are not being led through Vietnam's physical terrain this time but through the intrapsychic terrain of the self, replete with the emotional booby traps and dangers of Vietnam's guerrilla environment. Many veterans in psychotherapy have a need to know that they will be safe with their therapist–leader. Some feel they cannot take another chance with dangerous leaders.

Table 4 presents a few of the most common forms of leadership-related countertransferential inhibitions in therapists working with Vietnam veterans. These often undermine the very essential tasks of the treatment with Vietnam veterans: namely the working through of fears related to authority dominance and control (Parson, 1985a), increasing drive and boundary regulation, and attainment of ambition and ideals. The inhibitions noted are in contrast to another type of leader—the "gung-ho," narcissistic leader, who in Vietnam was motivated primarily by greed, and personal gain and comfort, with little regard, respect, or caring for his troops.

Paying strict clinical attention to countertransference issues can promote the climate of safety, healing, and psychic integration. Dr. Jacob Lindy (1987) in his work, *Vietnam: A Casebook,* offers an excellent example of the power of a relationship perceived by the veteran patient as safe, supportive, and integrative:

> among the 37 treatments . . . strong bonds developed between veteran and therapist. They were more durable, more intense, and more vivid than those to which we as a clinical group were accustomed. Another veteran described this bond in detail during his follow-up interview. "It was as if he [my doctor] were by my side and we were digging a foxhole together. I would go down a certain distance, and he would go down even further, so I would need to go deeper, and so it preceeded, going deeper than I ever imagined. It was as if *we weren't afraid together* of facing any of it until we were at the bottom; then, with his help I could climb out." (p. 213)

Table 4. Classification of Countertransferential Leadership Inhibitions

Assumed responsibility. Inhibitions over fears of taking responsibility for "losing" yet another soldier in his command; therefore, therapist may tend to "downplay" the leadership role in the therapy.

Direction "phobia." Inhibitions over fear of leading another soldier down the wrong path to unforeseen dangers; therefore, therapist may construe "safe" leadership in the veteran–therapist relationship.

Authority denial. Inhibitions over fear of being perceived by the veteran–patient as a hated "authority figure" and as an agent of "the system."

Competence doubting. Inhibitions over fear that the veteran knows more about his problems and is more knowledgeable about stress-related disorders than the therapist.

Mission avoidance. Inhibitions over fear of being overtly criticized for another "major" failed military enterprise or mission. Such therapists manifest high anxiety in the treatment, as their "containing" capacities disintegrate, while reciprocally inducing an increased sense of dyscontrol and avoidance in the patient.

CRITICAL PSYCHOTHERAPEUTIC CONSIDERATIONS

The first phrase of treatment is conceptualized for the veteran in acute distress, marked by affective storms and heightened psychophysiological arousal. We now bring our focus on patient variables. What does the veteran–patient bring to treatment? No matter what the patient brings, the therapist must be willing and able to provide the essential "recovery environment" (Green *et al.,* 1985) through the applied principles of diversiform psychotherapy. For veterans who have never experienced a pleasant, integrating homecoming, a traumatic stress-informed working alliance with a stable, transexperientially competent therapist can lead to positive movement toward the realization of an "emotional homecoming experience," a critical healing dimension in acquiring a cohesive self after Vietnam.

Elements of Post-Traumatic Crisis (P-TCr) Management

During the early stages of treatment, the goal is to first arrest post-traumatic regression and increase control, while bolstering regulation over the stormy flood of emotions. According to Horowitz (1986), the processing of trauma is marked by a completion tendency in resolving intrapsychic trauma elements. In severe cases, the unconsummated perpetual tendency to repeat trauma elements intrapsychically or motorically is in part motivated by the ubiquity of conditioned emotional stimuli capable of reactivating latent traumatic mental contents. Table 5 portrays the various "impinging precipitants" (or triggering events) that instigate crisis in many Vietnam veterans. Because many psychological crises among Vietnam veterans are frequently related to unresolved war experiences in one way or another, "post-traumatic crisis" (P-TCr) is the designation applied.

Narcissistic Regression Tendency and Wounded Masculine Narcissism

In order to optimize treatment efficacy at each phase of psychotherapy, the therapist is encouraged to identify, understand, and become sensitive to the veteran's narcissistic vulnerabilities, regardless of the conceptual or technical procedure or model being applied. The veteran's proneness to narcissistic regression in psychotherapy poses a real threat to the ultimate success of the treatment. Narcissistic regressions can occur during any phase of the treatment and are usually precipitated by perceived slights, rejections, threat of abandonment, confrontation, sense of failure, disappointments, and rebuffs. At the core of these *narcissistic sensitivities* is profound narcissistic vulnerability that keeps the patient in a constant state of inner tension, interpersonal discomfort, and defensiveness in warding off anticipated hurt. In this state of fragmentation

Table 5. PTsfD Crisis Precipitants in Vietnam Veterans

Classification of self-dimension as source of crisis response	Specific triggering event	Major PTsfD crisis symptomatology	
		Acute intrusive stress phenomena	Acute narcissistic intrusive phenomena
Intrapsychic: Affective	Spontaneous feelings: Unconscious guilt, survivor guilt, pathological grief states, feelings of terror, horror, and shame	Emotional agitation, depression, anxiety, suicidal impulses, withdrawal	Sense of "falling apart," reduced self-caring, undermined ambition, values, and ideals, withdrawal
Intrapsychic: Fragmented memory complex	Anniversary dates: Christmas, specific date of traumatic events, (e.g., being wounded, death of friends, first firefight, ambush, etc.)	Emotional agitation, suicidal feelings, depression, grief, high anxiety, rage, separation anxiety	Loss of cohesion, low self-esteem, feelings of depletion/emptiness, narcissistic injury
Interpersonal	Death of parents, mate, children, or friends, serious illness, loss of love and friendship, infant's incessant crying spells	Withdrawal, grief, separation anxiety, annihilation anxiety, rage, suicidal impulses	Low self-esteem, undermined ambition, values, and ideals, low self-care skills, impoverished self-regulation
Occupational	Sense of being betrayed, "put down," humiliated, shamed, and forced to "surrender" to authority persons	Resurrection of "fragging" impulses, homocidal impulses, need for revenge	Narcissistic mortification, narcissistic rage, low self-esteem, low ambition, ideals, and values
Social-environmental	Sociopolitical events: Return of Iran and Beirut hostages, "rumors" of war, and other violent social events (e.g., the McDonalds Restaurant and Oklahoman massacres)	Murderous rage, homocidal impulses, violent thoughts, need for revenge, fratricidal impulses, suicidal impulses	Seeks narcissistic reparations, narcissistic hurt and outrage, sense of inner fragmentation and loss of control
Somatic-sensory	Sensory activation: A rainy or hot day, smell of fuel, smell reminiscent of burnt human flesh, "somatopsychic flashbacks"	Anxiety, agitation, physiological arousal, physiological reliving	Somatopsychic regulation, sense of inner fragmentation, low self-esteem

proneness, the veteran may attempt to defend against feelings of vulnerability through hypersexual behavior and substance abuse.

A dimension of narcissistic vulnerability among Vietnam veterans is the "wounded masculine narcissism." This condition evolves from the sense of powerlessness, hopelessness, "subjective incompetence" (Figueiredo & Frank, 1972), and incapacity to stave off mentally intrusive, disrupting events such as flashbacks (Parson, 1982, 1984a). Moreover, patients lacking a sense of personal empowerment are often unable to develop initiative, ambitions, goals, or ideals essential for the development of a real and lasting change in their lives. Being unemployed or underemployed and feeling unable to care for their families is another source of narcissistic injury (Parson, 1985d). Unfortunately, a discussion of narcissism in survivors of trauma is absent in the clinical literature.

On the other hand, Vietnam veterans express two types of "narcissistic instrumental behaviors." The *passive* type is characterized as "withdrawn," "isolated," "alienated," or "passive." *Active* manifestations of narcissistic instrumental dynamics are exemplified in veterans who act out primitive feeling states in the form of *action addictions* (Wilson & Zigelbaum, 1986), "workaholism," hypersexuality, and flirtation with danger in death-defying, self-destructive practices. Thus, sensation seeking as discussed by Wilson and Krauss (1985) is relevant to the conceptualization of active narcissistic instrumental behaviors. They found Vietnam veterans exposed to injury and death in combat exhibited significant sensation-seeking tendencies. In both active and passive types of narcissistic expressions, Vietnam veterans may achieve some degree of structural cohesion, temporal stability, and positive affective coloring to their self-representations (Stolorow & Lachmann, 1980).

Techniques of the Diversiform Model in Treating PTsfDs in Phase 2, Cognitive-Phenomenological Techniques

These techniques involve the veteran's cognitive and experiential foundation of his presenting problems. The clinical formulation of Joe D.'s presenting problems (previous case study) incorporated the recognition that his entire psychological organization, which maintained current distress and fueled his post-traumatic deterioration, needed to be addressed in a comprehensive manner in Phase 2. For now, the task of treatment was to increase control over the patient's *traumatic affective stress syndrome* consisting of guilt, shame, suspiciousness, fear of punishment, distrust, and terror.

As part of an integrative clinical model of psychotherapy, the cognitive-phenomenological analysis plays a central role in this part of the treatment plan. The steadfast "containing" and calmative presence of the therapist provides a climate in which the veteran's subjective experiential world emerges. Joe's inner world of perceptions was reported directly as he was encouraged to talk at length about his problems. The patient was protected from sinking prematurely into the potentially overwhelming anxiety and pain of his Vietnam experience. The therapist instead asked him to focus on the *present* dimensions of his life, particularly those problems that led to his current psychological distress. Additionally, the therapeutic task emphasized the management of problematic beliefs (see Table 6). Through this "experiential replaying" of his problematic experiences in the presence of a steadfast, idealizable "container" (the therapist), Joe began to learn that—in his own words—"someone in this world has the guts, responsiveness and caring to tolerate me with all my faults and guilt". The therapist's encouragement and reassurance produced a calming effect on his inner state of chaos—a basic step toward ultimate integration and cohesion.

In understanding Joe's inner world of experience, it became clear that a number of his ideas about himself, his Vietnam experience, and about others were distorted and that this distortion was related to the mainte-

Table 6. Common Irrational Beliefs among Vietnam Veterans[a]

1. The belief that every significant person in America should approve of you because of your service and sacrifice in Vietnam.
2. The belief that one must continue "humping the bush" (or suffering) even today to be considered worthwhile.
3. The belief that other people should anticipate and meet one's needs expeditiously and unquestioningly.
4. The belief that people who avoided the draft, protested against the war, and who did not serve in Vietnam are "bad" and should be severely criticized, punished, or even condemned.
5. The belief that one's well-being is totally determined by local, state or federal government benefit and that one is totally helpless to make things better for oneself.
6. The belief that the VC or NVA were subhumans and that they had no right to their social, political, and wartime ideologies.
7. The belief that one's Vietnam history is the all-important determinant of present and future behavior, attitude, ambition, ideals, and values, and that there is nothing one can do about this.
8. The belief that there was the right and perfect strategy for winning the war.
9. The belief that were one to have a positive homecoming, all current emotional, career, and family problems would not have occurred.
10. The belief that while in Vietnam, one could have magically overcome time and space and been sufficiently intelligent, fast, agile, and omnipotent to prevent one's friend(s) from being killed by the enemy.
11. The belief that self-reliance and self-responsibility are no longer relevant to one's life because one did it in Vietnam once and for all time.
12. The belief that happiness is beyond one's reach because of killing done in Vietnam; that one does not deserve love, family, career, or friends.

[a]After Albert Ellis's concept of "irrational beliefs" in *Reason and Emotion in Psychotherapy*, 1962, New York: Lyle Stuart.

nance of his present affective stress state. Maintaining the "containing" attitude, the therapist introduces cognitive techniques tailor-made to deal with specific traumatic state-maintaining ideas, beliefs, values, personal philosophy, and guilt (Marin, 1981).

Psychoecological Interventions

Many Vietnam veterans seeking assistance for mental health concerns require services that extend beyond the therapist's repertoire, especially in cases of post-traumatic crisis. Psychoecological resources additionally expand the one-to-one treatment situation to meet the patient's needs more holistically. As "psychoecological therapy," these interventions serve the purpose of establishing *mutual engagement* of the veteran and aspects of social culture. The alienation and social antipathy experienced by Joe after his return from Vietnam made it inordinately problematic for him to seek assistance at private or public human services agencies. His anger and resentment in the past had always interfered with his desire to reach out and make emotional contact with the culture.

During his many years of solid employment and career success, prior to his post-traumatic regression, Joe stated he felt proud that he didn't need "a damn thing from the government or the VA." However, because of his dire financial need at the time, Joe was encouraged to visit the local public assistance office and the regional office of the VA after the therapist had made direct contact by telephone with appropriate persons who Joe would meet when he arrived at the regional office. The therapist also prearranged a meeting for Joe, his wife, and the school psychologist and medical personnel pertaining to his children's emotional and medical needs. Though many traditionally oriented therapists view such activities on the part of the therapist as overinvolvment and as possible indications of severe countertransferential conflicts, experience has shown otherwise. For, in the absence of these activities, the establishment of the therapeutic alliance and trust would be significantly undermined. Stated simply, offering the veteran concrete services that meet his needs on this level is ego bolstering. The veteran feels that the therapist really cares for him and is willing to "go all out" to give him the care he needs. During these types of negotiations, the veteran learns to deal with the culture, reducing his anxieties in such interactions, and experiencing his environment as less threatening to him while learning to negotiate for essential services and benefits he may be entitled to.

Mobilization of Social Alliances

Social support, especially emotional support from spouse, family members, and friends is an ameliorating factor in post-traumatic suffering in Vietnam veterans with PTSD symptomatology (Brende & Parson, 1985; Figley & Sprenkle, 1978; Kadushin, 1985; Parson, 1985e; Scarano, 1982; Smith, Parson, & Haley, 1983; Williams & Williams, 1985). Further, because research has established that 60% of male Vietnam veterans are involved in a relationship (Silver & Iacono 1986), any comprehensive treatment needs to incorporate the recognition that the veteran comes from an interpersonal matrix that should be examined and understood by the primary therapist. Thus, Joe's wife and children were invited by the therapist to participate in this phase of treatment to assess the nature of Joe's support system and determine the needs of the family-as-a-whole. The assessment revealed the need for family therapy. However, because of Joe's paranoid fears, narcissistic vulnerabilities, shame, and guilt, it was decided that it was constructive for family members to receive psychotherapy by another therapist for the present.

During Phase 2, other techniques and approaches are used on behalf of the patient. These include psychoeducational procedures and bibliotherapy, pharmacotherapy (as needed), biofeedback, and relaxation training.

Phase 3: Consolidation

After the veteran begins to exhibit control and regulation, he now embarks upon the next phase of the treatment aimed at consolidating the cognitive and emotional learning acquired during the previous phase. With the increased ego controls, reduced fragmentation, and trust in the therapist and in the therapeutic process, the consolidation phase offers greater opportunities for integration of traumatic elements. One of the chief objectives of this phase is the continued strengthening of ego functions in preparing for the essential *regression in the service of self-cohesion,* the fourth phase of the proposed treatment model.

Whereas in the preceding phase, the therapist was prescriptively active in ministering and managing a variety of therapeutic techniques in adapting to the psychological needs of the patient, this phase requires less activity on the part of the therapist. The therapist's relative inactivity places increased demands on the veteran's own inner resources in resolving and integrating the traumatic configurations within his personality. The patient is given increasing responsibility for the enterprise.

The veteran's presenting complaints of intrusion and affective flooding are by now better regulated. A fundamental task at this time is to assist the veteran in achieving a rapprochement with his emotional life. Because the veteran's self-structure is still relatively fragile, the treatment is geared to increase self-awareness in "tolerable dosages" (Horowitz, 1974). The therapist needs to be aware that reconnecting the veteran with his feelings is hazardous work: The therapist must be willing to risk self in the process (Parson, 1984a). Another notable goal of this phase is a synthesis of the veteran's *feeling, knowing, and doing,* a prerequisite for self-awareness or self-knowledge, self-esteem, and achievement of a sense of self-renewal through integration of self-identity and other self-elements.

Phase 4: Traumawork—Adaptive Regression in the Service of Self-Cohesion

Ernst Kris (1952) coined the phrase *regression in the service of the ego* to describe the formal mechanisms of wit and the creative process in general. This process partook of both id and ego forces, and, like the dreamwork, did not simply submit to the primary process but was under active regulation by ego functions (Schafer, 1954).

The phrase *adaptive regression in the service of self-cohesion* has been coined by this author to describe the formal mechanisms in the process of healing integrations in which fragmentation-born defenses related to deeply buried traumatic memories are regressively structured in an adaptive therapeutic context. The term *traumawork* is synonymous with this phrase. The traumawork employs a number of regressive therapeutic techniques and procedures in order to effect a *restructuring of faulty memory traces* and collateral abreactive expressions of "lost emotions." This objective of the traumawork phase goes beyond mere derepression of "lost memories"; it seeks to recover lost ideas, which have been "split off" from their associated affect through a systematic procedure referred to here as *post-traumatic events reconstruction.* Abraham Kardiner (1959), through the use of dreams, was able to reconstructively formulate the traumatic histories of two World War I veterans he treated successfully in time-limited therapy 7 years after combat. He also found the need to therapeutically fill in gaps in memory (amnesias) in order to bring about relief and change.

The specific techniques of the traumawork phase include *hypnosis* (Brende, 1985; Brende & Benedict, 1980; Brende & Parson, 1985; Brende & McCann, 1984; Parson, 1981, 1985e; Silver & Kelley, 1985; Spiegel, 1981; Watkins, 1949, 1971), *meditation* (Brende & Benedict, 1980; Brende & Rinsley, 1979; Delmonte, 1984; Delmonte & Kenny, 1986; Kenny & Delmonte, 1986; Parson, 1984a), *imagery procedures* (Parson, 1985c; Shorr, Sobel, & Connella, 1980); and a selected array of audiovisual "regressive aids" referred to as *therapeutic traumatic memory activators.* These consist of trauma-specific scenes and include battle sounds featuring rocket, mortar, M-60 machine gun fire, and auditory helicopter imagery.

In preparation for the traumawork, the adaptive regression to aid integration, a brief formal or quasi-formal assessment was conducted to determine whether Joe was ready for the journey back to Vietnam. Because Vietnam veterans with traumatic self-disorders are often terrified of losing ego-boundary control, regressive therapeutic techniques and procedures must be employed only following a period of self-structural building. The clinician must be careful to protect the patient against "dysadaptive regression" that, essentially, is contrasted with the ideal of an "adaptive regression" (Hartmann, 1939).

In this post-traumatic adaptive regression, ego boundaries are presumed to have achieved a high degree of flexibility. Brende and McCann (1984) highlight the critical elements and underlying assumptions of *integrative regression* that is the core function of the traumawork. These are (1) that the ego boundary can be "dissolved"; (2) that the regression is merely temporary and "reversible"; and (3) that the ego can remain intact while it journeys into deeper levels of the unconscious (p. 66). During this phase, Joe achieved the *healing recapitulation* (Figley, 1979) through *therapeutic revivification* (Brende, 1981) of buried traumatic memories. Joe was able to recollect precursor incidents in the war just prior to his being "hit." For example, he encountered the buried feelings related to grief over the loss of his eye and facial disfigurement, rage over these losses, as well as shame and guilt for leaving his men behind (upon his evacuation from the field). He also became aware of killing a child with a grenade and expressed his fears around child rearing and apprehensions that some day someone will kill his child in retaliation for the "murder" (of a child) he committed in Vietnam. In the regressed state, Joe reexperienced the moment in battle he was injured and could now "see the blood spray and mist in the air around me." After a series of regressive "excursions," Joe's memories and attendant feelings were now available to the treatment process.

Phase 5: Reintegration-Cohesion

Though Kohut's (1977) self-psychology was conceived for the treatment of narcissistic disorders in *nonextreme trauma* contexts, I have found his respect for the patient's *narcissistic vulnerabilities* an asset in working with traumatized persons. Most survivors of extreme stress are especially vulnerable to narcissistic upset and injury. Their self-protective withdrawal gives their self-structures a profound narcissistic bent, resembling Kohut's description of narcissistic personality syndrome and the avoidant, schizoid personality.

In this regard, the self-object's intuitive responses and management of mutual intersubjective expressions of cognitive, affective, and experiential elements in the therapeutic relationship lead to structural growth. This growth is mediated by the therapeutic provisions (referred to earlier) called "transmuting internalizations" (Kohut, 1971, 1977), which represent the gradual acquisition of new psychic structure. Some veterans, at this point in the treatment, may require additional cognitive, behavioral, relaxational, or psychological homework assignments, especially in cases in which the traumawork phase may have produced what I have called "disruptive emotional residuals." For the most part, however, this phase of the treatment emphasizes the structuring of the intersubjective frame of reference of veteran and therapist. Thus, through the self–other mutuality of the therapeutic relationship, all other self–other configurations in the veteran's experience stemming from *before, during* (in Vietnam), and *after* (homecoming and subsequent experiences) the war are examined in both nontransference and transference spheres of the relationship. The treatment progressed via two specific self-psychological "developmental lines" (A. Freud, 1939), discussed later in detail.

From Exhibitionistic Dependency to Matured Goals and Ambition

Early during the traumawork phase, Joe's intense feelings of shame over "falling short of my own standards of excellence" were prominent in the treatment. What Joe was feeling is distinguished from guilt (which stems from one's having transgressed a prohibition). As the various elements of his war stress and sanctuarial traumatic stress were explored under the illuminating influence of the therapy, buried feelings of shame and humiliation were unearthed. These feelings were related to his having "failed to save my high-school buddy in Khe Sanh"; to his being wounded so severely that he did not complete his 1-year tour in Vietnam; and to his "inferior combat service" compared to his father's and uncle's service in Germany and Iwo Jima in World War II. Feelings of shame and humiliation were also expressed in regard to his wife and children. Joe felt a failure in raising his children, in being a husband "deserving of his wife's respect and affection," and in failing to hold onto his job that he had worked so hard to secure for so many years. These feelings emerged as the result of a series of dynamic explorations of Joe's obsessive-compulsive-type perfectionism that became manifest during the period of his post-traumatic deterioration.

Utilizing the "structure-maintenance focus" (Parson, 1986a), the therapist attempted to demonstrated to Joe the purposes his perfectionistic behaviors served in maintaining self-esteem and structural cohesion. It became clear that Joe's perfectionism was not due to an unrelenting, harsh superego, typical of obsessional characters but rather to the archaic grandiose self-image that "a warrior never fails." Joe's fear of failure, shame, humiliation, and self-contempt motivated an overregulation of his self in order to forestall any chance of mishap, "where I would fuck up once again." His ambition could not attain any degree of maturity and realization as long as his narcissistic perfectionism remained unchanged. Later, this perfectionism gave way to more inner freedom, willingness, and capacity to "allow things to happen," without the need to compulsively control "everything I do."

From Archaic Idealization to Matured Ideals and Values

One aspect of Joe's presenting post-traumatic affective syndrome, in addition to shame, was guilt. As the self becomes increasingly integrated, however, guilt feelings and related memories acquire mental representation and salience in the treatment, in response to the traumawork and a cohesive "containing" relationship. As indicated earlier, Joe's self-structure had defects in both self-aspects. Though the positive, idealizing transference (by way of the idealized parental image) was always operative in the treatment, along with the mirroring transference (derived from the grandiose self), it was only later that strong authority conflicts emerged in the transference. Like many Vietnam veterans with problems in occupational leadership and/or occupational subordinate roles, Joe needed to resolve his conflicts in these areas. Related to these issues addressed through analysis of the idealizing transference were Joe's fragmented identity, lack of self-worth, fractured values, severe guilt and related work inhibitions, disinterest in family matters, poor initiative, industry, and sense of competency.

Joe unconsciously viewed the therapist as a "revered, great leader, who would lead" him safely from one victory to another. Through the idealizing transference (merger) with the omnipotent therapist–leader, he, too, was a great idealized leader he had once experienced himself to be in Vietnam. This self-view had been "spoiled" following his being wounded and evacuated out of "the bush." He had felt responsible for his platoon's welfare. And, because of shame and guilt, he had unconsciously "protected myself against leading anybody ever again," adversely affecting his chances for promotion to a supervisory or executive level in his firm. He felt he could not "ever tolerate the feelings of shame and guilt," and he had felt "uneasy and somewhat fearful with responsibility in any workplace after the War." In Vietnam, the leadership role had given Joe feelings of power and omnipotence. Now, through the idealizing transference, he once again connected with these grandiose feelings as he "safely" shared this power through dynamic merging with the therapist.

Through psychoanalytic interpretive activity, Joe was able to work through and integrate his pathological omnipotence, his death enthrallment (Parson, 1986b), his fragmented, labile self-esteem, as well as his shame and humiliation proneness, and guilt-driven defenses. Additionally, he worked through his "war anniversary reenactment tendency," his rage over the death of friends, and violent impulses related to his wounded masculine narcissism. He then felt less isolation as he embarked on the path to self-cohesion.

As a result of the treatment, the deficits in the idealized parental image due to both combat and sanctuarial traumatic stresses were psychiacally reorganized to acquire:

1. Adequate firming up of drive-controlling, drive-channeling and drive-neutralizing functions
2. Adequate development of the idealization of internalized values and guiding principles
3. Development of such highly differentiated psychological functions as empathy, creativeness, humor, and wisdom. (Ornstein, 1979, p. 187)

Key to this phase, additionally, was the therapist's use of "psychoanalytic listening" (Chessick, 1985) while minimizing the incidences of humiliation and other narcissistic "woundings" inherent in the treatment process (Fisher, 1985; Parson, 1984a; & Wilie, 1981). The therapist also monitored countertransference feelings while listening to the patient's moral pain (Marin, 1981; Parson, 1986b), over having seen and given tacit "approval" to atrocities in Vietnam (Frey-Wouters & Laufer, 1986; Haley, 1974), and allowing the patient to regressively merge with him (in both the mirroring and idealizing transferences). The foundation was then laid for Joe's gaining emotional and intellectual independence from Vietnam along with matured ideals and values.

Overall, Joe achieved a stable sense of self as active (self as "doer") as *connected to his affective world* (self as "feeling"), with a *sense of continuity* (identity) and *inner stability* (synthesis) and as *unique* (as a person and human being). Compared to earlier periods of the treatment, after 3½ years of psychotherapy, Joe's increased self-control manifested itself in his being less stimulus bound as he retrospectively mastered his war–home dual traumatic experiences on "the road to recovery" (Brende & Parson, 1985).

REFERENCES

American Psychiatric Association. (1980). *Diagnostic and statistical manual of mental disorders* (3rd ed.). Washington, DC: American Psychiatric Association.

Brende, J. E. (1981). Combined individual and group therapy for Vietnam veterans. *International Journal of Group Psychotherapy, 31,* 367–78.

Brende, J. O. (1985). The use of hypnosis in post-traumatic conditions. In W. Kelly (Ed.), *Post-traumatic stress and the war veterans patient* (pp. 193–210). New York: Brunner/Mazel.

Brende, J. O., & Benedict, B. (1980). The Vietnam combat delayed stress syndrome: Hypnotherapy of "dissociative symptoms." *American Journal of Clinical Hypnosis, 23,* 34–40.

Brende, J. O., & McCann, I. L. (1984). Regressive experiences in Vietnam veterans: Their relationship to war, post-traumatic symptoms and recovery. *Journal of Contemporary Psychotherapy, 14,* 57–75.

Brende, J. O., & Parson, E. R. (1985). *Vietnam veterans: The road to recovery.* New York: Plenum Press.

Brende, J. O., & Parson, E. R. (1987). Multiphasic treatment of Vietnam veterans. Psychotherapy in Private Practice, *5*(2), 51–62.

Brende, J. O., & Rinsley, D. (1979). Borderline disorder, altered states of consciousness, and glossolalia. *Journal of the American Academy of Psychoanalysis, 7,* 165–188.

Caplan, G. (1970). Psychological readjustment of Vietnam veterans. Statement to Senate Labor and Public Welfare Committees, Subcommittee on Veterans Affairs.

Chessick, R. (1985). Psychoanalytic listening II. *American Journal of Psychotherapy, 39,* 30–47.

Decker, D. (1985). On the devalued self and implications for treatment. *Journal of Contemporary Psychotherapy, 15*(2), 172–189.

Delmonte, M. (1984). Therapeutic effects of meditation: A psychometric, physiological and behavioral evaluation. *Irish Journal of Psychology, 6*(1), 79–80.

Delmonte, M., & Kenny, J. (1986). Conceptual models and functions of meditation in psychotherapy. *Journal of Contemporary Psychology, 17*(1), 80–89.

DesPres, T. (1976). *The survivor: An anatomy of life in the death camps.* New York: Oxford University Press.

Ellis, A. (1962). *Reason and emotion in psychotherapy.* New York: Lyle Stuart.

Figley, C. R. (Ed.). (1978). *Stress disorders among Vietnam veterans.* New York: Brunner/Mazel.

Figley, C. R. (1979). *Combat as disaster: Treating combat veterans as survivors.* Invited address to the American Psychiatric Association, Chicago.

Figley, C., & Sprenkle, D. (1978). Delayed stress response syndrome: Family therapy implications. *Journal of Marriage and Family Counseling, 6,* 53–59.

Figueiredo, J., & Frank, J. (1972). Subjective incompetence, the clinical hallmark of demoralization. *Comprehensive Psychiatry, 23*(4), 353–363.

Fisher, S. (1985). Identity of two: The phenomenology of shame in borderline development and treatment. *Psychotherapy, 22,* 101–109.

Fortescue in War. (1922). *Report of the War Office Committee of Enquiry into "shell shock".* London: Her Magesty's Stationery Office.

Fox, R. (1974). Narcissistic rage and the problem of combat aggression. *Archives of General Psychiatry, 31,* 807–811.

Freud, A. (1939). *Ego and the mechanisms of defense.* New York: International Universities Press.

Freud, S. (1955). *Psychoanalysis and war neurosis* (Standard ed. Vol. 17). London: Hogarth Press.

Freud, S., Ferenczi, S., Abraham, K., Simmel, E., & Jones, E. (1921). *Psychoanalysis and the war neuroses.* London: International Psychoanalytic Press.

Frey-Wouters, E., & Laufer, R. (1986). *Legacy of a War.* Armonk, NY: M. E. Sharpe.

Green, B., Wilson, J., & Lindy, J. (1985). Conceptualizing post-traumatic stress disorder: A psychosocial framework. In C. R. Figley (Ed.), *Trauma and its wake: The study and treatment of post-traumatic stress disorder* (pp. 142–172). New York: Brunner/Mazel.

Grinker, R., & Spiegel, J. (1945). *Men under stress.* Philadelphia: Blakiston.

Haley, S. (1974). When the patient reports atrocities. *Archives of General Psychiatry, 39,* 191–196.

Haley, S. (1978). Treatment implications of post-combat stress response syndromes for mental health professionals. In C. R. Figley (Ed.), *Stress disorders among Vietnam Veterans* (pp. 254–267). New York: Brunner/Mazel.

Haley, S. (1985). Some of my best friends are dead: Treatment of the PTSD patient and his family. In W. Kelly (Ed.), *Post-traumatic stress disorder and the war veteran patient* (pp. 54–70). New York: Brunner/Mazel.

Hartmann, H. (1939). *Ego psychology and the problem of adaptation.* New York: International Universities Press. (Tr. by D. Rapaport in 1958).

Horowitz, M. (1974). Stress response syndromes: Character style in dynamic psychotherapy. *Archives of General Psychiatry, 31,* 768–781.

Horowitz, M. (1986). *Stress response syndromes* (2nd ed.). New York: Jason Aronson.

Horowitz, M., & Solomon, G. (1975). Delayed stress response syndromes in Vietnam veterans. In C. R. Figley (Ed.), *Stress disorders among Vietnam veterans* (pp. 268–280). New York: Brunner/Mazel.

Jaspers, K. (1963). *General psychopathology.* Chicago: University of Chicago Press.
Kadushin, C. (1985). Social networks, helping networks, and Vietnam veterans. In S. Sonnenberg, A. Blank, & J. Talbott (Eds.), *The trauma of war: Stress and recovery in Vietnam veterans* (pp. 80–110). Washington, DC: American Psychiatric Press.
Kardiner, A. (1941). The traumatic neurosis of war. *Psychosomatic Medical Monograph* (pp. 11–111). New York: Paul Hoebel.
Kardiner, A. (1959). Traumatic neurosis of war. In S. Arieti (Ed.), *American handbook of psychiatry* (Vol. 1, pp. 120–143). New York: Basic Books.
Kenny, V., & Delmonte, M. (1986). Meditation as viewed through personal construct theory. *Journal of Contemporary Psychotherapy, 16,* 4–22.
Kohut, H. (1971). *The analysis of the self.* New York: International Universities Press.
Kohut, H. (1977). *The restoration of the self.* New York: International Universities Press.
Kormos, H. (1978). The nature of combat stress. In C. R. Figley (Ed.), *Stress disorders among Vietnam veterans* (pp. 4–58). New York: Brunner/Mazel.
Kris, E. (1952). The psychology of caricature. In E. Kris (Ed.), *Psychoanalytic explorations in the arts* (pp. 44–96). New York: International Universities Press.
Krystal, H. (1984). Psychoanalytic views on human emotional damages. In B. A. van der Kolk (Ed.), *Post-traumatic stress disorder: Psychological and biological sequelae* (pp. 2–28). Washington, DC: American Psychiatric Press.
Laufer, R., Brett, E., & Gallops, M. (1985). Dimensions of posttraumatic stress disorder among Vietnam veterans. *Journal of Nervous and Mental Disease,* 538–545.
Lifton, R. J. (1980). *The broken connection.* New York: Simon & Schuster.
Lindy, J. D. (1987). *Vietnam: A Casebook.* New York: Brunner/Mazel.
Lipkin, J., Blank, A. S., Parson, E. R., & Smith, J. R. (1982). Vietnam veterans and post-traumatic stress disorder. *Hospital and Community Psychiatry, 33*(11), 908–912.
Margolin, Y. (1984, August 26). *"What I don't know can't hurt me:" Therapist reactions to Vietnam veterans.* Paper presented at the 92nd Annual Convention of the American Psychological Association. Toronto, Canada.
Marin, P. (1981). Living in moral pain. *Psychology Today, November,* pp. 68–80.
Ornstein, P. (1979). Self-pathology in the psychoanalytic treatment process. In L. Saretsky, G. Goldman, & M. Milman, (Eds.), *Integrating ego psychology and object relations theory: Psychoanalytic perspectives in psychopathology* (pp. 180–195). Dubuque: Kendall/Hunt Publishing Company.
Parson, E. R. (1980, September). *The CMHC-based treatment of the Vietnam combat veteran: An alternative psychotherapy model.* Paper presented at the 32nd Institute on Hospital and Community Psychiatry, Boston, Massachusetts.
Parson, E. R. (1981, November 4). *"Still life": Psychological criticism of Vietnam's aftermath on the life of a veteran.* Invited commentary submitted to the American Film Institute, Washington, DC.
Parson, E. R. (1982). Narcissistic injury in Vietnam vets: The role of post-traumatic stress disorder, "agent orange" anxiety, and the repatriation experience. *Stars and Stripes, November 18,* pp. 4–8.
Parson, E. R. (1984a). The reparation of the self: Clinical and theoretical dimensions in the treatment of Vietnam combat veterans. *Journal of Contemporary Psychotherapy, 14,* 4–56.
Parson, E. R. (1984b). The role of psychodynamic group therapy in the treatment of the combat veteran. In H. Schwartz (Ed.), *Psychotherapy of combat veterans* (pp. 153–220). New York: Spectrum Medical and Scientific Books.
Parson, E. R. (1985a). Ethnicity and traumatic stress: The intersection point in psychotherapy. In C. R. Figley (Ed.), *Trauma and its wake: The study and treatment of post-traumatic stress disorder* (pp. 314–337). New York: Brunner/Mazel.
Parson, E. R. (1985b). The intercultural setting: Encountering black Vietnam veterans. In S. Sonnenberg, A. Blank, & J. Talbott (Eds.), *The trauma of war: Stress and recovery in Vietnam veterans* (pp. 362–387). Washington, DC: American Psychiatric Press.

Parson, E. R. (1985c). The black Vietnam veteran: His representational world in post-traumatic stress disorder. In W. Kelly (Ed.), *Post-traumatic stress disorder and the war veteran patient* (pp. 170–192). New York: Brunner/Mazel.

Parson, E. R. (1985d, November 15). *Unconscious guilt and fear of authority dominance as psychological impediments to economic mainstreaming in Vietnam veterans.* Invited presentation at a Continuing Medical Education Conference at the VA Medical Center, Montrose, New York.

Parson, E. R. (1985e, September 22). *Post-traumatic stress disorder in medical settings: What treatment personnel need to know.* Invited presentation at the University of Osteopathic Medicine, Des Moines, Iowa.

Parson, E. R. (1985f, September 22). *From post-traumatic crisis to identity: The role of the mental health practitioner in recovering from Vietnam.* Invited paper presented at Drake University. Des Moines, Iowa.

Parson, E. R. (1985g, September 24). *Race and trauma: The black Vietnam veteran in transition.* Invited paper presented at the Black Congressional Caucus Conference. Washington, DC.

Parson, E. R. (1986a). Transference and post-traumatic stress: Combat veterans' transference to the Veterans Administration Medical Center. *The Journal of the American Academy of Psychoanalysis, 14*(3), 349–375.

Parson, E. R. (1986b). Life after death: Vietnam veterans' struggle for meaning and recovery. *Death Studies, 10,* 11–26.

Parson, E. R. (1987, April). *Freud, veterans, and social policy.* Paper presented at the spring meeting of the Division of Psychoanalysis, American Psychological Association.

Parson, E. R. (1988). The unconscious history of Vietnam in the group: An innovative model for working through authority conflicts in guilt-driven Vietnam veterans. *International Journal of Group Psychotherapy.*

Penk, W., Rabinowitz, R., Bell, W., Patterson, E., Dorsett, D., Ames, M., & Peck, R. (1985). *Ethnic differences in family environments of Vietnam combat veterans seeking treatment for substance abuse.* Unpublished manuscript.

Piaget, J. (1954). *The construction of reality in the child.* New York: Basic Books.

Ransom, L. (1983). Black Vietnam vets: Study says they suffer more. *National Leader, 2*(16), 1–11.

Readjustment Counseling Service. (1984). *Report of the working group on black Vietnam veterans.* Washington, DC: VA Central Office.

Reik, T. (1949). *Listening with the third ear.* New York: Ferrar, Straus and Young.

Saretsky, T. (1981). *Resolving treatment impasses: The difficult patient.* New York: Human Sciences Press.

Scarano, T. (1982). Family therapy: A vviable approach to treating troubled Vietnam veterans. *The Family Therapist, December,* 4–9.

Schafer, R. (1954). *Psychoanalytic interpretation in Rorschach testing: Theory and application.* New York: Grune & Stratton.

Schwartz, H. (Ed.). (1984). *Psychotherapy of the combat veteran.* New York: Spectrum Medical and Scientific Books.

Scurfield, R. (1985). Post-trauma stress assessment and treatment: Overview and formulations. In C. R. Figley (Ed.), *Trauma and its wake, I: The study and treatment of post-traumatic stress disorder* (pp. 219–256). New York: Brunner/Mazel.

Scurfield, R., & Blank, A. (1985). A guide to obtaining a military history. In S. Sonnenberg, A. Blank, & J. Talbott (Eds.), *The trauma of war: Stress and recovery in Vietnam veterans* (pp. 263–295). Washington, DC: American Psychiatric Press.

Shatan, C. F. (1972, May 6). Post-Vietnam syndrome. *The New York Times,* p. 35.

Shatan, C. F. (1973). The grief of soldiers: Vietnam combat veterans self-help movement. *American Journal of Orthopsychiatry, 43,* 640–653.

Shatan, C. F. (1974). Through the membrane of reality: Impacted grief and perceptual disonance in Vietnam combat veterans. *Psychiatric Opinion, 10*(6), 6–15.

Shorr, J., Sobel, P., & Connella, J. (1980). *Imagery: Its many dimensions and applications.* New York: Plenum Press.

Silver, S., & Iacono, C. (1986). Symptom group and family patterns of Vietman veterans with post-traumatic stress disorders. In C. R. Figley (Ed.), *Trauma and its wake, II: Theory, research and intervention* (pp. 78–96). New York: Brunner/Mazel.

Smith, C. (1980). Oral history as "therapy": Combatant's accounts of the Vietnam war. In C. R. Figley & S. Leventman (Eds.), *Strangers at home: Vietnam veterans since the war* (pp. 8–34). New York: Praeger.

Smith, J. R., Parson, E. R., & Haley, S. A. (1983). On health and disorder in Vietnam veterans: An invited commentary. *American Journal of Orthopsychiatry, 53,* 27–33.

Spiegel, D. (1981). Vietnam grief work using hypnosis. *American Journal of Clinical Hypnosis, 24,* 33–40.

Stolorow, R., & Lachmann, R. F. (1980). *Psychoanalysis of developmental arrests.* New York: International Universities Press.

Van Putten, T., & Emory, W. (1973). Traumatic neurosis in Vietnam returnees. *Archives of General Psychiatry, 29,* 695–698.

Watkins, J. (1949). *Hypnotherapy of war neuroses.* New York: Ronald Press.

Watkins, J. (1971). The affect bridge. *International Journal of Clinical and Experimental Hypnosis, 19,* 21–27.

Williams, C., & Williams, C. (1985). Family therapy for Vietnam veterans. In S. Sonnenberg, A. Blank, & J. Talbott (Eds.), *The trauma of war: Stress and recovery in Vietnam veterans* (pp. 194–209). Washington, DC: American Psychiatric Press.

Wilson, J. (1977, August). *Identity, ideology and crisis: The effects of the Vietnam war on the psychosocial development among Vietnam veterans.* Paper presented at the American Psychological Association Conference, San Francisco.

Wilson, J. (1978). *Identity, ideology and crisis: The Vietnam veteran in transition* (Vol. II). Washington, DC: Disabled American Veterans.

Wilson, J. (1980). Conflict, stress and growth: The effects of war on psychosocial development among Vietnam veterans. In C. R. Figley & S. Leventman (Eds.), *Strangers at home: Vietnam veterans since the war* (pp. 123–165). New York: Praeger.

Wilson, J. (1986). The etiology, dynamics and principles of treatment of post-traumatic stress syndromes of Vietnam veterans. In F. Ochberg (Ed.), *Post-traumatic therapy* (pp. 130–157). New York: Brunner/Mazel.

Wilson, J. P., & Krauss, G. E. (1985). Predicting post-traumatic stress disorder among Vietnam veterans. !n W. Kelly (Ed.), *Post-traumatic stress disorder and the war veteran patient* (pp. 102–147). New York: Brunner/Mazel.

Wilson, J. P., & Zigelbaum, S. D. (1986). PTSD and the disposition to criminal behavior. In C. R. Figley, (Ed.), *Trauma and its wake: Theory, research and intervention* (pp. 305–323). New York: Brunner/Mazel.

Wylie, R. (1968). The present status of self theory. In E. Borgatta & W. Lambert (Eds.), *Handbook of personality, theory, and research* (pp. 81–94). New York: Rand McNally.

12

Treatment Issues in the Psychotherapy of Holocaust Survivors

PHYLLIS EHRLICH

INTRODUCTION

Treatment issues in the psychotherapy of Holocaust survivors for the 1980s and the future need to be based upon a continuum of underlying issues including Holocaust experiences, adjustment through the intervening years, and the aging process. Recomendations for treatment modalities and worker roles will be drawn from a review of issues of survivorship, issues in the process of aging, and the integration of these issues in a societal perspective for the survivor in late life.

With the "conspiracy of silence" somewhat behind us, a new approach to treatment models must be designed to integrate the survivors' Holocaust experiences with 40 years of adaptations. Incorporating this passage of time dictates that clinical services for Holocaust survivors and families should be provided within the boundaries of gerontological perspectives. Whether one is discussing Holocaust survivors who fled Europe as children or adults pre-1939, or those who survived the Nazi occupation in Europe post-1939, all approach or are well into their aged years today. Heterogeneity rather than homogeneity characterizes this population. Therefore, a variety of treatment approaches are needed in therapeutic interventions in order to meet the diverse needs of survivors of the Holocaust.

A literature search has indicated that there are a limited number of manuscripts or unpublished studies utilizing a gerontological perspective.

PHYLLIS EHRLICH • Benjamin Rose Institute, Cleveland, Ohio 44115.

Noteworthy are the descriptive manuscripts of Rosenbloom (1985) and Steinitz (1982); the service delivery articles of Hirschfeld (1977) and King (1977); and the studies of Kahana, Kahana, and Harel, (1985), Lutwack (1984), and Shanan and Shahar (1983). Unfortunately, the earlier psychodynamic literature (e.g., Berger, 1977; Bettelheim, 1943; Krystal, 1968; Niederland, 1965), though valuable as background and preparatory information for today's counselor, is inadequate for designing appropriate interventions for service to elderly Holocaust survivors and families in the 1980s and beyond. They deal neither with change over time nor with the effects of aging.

As a result, the concepts in this chapter have been developed from this author's gerontological therapeutic experiences, the current, albeit limited, literature, and interviews with therapists and leaders in the Oral History Program of the Southeastern Florida Holocaust Memorial Center. This chapter has been developed inductively, drawing its recommendations for treatment modalities and worker roles from a review of (a) issues of survivorship, (b) issues in the process of aging, and (c) the integration of these issues in a societal perspective for the survivor in later life. For ease of presentation, group descriptors such as *survivor* and *aged* are used throughout this chapter; the need for individualization, however, is recognized. The terms *clinician* and *client,* rather than *therapist* and *patient,* are used in an effort to broaden the treatment concept beyond the medical model with its high emphasis on pathology as ubiquitous in survivorship. Survivors will be considered as normal people who lived through an abnormal experience.

ISSUES IN SURVIVORSHIP

Newman (1979), synthesizing much of the early literature, suggests that regardless of predisposing personality factors and specific Holocaust experiences, all of the survivors experienced some of the following:

- A prolonged state of helplessness
- Deprivation in individuality and autonomy (i.e., numbered and catalogued as "things" and not "people")
- Loss of all reference groups (i.e., family, occupation, etc.)
- Physical and/or mental torture unrelated to individual behavior
- Recurrent episodes of terror.

Approximately 15 years after the war, Niederland (1968) listed the following traits that he defined as "survivor syndrome":

- A pervasive depressive mood
- Survival guilt complex
- Somatization, usually with hypochondriasis

- Anxiety
- Personality change
- Psychotic disturbance with depressed mood

He further suggested intensive psychotherapy as the treatment method of choice.

Assael (1984) and Leon (1982) report that aging survivors are more often and more seriously sick with poorer prognosis than control group respondents. They, as well as Eaton, Sigal, and Weinfeld (1982), report greater psychological stress among survivors. Eaton and associates also found that perceived anti-Semitism resulted in greater increase in stress levels for the survivor than the control group. Additionally, for many survivors the approach to one's own mortality appears to indicate both an acceptance of the inevitability of natural death along with a sense of invincibility in life for having faced death and survived.. Death of loved ones or separation from them, however, may reactivate the former sense of all-pervasive loss.

Recent studies have begun to examine the coping responses over time that have allowed large numbers of survivors and families to become integrated and contributing members of society—to recreate life. Rosenbloom (1985) presents the theoretical questions that underlie these studies: "Did pre-existing personality and value systems play a role? Did successful coping with extreme stress enhance adaptive capacities? Did meaning attached to survival make a difference?" (p. 186).

Rotenberg (1985) in a self-study attributes his survival to four primary factors: (a) pre-Holocaust loving, positive, strongly integrated family, (b) high intellectual ability that allowed for adaptation to new learning, (c) continued faith in his ultimate survival, and (d) ability to connect with others rather than remain alone. Though only a single personal case example and not generalizable, it is interesting to note the similarity of Rotenberg's factors to Rosenbloom's questions. Kahana and associates (1985), studying predictors of psychological well-being of 283 respondents, report that among survivors, positive affect is most strongly and significantly associated with post-Holocaust adaptations and life experiences such as (a) disclosure in the sharing of Holocaust-related experiences, (b) altruism, (c) a perception that survivorship aids the adjustment to aging, and (d) a survivor spouse. These researchers conclude that 40 years after the Holocaust, the mental health of survivors differs more by the manner of coping over time than the specific stresses and trauma they endured.

Lutwack (1984) found, in a study of the relationship between coping strategies and life satisfaction and adjustment to aging among 65 concentration camp survivors, that the specific stressors or the number of coping mechanisms did not have a significant influence life satisfaction. Therefore, the value of the specific coping mechanism should be considered.

The most effective coping mechanism identified in this study included (a) focus on the present in terms of immediate acts of accomplishment, (b) rejection of defenses such as fatalism, which prevent one from becoming an active participant in the process of counteracting stress, and (c) participation as a giver and receiver of help through a network or a social support system. Significant demographic variables impacting on life satisfaction were (a) date of arrival in the United States (sometimes referred to as new birth date), (b) year of birth, (c) current employment, and (d) for camp survivors, the number of months spent in the camp.

Shanan and Shahar (1983), studying long-term effects of exposure to prolonged massive trauma of 90 Israeli respondents, found that survivors who were successfully coping tended to (a) be more task oriented, (b) cope more actively, and (c) be more highly involved with social networks and their occupations than those in the study who had been Israeli residents during World War II. A lower (not pathological) level of cognitive functioning was interpreted as related to the compensatory mechanisms of denial and detachment as a means of coping with extreme stress. Overall, however, Shanan and Shahar found that the survivors reported more stability during the past decade and more satisfaction with their present situations.

Steinitz (1982), reporting data from 550 community-living Jewish survivor clients, suggests that successful coping mechanisms and adaptation requires (a) meaningful family roles, (b) voluntary activities and employment, and (c) concentration on the future.

These studies leave us with many unanswered questions about the relationship of survival coping mechanisms to later social adaptations. The overlapping coping mechanisms and adjustment patterns as described suggest, however, a direct relationship to adjustment to the aging process.

In summary, the themes of the preceding post-Holocaust studies suggest a pervasive sense of loss: loss of family and friend support networks, loss of control for even simple daily decisions, and loss of ability, through bodily changes and illness. Issues of loss of control, helplessness, dependency, and inability have been related to factors of illness and physical decrements for survivors. The pyschological literature today identifies the support network as a buffer to life's stressors; the extended family of parents, grandparents, siblings, children, and grandchildren primarily serves this function. For many survivors, this was not an option. As the data indicate, there were no parents to serve as role models, no siblings with whom to share, and no normal opportunity to mourn these losses. New family constellations had to be created; this was accomplished primarily through the survivors' network of social clubs and informal communication. The studies of lifelong coping mechanisms leave us with many unanswered questions about the relationship of survival coping mechanisms to later social adaptation.

One caveat to the clinician is to be aware that battle lines may be too easily drawn between the defenders of the early psychodynamic analysis of survivorship that identified the characteristics of "concentration camp" and "survivorship" syndromes (Bettleheim, 1943; Niederland, 1968) and the defenders of the belief that the successful societal integration of so many survivors suggests a lack of effect of post-traumatic disorders (Peskin, 1981). The critics of early psychiatrists explain the highly pathologic nature of this initial material by the fact that psychiatrists wrote of self-selected patients who came to the therapist for counseling and who also had as another agenda the necessary assessment of pathology to obtain reparations. The defenders of the latter interpretation point with pride to the case studies that abound regarding socially and economically successful Holocaust survivors and children of survivors. The arguments of neither side appear generalizable to the total survivor population. Just as survivor samples were biased in the pathology studies, so too are they in the "healthy" studies, thus rendering only limited applicability to the population of survivors and children at large. This either/or debate is of little value to the clinician who explores all areas for potential causal and adaptive factors in the determination of appropriate interventions. The overlapping coping mechanisms and adjustment patterns as described suggest, however, a direct relationship of adjustment to the aging process, a process in which many survivors are engaged today. The following section outlines the issues in the aging process in order to examine the integrative factors of survivorship and aging.

ISSUES IN THE PROCESS OF AGING

Monk (1985) theorizes that

> even when conceptually isolating aging, youth or middle age, each must be viewed in light of the entire life continuum, the pathways of a person's entire life and how they were shaped in each instance by social and historical circumstances. (p. 12)

Within this life-course approach, each period of life still retains its distinct characteristics (Erikson, 1982).

Peck (1968), acknowledging his debt to Erikson's conceptualization of the final crisis period of integrity versus despair, poses three developmental tasks for late life.

1. *Ego differentiation versus work role preoccupation.* One redefines one's worth as separate from a prior role such as work and shifts to new, accepting roles of intra- as well as interpersonal relationships.

2. *Body transcendence versus body preoccupation.* One handles physical power decline, lowered resistance to illness and recuperative powers by defining well-being in terms of satisfying relationships and activities.

3. *Ego transcendence versus body preoccupation.* One adapts positively to

the inevitable prospect of death and devotes one's energy to helping others so they may be happy now and after one's death. This approach not only ensures others' well-being but develops a satisfying and preferable alternative to denial of mortality.

Peck's triad of tasks is useful in that it takes a positive approach to what are usually considered unwelcome aspects of aging and supports personality change as possible in old age. This understanding indirectly supports the potential for relationship realignments as a natural outgrowth of readjustment to self in an old-age perspective.

Adaptation to these psychological tasks is the challenge of positive aging. This must be accomplished in spite of the social, physical, and environmental pressures that negatively impact upon the aged person today. Major pressures affecting adaptation are the following:

1. *Societal stereotypes.* The aged years of life (60+) continue to be seen as a downward spiral in which aging is synonymous with frailty, nonproductivity, and withdrawal. In spite of an ever-increasing number of active, productive, and alert older people, many accept this philosophy for themselves; many young persons shun the aged out of fear of their own aging process.

2. *Societal changes.* The spiral of technological change challenges the ability of elderly persons to adapt their own lives and contribute to integenerational relationships on other than an affective level. Toffler (1970), in *Future Shock,* dramatically presents the issue of the speed of change in our society to which the aged, as all of us, must continually adjust:

> The world of today . . . is as different from the world in which I was born as that world was from Julius Caesar's. I was born in the middle of human history, to date, roughly. Almost as much has happened since I was born as happened before. (p. 13)

That was 1970. The speed of change continues forward.

3. *Losses.* Losses exert a negative impact at any age. Adaptation to the multiple losses of aging necessitates expending a considerable amount of psychic and physical energy. The reality of the problems of adapting to the intrinsic and extrinsic losses of late life is compounded by the need to deal simultaneously with the social stereotypic attitudes and technological changes previously mentioned.

Butler and Lewis (1982) provide an excellent list of the most significant extrinsic and intrinsic factors that one in the aging process must generally confront. These factors include personal and social losses, socioeconomic adversities, physical illness, and bodily decline as well as the expectable changes that come with aging.

4. *Environmental dependency.* Lawton (1980) conceptualized differential changes in vulnerability. His "theory of environmental press" points out that, as the competence of the individual decreases, the proportion of behavior attributable to the environment increases; that is, the less compe-

tent person's behaviors are more controlled by environment than by intrapersonal forces.

In Lawton's theory, there is generally a balance between demand and individual competence. If the balance is there, the effect is positive. If the demands are too great, then this will result in distress and negative reaction. Concommitantly, if the environmental demands are too low (a boring, unstimulating environment), this too can have a negative effect. The issue is the fit of interaction; that is, low competence and low press equals adaptation.

Though environmental press affects all ages, the higher physiological competence level of younger people generally enables them to rise above this. With elderly persons and families dealing with adjustments to lowered mobility and competence, the issue of environmental dependency frequently reaches crisis proportions as relocation to congregate or institutional sites are considered.

5. *Intergenerational dependency.* The myth that children as a group desert their elderly parents has long been disproved (Brody, 1985; Shanas 1979); intergenerational support is prevalent for nearby, as well as dispersed families (Moss, Moss, & Moles, 1985). These positive findings have associated with them, however, the fear of dependency on the part of the elderly and frequently, for significant others, the pressures of caregiver burden (Zarit, Rever, & Bach-Peterson, 1980). Working through the issue of dependency requires for elderly the ability to develop "responsible dependency"—a concept developed by Myrna Lewis (Butler & Lewis, 1982). Lewis described this concept as:

> the realistic evaluation of when one begins to require help from others and an ability to accept that help with dignity and cooperativeness, rather than denying the need or abusing the opportunity to be dependent. (p. 58)

To achieve a level of "filial maturity" (Blenkner, 1965) in which the child recognizes both personal and parental limitations and, in that perspective, offers support without the demand for control or dependency, is the task of the younger generation.

These five categories of pressures underlying the elderly person's ability to adjust to the life crises of old age generally occur regardless of one's educational, social, or economic status. Specific crises common to late life may include widow(er)hood, retirement, reduction in household size, sensory decrements, physical pain, decreased mobility, spouse caregiving, hospitalization, institutionalization, lowered income and social status, and significant others' death. Common emotional reactions that may occur in the adjustment to late life changes include loneliness, depression, anger, guilt, grief, anxiety, and helplessness. Rosow (1974) hypothesized that late life stressors have a greater effect on elderly persons as they are experiencing an increasing number of losses at a time of diminishing resources and abilities. Despite the potential for greater negative impact from a list of stressors that could be overwhelming for even the young, it is encouraging to note that most elderly persons do adapt to late life changes. Coping mechanisms (stress reducers) are not necessarily age-related.

Effective coping strategies for elderly persons are an interaction of instrumental activities and personality characteristics. Key among the instrumental strategies is the ability to maintain a formal/informal support network and the ability to modify environmental press to a level of "person–environment" fit (Kahana & Kahana, 1983). Limited resources may hinder the ability of some elderly to utilize all instrumental options. Equally effective as positive coping strategies are personality characteristics that may include an insistence on an ongoing role in problem solving, and an open, flexible state of mind. These latter personality coping strategies for late life adjustment are most powerful in that they remain in the control of the aged person.

In summary, differing cognitive and behavioral coping styles developed over the course of a lifetime of experiences allow elderly persons to respond differentially to stressors. Too frequently, helpers, in their desire to protect, fail to remember that elderly people have brought to their later years the experiences and knowledge of younger days. Aging is a process; old age is not suddenly superimposed upon life.

As Holocaust survivors enter late life, the experiences of survivorship and those of "old aging" appear to mesh. Inadequate coping mechanisms of the former period interfere with successful coping strategies at this period; a high functional level in the past provides no assurance of avoidance of present dysfunction. For example, one whose manner of survivorship coping strategy was repression through high investment in economic gain, may find retirement to be a period of return to high stress. Effective treatment is built upon an integration of survivor and aging issues as outlined in the next section.

INTEGRATING SURVIVOR AND AGING ISSUES: THE FRAMEWORK FOR TREATMENT

The overlapping issues of survivorship and aging can be conceptualized as consisting of five global areas encompassing attitudinal factors for therapists and clients and client effective and instrumental behaviors.

1. *Requests for service.* Survivors, as a rule, did not seek out mental health services in their younger days. This would appear to be illogical behavior considering the psychic/physical devastation brought by the Nazis. Survivors did not seek help because of lack of trust that anyone could help them; they had faith only in themselves and other survivors. The silence of the Jewish and professional community reinforced this sense of social marginality and alienation. Those who enter the system today are

frequently motivated by aging issues that are expressed by requests primarily for concrete assistance.

This reluctance to seek help is magnified in later life as older persons in general frequently deny the need for counseling as this concomitantly suggests to them a loss of autonomy. The entré for the clinician then is frequently the provision of a concrete service(s) into which he/she integrates opportunities for counseling with a goal of late life adjustment.

Zarit (1980), recognizing that therapists frequently reject this approach and therefore avoid providing service to elderly persons, suggests that:

> many older clients may not perceive the potential benefits of counseling or may be unwilling to request counseling because of its negative connotations. When given assistance with other matters, like physical or housing problems, they may spontaneously engage the staff person in a counseling process. When a program is organized in this practical way, clients will neither have an unnecessary label attached to their concerns, nor will they feel shuffled around from one person to another, and the trust established in working on other difficulties can facilitate the counseling. (p. 272)

2. *Counselor attitudes.* It is considered axiomatic that a counselor cannot work effectively with a client he or she neither likes nor understands. This issue is compounded for those working with aged survivors and/or aged persons in general. Most workers have not experienced the Holocaust and are too young to be personally dealing with the issues of "old aging." Dreifus (1980), addressing the Jewish therapist, suggested that "in order to be able to help, . . . one has to wrestle with the problems of the Holocaust brought into the consulting room" (p. 40). This in itself may be an insurmountable challenge. However, to work with the aged, the clinician must also be ready to wrestle with his or her own finiteness and declining sense of invincibility.

3. *Life course development.* Survivor means strength; aging is built on strength. The longer people live the greater the strengths that are developed to adapt to change, both societal and personal. The Holocaust survivors, many of whom became productive, contributing citizens in the United States, Israel, and elsewhere, are certainly a testament to this phenomenon. Practitioners with older clients recognize that though they may be resistant to change, the elderly as a group do adapt and integrate change into their lives. The clinical issue is to identify, respect, and build upon the strength rather than to overprotect and reinforce only the residual scars of survivorship.

4. *Common emotional reactions.* Emotional reactions most common to elderly persons dealing with the negative stressors of aging include loneliness, depression, anger, guilt, grief, anxiety, and helplessness. Steinitz (1982) identified and charted similar reactions in greater intensity for the survivor under headings of psychological depression, paranoid reactions, sleep disturbances, and severe loneliness or isolation.

5. *Coping strategies.* The stressors of survivorship and those of old aging

appear similar in content though perhaps not in intensity. The following typify those pressures to be confronted and resolved:

- *Societal stereotype and internalized rejection.* Society rejected the survivor through silence and continues to reject the elderly population through reinforcement of negative stereotypes. In both groups, this has led to an inability to let one's guard down and, too frequently, to an internalization of the societal rejection.
- *Ongoing losses.* Ongoing losses of all types were a concomitant part of the Holocaust experience that is repeated in old age. Whereas loss of loved ones was an unnatural process for the survivor, it is a natural process for the aged. Chronic illness with its downward trajectory is also part of the aging process. The elderly tend to deny illness in order to remain independent; the survivor has problems in accepting a second period of decline. Luck may have been a rationale for survivorship; luck has far less credence in old age.
- *Autonomy versus dependency.* The right to your own decisions—to your own folly—was the driving force for the survivor in the building of a new life. It remains the overriding issue of aging in which economic resources and physical acumen decline. Institutionalization, then, becomes the ultimate loss of control.
- *Alienation.* Society had no role models for understanding survivorship. There are few role models for successful aging. This lack of understanding has frequently led to group rejection.

Thus, it bears reinforcing to say that coping mechanisms are not age-related. The strategies already isolated as successful for survivorship such as disclosure, altruism, involvement in network reciprocity, and forward thinking are replicated for successful aging.

The perspective of time provides the most salient framework within which to examine the coping strategies for both groups. The Holocaust was not one event but a series of traumatic events acted out over time; old aging is not of a moment but a process over time. In the aged survivor, then, dealing with late life issues is a return to the past that may magnify the issues and deter the adjustment to aging. Intervention provides the means to differentiate between, rather than fuse, old and current traumata. Treatment interventions adapted to meet the idiosyncratic needs of the aged Holocaust survivor are presented in the final section of the chapter.

TREATMENT INTERVENTIONS FOR AGED HOLOCAUST SURVIVORS AND THEIR FAMILIES

The early clinical writings on treatment interventions were all psychoanalytically oriented; long-term psychotherapy was the professional's treatment of choice for the adult survivor. This recommendation for the relatively small percentage of survivors requesting mental health care post-World War II may have been appropriate; it is still one treatment of choice.

Today, a broader segment of both young/old (60–74 years) and old/old (75+ years) survivors are seen by the clinician. Many have made their own idiosyncratic adjustments to past experiences but now appear more vulnerable to the processes and pressures of normal aging that replicate so much of their past.

Clinicians, to be effective with this target group, must recognize the interactive effect of survivorship and aging in terms of psychosocial experiences and successful coping mechanisms. At the same time, they should not assume that all late life adjustment issues are only survivor-related or that all survivors need to address these issues. It follows, therefore, that case management and treatment modalities must be individualized. Intensive psychodynamic therapy will not be discussed here as it has been adequately addressed throughout the literature.

Case Management

The case management interventive model responds to the complex situation for the frail or at-risk elderly who generally enter the system at the time of crisis in daily management. As a community-based service, it may avoid or at least delay institutionalization. The case management process includes (a) assessment, (b) development of a care plan, (c) implementation of a plan through resource coordination to meet both psychosocial and concrete needs, and (d) facilitation and monitoring of service delivery to the client (Steinberg & Carter, 1984).

The coordination of informal and formal resources as an immediate crisis response is appropriate to counteract the frequently overwhelming feeling of helplessness as elderly persons grapple with the reality of declining abilities and increasing dependence. As Zarit (1980) indicated, case management provides the entrée to a population that is generally not socialized to trust the mental health system nor see much value in "talking" therapies. Meeting crisis needs stabilizes the daily living issue, thereby opening the door for the clinician to assist the client at the psychological level as well.

Though a case management model must be included as one service for aged survivors, it should be noted that the provision of this service is frequently frustrating for both clients and workers. Clinicians resist it because it is time-consuming in terms of locating and coordinating resources, if they exist, or creating alternatives to those that are not available. At the same time, case management without the counseling component frequently leads to failure, regardless of the availability of resources as many elderly clients are quick to refuse service due to a resistance to dealing with issues of dependency, changed body image, and long-term financial demands on already limited incomes.

Planned Short-Term Treatment

A time-limited, brief approach to clinical interventions regardless of the specific treatment modality used (i.e., psychodynamic, behavioral, supportive) appears to meet the needs of the aged survivor. The brief treatment approach has a distinct process and goal. Its aim is to quickly engage the client in the problem-solving activity through a transactional approach that enhances autonomous functioning and maximizes client responsibility for treatment outcome (Lemon, 1983). Implicit in the short-term treatment approach is (a) the determination of specific workable problems that are generally conceptualized as problems in living rather than in history or pathology; (b) the setting of clear, measurable goals; and (c) the establishment of a contract to work on the designated problem(s).

The rationale for the short rather than extended treatment model for the aged survivor is that it is built upon the concept of client autonomy, maximizes the client's sense of control, and meets the reality that most elderly persons do not choose to stay in treatment for a long period of time. Short-term treatment can respond more rapidly to the need for reduction in the social and interpersonal stressors related to daily living issues. It helps reestablish lifelong coping mechanisms that may not have been the best but have gotten the person through. It demands less physical investment for the more frail elderly person and does not require long-term commitments of money and time. The elderly client sees an end in investment of energy, time, and money. The focus is on the process of client involvement and responsibility for decision making rather than on therapist analysis.

Various interventions relating to specific clinical treatment paradigms are suggested in the remainder of this chapter; all are applicable to the brief treatment model. There is no priority ordering and, in fact, more than one intervention may be used simultaneously. One caveat is that the clinician must be motivated to learn and apply differing techniques and roles from those of long-term intensive psychotherapy to a population whose present and past experiences are frequently unrelated to those of the clinician.

Cognitive Therapy

Reactive depression is one of the most prevalent conditions of elderly persons due to an inability to cope with the pressures of aging in our society. It is frequently, however, not the clients' primary presenting problem at the initial clinical session. In this perspective, a behavioral treatment model such as cognitive therapy is appropriate.

Cognitive therapy is a relatively recent, structured, time-limited treatment for depression developed by Aaron Beck, Rush, Shaw, and Emery (1979). Beck's studies were completed with young adults; Gallagher and

Thompson (1981) and Breslau and Haug (1983) applied the model to treatment of older adults. Cognitive therapy not only is a treatment of choice for the aged Holocaust survivor because of its time-limited nature and applicability to depression but also because it offers the client the opportunity to restructure thinking by examining options. As a general pattern, survivors do not see that they have options.

The cognitive model is built upon the premise that a person's behavior and affect is determined by the way he or she cognitively perceives the world. In the depressed person, the process is generally a reinforcement of the negative; cognitive treatment provides a means of breaking the vicious cycle of negativeness by exposing faulty logic and replacing the thoughts with more realistic, constructive, and adaptable ones.

The client is given the behavioral assignment of completing at home a daily dysfunctional thought record. This record requires the documentation of the (a) situation of concern, (b) immediate emotional reactions, (c) automatic thoughts and responses, and (d) alternative rational response(s). Through analysis of repetitive destructive behaviors or thoughts, the client can begin to give himself or herself permission to act differently.

The cognitive method is not an intensive process for personality change. It is, therefore, very applicable to the resistance of elderly persons to therapy. The clinician must spend time at the beginning to educate the client to the process in terms of the client's responsibility to work on change, the value of completing homework assignments, and the positive outcome of taking a few risks in the protected setting of a therapy session. At the same time, the clinician must bear in mind the overlay of societal stereotypes and pressures that, if internalized by the depressed client, become a catch-22 for change and adjustment. The clinician using the cognitive model generally plays a very active role in therapy; with the aged survivor, it is very important to remember that the client, though working as an investigative team member with the clinician, must maintain a sense of autonomy and control of the process.

Grief Counseling

Grief reaction refers commonly to the loss of loved ones through death but is a term applicable to losses of all types and at all ages. In this perspective, grief can be considered as the gradual process of severing the intense ties to a specific loss through acknowledgment of the reality while simultaneously rebuilding a new life and identity. Natural grieving is a before, during, and after process; many survivors grieved only long after the trauma or possibly not at all. For some, the issue of "survivor guilt" in old age may be related to a lifelong unresolved grief process.

Coping with losses, along with the concomitant emotional reactions of helplessness, hopelessness, anxiety, anger, rage, guilt, and the like, was a major task for survivors. In "old aging," the survivor again has to deal with similar stressors of loss. This replication of former losses in old age may either assist the survivor to adapt because of learned lifelong patterns or may exascerbate a rather tenuous adjustment. The clinician must recognize that coping with loss in late life differs from that of earlier days as there is no longer an extended future orientation with its greater potential for replacement. Grief counseling is an appropriate clinical task responding to loss as a predominant theme of old age; it provides permission to show grief.

Warden (1982) outlines the principles for effective counseling in acute grief situations following death. His model requires the active involvement of the client in the change process and encourages movement out of the clinical setting as soon as possible. At the same time, he suggests the appropriateness of an extended supportive role for the counselor. This apparent inconsistency in clinician roles is appropriate as it reinforces the aged client's autonomy, whereas, at the same time, recognizing the reality of declining abilities, networks, and other resources that may necessitate a more supportive role in the rebuilding of new resources and relationships. The Warden model adapted for generic grief counseling with aged survivors includes the following steps:

1. *Help the survivor actualize the loss.* Assist the survivor to internalize the reality and finality of loss, that is, retirement, loss of a limb, death of a child, and the like.

2. *Help the survivor identify and express feelings and grief.* Open expressions of feelings and sharing of experiences assist the survivor to adjust and build a new life. Disclosure remains a significant component of the late life grief process, as well.

3. *Assist the survivor to plan.* Problem solving for self and with others is an essential step in moving through a normal grieving process as it was for survivor life adjustment.

4. *Facilitate emotional withdrawal.* The role of the counselor is not only to facilitate the withdrawal from past ties or roles but also to enable the elderly client to find and maintain new relationships—an effort frequently difficult, particularly for elderly people to accomplish alone due to declining physical resources and energy. The maintenance of a social network no matter how small has been documented as a significant coping factor for survivors—the avoidance of aloneness and helplessness is paramount.

5. *Interpret the normalcy of the behavior.* Holocaust survivors feel most comfortable in a reference group of other survivors, and positive adjustment has been related to a survivor spouse. In old age, their reference group is much larger; survivors need help to understand that their issues now are also those of the larger cohort of which they are a part. Their lifelong identification as a "unique" group makes this task especially difficult.

6. *Allow for individual differences.* Room must be left for individuality of

grief reactions, processes, and solutions. In summary, all survivors, as well as many others, bring some of life's scars to old age. The scars of unresolved issues affect today's adjustment and the therapy. Grief counseling for social, physical, and psychological losses is one response.

Life Review

Butler (1963) suggests that "life review" is a process that occurs universally for all persons in late life. "Life review as a looking-back process that has been set in motion by looking forward to death, potentially proceeds toward personality reorganization" (p. 67). Although he considers it a normative process. Butler recognizes that for some, life review can lead to increased anxiety, depression, guilt, and despair. This is the catch-22 for the counselor with the aged survivor.

Life review, as an informal reminiscence process, proceeds naturally in counseling of aged persons. The clinicians' role is to listen and recognize that this narrative process allows the elderly person to adjust to the present through a review of the past, builds self-esteem and ego integrity, and links generations.

The counselor may also use reminiscence as a therapeutic tool through the development of more structured life review/reminiscence therapy sessions or groups. In general, life review as a therapeutic technique for elderly persons must be used selectively. It is recognized that it is best used with those who are articulate, have some insight, and a history of adequate coping capacity. Therefore, it is essential to obtain a client history before suggesting this specific therapy. Whether life review is pursued as the more formal therapy, or voluntary oral history, the following concerns remain. The greater openness of our society today to discuss the Holocaust experiences may exert undue pressure on the survivor for whom there remains unresolved tensions between the desires to remember and those to forget. The outcome may be greater psychological fallout. There may be an idealization of the past on one hand or an inability to justify uncomfortable personal behaviors on the other. Frequently, survivors talk of the experience in the third person as if it happened to someone else; the difference lies in the meaning of describing what happened to everyone and describing one's personal experiences. Nevertheless, the emphasis on "to bear witness" would suggest the appropriateness of this clinical tool in a therapeutic perspective for the Holocaust survivor. However, the experience of the Southeast Florida Holocaust Memorial Center's Oral History Program suggests that this tool, even in a nontherapy setting, is used very selectively by survivors. Of the thousands of survivors living in the South Florida area, only 375 have volunteered to formally provide taped oral histories. Disclosure has been documented as a significant coping mechanism; however, the formal setting may not be the most appropriate site for this activity.

Life review/reminiscence as a normative memory process may be part of the counseling process with aged survivors. However, the counselor must be comfortable leaving the decision to share these memories totally within the control of the survivor. Oral history to encourage self-healing rather than therapy should be the perspective of the clinical intervention for this target population.

Caregiver support groups. Children's caregiving responsibilities may range from the need for no more than a phone call to daily in-home responsibility, institutionalization, and/or guardianship. As caregiver responsibilities increase, the unresolved issues of survivor children tend to magnify the feelings of caregiver burden. The problem solving educational process of a support group with its focus on peer leadership is an appropriate and popular intervention.

Steinitz (1982) suggests that long-term care, loss and mourning, and intergenerational communication are of particular concern to survivor families. Though there may be differences in degree, these issues surface in every "sandwich generation" support group as children in the middle struggle to help parents within the framework of meeting their own and their children's psychosocial needs. It should be noted that frequently today the children caregivers are themselves elderly and may also be dealing with their own aging issues. In survivor families, however, due to later marriages, the caregivers are younger and generally have fewer, if any siblings. Though the issues may vary in degree of intensity and/or content, it is suggested that children of survivors participate in mixed "sandwich generation" support groups in order for them to develop an awareness of the normalcy of the problems and the breadth of alternative solutions.

Family Therapy

Since the 1970s, clinicians have recognized the importance of an intergenerational approach to family therapy. Considering the very close, possibly enmeshed nature of the survivor family and the priority given to the informal rather than the formal care system by the survivor family, a family therapy approach provides the means to modify unrealistic expectations within a family communication model.

Bonjean (1983) developed a problem-solving family model for counseling caregivers of dementia patients. This model is easily adaptable to intergenerational family therapy. In this process the worker (a) explores family interactions in terms of individual behaviors with or without the identified problem, (b) probes for ageist assumptions, and (c) enables the family to develop realistic goals by thinking about what it would be like when the problem is not there. The initial session moves quickly from the problem(s) to the solution(s). The focus of all other sessions is also on solutions in a behavioral perspective. What can each family member do to make things better, worse, or maintain the status quo?

A problem-solving family model provides the means to dispel dysfunctional family role expectations that are exascerbated by the greater enmeshment of the survivor family. Through improved intergenerational communication, families can dispel myths that affect attitudes and behaviors. Such myths include (a) the child caregiver/elderly care recipient as the only dichotomy, (b) tangible rather than affective support is more essential to elderly persons, and (c) support for parents is discrepant with needs of other family members. Each family member is responsible for self-clarification of expectations, communication of expectations, examining outcomes of expectations, and, when necessary, modifying or developing new or more approriate expectations (Scharlach, 1985).

CLINICIAN ROLES

The primary tool of the clinician is the self. Knowledge of steps in treatment interventions is of limited value without the personal projection of sincerity that encourages the client to trust and risk. Some guidelines for refining the clinical role with the aged survivor include:

1. Investment in developing knowledge of the history and experiences of the Holocaust and the prewar environments.
2. Learning from the client about his or her unique and shared experiences during the Holocaust.
3. Understanding the heterogeneity of the group and individualizing the needs and services.
4. Being aware of the total countertransference reaction to both person and issues.
5. Empathetic and senstive listening to what the client cannot disclose or is anxious about disclosing.
6. Being open to experience in order to understand the depth of the Holocaust experience.
7. Refraining from assuming the enforcer/authority role—that is, understand the hesitancy of the survivor to establish new and trusting relationships. Being patient for change.
8. Being able to accept anger, frustration, and intense demands.
9. Being nonjudgemental—respecting each person's history and coping styles.
10. Exploring individuality in the grieving process.
11. Refrain from overprotecting, rescuing, or victimizing the client and aid in problem solving.

Monk (1985), talking to all "helping professionals," suggests that

> Filial maturity ought not to be confined exclusively to the family domain. It has a comparable place in the processional helping relationship as a form of "therapeutic maturity" that begins by precluding all condescension, pseudofamiliarity, and attacks

> on the older person's sense of privacy. . . . Therapeutic maturity is launched with the emphathetic endeavor of reaching out to the client's feelings of self-esteem and playing them out as one's own. It continues with the helpers' reflecting on their own feelings and attitudes toward aging as a life process and toward the aged as people. (p. 8)

Though the period of the "conspiracy of silence" may be behind us, the challenge to develop services of "therapeutic maturity" to meet the needs of the aged Holocaust survivor and family remains. The population of Holocaust survivors deserves this professional commitment. The value of such service development goes far beyond meeting this population's needs; it provides the foundation for the analysis design, and/or replication of therapeutic interventions for wartime veterans, rape victims, and members of other victim groups who experienced trauma in their past and now deal with life's aging issues as well.

REFERENCES

Assael, M. (1984). The aging process in Holocaust survivors in Israel. *American Journal of Social Psychiatry, 4,* 32–36.

Beck, A., Rush, J., Shaw, B., & Emery, G. (1979). *Cognitive therapy of depression.* New York: Guilford Press.

Berger, D. (1977). The survivor syndrome: A problem of nosology and treatment. *American Journal of Psychotherapy, 31,* 238–251.

Bettleheim, B. (1943). Individual and mass behavior in extreme situations. *Journal of Abnormal and Social Psychology, 33,* 417–452.

Blenkner, M. (1965). Social work and family relationships in old age. In E. Shanas & G. Streib (Eds.), *Social structure and the family: Generational relations* (pp. 46–59). Englewood Cliffs, NJ: Prentice-Hall.

Bonjean, M. (1983). *Brief systematic psychotherapy with caregivers of demented family members.* Paper presented at the annual meeting of the Gerontological Society of America, New Orleans, LA.

Breslau, L., & Haug, M. (1983). *Despression and aging: Causes, care, and consequences.* New York: Springer.

Brody, E. (1985). Parent care as a normative family stress. *The Gerontologist, 25,* 19–29.

Butler, R. (1963). The life review: An interpretation of reminiscence in the aged. *Psychiatry, 26,* 65–76.

Butler, R., & Lewis, M. (1982). *Aging and mental health: Positive psychosocial and biomedical approaches.* St. Louis: C. V. Mosby Co.

Dreifus, G. (1980). Psychotherapy of Nazi victims. *Psychotherapy and Psychosomatics, 34,* 40–44.

Eaton, W., Sigal, J., & Weinfield, M. (1982). Impairment in Holocaust survivors after 33 years: Data from an unbiased community struggle. *American Journal of Psychiatry, 139,* 773–777.

Erikson, E. (1982). *The life cycle completed.* New York: W. W. Norton.

Gallagher, D., & Thompson, L. (1981). *Depression in the elderly: A behavioral treatment manual.* Los Angeles: University of Southern California Press.

Hirschfeld, M. (1977). Care of the aging Holocaust survivor. *American Journal of Nursing, 77,* 1187–1189.

Kahana, B., & Kahana, E. (1983). Stress reactions. In P. Lewinson & L. Teri (Eds.), *Clinical geropsychology: New directions in assessment and treatment* (pp. 139–169). New York: Pergamon Press.

Kahana, B., Kahana, E., & Harel, Z. (1985). *Predictors of psychological well-being among survivors of the Holocaust.* Paper presented at the annual meeting of the American Orthopsychiatric Association.

King, S. (1977). Counseling the younger elderly. *Journal of Jewish Communal Service, 54,* 26–31.

Krystal, H. (1968). The problem of the survivor. In H. Krystal (Ed.), *Massive psychic trauma.* New York: International Universities Press.

Lawton, M. P. (1980). *Environment and aging.* Monterey: Brooks/Cole.

Lemon, E. (1983). Planned brief treatment. In A. Rosenblatt & D. Waldfogel (Eds.), *Handbook of clinical social work* (pp. 401–419). San Francisco: Jossey-Bass.

Leon, G. (1982). The mental resiliency of Holocaust survivors. *Psychology Today, 16,* 18.

Lutwack, P. (1984). *The psychology of survival: Effective coping strategies used in Nazi concentration camps (Implications for the elderly).* Unpublished doctoral dissertation, University of Florida, Gainsville, Florida.

Monk, A. (1985). *Handbook of gerontological services.* New York: Van Nostrand Reinhold Co.

Moss, M., Moss, S., & Moles, E. (1985). The quality of relationships between elderly parents and their out-of-town children. *The Gerontologist, 25,* 134–140.

Newman, L. (1979). Emotional disturbance in children of Holocaust survivors. *Social Casework, 60,* 43–50.

Niederland, W. (1965). Clinical, social, and rehabilitation problems in concentration camp survivors. *Journal of Jewish Communal Service, 42,* 186–191.

Niederland, W. (1968). The psychiatric evaluation of emotional disorders in survivors of Nazi persecution. In H. Krystal (Ed.), *Massive psychic trauma.* New York: International Universities Press.

Peck, R. C. (1968). Psychological developments in the second half of life. In B. L. Neugarten (Ed.), *Middle age and aging: A reader in social psychology* (pp. 88–92). Chicago: University of Chicago Press.

Peskin, H. (1981). Observations on the first international conference on children of Holocaust survivors. *Family Process, 20,* 391–394.

Rosenbloom, M. (1985). The Holocaust survivor in late life. *Journal of Gerontological Social Work, 8,* 181–191.

Rosow, I. (1974). *Socialization to old age.* Berkeley: University of California Press.

Rotenberg, L. (1985). A child survivor/psychiatrist's personal adaptation. *Journal of the American Academy of Child Psychiatry, 24,* 385–389.

Scharlach, A. (1985). *Treating the aging family: Demystifying dysfunctional role expectations.* Paper presented at the annual meeting of the Gerontological Society of America, New Orleans, LA.

Shanan, J., & Shahar, O. (1983). Cognitive and personality functioning of Jewish Holocaust survivors during the mid-life transition (46–65) in Israel. *Archiv for Psychologie, 135,* 275–294.

Shanas, E. (1979). Social myth as hypothesis: The case of the family relations of old people. *The Gerontologist, 19,* 3–9.

Steinberg, R., & Carter, G. (1984). *Case management and the elderly.* Lexington, MA: Lexington Books.

Steinitz, L. (1982). Psycho-social effects of the Holocaust on aging survivors and their families. *Journal of Gerontological Social Work, 4,* 145–151.

Toffler, A. (1970). *Future shock.* New York: Random House.

Warden, J. W. (1982). *Grief counseling and grief therapy.* New York: Springer.

Zarit, S. (1980). *Aging and mental disorders: Psychological approaches to assessment and treatment.* New York: The Free Press.

Zarit, S., Rever, K., & Bach-Peterson, J. (1980). Relatives of impaired elderly: Correlates of feelings of burden. *The Gerontologist, 20,* 649–655.

13

The Psychiatric Effects of Massive Trauma on Cambodian Refugees

J. D. KINZIE

INTRODUCTION

From 1975 to 1980 the brutal Pol Pot regime in Cambodia brought destruction, death and extreme suffering to the Cambodian people. From that tragedy, we have learned some of the personal and clinical effects of extreme trauma. The Cambodians, surviving such adversity without knowledge of Western psychiatric concepts and without recourse to financial compensation, have given us a unique opportunity to study the outcomes of stress. Our research and clinical goals are to improve clinical treatment of these victims who now make their homes in many American communities.

The goals of this paper are to describe in this victimized population:

- The clinical syndromes
- The symptom patterns clarifying the diagnostic implications of these symptoms in relation to post-traumatic stress disorder (PTSD)
- The natural history of the course of PTSD among Cambodians
- The treatment implications of these findings

HISTORY OF CAMBODIAN AUTOGENOCIDE

Until 1970, Cambodia was a relatively rich and stable Southeast Asian country. The majority of the people lived in small villages, engaged in

J. D. KINZIE • Department of Psychiatry, Oregon Health Sciences University, Portland, Oregon 97201.

agriculture, and followed the Buddhist religion. The Indochinese was expanded into Cambodia in 1970 and subsequently the Western-oriented government was replaced by the Communist government of Pol Pot (Khmer Rouge) in 1975. In the next 4 years, between 1 million and 3 million of Cambodia's population of 7 million died. Hundreds of thousands were executed, whereas others died of starvation and disease in forced labor camps. In this radical revolutionary movement to make a new society, many influential citizens representing traditional values were killed or displaced. These included Buddhist monks and medical, legal, and educational professionals as well as urban business leaders. The infliction of atrocities by one group of Cambodians on another resulting in one of the most violent blood baths in the twentieth century was termed *autogenocide.* The violence ended finally in 1979 when the Vietnamese ousted the Khmer Rouge government.

The revolution not only caused the deaths of millions of people but destroyed the basic pattern of Cambodia's culture. The destroyed basic values of Cambodian society included a strong family identity, respect for ancestors, a need for smooth interpersonal relationships, and a willingness to accept things the way they were. Because much of Buddhist doctrine teaches that personal misfortune is inevitable, many Cambodians sought comfort and relief from unhappiness in supernatural beliefs and ancestral or animistic worship. These provided a more satisfying alternative to Buddhism that offered no escape from one's destiny or Karma (Boehnlein, Kinzie, Bath, & Fleck, 1985). After the Vietnamese invasion, thousands of refugees escaped to Thailand where they spent 2 to 5 years. Now over 104,000 have resettled in the United States, continuing to face other challenges such as adjusting to a new culture, learning a new language and new occupational skills, facing poverty, and dealing with familial conflicts over traditional versus American values.

BRIEF HISTORY OF THE INDOCHINESE CLINIC

Since 1978, the department of psychiatry, Oregon Health Sciences University, has sponsored a weekly Indochinese Refugee Clinic (Kinzie & Manson, 1983; Kinzie, Tran, Breckenridge, & Bloom, 1980;), evaluating almost 500 new patients. Our current caseload is over 220. Although the numbers of Cambodians originally seen were small, currently, 20% of the patients and a majority of the new patients are Cambodians. The clinic emphasizes thorough psychiatric evaluations, supportive ongoing psychotherapy, the use of appropriate psychotropic medicine. and regular counseling with mental health counselors who represent each ethnic group. Emergency room facilities and inpatient hospitalizations are available. During this time, about 85 Cambodians have been evaluated. In the current caseload of over 60 Cambodian patients, almost all suffer from PTSD. The majority of these have been followed for at least 2 years and, in some cases, for over 4 years. The interviews and therapy sessions involving patient and psychiatrist are emotionally charged, and this report does not do justice to the intensity of the shared experience.

CAMBODIAN CLINICAL STUDIES

In 1982, we became aware of the severe post-trauma reaction suffered by survivors of the Cambodian labor and concentration camps. The diagnosis was not straightforward as the original patient presentation was marked by depressive symptoms with an avoidance of talking about event in Cambodia, which we later realized was part of the syndrome. Through the structured interview and knowledge about the traumatas in Cambodia, however, we were able to report on 13 patients with PTSD (Kinzie, Fredrickson, Ben, Rleck, & Karis, 1984). The amount of trauma suffered by these patients was massive—all had family members who were executed, had disappeared, or starved to death. All were forced to evacuate their homes; their families were separated, and they endured forced labor with inadequate food, shelter, or medical attention. Indiscriminate and unpredictable killings were frequent. Although the Pol Pot camps were discontinued after 4 years, in the beginning no end was in sight, and no hope was given. The experiences of a sample of 35 patients and 40 nonclinical Cambodian children (described later) are summarized in Table 1.

Table 1. Cambodian Pol Pot "Work Camp" Experience

N	(%)	Type of experience
Adult clinic population (*N* = 35)		
35	100	Forced labor often 15 hours a day, 7 days a week for 4 years
26	74	Separated from family
28	80	Went long time without food
31	88	Violent deaths reported of family member, usually executions
20	57	Death by starvation to family members
13	37	Family members "lost," whereabouts unknown
5	14	Beaten severely
Nonclinical adolescents (*N* = 40)		
39	98	Forced labor often 15 hours a day, 7 days a week
33	83	Separated from families
33	83	Went long time without food
32	80	"Lost" family members by execution, starvation, or whereabouts unknown[a]
25	63	"Lost" fathers
15	38	"Lost" mothers

[a]Average adolescent lost 3 members of nuclear family.

Table 2. PTSD in Cambodian Clinic Patients

First study (N = 13)[a]
Present in over 75% of patients
1. Depressive symptoms
2. Avoidance of memories or activities of Cambodia
3. Nightmares
4. Recurrent, intrusive thoughts
Present in over 50% of patients
1. Detachment from others, emotional numbing
2. Exaggerated startle response
3. Intensification of symptoms by exposure to events that symbolize trauma
4. Intensification of symptoms with stress
1-year follow-up (N = 12)
Present in over 75% of patients
1. Avoidance of memories or activities of Cambodia
2. Shame or guilt about surviving
3. Intrusive thoughts (but most improved)
Present in over 50% of patients
1. Depressive symptoms (but improved in most)
2. Nightmares (but improved in most)
3. Startle reaction

[a]10 patients had a diagnosis of depressive disorder.

Depression, defined by *Diagnostic and Statistical Manual of Mental Disorders* of the American Psychiatric Association (DSM-III), was very common (see Table 2). Ten patients had a depressive diagnosis, and 9 experienced major depressive episodes. Nightmares and recurrent intrusive thoughts were frequently reported. Intensification of symptoms by events that represented the trauma (for example, news articles about Cambodia) occurred in most patients. Avoidance behavior was ubiquitous: an active conscious suppression of any memories or avoidance of activities that would remind the patients of events in Cambodia. Even so, the patients were often in turmoil because their attempts at avoidance were unsuccessful and did not prevent intrusive, disturbing thoughts. It was clear that these patients were severely impaired and that their symptoms were similar to severe PTSD, chronic type. Their symptoms were also similar to those of other victims of concentration camps such as were described after World War II.

We were able to follow 12 of the 13 patients with PTSD 1 year later (Table 2). Of these, 5 no longer met PTSD diagnosis, and 3 were much improved (Boehnlein *et al.*, 1985). Notably improved were the depressive symptoms such as interrupted sleep, poor appetite, and loss of interest in outside activities. The nightmares were markedly reduced in almost all patients, and intrusive thoughts were reduced in the majoirty. Avoidance memories or activities related to Cambodia did not change in most patients. Shame or guilt about surviving was more noticeable at follow-up than when the patients were originally evaluated. At the 1-year follow-up, we were encouraged by evidence of recovery and had more hope that some of the impairment from this disorder would be ameliorated with time. Subsequent experience did not bear this out, as will be discussed later.

CAMBODIAN CHILD VICTIMS STUDIED AS ADOLESCENTS

With the cooperation of a local high school, our group studied 46 Cambodian high-school students (out of 52 in the school), 40 of whom had been victims of the Pol Pot regime. The study used operationally defined criteria, that is, research diagnostic criteria (RDC) and the standardized interview (part of the Schedule for Affective Disorders and Schizophrenia [SADS]) by psychiatrists (Kinzie, Sack, Angell, Manson, & Rath, 1986). The students averaged 17 years of age and had been in the United States for an average of 2½ years. Previously they had spent an average of 3 years in refugee camps and had been under the Pol Pot regime for 4 years. This started at about the age of 8. The amount of trauma suffered by these students was massive (Table 1). Almost all had been in age-separated camps away from their families and had endured forced labor, often 15 hours a day, 7 days a week. They lived under starvation conditions and suffered the effects of malnutrition. The sight of corpses was common, and many children knew that members of their groups had been killed while escaping. Thirty-eight percent described beatings to themselves or members of their families; 43% saw people killed; 14 of the 40 had no family members living. The average student had lost three members of the nuclear family to death.

The results of our interviews indicated that 50% (20) fitted the full DSM-III PTSD diagnosis; 21 of the total group also had depressive disorders. Other less common disorders were panic disorders (3) and generalized anxiety disorders (7). The clinical experience involving American adolescents undergoing stressful events indicates that a common result is antisocial behavior and drug abuse. However, no cases of either were found among these Cambodian adolescents. This suggests that cultural factors strongly influence some symptom formation.

We were somewhat surprised that the full PTSD syndrome was only present in 50% of the students after such massive trauma. On reevaluation, using DSM-III criteria, it was found that 5 missed the full diagnosis because of no numbing symptoms (Criteria C). An additional 13 had other symptoms, the avoidance of activities that aroused recollection of the events, trouble concentrating, or survivor guilt but did not have the intru-

Table 3. Cambodian High School Students (N = 40)

DSM-III criteria	N	Depressive diagnosis	Complete avoidance
Full PTSD	20	17	9
PTSD (no numbing symptoms)	5	1	4
"Avoidance" symptoms only	13	5	9
Major depression only	1	1	0
No symptoms, no diagnosis	1	0	0
Total	40	24	22

sive memories or recurrent dreams. One other student had a major depressive disorder without any other symptoms, and only 1 student had no symptoms and no diagnosis. Thus, 38 out of the 40 had some symptoms of PTSD, in addition to 1 with a major depressive disorder. As is seen in Table 3, the depressive diagnoses were extremely common (RDC criteria; major, minor, and intermittent). They were most common in those who had the full PTSD. Depressive diagnoses were uncommon in those who did not have the numbing symptoms. Our impression was that, in this group and perhaps in many other Cambodians, the numbing and depressive symptoms were extremely difficult to distinguish from each other. Only when depression was present did the numbing get scored and the patient received a PTSD diagnosis. This raises further questions about the validity of DSM-III criteria as currently formulated.

In this group of students, avoidance symptoms were extremely common. From our interviews, we noticed the presence of statements of complete avoidance of any thoughts, memories, or activities about Cambodia. Twenty-two students had complete avoidance, and 9 others reported lesser degrees of avoidance, such as not specifically thinking about Pol Pot or avoiding TV and news reports about Cambodia. Additionally, 16 students said they had never talked to anyone before about their Cambodian experience, indicating further avoidance behavior. Thus it was clear that the great majority of students who had these experiences under the Pol Pot regime had some long-term effects. The full syndrome was not always present, but depressive and avoidance symptoms were common. Few escaped unaffected.

CONTINUING CLINICAL STUDIES

We have continued to evaluate our patients, particularly following the differential response to their treatment over time. Currently, we are using

DSM-III-R (a revised version of DSM-III) as our criteria for PTSD and find that it provides diagnostic criteria that more clearly follow the patterns that we see in the clinic. In our current group of over 30 patients, we have found, using DSM-III-R, that the diagnosis persists much longer than under DSM-III. This is because numbing symptoms are not a criteria in DSM-III-R. The numbing symptoms are related to or indistinguishable from depressive symptoms. Thus, as depression improves, so do the numbing symptoms, and therefore the diagnosis of PTSD is not met on DSM-III. In a review of 18 patients who had been in treatment from 6 months to 4 years (using DSM-III-R), 16 still met PTSD criteria, whereas 2 did not. The depressive symptoms improved in many of the patients, but the persistant avoidance of stimuli continued in all 18—they continued to avoid activities or situations that aroused the trauma or made deliberate efforts to avoid thoughts or feelings associated with the trauma. Further work was temporarily interrupted by an unfortunate event.

We had always been impressed by the particular vulnerability of all our PTSD patients to increased stress. Although many had improved, under academic, financial, or vocational pressures they experienced a return of all their symptoms. This was not only true of the intrusive thoughts and nightmares but also the depressive symptoms. It seemed that symptoms, particularly intrusive ones, waxed and waned over time and were reduced with treatment and increased with stress.

Because of the threats of funding cuts, our Cambodian mental health worker who had been on this project for over 5 years could not remain on the clinic staff. This meant the program would lose him as an interpreter and as counselor and therapist for the refugee patients. Many of the patients were told of this possibility by the mental health worker.

The results of this information were clearly visible by the next clinic visit in an extremely dramatic and disturbing way. All patients had a marked increase in symptoms, not just the return of nightmares and depressive symptoms but more anguish and suffering. It was as if they had given up hope, lost all security, and were reexperiencing the threats and suffering of Cambodia. Most reported onset of nightmares involving threats to themselves, death to family members, and a profound sense of being abandoned. They suffered a painful reexperience of extreme hopelessness. Of the first 13 patients evaluated following this news, 11 had a marked increase in nightmares and intrusive thoughts. The nightmares vividly relived events in Cambodia, including the torture and death of relatives. Eleven patients had an increase in depression with poor to almost absent sleep, reduced appetite, increased crying spells, and fatigue. Eight had many somatic complaints, that is, headaches and backaches—3 went to emergency rooms for alleged somatic difficulties. Two of the 13 patients had a marked increase in blood pressure. This occurred in patients who had been stable for years as well as those who were recently stabilized. Due to their continued vulnerability to stress, there was a rapid return of all symptoms even after some success in treatment.

As a postscript to the preceding, funding was secured on a relatively permanent basis. After this information was given to the patients, most, but not all, returned to their prior level of functioning.

DISCUSSION

The concentration-camp syndrome described after the Nazi Holocaust showed a particular psychopathology (Chodoff, 1975; Eitinger, 1961; Trautman, 1964). The massive trauma suffered by Holocaust victims has continued to demonstrate the near universality of symptoms and devastating long-term effects (Arthur, 1982; Klein, 1974; Kral, Pazder, & Wigdor, 1967; Oswald & Bittner, 1968). Our Cambodian patients showed almost identical symptoms, even though they came from a different culture, involving a different belief system, and lacked the knowledge and verbal ability of Western language to describe their symptoms as vividly as did the Jewish victims. Although the Cambodians' symptoms met the criteria of DSM-III for post-traumatic stress disorder, this diagnosis seems different, both quantitatively and qualitatively, from that of victims who have suffered discrete traumata such as accidents, rape, or perhaps isolated combat stress. The universality and persistence of symptoms for at least 10 years indicate the devastation these patients suffered; there is no sign of abatement. At the present time, the Cambodians represent the largest group of new patients in our clinic population.

The question has been raised of how much the Cambodians with PTSD differ from other refugees who only suffer the effects of immigration. Our clinical experience shows that the Cambodian patients are different than the Vietnamese, the Lao, and the Mien. The symptoms not present among other refugee groups include nightmares, intrusive thoughts, startle reaction, and a vulnerability to stress. The persistence of the symptoms over time also differs. Individual refugees from other cultures may have had very traumatic experiences with some PTSD being diagnosed, but these cases are relatively rare. Only 4 out of approximately 200 Vietnamese have been diagnosed as having PTSD. It had been found in other community surveys that the Cambodians are significantly more frequently depressed than any other refugee group (Rumbaut, 1985).

The symptoms of PTSD tend to overlap with those of depression. Although PTSD is listed in DSM-III as an anxiety disorder, it is not anxiety that is subjectively experienced by our patients. This may be due partly to difficulty separating the numbing response from the depressive response. In patients who suffer from massive trauma but do not have depressive symptoms, the diagnosis of PTSD by DSM-III criteria is difficult. DSM-III-

R captures the syndrome present in our clinical work more clearly because it does not require the numbing symptoms and gives more emphasis on avoidance symptoms.

The work of Horowitz (Horowitz, 1974; Zilberg, Weiss, & Horowitz, 1982) has provided the impetus for dividing the symptoms of PTSD into intrusive and avoidance categories. This is consistent with our clinical experience and has been a useful pattern. This concept was recently advanced by Laufer, Brett, and Gallops (1985), who found that distinguishing between "denial" and "reexperiencing" is an alternative approach for understanding PTSD. We have found that the two patterns exist in the nonclinical population, that is, among those experiencing intrusive symptoms and those with denial or avoidance symptoms. But all of our subjects with intrusive symptoms also had avoidance symptoms. Furthermore, in our patient population at clinic admission, the full syndrome with avoidance and intrusive symptoms plus depression was present. With treatment and time, however, the depressive component as well as the intrusive "reexperiencing" components markedly diminished, whereas avoidance behavior remained as the patients deliberately and actively attempted to avoid thinking about Cambodia or the traumata they had suffered. It would appear that the two subtypes of symptoms, in our experience, represent part of the longitudinal natural history rather than separate and independent symptoms.

Our patients are dramatically vulnerable to stress. Intensification of symptoms, especially intrusive thoughts, nightmares, and depressive symptoms, occurs under stress—financial, interpersonal, or even symbolic. This may be a major component of the syndrome. Recent reports indicate full PTSDs have occurred in World War II veterans up to 30 years after the end of the war (Christenson, Walker, Ross, & Malthie 1981; VanDyke, Zilberg, & McKinnon, 1985). These reports give added significance to the suggestion by Green, Lindy, and Grace (1985), who note the need for classifying the symptoms over time and a need for longitudinal studies on changes in PTSD symptoms. This approach is helpful in our current clinical findings. Originally, we were impressed by the persistence of our patients' symptoms. Then, in our first year of follow-up, we were greatly encouraged by the improvement. Further follow-up has shown the return of many symptoms in many patients despite stabilization through treatment and consistent financial and social support. The new episodes may be short-lived but can be long-lasting and intense. Vulnerability to stress is one of the major components in the concentration-camp syndrome and clearly needs to be considered in chronic PTSD. Our suggestion is that the designation PTSD, residual type, by given after the full PTSD syndrome has been diagnosed but during the time the patient exhibits only partial symptoms such as avoidance behavior. This is analogous to schizophrenia and implies that, in the past, the full syndrome was present, some residual

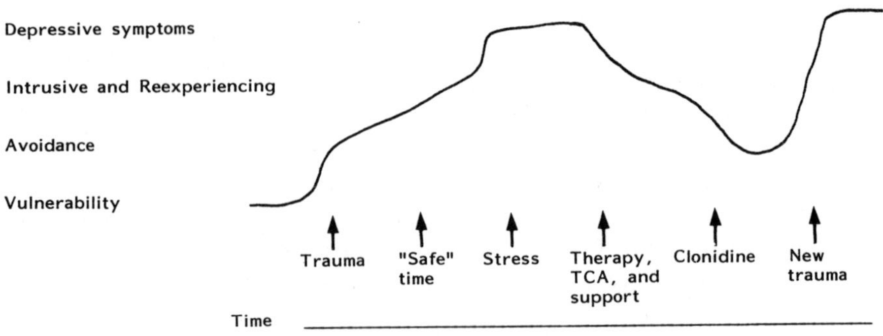

FIGURE 1. Symptoms of PTSD over time.

symptoms remain, and that there is an ongoing vulnerability for exacerbation of the disorder.

We illustrate the course of the disorder in Figure 1. The symptoms did not develop during or immediately after the trauma but only when the patients were "safe" in a refugee camp or in the United States. The symptoms of nightmares and intrusive thoughts occurred at that time and despite attempts at avoidance behavior, Often, there was discrete stress—job pressure, loss of family members through moves, or health problems—that then caused depressive symptoms. It was at this time that the patients were referred to the clinic for evaluation and therapy. With the initiation of treatment, which involved support and antidepressant medicine, the symptoms were gradually reduced. This is particularly true of the depressive symptoms and some of the intrusive and reexperiencing symptoms. Adding clonidine therapy in some patients gave further reduction of symptoms. Nevertheless, the patient always maintained avoidance behavior and remained vulnerable to stress. With new trauma, the full symptoms developed again, including depression. We have several patients to whom this cycle has recurred many times in a four-year period.

CASE EXAMPLES

A 30-year-old widowed female was originally evaluated 4 years ago. Her history revealed a very traumatic 4-year experience in Cambodia. Her husband and father were both killed, and one child died of starvation. She spent 4 years in forced labor and continually faced starvation herself. When originally seen, she was hypervigilant, moving from house to house because something in the neighborhood reminded her of Cambodia. Nightmares, insomnia, poor concentration, poor appetite, and anhedonia were present. She was begun on antidepressant medicine, and 1 year later she had improved and no longer met the criteria for PTSD. The nightmares, insomnia, poor concentration, and social withdrawal had ceased entirely. However, there was a sense of shame, decreased interest, and avoidance of all past events. Six months later, she lost her job and had somatic symptoms, the return of nightmares, startle reaction, and depression. She continued on imipramine; clonidine was added, and again she had a remission of most of her symptoms. She started back to work but immediately found the job stressful. All the PTSD symptoms returned, including nightmares, startle reaction, sleep disorders, and further avoidant behavior. Interventions enabled her to quit work, and there was a reduction in her intrusive symptoms. She remained markedly improved, although she still had PTSD. About a year later, 3 years after the original diagnosis, she was found to have mild hypertension. She remained vulnerable and was unable to work but was overtly functioning in her home. Recently, she was told that our Cambodian mental health worker who had worked with her 4 years might not be able to continue in his job. Ten days after she was told this, she was seen in our clinic, visibly upset. She trembled throughout the interview and had a dramatic increase in her blood pressure to 140/110. There was a marked increase in intrusive thoughts, nightmares, and startle reaction and she felt intensely hopeless.

A 56-year-old woman was originally evaluated 4 years ago. She had endured 4 years of forced labor under the Pol Pot regime. Her siblings were executed during this time, and some of her children died of starvation. She watched her husband die as a result of not being able to receive adequate medical treatment. When we originally evaluted her, she had a major depressive disorder and PTSD with intrusive thoughts, nightmares, some emotional numbing, poor concentration, and avoidance of any reminders of her past. She was treated with antidepressant medicine (doxepin), and after a year she was so improved she did not qualify for PTSD diagnosis. Insomnia and low interest had decreased entirely as had the hypervigilance. The nightmares and startle reaction were markedly reduced. She was subsequently seen only for supportive visits periodically, and her antidepressant medicine was stopped. During the next 2 years she did remarkably well. When told of the possible loss of our Cambodian mental health worker, she had an immediate reaction. She did not sleep for 10 days until seen in clinic. She had nightmares that involved the death of her husband "just like it was happening again." She also remembered some of the deaths of her children who died of starvation. These thoughts intruded in the daytime as well as at night. She had an increase in startle reaction and was markedly depressed. She requested multiple medications to help her cope. She felt helpless and said, "It was just like an arm and a leg had been cut off," an actual threat made to her during the Pol Pot regime.

TREATMENT IMPLICATIONS

Treatment of severely traumatized patients, who are also refugees, is an extremely difficult task. Some general principles of treatment can be briefly described. Because PTSD is a chronic disorder, therapy must be initiated only after a long-term commitment by the therapist. Time-limited therapy is contraindicated because of the pressure to achieve goals rapidly and the patient's sense of abandonment after the therapy is terminated. Therapy should be supportive. Explorative or dynamic approaches should be used only to the extent they provide clarification or meaning of the trauma to the patient. Stabilizing the environment through financial assistance and social support are necessary components of the treatment. Medications can be extremely important in reducing symptoms, for example, tricyclic antidepressants are very useful in reducing associated depression and some symptoms of PTSD; clonidine can augment the effects of the antidepressants. Because the symptoms of PTSD wax and wane, it is important for the therapist to better understand the course of the disorder and to be flexible in adjusting to the patients' needs over time.

In summary, the horrible trauma in Cambodia from 1975 to 1979 left enduring effects on its victims. These effects persist many years later and present as DSM-III diagnoses of PTSD usually accompanied by major depressive disorder. The major symptoms of PTSD include both intrusive and avoidant types. Following patients longitudinally reveals the depressive symptoms are most responsive to change and therapy. The intrusive symptoms also respond to treatment, but avoidant symptoms usually remain. Despite therapy and social support, the intrusive symptoms return at times of stress. It is hoped that further clinical experience with these unfortunate people will not only delineate the syndrome further but will reveal better treatment methods.

REFERENCES

Arthur, R. J. (1982). Psychiatric syndromes in prisoner of war and concentration camp survivors. In C. T. Friedmann & R. A. Faguet (Eds.), *Extraordinary disorders of human behavior* (pp. 47–63). New York: Plenum Press.

Boehnlein, J. K., Kinzie, J. D., Rath, B., & Fleck, J. (1985). Post-traumatic stress disorder among survivors of Cambodian oncentration camps: One year later. *American Journal of Psychiatry, 142,* 956–960.

Chodoff, P. (1975). Psychiatric aspects of the Nazi persecution. In S. Arieti (Ed.), *American handbook of psychiatry* (2nd ed., Vol. VI, pp. 932–946). New York: Basic Books.

Christenson, R. M., Walker, J. I., Ross, D. R., & Malthie, A. A. (1981). Reactivation of traumatic conflicts. *American Journal of Psychiatry, 138,* 984–985.

Eitinger, L. (1961). Pathology of the concentration camp syndrome. *Archives of General Psychiatry, 5,* 371–379.

Green, B. L., Lindy, J. D., & Grace, M. C. (1985). Post-traumatic stress disorder: Towards DSM-IV. *Journal of Nervous and Mental Disease, 173,* 406–411.

Horowitz, M. (1974). Stress response syndromes: Character style and dynamic psychotherapy. *Archives of General Psychiatry, 31,* 768–781.

Kinzie, J. D., & Manson, S. M. (1983). Five-years' experience with Indochinese refugee patients. *Journal of Operational Psychiatry, 14,* 105–111.

Kinzie, J. D., Tran, K. A., Breckenridge, A., & Bloom, J. D. (1980). An Indochinese refugee psychiatric clinic: Culturally accepted treatment approaches. *American Journal of Psychiatry, 137,* 1429–1432.

Kinzie, J. D., Fredrickson, R. H., Ben, R., Rleck, D., & Karis, W. (1984). Post-traumatic stress syndrome among survivors of Cambodian concentration camps. *American Journal of Psychiatry, 141,* 645–650.

Kinzie, J. D., Sack, W., Angell, R., Manson, S., & Rath, B. (1986). The psychiatric effects of massive trauma on Cambodian children I. The children. *Journal of the American Academy of Child Psychiatry, 25,* 370–376.

Klein, H. (1974). Delayed affects and after-effects of severe traumatization. *Israeli Annals of Psychiatry, 12,* 293–303.

Kral, V. A., Pazder, L. H., & Wigdor, B. T. (1967). Long-term effects of a prolonged stress experience. *Canadian Psychiatric Association Journal, 12,* 175–181.

Laufer, R. S., Brett, E., & Gallops, M. S. (1985). Symptom patterns associated with post-traumatic stress disorder among Veterans exposed to war trauma. *American Journal of Psychiatry, 142,* 1304–1311.

Oswald, P., & Bittner, E. (1968). Life adjustment after severe persecution. *American Journal of Psychiatry, 124,* 1393–1400.

Rumbaut, R. G. (1985). Mental health and the refugee experience: A comparative study of Southeast Asian refugees in Southeast Asian mental health. In T. C. Owan (Ed.), *Treatment, prevention, sources, training, and research* (pp. 433–486). Bethesda: NIMH.

Trautman, E. C. (1964). Fear and panic in Nazi concentration camps: A biosocial evaluation of the chronic anxiety syndrome. *International Journal of Social Psychiatry, 10,* 134–141.

VanDyke, C., Zilberg, N. J., & McKinnon, J. A. (1985). Post-traumatic stress disorder: A thirty year delay in a World War II veteran. *American Journal of Psychiatry, 142,* 1070–1073.

Zilberg, N. H., Weiss, D. S., & Horowitz, M. J. (1982). Impact of event scale: A cross-validation study and some empirical evidence supporting a conceptual model of stress response syndromes. *Journal of Consulting and Clinical Psychology, 50,* 407–414.

14

Diagnosis and Treatment of Survivor Guilt

The Bad Penny Syndrome

TOM WILLIAMS

After seeing over 2,000 trauma victims, it appears to me that the ones who do not improve in treatment are those who have not resolved their survivor guilt. At the Post-Trauma Treatment Center, we call this the "bad penny syndrome," because these clients tend to return to treatment periodically and do not seem to resolve their traumatic experiences. The DSM-III omits survivor guilt as a diagnostic criterion because some believe that it does not fit with psychically reliving behavioral symptoms or autonomic responses, but many clinicians working with trauma groups report that some form of survivor guilt is indeed a major concern for both diagnosis and treatment of trauma survivors.

THEORETICAL MODELS FOR UNDERSTANDING PTSD

In looking to theory to try to understand what seems to perpetuate symptoms of post-traumatic stress disorder (PTSD) over time, two particular models appear to be important in understanding this phenomenon. After 2 years of experience in treating armed robbery and assault victims, police officers, war veterans, and ex-POWs, we developed an acute trauma model. We have treated some 350 people utilizing the trauma team concept, which includes intervention as quickly as possible after the trauma, preferably minutes, but certainly no more than hours later. The model

---

TOM WILLIAMS • Post-Trauma Treatment Center, Aurora, Colorado 80014.

delineates three distinct phases of acute post-trauma reactions: the shock phase, the impact phase, and the recovery phase.

Two distinct emotional responses normally characterize the *shock phase:* (1) immobilization, confusion, and disorganization and (2) denial. However, people who are well-trained, such as military police or emergency medical workers, may bypass these reactions, although residual elements of them are often evident. In the *immobilization phase,* the typical response is one of confusion, disorganization, and an inability to perform such simple routine tasks as opening a cash register for a robber. In the *denial phase,* the person does not believe that the trauma is actually happening. Some victims report perceptual changes in which time is altered and events seem to be happening in slow motion. Visual perceptions may be modified so that people sometimes have a derealized "out-of-body" experience or at least feel that they are simply observing rather than participating in the trauma. Another common perceptual alteration is a hystericallike tunnel vision that focuses on the trauma scene itself to the exclusion of the rest of the environment. For example, a robbery victim focuses on a weapon directed at him or her and does not recollect what the robber looked like, what was happening, or who was standing next to the robber.

The *impact phase* starts with a period of anger and/or extreme anxiety that is manifest as trembling, or crying, or subjective feelings of tension, anxiety, outrage, or anger. Initially, this anger may be displaced as in the case of a store employee who gets angry with the store's owners for allowing themselves to be robbed instead of with the armed robber. Some war veterans have a difficult time blaming the enemy for the chaos of combat and the death and destruction and instead may blame themselves or their government or be angry at inappropriate targets.

The next step in the impact phase we call the "what-if-and-maybe" phase, or, stated simply, a process of self-doubt. This is a form of survivor guilt in which the individual questions his or her behavior during the trauma in order to try to change history and avoid facing the reality of the trauma situation. For example, a woman whose child was killed in an automobile accident may say things to herself such as, "If I hadn't been going down the road at that time, if I had not had him in the car, if only I had been on the road 10 minutes earlier, the drunk driver wouldn't have hit me." Trauma victims will go to great lengths to invent different scenarios that ignore the actual fact and outcome of the trauma. Thus, we often see self-blame in rape or robbery victims or self-doubt in police officers or war veterans who have been involved in shootings. This survivor guilt is a way in which the trauma victim avoids the facts of the trauma and may last indefinitely as the victim embroiders more and more elaborate" if-only" stories (Bard & Sangrey, 1986).

The final aspect of the impact phase is depression in its classical sense. The trauma victim generally shows the typical vegetative signs and is irritable, isolated, and feels misunderstood and hopeless and helpless about the future. If the self-doubt portion is not resolved in the impact phase, the trauma victim will continue to alternate between anger, anxiety, and depression. Hence, the victim cannot progress to the recovery phase and attempt to reestablish a normal life. Over the last several years of treating trauma victims, it has become apparent to us that surviving a trauma and dealing with it does not make a person less susceptible to additional traumata. On the contrary, we find that survivors are more sensitized and more susceptible to new trauma. If the traumata are not dealt with, understood, and put into perspective, additional stresses accumulate more easily.

In Horowitz' (1986) model of chronic stress, there is a period in which a person appears to be free of symptoms but, upon close investigation and careful discussion and observation, one notes that a trauma victim is never completely symptom free. The victim usually has difficulties with relationships, sleeping, and authority relationships and has a general feeling of being misunderstood and living a life perpetually altered by the traumatic event. I have modified Horowitz's model to describe clinical experiences with real-life trauma victims rather than theoretical models because the latter lack the overlapping phases we have seen with actual victims. This model indicates that anxiety and depressive symptoms often overlap and yet, at other times, are distinct separate stress response symptoms.

Normally, the next phase is that of intrusive imagery. We call it the *anxiety phase* because predominant mood as displayed is one of tension and anxiety. The unconscious thoughts as well as conscious memories of the trauma intrude on the mind in the form of daydreams, flashbacks, nightmares, or daytime intrusive imagery. They appear to be anxious, and their physiological arousal state is higher than normal, leading to hypervigilance, exaggerated startle response, trouble in concentrating, sweaty palms, advanced heart rate, and other traditional signs of autonomic nervous system response. Further, they complain of sleep disorders, especially initiation of sleep and, in the most severe cases, middle sleep disturbance—being awakened by nightmares—although some victims do sleep through the dream state. This phase is particularly distressing because of the psychic pain from being in a chronic, anxious state.

The next phase is the *denial phase* that we call the depressive phase. The subjective mood is one of depression. Victims have poor quality of sleep regardless of the amount of sleep, lose interest in the normal activities, and are irritable with others. They tend to be extremely isolated, psychologically distant from others, uncommunicative, and nasty. Life simply has lost its flavor for a person in this phase. Persons in the denial phase often use antidepressant-type drugs (including alcohol) or routinely have high risk vocations or hobbies that generate excitement to counter the depressive symptoms.

In our work, we have found the most difficult part of this disorder occurs when the anxiety and depressive phase overlap to create a mixture of anxiety and depression. For example, individuals may have difficulty getting up in the morning in spite of early morning awakening, will get through the day somehow in a depressed and grumpy mood, and then become tense and anxious in the evening. Following this, they may start to daydream about the trauma, becoming hypervigilant, which in turn interferes with their sleep, during which nightmares may occur. This phase is generally the one that brings people into treatment. They fear they are going crazy, because they are suffering from mood swings associated with the traumamatic event.

In the acute trauma model, self-doubt or survivor guilt keeps a person cycling between anxiety and depression. In the chronic model, people who are stuck in the mixed anxiety and depression mode maintain this position of cyclical alternation because they are unable to resolve their survivor guild. This is, of course, an exceptionally self-punitive way of coping with what happened.

If a person is able to resolve the survivor guilt and return to a relatively symptom-free mode of functioning, he or she may remain there for some time. However, we do find that a new trauma or a reminder of the original event tends to cause the victim to become symptomatic again. Similarly, an accumulation of stressors of daily life, marital or financial problems, employment difficulties, ill health, or relationship tensions may also cause the trauma survivor to become symptomatic and revert to patterns of cyclical alteration. With effective treatment, survivors can learn to control many of the symptoms of anxiety and depression and function more adaptively. However, persons who are subject to constant high levels of stress, such as emergency response workers, seem unable to remain in a symptom-free mode and experience much intrusive imagery because of constant immersion in trauma.

Another way of coping with prolonged stress is through sensation seeking to generate a high arousal state and get symptom relief through an adrenaline rush (Wilson, 1983). People suffering post-traumatic stress disorder who work in high-risk occupations frequently have interests in high-risk activities such as sports parachuting, motorcycle driving, rock climbing, car racing, or they constantly seek excitement through numerous sexual encounters.

Survivor guilt expresses itself in many ways. For example, the officer in a police shooting may be consumed with self-doubts; the rape victim may feel shame; the emergency medical person feels responsible for the death of a patient; the one who survived while others died is consumed with grief; the soldier is ashamed of his participation in battlefield atrocities. Typically, we often see these persons in the stage of alienation between anger/anxiety and depression, unable to continue the natural stress recovery process and achieve some sort of peace and understanding of their involvement in the trauma.

IDENTIFICATION OF FORMS OF SURVIVOR GUILT

Existential survivor guilt was first identified by Cobb and Lindemann (1947) in their study of survivors of the Coconut Grove fire in New York in 1942. Such guilt is characterized by the survivor's confusion over his or her having lived and the meaning of survival: "Why did I live when other people died?" With war veterans and Holocaust victims, we sometimes see variations on this theme: The survivor wishes to change places with the person who died, and the guilt is expressed as, "I should have died, and they should have lived." Often their own lives have been chaotic since the event, and they feel that the person who died would have had a better life and more to life for. War veterans frequently say that the ones who were killed in war were the lucky ones—their pain and suffering is over and their names are on a monument. After hearing about the trauma in an interview, I frequently ask, "How come you lived through that?" Often I get the response, "I don't know. I ask myself that question all the time," or "Perhaps there is some purpose for my life after facing the probabilities of my own death."

Content guilt, as contrasted with existential survivor guilt, is a result of a person's having done something to ensure his or her survival. This might include avoiding responding to others in need, having made a decision that resulted in others' deaths, and seeking refuge for oneself when others remained threatened or suffering. This is a much easier form of survivor guilt to treat because the avoidant nature of this form of guilt implies a conscious decision to act, to survive, or operate efficaciously in the traumatic environment.

Because survivor guilt has both emotional and intellectual components, a major treatment goal is to separate out the affective and cognitive elements. The survivor must learn that it is okay to feel sad about someone's having died in a traumatic situation, but it is not rational or appropriate to feel total responsibility for that person's death. A war veteran, failing to comprehend that, will blame himself for the death of a friend, whereas it was the enemy who actually killed him. Thus the patient learns that war should be blamed, not those who lived through it.

TREATMENT IMPLICATIONS

Uncorking the Bottle

The course of treatment at the Post-Traumatic Treatment Center is individual therapy followed by group or marital therapy, depending on the individual and the presenting problems. I have found that it is essential to get as complete a story as possible before putting a person in a group. Although much of the real healing often takes place in group, its precursors are in individual treatment. Putting a person in a survivors' group without knowing the story is like an attorney's examining a witness on the stand without knowing in advance what the witness would say. Not all survivors are appropriate for all groups, and most groups are homogeneous and trauma-specific (e.g., combat veterans, special operations operatives, rape victims, medical personnel, etc.).

Getting the Story of the Traumatic Event

As noted earlier, trauma victims tend to remember the actual event in a slow-motion "time warp" and often have tunnel vision—they forget many of the environmental factors in the trauma situation. The longer the trauma has been in the past, the less they seem to remember of the environmental situation.

For a therapeutic intervention to be successful, one must get the story of the trauma in precise detail. For example, it is helpful to know the details about environmental conditions, particular smells, articles of clothing, and other situational cues. It is important for them to tell you about the trauma scene as clearly and vividly as possible. It may be important for them to bring in memorabilia, such as newspaper clippings, photographs, letters written home, or perhaps audiotapes. Sometimes it is important to remind them that people do not die from crying and that once they start crying they will stop. The more they tell the story and the more successful you are with them in resolving the guilt issues, the less intense the emotions become.

Here is an excerpt from an interview that will illustrate the points just made.

TOM: When were you in Vietnam?

PAUL: 1967 to 1968. I got hit February 14, 1968.

TOM: Where?

PAUL: In Nui Nah Dinh. We were in there on a LRRP to do some reconnaissance for the 25th division.

TOM: Where in your body?

PAUL: All over. I had second and third degree burns over the upper 40% of my body. Shrapnel right-hand side of face, skull. I was shot three times, kneecap.

TOM: Bullets or fragments?

PAUL: Both. Fragments from the waist up.

TOM: Was it a .51?

PAUL: No, it was an AK-47. I got hit in the left ankle, right knee, left thigh, shrapnel right-hand side, from the waist up—it was from a grenade. I think it was made in Czechoslovakia.

TOM: How did you get the burns?

PAUL: They set the grass on fire and burned me. Trying to get me to come out—they wanted to have a party with me.

TOM: Start from the top.

PAUL: We went in, right? They had a canopy [dense tree and foliage].

TOM: How did you get in?

PAUL: We rappelled in [slid down ropes from the helicopter].

TOM: Out of what?

PAUL: I think it was a UH-4D if I remember right. We rappelled in, that was like 4:00 in the morning.

TOM: OK, how many went it?

PAUL: There was 12 of us.

TOM: A whole team.

PAUL: Yea. There was a major, a captain, I can't remember all the guys now. At daylight we started to move. Thanks to the Air Force with their recon they said that we would run into light resistance, maybe VC. The 337th NVA regimental headquarters happened to be there. Needless to say, bad day. Everybody was killed but me. Because I was point [lead man].

TOM: You were let through the killing zone?

PAUL: Yea. Standard setup. You know that as well as I do. Uh, after I got hit, I laid in the woods for 3½ days, something like that, 4 days, I lost track of time. I gave myself morphine.

TOM: You were fragged and shot.

PAUL: And burned. You know what elephant grass is? They set it on fire to smoke me so they could butcher me. I didn't come out real quick.

TOM: What happened?

PAUL: I'm on point. And we're talking daylight. About 5:30, 6:00 o'clock.

TOM: So it's light.

PAUL: Yea, it's light. They were waiting for us.

TOM: How long? Did you walk before you were hit?

PAUL: Oh, shit. Maybe, anywhere from 3 seconds to 30 minutes. We were just getting our shit together. Evidently there was a leak. They were waiting on us.

TOM: You were walking point. How far away from your slack man [the man behind the point or lead man]?

PAUL: 50, maybe 60 yards at most.

TOM: You were in elephant grass?

PAUL: I hit the grass. I was just going into the grass when we got ambushed. Then all of a sudden, you know, they hit them. I turned to go back.

TOM: What kind of fire?

PAUL: Very heavy fire. AKs. Yea, heard a few grenades go off but they were ours. Fire fight lasted maybe 3 minutes. Maybe 4. I'm not sure.

TOM: So you went back.

PAUL: I started back and then I got hit.

TOM: What hit you first?

PAUL: The gunshot hit me first. I got hit first in the left ankle. Then I went down. It was like it was in a dream. You know, it was slow motion. I got up to my right leg. I remember that clearly. Then I tried to set up. I was wanting to get back to my team. And then I got hit in the left thigh. And it wasn't real serious, just enough to knock me down again. Scrape—they call it a flesh would. I got back up and the other one hit me just, well damn near dead center in the knee but had a glancing blow and hit the bone. I went back down again. And then I remember the gooks coming out of the woods. They came after me. I got off in the grass, low crawl, dragging. Went into the grass and tried to set myself up to where I could do some business. Then all of a sudden it was real quiet, it was like in a church during a high mass. And then I remember smelling something burning, I was on fire. It may have been 30 seconds to 30 minutes, I'm not sure of time. I got hot, started burning, so I ran through the fire or crawled or whatever I done. I think I ran. Out of the woods and crawled up under some bushes and stuff and foliage and that was it.

TOM: NVA?

PAUL: NVA. They were already busy butchering what was left of the team. They had a bad habit of cutting our dicks off and stuffing them in our mouths.

TOM: Is that what happened?

PAUL: I don't know. I didn't see it. I went into shock or whatever. Mother Nature's anesthetic.

TOM: So you didn't see it.

PAUL: No. I couldn't get back to the team. Man, it was called self-preservation. Maybe I was chicken. I should have went back. But I didn't.

TOM: Why?

PAUL: I was scared. And I don't think I could have really made it. Just to be honest. Because I remember looking at my arm, the flesh was hanging off of it, the skin. And this side of my face, it was, I was bleeding really bad. I don't know if I got the blood stopped or not before I passed out. I'm not sure. Three days later the 25th division picked me up. I remember the medic saying, "this one's still alive." And then I passed out. I woke up in the 3rd Field Hospital.

Probing for Survivor Guilt

Paul gave me the facts of the story. Probing the feelings is often more difficult. While doing interviews with the trauma victims, it is helpful to be acutely aware of the subtle hints of survivor guilt. As the interview continues, note the connection between death and guilt:

TOM: What do you feel so guilty about?

PAUL: I don't feel guilty about a fuckin' thing. And even if I did, I wouldn't tell you, I would go tell the people that I feel bad about if, if I can find out where they're buried.

TOM: What's all this "if" shit?

PAUL: What do you mean *if*? If I could find out where they're at? I would. I let my partners down. I never made it back.

TOM: Tell me about it. What do you tell yourself?

PAUL: I didn't make it back.

TOM: What do you tell yourself?

PAUL: I was wounded, but I should have been with my partners. I don't want to talk now. You hear? All right? That's none of your business. Okay?

The Use of Trauma-Related Stimulus Material to Evoke Guilt and Other Emotions

An additional technique to surface guilt is to use some type of audiovisual stimulus to provoke memories. Utilizing some sort of stimulus to provoke the survivor guilt has been helpful in individual work and is especially useful in the therapy in group work. I have used some emotion-laden material, such as the Viet Vet Video production, *Wall of Tears,* to get Vietnam veterans talking about the experiences that distress them the most. Another audiovisual I have used is the last episode of *M.A.S.H.,* where Hawkeye suffers from survivor guilt when a Korean mother smothers her child in a tense situation.[1] It is much better to hear these stories in individual counseling than to have them erupt unexpectedly in group. It is my standard practice to ask group members whether they have seen anything in the media, read any books, or seen any movies that were distressing to them in order to get them to start talking.

Suppressed Survivor Guilt Requires Time to Emerge

Many stress victims are reluctant to discuss their guilt feelings or the trauma that they experienced. It is often necessary to spend several hours with them in order to uncover the traumatic situations involved. The following transcript is an interview with a Vietnam veteran. He had an abreac-

[1]I have heard several similar stories where that actually happened: from an intelligence agent during the Berlin crisis, an American U.D.T. sailor in North Vietnam during the Bay of Tonken "shoot-out," and a regular combat soldier hiding in a hut in Vietnam.

tion after about 3 years of interview. The material that came forth in that interview had been long suppressed and was so dramatic that, when it came out, he vomited.

JOHN: I'm a little leery of going to the vet center because there's a lot of Marines there and . . . it's one thing to talk about what you did over there, but it's another thing to say something you didn't do or should have done. I don't want to get anybody mad or ticked off.

TOM: Because?

JOHN: Well, I got people hurt, you know.

TOM: How?

JOHN: Well, you know, I didn't fire.

TOM: What difference would that have made?

JOHN: A lot of difference.

TOM: Why?

JOHN: A lot of people wouldn't have got hurt.

TOM: Why?

JOHN: Because I didn't fire.

TOM: How long was it between seeing movement and when the RPG [rocket-propelled grenade) hit?

JOHN: About 5 seconds.

TOM: Do you think that 4 or 5 seconds would have made any difference?

JOHN: Yea.

TOM: You think you would have killed the NVA with an RPG before they squeezed it off?

JOHN: . . . I certainly don't know . . . all I know is that I didn't do what I was supposed to do.

TOM: Afraid to fire? Or you just weren't sure?

JOHN: I wasn't sure.

TOM: You didn't know where the two guys were from the LP [listening post]. The people on the line were alerted that there was movement, right?

JOHN: Right. The jerk that was on with me fell asleep and the men on the lines were throwing rocks at us to wake us up. I woke up, you know, and all I remember was I got up and started running towards the lines.

TOM: What happened then?

JOHN: I don't know what happened to the other two guys. I don't know what happened. I just got up.

TOM: Were they there?

JOHN: I don't know. Don't ask me. [crying] I don't know.

TOM: Tell me, John.

JOHN: [crying] I can't remember.

TOM: Tell me. What went on that night? What do you keep telling yourself? What are you seeing right now?

JOHN: [sobbing/crying] They're all over us. [crying] They're all over us.

TOM: What do you mean they're all over us? What are you seeing?

JOHN: [crying] They were all over us. I . . . I don't know. I don't want to remember.

TREATMENT CONSIDERATIONS

One goal of counseling is to separate the rational or cognitive component from the emotional "grief" component. If you directly attack the survivor guilt, you may not get anywhere. Trauma victims seem to have a great need to hang on to the guilt; so to make them accessible to treatment you must let them maintain that affective component while you attack the issue of responsibility. I will often make the comment, "Gosh, that was a horrible thing. That must make you feel very sad," to give words to their feelings of grief. People with survivor guilt really don't think that others can understand them. As you continue in treatment with them and continue to give them the affective part of the survivor guilt, the anguish will diminish over time. The intensity of their sadness begins to diminish as they begin to understand more about the trauma situation. The main goal in counseling with survivor guilt is to allow them to feel sadness but to attack the issues of responsibility. There are a variety of ways of doing this, and the therapist is limited only by his or her imagination. Some suggestions are explored next.

Shared Responsibility

The technique of getting survivors to share responsibility for what happened starts with pointing out other factors involved in the incident itself. One of the factors may simply be one of time and space: They may have been in the wrong place at the wrong time; they may simply have been victims of a random act. Many people who have been raised in organized religions tend to feel that what happened to them was a consequence for some past sin. With war victims, it is important to focus on the fact that the war was responsible for the deaths; the war was responsible for the situation in which the trauma occurred. However, one must be careful to try not to absolve them of all responsibility.

Cognitive Restructuring

Survivors of trauma tend to remember the traumatic situation in an unchanged way. Their initial perception of the event is the way they continue to view it, as if the traumatic event were frozen in their memories. The healing process involves thawing out those memories and looking at them realistically. Because the memories have a very negative focus, the goal of cognitive restructuring is simply to look at the trauma in a different light. For example, a Navy SEAL (Navy special warfare team highly trained to work behind enemy lines) whom I was treating was the assassin for his SEAL team. He called himself a "murderer" and, in discussing the concept of a *murderer* with him, I suggested that, in fact, he was a *killer,* a less pejorative and more accurate term. What he was doing was not illegal and was in fact not only condoned but ordered by his seniors. It was a major breakthrough in therapy when he started to call himself simply a "killer" instead of a "murderer."

The first step a client seems to go through in cognitive restructuring is one of confusion that is an indication of cognitive disequilibration. Typically, confusion is a very positive sign that he or she is beginning to doubt the original perceptions of the situation and is realizing that perhaps the trauma has other aspects that have been ignored, forgotten, or devalued. I make a point of letting my clients know why this confusion is a good sign, a positive sign of change. When dealing with survivor guilt, it is important to find out what kinds of words people use to talk to themselves when they are thinking about the trauma situation and to help change these words to reflect the realities of their role in the traumatic event.

Clergy Referral

As many clinicians have noted, survivors of war and other traumata sometimes lose their religious beliefs. For others, religious beliefs are often strengthened by survivorship. For example, they may say, "Where was God when I needed Him?" It is my belief that trauma counselors should have contact with the clergy in their community. It is important to have a clergyman who can listen to these rather dramatic and sometimes gruesome stories in a nonjudgmental and practical way but with a sensitivity to the theological implications for the victim (Capps, 1982). In some cases, cognitive restructuring may take place within a religious ideology.

The Message Is That Victims Did the Best They Could

The central point of many of these concepts in treating survivors is to leave the person feeling that he or she did the best job in the situation that could have been done, considering the circumstances and the resources available at the time. As the individuals start to realize this, they often feel a need to do some form of restitution, such as reaching out to other trauma survivors, making themselves available to the media for discussions about their experiences, or engaging in other prosocial behavior. One way to help them get to this point is to ask them how long they need to continue to make themselves suffer. Certainly the trauma survivor feels that no amount of retribution or restitution can make up for the loss of a friend or loved one, and perhaps the best they can do for that lost person is to pull themselves together and make their own lives positive and productive.

TECHNIQUES AND SPECIAL POINTS

We have observed a variety of techniques that have been found useful with individuals suffering survivor guilt.

Developmental Considerations

Many people suffering from survivor guilt can be helped substantially if the trauma happened when they were young and their youth becomes a subject for discussion. Many Vietnam veterans were quite young when the trauma occurred, and they acted in a way that is now causing them the stress. With them, as with other young trauma victims, pain revolves around self-punitive survivor guilt that results from the way they behaved during the trauma. I discuss with them the moral development of adolescence. Essentially, adolescent idealism means that people in their late teens and early 20s hold to very high moral standards. They tend to see the world in black and white terms, but, when they find themselves in a trauma situation such as war, they soon learn that there are many gray areas. Nonetheless, they still judge themselves years later rather harshly because their moral development was, like the memory of the trauma, frozen in time in their minds. I tell them that judging themselves according to this adolescent idealism results in their being overly harsh with themselves because their moral development was sort of "frozen in time." Now they need to look at the moral aspects of their trauma behavior in light of their adult experiences in life. Adolescent idealism holds that life is fair, that good things should happen to good people and bad things should happen to bad people. Clinging to this adolescent belief system obviously leads to a very self-punitive position. As an adult they now know that life is frequently unfair.

Included in the discussion of age in relation to the trauma, it must also be noted that there were often massive amounts of peer pressure from others in the group. For instance, many combat units in the Vietnam War would cut off the ears of the enemy or slit the throat of the dead enemy soldier and "patch them" with a unit insignia so that the enemy who found the bodies of their comrades would know who killed them. Other rituals occurred, such as cutting off and braiding the hair of dead enemy women or sleeping in a body bag, that were locally designed and generally unknown to persons in command authority positions.

Empty Chair/Reversal

Gestalt techniques tend to be particularly effective in dealing with survivor guilt when one can pose such questions to the client as, "If Joe were here and alive now, sitting in that chair, would he blame you for your actions, or if you had died instead of Joe, would you blame him for your death?" One is limited only by one's imagination in utilizing such reversal techniques as writing a letter to a person who did not survive a trauma or to a dead relative with whom there is "unfinished business."

Time

As discussed earlier in the chapter, some individuals experience perceptual distortions in trauma. Events seem to unfold in slow motion, and, retrospectively, the persons tend to think that they had more time to make decisions than they actually had. It is important to clarify how much time was actually available, how quickly the decision had to be made, and that, given the information that they (not someone else) had, they were in the best position to decide how they should act and likely did the best they could. It is also important to discuss the amount of experience they had had in similar trauma situations: If they had been in combat for 6 months, one would expect a different type of response than if they were on their first day in combat. Very similar parallels can be drawn with police officers and other emergency workers.

Technical Aspects

In working with victims who have on-the-job traumata, such as military, police, medical, and other emergency workers, it may be very important to look at a trauma from a very technical sense. Did they in fact act correctly in that situation? Did they react according to procedures and standard policies? For example, I have found in working with police, military, and medical persons that in certain trauma situations they have found themselves having to make decisions that are normally made by persons much higher up in the line of authority. Consider the case of the young soldier who must call artillery fire because all of the officers are dead and the forward observer team has been killed, who gives the wrong coordinates and fires on friendly troops. Part of his therapy was to point out to him that the fire command was checked by two different organizations before the firing was actually done and there were at least two other organizations whose job it was to clear the coordinates, which they in fact did. He was therefore able to share some of the responsibility for the friendly fire with other persons and units who were equally incompetent.

Pride

It is helpful to maintain a positive focus and glean as many positive aspects of the person's behavior during the trauma as possible. The therapist should search for things in clients that can reinforce pride in their unit, their profession, or their behaviors. A client who felt guilty about following the drag marks of his friend for 3 days and finally finding him freshly killed could be helped only by being commended for recovering his friend's body. Sometimes this pride can be encouraged by making comments like, "If that had been me, I would have been pleased that you had gone to that much effort to try to save me and that you recovered my body for my family."

Symbolic Memorials

There are many ways to ameliorate guilt. We have found that many of our trauma victims have used arts and poetry to express some of the feelings they have had toward the missing person or their feelings about the involvement in that situation. In working with suicidal people with survivor guilt, some of the better interventions have included the communicating that "as long as you are alive, the memory of the victim remains." With some trauma victims, it may be necessary to visit the graves of buddies or loved ones who died or review newspaper or other media reports of the trauma to facilitate completion of stress recovery. Vietnam veterans may need to look at the Book of Friends (a registry of all those who died in Vietnam), see the videotape, *Wall of Tears,* visit "The Wall," or the DAV Vietnam Memorial in Angel Fire, New Mexico, or perhaps participate in some other form of recognition that someone acutally did die. In group therapy, we frequently have some sort of memorial symbol at the last group session. It has been as simple as having a moment of silence and as complex as having a ceremony of lighting candles, talking about the death of a friend, and burning his or her name into a piece of plywood with a map of Vietnam sketched on it.

SUMMARY

One of my clients was a medic in Vietnam. In October 1967, after losing many men in Vietnam, Jim went to a small village near where the action had been and wiped out the entire village by himself. The anniversary date has always been particularly important for Jim. He had been out of treatment for approximately a year when he called to remind me that his anniversary date was approaching and to request a meeting with me on that day. He told me that he was going to come in full combat gear, and I reminded him that I felt particularly uncomfortable with that idea and suggested that he wear civilian clothes. He said he did not know what he was going to do, but we made our appointment. The next morning Jim came to my office wearing a three-piece suit. The following transcript is typical of Jim's journey in attempting to deal with his survival guilt.

TOM: What helps deal with guilt? When guys keep showing up repeatedly like bad pennies, it means they've not been able to deal with their guilt.

JIM: That's true, I agree with you. I wouldn't say that I've totally solved the guilt. I think I've probably got a handle on it, and recognize it for what it is. For me, at least, it was so many years ago, October 1967, it was a bad scene, it happened, and made such an impression on me that it ruined me for so many years. Being a kid, an 18-year-old kid at the time, it made such an impression on me that I didn't know how to deal with it so what did I start doing? I started striking out to make up for my failure.

TOM: You started drinking.

JIM: I started drinking. To get over that pain. But seeing for the first time, actual, actual total obliteration of a human body and I couldn't do anything about it.

TOM: As a medic.

JIM: As a medic. So, as those years past, when I'd stike out and I'd drink, it all went back to a clearing, went back to a village and I had to make up for the deaths that I felt that I caused and I had nothing to do with it. As I didn't fire the bullets, I didn't fire the rockets, the mortars, or anything. Recognizing that now puts me at ease. It's taken a long, long time to understand it for what it is. And for what it did. I volunteered to go. I went. Maybe I didn't really know what I was getting into because. . . . I'm a soldier, I'm the best, I'm conditioned for this. By God, I individually can stop this war. Just like every other soldier I was with thinking the same thing, but we never said it. My job wasn't to kill. Introspective, my job was to fix.

TOM: But you did kill.

JIM: I did. And maybe that's what's hurt me more than anything. The fact that I did kill. Me? Taking a human life? Me? There's no rhyme or reason to that. I'm not that way. I'm not a murderer. I'm not a killer. I'm just a kid, but I turned out to be a man, a hard-core, hard-faced individual.

TOM: And what you did lately was to tape-record all of your recollections about that day in the clearing.

JIM: That day in the clearing. And I can talk about my pain. I can't speak for others, I can only speak for myself and the pain that I have been going through, for so many years. . . . The pain! Going to see the docs and having them talk about it and so forth and getting into groups, that's great, but I'm still within myself because I make the decision, you don't make the decision, the group doesn't make the decision, I make the decision.

TOM: Does the group help in talking about it?

JIM: It brings it out. . . .

TOM: Makes it available for you to deal with? Or gives you ways of dealing with it? Gives you different ways of looking at it?

JIM: It gives me the opportunity to hear how others are doing it.

TOM: OK, like when Joe finally said, "I did the best job I could to try to save John."

JIM: But he didn't say that, we had to tell him.

TOM: But he finally said that, he recognized it. And did that do something for you?

JIM: Yea.

TOM: So you got some vicarious learning from it. You said, wait a minute, maybe that works for me. Maybe I can take a look at it and see if I did the best job I could.

JIM: I got to go along with that.

TOM: Because you hadn't thought of that before by yourself over the last 17 years. Want to read your poem?

JIM: Sure. I may cry a little bit but it's over.

Another Soldier Down

Heat of the day,
A heavy mugginess fills the air.
Clothes drenched with sweat and the sound swoosh, swoosh.
Commands yelled in quick order.
To the sides everyone.
Watch the flanks.
Joe, give me the damn phone.
Those sons of bitches.
The sound is gone with stillness all around . . .
Doc . . . Doc
I grab my bag because there's
Another soldier down.
Now it's dusk with
Coolness but mugginess still lingers
Entering heavy jungle foliage
Commands passed quietly. Keep alert.
Booby traps heavy in this area.
We'll sit in about two clicks and wait for Caldwell's orders . . .
Doc, stay close.
We do as told . . . then a sound fifty yards ahead . . .
Twang . . . screams from point . . . help . . .
Hit a punji—voices gurgle
Grab my bag.
Lieutenant yells "Trap, . . . Hold position. . . ."
I move anyway cause all I know is
Another soldier down.
Early morning. Chilly.
Think awful strange for such a hot country.
Move to an edge of a clearing.

Point man taking right out on evac . . .
Don't know if I did right . . .
Never saw holes like those before.
Ears perk up. Hear blades and choppers come in.
For an evac Jeff, didi (hurry away) and take them.
To LZ. Others guard perimeter
HQ says activity heavy on all sides.
Be alert.
Evac hovers. We start forward and all hell breaks loose.
Ratatat-tat. Swoosh. Ping. Ping. Chopper twenty-five,
thirty yards away. Two, maybe three, other ships above.
Covering fire from ground and above ground "WHOMB", evac blows.
Bodies and screaming.
Grab my bag. Another soldier down.
Later, hot again, a heavy mugginess in the air.
The stench of death wraps around like a blanket.
Shambles inside, confusion and anger and fear.
Yet I know when I hear . . .
I'll grab my bag.
Another soldier down.
Later, hot again, a heavy mugginess in the air.
The stench of death wraps around like a blanket.
I'm a shambles inside, confusion and anger and fear.
Yet I know when I hear or see pain
I grab my bag.
For all I know is,
Another soldier down!

JIM: That's reality. There's more to that poem. Because of my shambles, confusion, and anger, fear, I went to a village to make up in the sense of an eye-for-an-eye and a tooth-for-a-tooth. But I couldn't write that essay.

TOM: Have you?

JIM: In my mind. And I think it's best where it's at. The day will come I'll put it to a piece of paper.

REFERENCES

Bard, M., & Sangrey, D. (1986). *The crime victim's book.* New York: Brunner/Mazel.

Capps, W. (1982). *The unfinished war: Vietnam and the American conscience.* Boston: Beacon Press.

Cobb, S., & Lindemann, E. (1947). Neuropsychiatric observations. *Annals of Surgery, 177,* 814–824.

Horowitz, M. J. (1986). *Stress response syndromes* (2nd ed.). New York: Jason Aronson.

Wilson, J. P. (1983). Vietnam veteran on trial: Relationship of post traumatic stress disorder to criminal behavior. *Behavioral Sciences and the Law, 3,* 69–84.

15

Native American Healing and Purification Rituals for War Stress

STEVEN M. SILVER and JOHN P. WILSON

INTRODUCTION

This chapter addresses certain features of Native American healing practices that have relevance to the treatment of traumatic stress syndromes and other mental states of distress. The major focus will be on American Indian healing practices used for survivors. To those unfamiliar with the ways of American Indian shamans, these practices may seem strange and initially somewhat foreign or even threatening. However, for those willing to learn and be open to experience, there is psychic encounter in ritual that some would term *metaphysical* or perhaps *supernatural*. To Native Americans, they are both religious and sacred.

As an introductory remark, we must point out, this is not a presentation on vanished peoples and traditions. Since the end of World War II, there has been an American Indian Renaissance taking place in spite of forces in the Anglo culture to eliminate it and often without the awareness of "outside" observers and health care providers. An integral part of this resurgence is the increased emphasis on the use of traditional healing and purification practices. Moreover, although many divergent cultures exist within tribal societies, striking commonalities can be found in their ways of integrating warriors.

STEVEN M. SILVER • PTSD Program, Veterans Administration Medical Center, Coatesville, Pennsylvania 19320. **JOHN P. WILSON** • Department of Psychology, Cleveland State University, Cleveland, Ohio 44115.

ON THE NATURE OF WAR

In the study of war and its aftermath, one must not be blinded by the need to overly quantify and analyze its various dimensions. Clearly, the effect of war is more than an individual's conditioned reactions to horrific and traumatic stimuli. Wars are complex socioeconomic-political phenomena that contribute to and affect the entire culture (Mansfield, 1982). The impact of war on a nation parallels, to some degree, the impact of injury and death on members of a family. The legacy of the experience affects everyone, in one way or another and is often transgenerational. There are elements in war not ordinarily found in other traumatic situations. One of these is its potential for producing a form of emotional "addiction." Here we do not rely solely on the postwar desires of some survivors to recapture the thrill of combat, though this may be present in the vicissitudes of risk taking or sensation-seeking behavior (Wilson & Ziegelbaum, 1986).

War often produces complex, confusing, and exhilarating emotional experiences. Inevitably, these are part of war's addictive quality to the combatant. Like all substances of addiction, war taps into receptor sites already existing in the organism, doing so in an extremely efficient, powerful, and biosocial manner. The quality of addiction is the intensity of feelings, an intensity rarely matched in the course of ordinary living. However, the intensity of warfare can be subtley traumatizing at the same time as it demands the utmost of emotional responsiveness in dilemmas of life/death survival situations. Thus, one of the central problems of combatants after war is to regain a healthy sense of both emotion and morality.

Traumatic events such as war often are chaotic. However, one should not view them as unreal or apart from the possible range of human experience. Indeed, because the ordinary world is marked by a mythos that often denies the possibility of random, arbitrary, and amoral physical and psychological violence, it might be argued that the deillusionment that accompanies trauma (Janoff-Bulman, 1985) may cause individuals to develop an objectively more realistic basis by which to appraise reality. Only from the perspective of a peaceful, civilized society is the nature of modern guerilla warfare viewed as bizarre, surreal, immoral, and nonhuman. Yet it is a truism to state that war alters the survivor's perspective of reality. For some veterans, their old view of reality is forever shattered by war trauma, inevitably creating the need to reformulate the existential meaning of life itself as well as their role in it. Thus, war can alter individuals in many ways, depending on events in the postwar recovery environment. Some men never come home from war. Others become more fully human and wiser.

Sanctuary Trauma

As with other trauma survivors, warriors run the risk of returning to a post-traumatic world that may be indifferent or even hostile. Part of the mobilization of resources needed to cope with the trauma may involve construction of an idealized picture of the post-trauma world. The inability of the post-trauma world to measure up to this idealization may be both stressful and disappointing, especially if the defenses used to survive the trauma are dropped prematurely in relief. Silver (1985c) has termed this phenomena *sanctuary trauma.* If the post-trauma world is indifferent or actively hostile, the individual may form powerful feelings of alienation that, in turn, may be responded to by isolation and withdrawal or angry, forceful attacks against those who fail to understand the painful inner struggle. And although the warrior often has experiences that are both unusual and extraordinary, he runs the risk of maintaining a psychological state of being that is "warriorlike." The risk involves the adoption of a war-conditioned identity that includes the qualities of being angry, numb, terrorized, and hyperaroused. Traditionally, American Indian medicine men developed rituals to detoxify the warrior or others whose spirit was afflicted and diminished by stressful life experiences.

AMERICAN INDIAN HEALING: A CAVEAT

When considering Native American healing practices, we immediately encounter the idea of "spiritual healing" through culturally determined forms of meaning and religious significance that many mental health professionals tend to avoid or view as "primitive" or magical. As we examine Native American healing, we find cultures thoroughly permeated by spirituality to the extent that they usually do not have a single word for what mainstream American culture defines as religion. Hultkranz (1979) pointed out that "to the extent that Indian languages use an experssion for exclusively religious customs there is often reason to suspect influences from Christian preaching and Christian practice" (p. 9). This permeation is so complete that observers have initially thought some American Indians were without religion (Locke, 1976).

As noted elsewhere (Silver, 1985a), it is often difficult for non-Indian mental health professionals to "hear" what Native American healers have to say. This problem arises from two sources. First, the non-Indian mental health profession is involved in an ongoing struggle to be accepted as a science. The emphasis on quantifiable, standardized research methods reflects this struggle. Unless it can be stated in "hard data" terms, there is a reluctance to become involved in such "soft" and "nebulous" areas as religion. Perhaps more important, there is a reluctance to be perceived by peers as taking religion seriously. The second source is the tendency of non-Indians to view the spiritual beliefs of Native Americans as being primitive, and, therefore, having less to offer the student coming from the mainstream of the American culture.

We do not wish to overstate the case, but a number of non-Indian mental health professionals recognize and accept, through their personal contact and professional work, not only the dynamic quality of healing practices but also the usefulness of blending these practices into their own work (Bergman, 1973, 1974; Jilek, 1971). Nevertheless, the merger of religion and psychological practice is a problem for many clinicians. From our perspective, this is due to a failure to understand the implicit psychological processes at work in various healing rituals and religious practices. Adding to the difficulty for non-Indian observers is the fact that American Indians do not separate religion from psychology, and within the psychological healing practices, there is no separation of body and mind. Further, American Indian psychology tends to blend cognitive, emotion, behavioral, and existential orientations. If nothing else, it is a holistic and integrated approach to understanding behavior.

Historical Background

Traditionally, American Indian cultures heavily emphasized the family and, to a lesser extent varying among tribes, the tribal community. The extended family, which frequently incorporated as virtual relatives those not immediately blood kin, served to educate and support its members, especially the children (Red Fox, 1971; Stands in Timber & Liberty, 1967). Similarly, large-scale group involvement was usually a part of all ceremonial healing.

As no sharp distinction is made between body and mind, typically both areas are attended to in healing rituals that may include extremely long and complex ceremonies, such as in the Navajo Night Way used to treat overt insanity. The Night Way lasts 9 days and requires the Navajo singer to recite over 500 songs without error, a task comparable in length to reciting the diagnostic manual of the American Psychiatric Association (DSM-III-R) verbatim.

In addition, if the individual was to be exposed to the possibility of harm such as combat, prophylactic treatment and preparation was provided. Often "war dances" were part of a long preparation period designed to reaffirm the individual's strength, purpose, and community membership (Underhill, 1965).

War and Warriors

On the surface, it appears that a wide range of views on war and the role of the warrior exist within the 300 American Indian tribal cultures examined. However, closer scrutiny reveals common principles.

Among the Iroquois, for example, war was an instrument of policy, used to eradicate competitors for the same territory. Their wars were total and unrelenting. Smaller tribes from New England were destroyed when they were forced into Iroquois lands by the colonizing whites. The Iroquois conducted war in much the same way as did European nations. They saw war as a necessity, and killing the enemy was the primary goal. Warriors who killed many of the enemy were particularly valued and honored (Dillon, 1983).

Among the Apache, combat was an adjunct to economic survival. Honor was found in being able to seize horses and goods without having to enter into combat. They viewed fighting as a poor tactic among a people for whom day-to-day survival was a continuous struggle. Only once in their history did they engage in total war: a two and a half century campaign against the Spanish and Mexicans. For these people, war was for economic gain or survival, and, therefore limited in scope. Warriors who captured booty without losing men were particularly valued and honored (Terrell, 1972; Worcester, 1979).

Among the Cheyenne, combat was a highly ritualized affair designed to give the participants an opportunity to demonstrate courage by counting coup on an enemy. More honor was to be found in striking an enemy warrior without killing than in actually drawing his blood. This display of courage in the face of the enemy conferred upon the warrior high prestige within the tribe. For example, The Battle Where the Girl Saved Her Brother was immortalized among the Cheyenne not because it was a victory over the U.S. Army just before the defeat of Yellowhair but because a Cheyenne woman named Buffalo Calf Road Woman saved her brother from the middle of the battle after being dismounted.

Among the Papago, a settled tribe strongly invested in agriculture, war was considered to be so disruptive to the natural order of life that its participants were considered insane. Indeed, the Apache, who raided them from time to time, were considered to be nonhuman because they initiated such actions. Fighting was the absolute last resort, and those who participated in it stood in severe danger of so contaminating themselves as to be virtually untouchable unless properly cleansed (Hagan, 1979).

A clear distinction between states of war and peace kept war from dominating the other aspects of tribal life. Ritual and ceremony divided leadership responsibilities between states of war and peace. For the individual, the divisions compartmentalized the combat experience and maintained the social structure of the tribe.

In these four different tribes, we see four different views on war and warriors. American Indian cultures entered into armed conflict with attitudes ranging from reluctance to economic necessity. Their style of war ranged from episodic conflict to constant warfare. To argue that they did not wage war because they did not have the political and economic organization of European countries is among many mistaken conceptions of Indian societies (Underhill, 1965).

Traditional Preparation and Reintegration

Tribal ceremonies served several functions for preparing warriors for war. First, they conferred power upon the warriors for success in the coming struggle. Second, they reaffirmed the contract existing between the people and their warriors. Ritual, in which family and other tribal members participated, clearly demonstrated support of the warrior's upcoming efforts and ordeal (Mails, 1985). These preparatory rituals also served the purpose of confirming the membership of the warrior in his culture and promised his reintegration after the war. Ceremonies involving the whole tribe made the social contract pretty explicit; there was social recognition guaranteed both before and after battle.

All tribes, regardless of the degree of emphasis they placed on the opportunity for achievement offered by war, saw the warrior as sacrificing on behalf of the people. To enter into warfare in order to put an end to the disruption of the natural order was to take on a special role worthy of the highest respect. Likewise, to go to war against those forces that might destroy the people, to demonstrate courage in the face of danger, to be willing to fight and die for one's people, was again recognized as a role worthy of the highest respect.

When a young Papago warrior drew blood for the first time, he underwent a 16-day purification ritual. Each night an older warrior would formally say to him, "Verily, who desires this experience? Do you not desire it? Then you must endure its many hardships." (Underhill, 1965, p. 179). Impressed on the young warrior was the perspective of his experience as events requiring cleansing. The emphasis of the purification ritual was on returning the warrior to his people. After the purification he would be returned and would be regarded as somehow superior to his peers who had not been exposed to war. There were two important reasons for this, shared by peaceful Papago and the most war-like tribes. First, the reintegration process healed both warrior and community. Second, survivors were recognized as holders of uniquely acquired wisdom.

Mansfield (1982) found that tribal cultures utilize ceremony to provide the tribe and the warrior a structure in which mourning is shared. While the warriors were on the battlefield, their people endured their absence, wounding, and death. For example, from the perspective of American Indians, all Americans, not just the warriors, are spiritual veterans of the Vietnam War and all are in need of healing. However,

> tribal people go a step further. *Their ritual explicitly embraces and approves the killer's psychic numbing and prescribes a way for dealing with it.* The fear of intimacy, touching and being touched that is common in battle survivors and that in the twentieth century is labeled a sickness ("shell shock," "Vietnam Vet Syndrome," etc.) is accepted and even enforced in ritual warfare as an appropriate response to the experience of inflicting death in battle. The successful warrior is usually isolated from everyone except older killers and is specifically forbidden to touch or feed himself, to experience sexual intimacy, to

> touch the ground, and so forth. In effect, the numbing is externalized and formalized in a series of taboos; it is prescribed as a chosen response to the ordeal (Mansfield, 1982, pp. 38–39).

Thus, by ritualizing common trauma reactions, their power is reduced by reframing and suggestion. The wisdom of such rituals lies in their ability to decondition the intense emotions produced and learned in combat. *Ritual purification, embedded in cultural meaning, begins a process of transformation in identity and role expectation.* Moreover, ceremonies and rituals for both preparing warriors for battle and reintegrating them into the tribe not only acknowledge combat reactions but also rely heavily on the participation of the family, clan, and tribe. For example, the Navajo Enemy Way Ceremony, lasting several days, was and is used for purification and reintegration after the warrior encounters the violence of war. The ritual is usually sponsored by the individual's family and the participation of the entire community in the prayers and ceremonies is encouraged and expected.

Within many tribes there existed warrior societies, such as the Cheyenne Dog Men (often called "Dog Soldiers" by whites) and the Sioux Kit Fox. These societies provided the tribe "a source of control, fostered and answered the need for a military spirit and became the social centers" (Mails, 1985, p. 55). For the warrior, it is clear they provided the vehicle for his reintegration into the tribe by ritual, ceremony, and recognition.

Finally, the traditional ceremonies served to provide the warrior with a new mythos, one that could supply a purpose in life and balance the emotional impact of exposure to injury, death, and dying. The development of such a mythos appears to be an important part of any reintegration into a warrior's culture because the old values and belief systems are frequently challenged, even overthrown, by traumatic stressors. A new perspective on self and the world is frequently sought and may be a requirement for healing post-traumatic stress reactions (Silver, 1985b).

Modern Practices

Mental health professionals have noted the many problems existing for American Indians and how the use of mainstream resources has had only marginal impact on these ongoing difficulties, such as alcoholism, depression, and suicide (Barter & Barter, 1974; Dizmang, Watson, May, & Bopp, 1974; Leighton, 1968; May & Dizmang, 1974; Shore, 1974; Westermeyer, 1974; Weibel-Orlando, Weisner, & Long, 1984). Although we do not propose to present Native American healing rituals as a panacea, their effectiveness in treating mental illness cannot be overlooked.

At times, the traditional healing practices of American Indians were so ignored by mainstream culture as to become virtually invisible. However, although some ceremonies, rituals, and warriors' societies have ceased, many remain intact and in use today (Attneave, 1974; Mails, 1978). The surviving practices were not preserved rigidly; rather, they were adapted to deal with new problems besetting American Indians. Further, because of the holistic view discussed earlier, American Indians typically are able to make use of services offered by mainstream institutions while at the same time using and adapting traditional healing practices (Fuchs & Bashshur, 1975). Drawing from two cultures is often encouraged by enlightened mainstream healers (Isaacs, 1978; Jilek, 1974; Meyer, 1974). In a few instances, mainstream healers actively encourage the preservation and dissemination of the traditional healing techniques (Bergman, 1973).

As a function of deliberate federal policy, traditional American Indian ceremonies were secularized or suppressed. For example, for 40 years the piercing of the flesh, an important part of the Sioux Sundance, occurred only in "underground" ceremonies (Mails, 1978). Nevertheless, American Indian cultures that survived the nineteenth century appear to be undergoing a resurgence, in part because these cultures traditionally have had to accommodate change. Their members are often able to draw from tools of mainstream culture to aid the preservation of their traditional cultures by organizing and representing themselves (DeMallie, 1984; Hagan, 1979; Hultkranz, 1979; McNickle, 1968).

To a great extent, it appears this resurgence developed in response to needs of American Indian war veterans. Following both world wars, large numbers of returning American Indian veterans made use of the honoring ceremonies and purification rituals. Many American Indian veterans adopted ceremonies from other tribes, such as the Kiowa *Tiah-piah's* Gourd Dance that is now regarded as an intertribal veterans' ceremony (Holm, 1986). Over the past 5 years, the Vietnam-Era Veterans Inter-Tribal Association has organized a yearly powwow open to all veterans of all races. The Gourd Dance has been present in these gatherings (Holm, 1982) as have Sioux sweat lodges.

Mental health and medical professionals working with American Indians emphasize the usefulness of tapping into the healing strength provided by direct community involvement in helping troubled individuals with a broad range of ailments (Dizmang *et al.,* 1974; Weibel-Orlando *et al.,* 1984). One step beyond this is the deliberate utilization of American Indian healers for various mental disorders, such as depression (Jilek, 1974).

Trauma Treatment

The purpose of the ceremonies and rituals provided for returning American Indian warriors is to reintegrate them within the tribe. However, this does not mean returning them to their previous status as if nothing had taken place. To the contrary, the purpose is to recognize their experience and provide them with a new role. As DeMallie (1984) described the process:

> Warriors had to be recognized and were charged with the responsibility to take care of others, to practice self-discipline, and provide leadership. The social contract was assumed now as a *wichasha yatapika* ("man" plus "they praise"). (pp. 389–390)

Along with giving the warrior psychological support through formal purification, he assumed a new position within the tribe based on wisdom gained through experience. This provides the tribe a social and political structure in which to use warriors as leaders. This is a recognition of the acceleration of development that often accompanies exposure to massive trauma. Survivors typically have to deal with issues of life and death most people do not have to consider under late in life (Wilson, 1980). There is a wisdom in survivorship worth salvaging.

For the individual warrior, this change in status provides not only a powerful reframing of what might be perceived as a negative experience but also supplies a method for effectively addressing one of the more painful aspects of war trauma—survivor guilt. The typical response to some form of guilt is some form of self-punishment. Being placed in this new position provides the warrior with an opportunity to make atonement, to make a positive contribution, and, thereby, to respond with generativity to negative emotional feelings. The warrior is not asked to give up his experiences; they are the basis for assuming new responsibility, rank, and prestige. In this way, the emotional trauma of war is potentially transformed by new role opportunities within the social matrix of the tribe.

Tribal leaders accept the concept of unconscious functioning. Dreams and trance states, produced by a variety of techniques that create altered states of consciousness (Wilson, Walker, & Webster, in press) are used to obtain information that is stored symbolically and otherwise in the unconscious. Likewise, the surfacing of this repressed material by trance and self-hypnotic states may produce catharsis or an avenue for ego-enhancing suggestions. These techniques of treatment are cultural parallels to approaches used in mainstream psychotherapy, psychopharmacology, and hypnotherapy (Bergman, 1971, 1974; Silver, 1985a; Silver & Kelly, 1985).

Vietnam Veteran Powwows

The yearly powwows of the Vietnam-Era Veterans Inter-Tribal Association provide the interested clinician with an opportunity to observe first-hand the principles utilized by a broad cross-section of American Indians to heal their warriors by ceremony and ritual. These powwows have been attended by American Indian veterans from over 90 tribes as well as many non-Indian veterans.

Extended families often accompany the veterans, and, at any one time, several thousand might be present on the powwow grounds. In addition to the ceremonial dances and other rituals, such as sweat lodges, informal activities take place concurrently with the powwows, such as rodeos, foot races, and softball games. Within the powwow arena, however, only ceremonies and dances are held. In other circumstances, powwows serve as focal points for social gathering. The powwows of the Inter-Tribal Association are different in that they are organized to recognize, honor, and heal a specific group—Vietnam War veterans. The arena area is treated with respect by all who attend. Tribal and racial rivalries are suppressed in the service of providing recognition and acceptance of veterans' sacrifices. All Vietnam War veterans are welcome at the powwows. When the powwows were held in Oklahoma, Gourd Dances were continuously conducted except when special ceremonies took place. The Gourd Dance, named after the gourdlike rattle carried by warriors, is circular with the participants facing inward toward the chanters and drum. Typically, many warriors wore long, narrow, blue-and-red cloaks over their shoulders, with the red side over the heart if they were combat veterans. Most wore military emblems and combat decorations on their cloaks.

Family and community involvement in the healing ceremonies is particularly demonstrated during the Gourd Dances. The veterans, including the veterans of other wars and other eras of service, form an inner circle, slowly approaching the drum, "drawing power" from it, and withdrawing together. In an outer circle are the nonveterans, including family members, friends, and others demonstrating their support of the veterans. Others, including children, always dance with the warriors.

Among other rituals designed to reduce the isolation of the veterans is the processional dance of triumph over the enemy. The warriors, leading the column, drag captured enemy flags behind them in the dust as their forefathers had done with U.S. Army flags and pennants in the nineteenth century. Women relatives dance on the enemy North Vietnamese and Viet Cong flags as was also done by women to enemy symbols in the last century.

The involvement of the families and community serves several additional functions: (1) it affirms the recognition of the warrior in his new role in the tribe; (2) it provides group support for the surfacing and integrating of traumatic experiences; (3) it underlines the bond existing between the community and those who might be warriors in the future by demonstrating the nature of the support that would be available to them if called into military duty.

Sweat Lodge Rituals

In different cultures around the world, religious and ritualistic practices have been developed to treat emotional illness, stress, and states of "dispiritedness."

These rituals have, of course, both specific and general purposes in terms of cultural values and psychological adaptation. There are rituals surrounding death (e.g., sitting wake) that are designed to facilitate the expression of grief and the loss of a loved one. In various rites of passage, the ritual serves to change status and identity within a group, such as the confirmation of manhood. Similarly, there are rituals that prepare men for battle and return from it. Among some Native American groups, war is regarded as an abnormal condition and aberration of the harmonious order of the universe. Thus, those who become warriors must of necessity assume a changed psychological state in order to kill the enemy and win victory so as to restore harmony and balance in nature. However, after battle, the community recognizes the need to return the warrior to a new role and identity in the culture. To do so, the culture honors the warrior's acts of bravery and provides rituals to purge, purify, and heal the physical and psychological wounds of war. In addition to providing a supportive and caring milieu for the warrior, there is the awareness, often tacit and intrinsic to the group, that the warrior identity must be transformed into a new identity that demands maturity and responsibility. Failure to achieve this transformation of the warrior identity may lead to alienation and the adoption of the victimized state with debilitating psychological behaviors (e.g., alcoholism, depression, and self-destructiveness).

Generally, the shaman of the culture, assumes the role of healer or medicine man and performs rituals of various types designed to cure suffering and restore good health and spirituality to the victim. Anthony F. C. Wallace (1966), the distinguished anthropologist, has written that

> efforts to induce an ecstatic spiritual state by crudely and directly manipulating psychological processes are found in every religious system. Such manipulations may be classified under four major headings: (1) drugs, (2) sensory deprivation, (3) mortification of the flesh by pain, sleeplessness, and fatigue, (4) deprivation of food, water and air. (p. 55)

The last three dimensions are commonly employed by various Native American groups as part of healing and purification rituals, especially by Lakota Sioux Indians in their sweat lodge ceremonies. Recently, Wilson *et al.* (in press) have written on efficacy and applicability of the sweat lodge ceremony as a form of treatment for PTSD, especially for war veterans. The sweat lodge ceremony possess physical, psychological, group-oriented, and spiritual dimensions that are especially useful in treating PTSD. More precisely, these dimensions are summarized briefly as (1) transforming the warrior identity into a more generative mode (Erikson, 1968), (2) establishing individual and cultural continuity, and (3) promoting of self-disclosure while physically and emotionally bonded to others in an environment of intense heat, sensory deprivation, and shared collective pain. Table 1 summarizes the changes in PTSD symptom clusters produced by the sweat lodge ceremony.

In writing about various cultural and religious practices as a form of

Table 1. The Effects of Sweat Lodge Purification Rituals on PTSD among Vietnam Veterans

PTSD symptom dimension	Change in symptom cluster produced by purification ritual
Depression, search for meaning, identity diffusion	Reformation of self, positive mood, enhanced sense of centering, and identity
Physical symptoms, memory impairment	Tension release, relaxation, awareness focused on internal states, ability to concentrate
Stigmatization/alienation	Sense of unity, bonding, communality, and continuity
Anger/rage	Inner calmness, acceptance of fate, release of destructive thoughts
Sensation seeking/hyperarousal	Creative channeling of need to enhance feeling of vitality
Intrusive imagery/affective flooding	Reformulation of reason to enter ritual transformation of imagery in less distressing direction, emotional calm
Intimacy conflict	Strong physical, psychological and spiritual bonding
Isolation	Enhanced sense of unity, bonding that contavenes isolation and aloneness
Emotional constriction/avoidance	Emotional expressive, reduced numbing, counterphobic tendency reduced, interpersonal trust

Source: John P. Wilson *et al.* (in press).

psychotherapy for the mentally ill, Wallace (1966) observes that they are designed to transform identity crises and maladaptive behavior.

> These rituals of salvation are, in a sense, similar to rites of passage because they seek to effect a change in the career line of their subject; conversely, rites of passage, such as the Plains Indians' vision quest, may involve mystical phenomena in the course of identity change. The justification for setting aside a special category of salvation rituals lies in the fact that some identity crises are not universally anticipated in a society and are not treated with universally applied rites of passage, but rather are more or less ad hoc ceremonies performed by and upon only those persons who "spontaneously" enter into the experience for the sake of spiritual enrichment or salvation. . . . The function of ritual, in these cases, is undoubtedly to provide a pattern for a process in remission of psychopathology which will bring the victim of severe mental illness out "on the other side," . . . if the ritual is effective, he will arrive at a condition that will permit him to take care of himself and perform useful services (often ritual services) for the other members of the community. (pp. 206–207)

Considering the perspective ritual transformations, we can ask how the sweat lodge ceremony facilitates a remission of PTSD and new vision of the self in society.

THE LAKOTA SWEAT LODGE PURIFICATION RITUAL[1]

The Sioux Indian Sweat Lodge Purification Ritual is a religious event of thanksgiving and forgiveness that is typically led by a medicine man of the tribe. It is regarded as a serious occasion in which spiritual insights, personal growth, and physical healing may take place. The process of purification is physical, symbolic, and metaphysical.

The Sweat Lodge

The sweat lodge is a dome-shaped tent whose frame is constructed out of three branches. The lodges vary in size and can hold between 7 and 20 men. The frame is covered with layers of blankets and topped with heavy canvas. The ground floor inside of the dome is often covered with old carpeting or soft pine boughs to make the seating more comfortable. In the middle of the dome floor is a shallow pit that has been dug out to a depth of about 4 to 12 inches. The pit holds rocks that have been heated in a fire located outside the sweat lodge. The opening to the lodge consists of a small door that is covered by a canvas flap. To enter the lodge, the participants must kneel down and are instructed to crawl into the tent clockwise fashion. At the apex of the dome hang different colored cloth strips that symbolize the sacred colors of the Sioux and the races of humankind.

Prior to the arrival of the participants, a fire is made by placing about 16 to 30 rocks into a mound that is encased by logs stacked upright in a conical shape. The fire is heated to a very hot temperature in preparation for the sweat lodge pit. Located between the fire and the dome are the ceremonial instruments that include the sacred pipe, an eagle wing, and feathers that lean against a small altarlike construction made out of Y-shaped supports and a small tree branch that lies between them.

When it is time to begin the ceremony, the medicine man lights a small amount of sage in a bowl. The smoke is fanned by the participants over the head and chest to purify the body before entering the sweat lodge.

The Sweat Lodge Ritual

Inside the sweat lodge, the participants sit cross-legged in a tightly packed circle around the rock pit. Using the antlers of a deer, the medicine man places the first six rocks into the pit. These rocks represent the "Six Grandfathers" or the different powers of the universe (the Four Winds, Earth, and Sky). Additional rocks are added before the flap to the door is closed. The inside of the tend is now completely dark except for the dim

[1]The authors have both participated in sweat lodge rituals.

glow from the red-hot rocks. The medicine man speaks in a calm and soothing voice about how things can happen if everyone puts their minds together. He states that healing and purification can happen and that the members can grow stronger by praying and overcoming pain and suffering. He explains that all of the participants will suffer together in the intense heat and that all of life is a struggle with pain and suffering. Water is then ladled onto the rocks for each of the "Grandfathers" as the medicine man sings a song of prayer that is then sung collectively by the participants.

One by one, in a clockwise manner, each of the participants offers his individual prayer that often begins with the words, "Thank you, Grandfather," and ends with "*Mitakuye oyasin*" ("with all beings and all things let us be relatives"). During the ceremony, there are "four doors" or four belief intervals during which the flap to the lodge is opened. The medicine man speaks words of wisdom and guidance at this time while the participants pass the wing of the eagle to fan themselves. Then, once again, there is darkness as the ceremony continues as more water is poured onto the rocks and the prayers resume. At the end of the "fourth door," the ceremony concludes as the individuals emerge into the cool air after an hour or longer in the sweat lodge. At this time, the medicine man lights the sacred pipe that is passed among the participants in a closing ritual.

Psychological Dimensions of the Ceremony

When analyzing the psychological dimensions of the sweat lodge ceremony, it must be recognized that each participant's perception and experience of the event will be affected by his unique personality characteristics, religious orientation, and cultural values. However, the ceremony does possess its own process and internal structure that bonds the participants together in a common group experience. In this regard, the sweat lodge ceremony contains a set of implicit psychological processes that involve group dynamics and individual modes of experience that are facilitated by the leadership and skill of the medicine man. To the student of group dynamics, much of what happens in the sweat lodge ceremony bears much similarity to group psychotherapy, intense interpersonal encounter, and other forms of social influences. On the other hand, it must be acknowledged that the scientific tradition of studying group dynamics may not be sufficient when trying to understand the total reality of the ceremony, much of which is regarded as a spiritual encounter by Native Americans. Nevertheless, we believe that ritual is potentially a valuable therapeutic treatment for PTSD among victims who are not Native Americans.

Table 2 summarizes the dimensions of the sweat lodge ritual and their psychological effect. Elsewhere, Wilson *et al.* (in press) have discussed the psychological aspects of the sweat lodge in more detail. However, due to

Table 2. Psychological Dimensions of Sweat Lodge Ritual

Dimension of ritual	Psychological effect
Sensory deprivation (lack of light)	Attention focused on inner state and words of others, lack of social cues and external stimuli, loss of time
Extreme heat	Struggle with pain, dehydration, altered states of consciousness
Small interior space	Womblike atmosphere, claustrophobic, urge to leave, no physical movement
Participants seated tightly in circle	Collectively joined and physically bonded
Individual prayers	Self-disclosure of personal concerns and needs, catharsis, acceptance of others, release
Four "doors" or rounds of prayer	Unity theme, collective suffering, collective sharing, enhanced sense of inner strength
Leadership of medicine men	Create expectations for healing, share wisdom of ritual, provide sense of continuity, role model of spiritual strength
Crawl in and out of tent naked	Humbleness, smallness, release, rebirth, renewal

Source: John P. Wilson *et al.* (in press).

space limitations in this chapter, we will briefly discuss the mechanisms by which the sweat lodge can serve as a therapeutic technique in treating post-traumatic stress disorder among victimized persons, especially war veterans. And although it is undoubtedly the case that the ceremony is more powerful in terms of its symbolic and culturally specific meaning to Native Americans, it is our belief that it has a core psychological process that is universal in its effects. Although we do not wish to diminish the spiritual aspects of this ritual to Native Americans, it is believed that controlled scientific studies would demonstrate the efficacy of this ritual as a therapeutic tool for the treatment of PTSD.

Inside the sweat lodge there is a feeling of sensory deprivation caused by extreme heat and the absence of light. As a result, attention becomes focused on one's inner state and the words of the other members as they pray. There is a lack of external stimuli and a struggle with the pain induced by the heat and the cramped conditions. As the ceremony proceeds, there is typically a loss of sense of time, near and actual dehydration, and many members report experiencing altered states of consciousness (see Harner, 1980, for a discussion).

The interior of the lodge creates a womblike environment that produces feelings of claustrophobia and an urge to escape. However, as the members are tightly packed in a circle, there develops a sense of being collectively joined and physically bonded to others. It is difficult to change position. Thus, consciousness is focused on one's inner state while listening simultaneously to the self-disclosure of the other participants. There is catharsis, the release of powerful emotion and the acceptance of others as humans who are struggling with special pain. Perhaps for these reasons, a sense of unity emerges out of the collective physical suffering and sharing of oneself with others. By the end of the fourth round, there emerges an enhanced sense of inner strength that one has overcome the pain, extreme heat, and darkness of the lodge to see new "light" in the self. The ritual is its own symbol and process: The members enter naked, crawl in a humble and humiliating position into the womblike tent. Then, through the guidance of the medicine person and the process of the four rounds of prayer, they emerge again from the interior of the womb with a profound sense of release, rebirth, and a personal renewal of spirit. Thus, as Table 2 summarizes, the dispirited state of PTSD is transformed by the ritual in ways that can be characterized as enhanced sense of centering, identity, connectedness, and emotional well-being.

Red Feather Ceremonies

American Indian cultures look on the role of a warrior as one that needs both continuity and transformation. Following combat, the warrior is expected to assume a position of leadership within the community, a position often not attainable until later in life. This intelligent utilization of the strengths gained through survivorship is more than simply reframing a negative experience into different cognitive perspective. It is also providing the individual with an opportunity to balance complex emotional states that were produced during the war. For those warriors who have suffered greatly from warfare, special rituals and ceremonies create the opportunity to transform the self in healthy ways.

One example is the induction of warriors into the Red Feather Society. A traditional warriors' society greatly reduced in numbers since the turn of the century has been revived in recent years. As a precursor to membership, Red Feathers are sworn to abstain from drugs and alcohol and pledge themselves to the care of others in the community.

During the Inter-Tribal Association powwow in South Dakota, two new members were inducted. The society is open only to multiply-wounded veterans. As a part of the ritual of induction, the members are publicly honored by ceremonial dancing in the powwow arena. The next day the candidates participate in a sweat lodge and the formal induction, during which they are presented with eagle feathers smeared with blood of other members. An additional requirement of induction includes the responsibility to provide a meal for some old people upon returning home.

It is interesting to note that this society has inducted veterans from a range of tribal backgrounds. Further, the rebirth of the society was in response to the needs of the newest generation of combat veterans.

PRINCIPLES FOR EXAMINATION

Among American Indian Vietnam War veterans, reintegration and intervention in traumatic stress reactions are facilitated by the utilization of the survivor's group and community. There is a driveby many to make contact with their elders and gain their support in reentering the tribal community through traditional healing practices (Holm, 1984).

Both sanctuary trauma and the potential fixation on war trauma are dealt with by the utilization of ceremonial and ritual treatment. The support and involvement of the community not only honors the sacrifices of the warriors but also diminishes isolation, withdrawal, and prevents the assumption of the victim role. The various rituals, individual and collective in nature, attempt to reintegrate the warrior and provide new opportunities to transform the self in a meaningful cultural context.

Although other techniques in traditional healing have their mainstream counterparts, such as hypnotherapy, catharsis, reframing, dream interpretation, and so on, the key element in American Indian healing practices is the involvement of the individual's social system. There is a recognition of true relatedness between the individual and the universe. The heart of American Indian healing rituals is to make use of this wholeness. Thus, it is the totality of the cultural rituals that create a sense of unified connectedness in time, space, and group identity. Psychological healing, when it occurs, does so by the power produced in ritual forms. These forms, in turn, empower the person's spirit to once again be with "all relations on earth and above."

In summary, there are rich traditions of healing and purification practices in Native American cultures. Despite the onslaught of mainstream American culture, many of these traditions have survived and actually grown in usage. There is much of value for survivors of war and other trauma to be studied in these cultures. For hundreds of years, various Native American groups evolved healing rituals embedded within a meaningful cosmology and group identity. Deeper insights into these practices may very well reveal the components of forms of "natural healing" of war trauma and psychic distress.

Toward the end of his life, Black Elk, one of the holiest medicine men of the Sioux Nation spoke:

> These rites of the *Inipi* are very wakan and are used before any great undertaking for which we wish to make ourselves pure or for which we wish to gain strength; and in many winters past our men, and often our women, made Inipi even everyday, and sometimes several times a day, and from this we received much power. Now that we have neglected these rites we have lost much of this power; it is not good, and I cry when I think of it. I often pray that the Great Spirit will show to our young people the importance of these rites. (Brown, 1971, p. 43)

REFERENCES

Attneave, C. L. (1974). Medicine men and psychiatrists in the Indian health service. *Psychiatric Annals, 4*(22), 49–55.

Barter, E. R., & Barter, J. T. (1974). Urban Indians and mental health problems. *Psychiatric Annals, 4*(11), 37–43.

Bergman, R. L. (1971). Navajo peyote use: its apparent safety. *American Journal of Psychiatry, 128,* 695–699.

Bergman, R. L. (1973). A school for medicine men. *American Journal of Psychiatry, 130,* 663–666.

Bergman, R. L. (1974). The peyote religion and healing. In R. H. Cox (Ed.), *Religion and psychotherapy* (pp. 296–306). Springfield, Il: Charles C Thomas.

Brown, J. E. (1971). *The sacred pipe.* Baltimore: Penguin Books.

DeMallie, R. J. (Ed.). (1984). *The sixth grandfather: Black Elk's teaching given to John G. Neihardt.* Lincoln: University of Nebraska Press.

Dillon, R. H. (1983). *North American Indian wars.* New York: Facts on File.

Dizmang, L. H., Watson, J., May, P. A. & Bopp, J. (1974). Adolescent suicide at an Indian reservation. *American Journal of Orthopsychiatry, 44,* 43–49.

Erikson, E. (1968). *Identity, youth and crisis.* New York: W. W. Norton.

Fuchs, M., & Bashshur, R. (1975). Use of traditional Indian medicine among urban Native Americans. *Medical Care, 13,* 915–927.

Hagan, W. T. (1979). *American Indians* (Rev. ed.). Chicago: University of Chicago Press.

Harner, M. (1980). *The way of the shaman.* New York: Harper & Row.

Holm, T. (1982). Indian veterans of the Vietnam War: Restoring harmony tribal ceremony. *Four Winds, Autumn,* 3, 34–37.

Holm, T. (1984). Intergenerational reapproachment among American Indians: A study of thirty-five Indian veterans of the Vietnam War. *Journal of Political and Military Sociology, 12,* 161–170.

Holm, T. (1986). Culture, ceremonialism and stress: American Indian veterans and the Vietnam War. *Armed Forces and Society, 12,* 237–251.

Hultkrantz, A. (1979). *The religions of the American Indians* (Monica Setterwall, Trans.). Berkeley: University of California Press.

Isaacs, H. L. (1978). Toward improved health care for Native Americans: Comparative perspective on American Indian medicine concepts. *New York Journal of Medicine, 78,* 824–829.

Janoff-Bulman, R. (1985). The aftermath of victimization: Rebuilding shattered assumptions. In C. R. Figley (Ed.), *Trauma and its wake: The study and treatment of post-traumatic stress disorder* (pp. 15–36). New York: Brunner/Mazel.

Jilek, W. G. (1971). From crazy witch doctor to auxiliary psychotherapist—the changing image of the medicine man. *Psychiatric Clinic, 4,* 200–220.

Jilek, W. G. (1974). Indian healing power: Indigenous therapeutic practices in the Pacific Northwest. *Psychiatric Annals, 4*(11), 13–21.

Leighton, A. H. (1968). The mental health of the American Indian—Introduction. *American Journal of Psychiatry, 125,* 217–218.

Locke, R. F. (1976). *The book of the Navajo.* Los Angeles: Mankind.

Mails, T. E. (1978). *Sundancing at Rosebud and Pine Ridge.* Sioux Falls: Center for Western Studies.

Mails, T. E. (1985). *Plains Indians: Dog soldiers, bear men, and buffalo women.* New York: Bonanza.

Mansfield, S. (1982). *The gestalts of war.* New York: Dial Press.

May, P. A., & Dizmang, L. H. (1974). Suicide and the American Indian. *Psychiatric Annals, 4*(11), 22–28.

McNickle, D. (1968). The sociocultural setting of Indian life. *American Journal of Psychiatry, 125,* 219–223.

Meyer, G. G. (1974). On helping the casualties of rapid change. *Psychiatric Annals, 4*(11), 44–48.

Red Fox, W. (1971). *The memoirs of Red Fox.* New York: McGraw-Hill.

Shore, H. H. (1974). Psychiatric epidemiology among American Indians. *Psychiatric Annals, 4*(11), 56–66.

Silver, S. M. (1985a). *Lessons from child of water.* (ERIC Document Reproduction Service No. CG 018 606.)

Silver, S. M. (1985b). Post-traumatic stress disorder in veterans. In P. A. Keller & L. G. Ritt (Eds.), *Innovations in clinical practice sourcebook* (Vol. 4, pp. 23–34). Sarasota Professional Resource Exchange.

Silver, S. M. (1985c). Post-traumatic stress and the death imprint: The search for a new mythos. In W. E. Kelly (Ed.), *Post-traumatic stress disorder and the war veteran patient* (pp. 43–53). New York: Brunner/Mazel.

Silver, S. M., & Kelly, W. E. (1985). Hypnotherapy of post-traumatic stress disorder in combat veterans from WW II and Vietnam. In W. E. Kelly (Ed.), *Post-traumatic stress disorder and the war veteran patient* (pp. 211–233). New York: Brunner/Mazel.

Stands In Timber, J., & Liberty, M. (1967). *Cheyenne memories.* Lincoln: University of Nebraska Press.

Terrell, J. U. (1972). *Apache chronicle.* New York: World.

Underhill, R. M. (1965). *Red man's religion: Beliefs and practices of Indians north of Mexico.* Chicago: University of Chicago Press.

Wallace, A. F. C. (1966). *Religion.* New York: Random House.

Weibel-Orlando, J., Weisner, T. & Long, J. (1984). Urban and rural drinking patterns: Implications for intervention policy development. *Substance and Alcohol Actions/Misuse, 5,* 45–57.

Westermeyer, J. (1974). "The drunken Indian:" Myths and realities. *Psychiatric Annals, 4*(11), 29–36.

Wilson, J. P. (1980). Conflict, stress and growth. In C. R. Figley & S. Leventman (Eds.), *Strangers at home: Vietnam veterans since the war* (pp. 123–166). New York: Praeger Press.

Wilson, J. P., & Zigelbaum, S. D. (1986). Post-traumatic stress disorder and the disposition to criminal behavior. In C. R. Figley (Ed.), *Trauma and its wake: Theory, research and intervention* (pp. 305–321). New York: Brunner/Mazel.

Wilson, J. P., Walker, A. J., & Webster, B. (in press). Reconnecting: Stress recovery in the wilderness. In J. P. Wilson (Ed.), *Trauma, transformation, and healing.* New York: Brunner/Mazel.

Worcester, D. E. (1979). *The Apaches.* Norman: University of Oklahoma Press.

16

Complicated Postcombat Disorders in Vietnam Veterans

Comprehensive Diagnosis and Treatment in the VA System

ROLAND M. ATKINSON, MICHAEL E. REAVES, and MICHAEL J. MAXWELL

INTRODUCTION

Postcombat adjustment of Vietnam veterans is highly variable (Egendorf, Kadushin, Laufer, Rothbart, & Sloan, 1981; Wilson, 1978). Most workers would agree with Egendorf (1982) that among persons exposed to the war, there is probably a spectrum of stress response problems varying from subtle forms to severe, chronic disorders. Although accurate prevalence data are not yet at hand, certainly only a portion of these veterans would meet the DSM-III (American Psychiatric Association, 1980) criteria for post-traumatic stress disorder (PTSD), and an even smaller proportion would be expected to show, in addition, features justifying other psychiatric diagnoses.

Few workers would disagree with the assumption that PTSD-positive clinical samples, especially in the VA system, are more likely to demonstrate associated psychopathology than cohorts surveyed in the community (for example, Escobar *et al.*, 1983; Lindy, Grace, & Green, 1984; Sierles,

Views expressed by the authors of this chapter do not necessarily reflect official policies of the Veterans Administration.

ROLAND M. ATKINSON and MICHAEL E. REAVES • Psychiatry Service, Veterans Administration Medical Center, Portland, Oregon 97201. **MICHAEL J. MAXWELL** • Vietnam Veterans Readjustment Counseling Center, Portland, Oregon 97214.

Chen, McFarland, & Taylor, 1983). Such data tend to be deemphasized by epidemiologists whose primary interest is to discern a more representative picture of PTSD in the entire combat veteran population. The purpose of our report is different. We wish to highlight the complex cases that come to our attention in the VA clinical setting. It is important that these cases not be mistaken as representative of all combat veterans. But it is equally important to acknowledge the special, challenging needs these veterans present to clinicians as well as the professional and organizational resources within the VA for comprehensive diagnosis and treatment of complicated postcombat cases.

The VA has rightfully, if belatedly, undertaken broad responsibility for assessment and treatment of Vietnam veterans for postcombat disorders through its specialized, community-based outreach centers (Blank 1982a, 1985) and hospital-based mental health services (Atkinson, Callen, Reaves, & Drummond, 1985). We suggest that VA programs offering multiple alternative treatment environments and a multidisciplinary team approach are—potentially if not always in fact—uniquely equipped to arrange the individualized, often sequential treatments required to rehabilitate highly dysfunctional combat veterans. We will first discuss differential diagnosis of PTSD, next describe some of the diverse treatment strategies that have been created in the VA system, and finally illustrate the course of treatment in several complicated cases from our own experience.

DIFFERENTIAL DIAGNOSIS

Modeling the Complex Case

Among workers who have studied Vietnam war veterans, opinion varies on the features that should rightfully be included in the specific disorder termed PTSD. There is empirical support for the DSM-III definition (for example, Atkinson, Sparr, Sheff, White, & Fitzsimmons, 1984; Boulanger, Kadushin, Rindskopf, & Carey, 1986). Others, although in general validating DSM-III criteria, have also found evidence for additional specific features, for example, depression (Fairbank, Keane, & Malloy, 1983; Silver & Iacono, 1984), rage (Silver & Iacono, 1984), or an avoidant subtype (Laufer, Brett, & Gallops, 1985). Still others, arguing that it is false to separate particular facets from the nexus of postwar maladjustment, have advocated a much broader definition of PTSD to include such behavior patterns as nomadism, antisociality, and substance abuse (for example, Blank, 1982b; Friedman, 1981; Rosenheck, 1985).

This latter, highly inclusive model lacks empirical underpinnings. Further, the etiology of PTSD as defined by DSM-III may differ in significant aspects from the etiology of associated disorders, for example, depression (Boulanger, 1986; Breslau & Davis, 1987), and mania and panic disorder

(Breslau & Davis, 1987). Most important for clinical purposes, specifying all diagnosable disorders invites consideration of appropriate therapeutic steps for each. On the other hand, it is known that PTSD can masquerade as another disorder (Arnold, 1985; Domash & Sparr, 1982; van Putten & Emory, 1973), either as another anxiety, affective, schizophrenic, dissociative, or personality disorder. Arnold (1985) has also called attention to the "affective stress response," typically feelings of grief, guilt or terror, associated with unassimilated traumatic experiences.

Consideration of theoretical models for psychosocial adaptation to extreme stressors (see Green, Wilson, & Lindy, 1985; Horowitz, 1986; Keane, Zimering, & Caddell, 1985, among others) will inform diagnostic assessment, as will knowledge of studies on etiologic factors in post-Vietnam PTSD cases. Exposure to combat or to its consequences (for example, field hospital nurses, graves registration workers) has been the factor most often demonstrated to correlate with postwar psychological distress in clinical (Callen, Reaves, Maxwell, & McFarland, 1985; Foy, Sipprelle, Rueger, & Carroll, 1984; Penk *et al.*, 1981), compensation seeking (Atkinson *et al.*, 1984), and community (Boulanger, 1986; Card, 1983; Egendorf *et al.*, 1981; Wilson, 1978) samples. Participation in atrocities confers especially high risk for PTSD (Breslau & Davis, 1987; Laufer *et al.*, 1985). Other factors related to military service may also be associated with subsequent adjustment, for example, the individual's perception of the meaning of combat (Hendin, Pollinger, Singer, & Ulman, 1981; Hendin, Pollinger, & Haas, 1984), general pattern of conduct during duty (Foy *et al.*, 1984), and mode of discharge after combat (Frye & Stockton, 1982). Secondary avoidance mechanisms (Keane, Zimering, & Caddell, 1985; Laufer, Brett, & Gallops, 1985) and postwar family and social supports (Frye & Stockton, 1982; Kadushin, 1985; Keane, Scott, Chavoya, Lamparski, & Fairbank, 1985) may influence symptoms of PTSD. The role of predisposing factors is controversial. Family instability during the veteran's early years is commonly identified in PTSD-positive VA clinical samples (for example, Sudak, Corradi, Martin, & Gold, 1984). Studies of nonclinical samples either tend not to support this association (for example, Card, 1983) or to place significant qualifications upon it (for example, Boulanger, 1986, who found the association only under conditions of low exposure to combat stressors).

Assessment

It follows from these considerations that the diagnosis of PTSD and concurrent disorders will be facilitated by seeking several varieties of information from multiple sources as outlined in Table 1. Arnold (1985) has recently discussed psychosocial and military history taking and the cardinal features of PTSD in a particularly useful manner. Acquisition of such information requires an empathic, often unstructured approach. However,

Table 1. Diagnosis of PTSD: Sources of Information

Psychosocial history
Veteran, significant others
Military history
Veteran, significant others
Department of Defense records
Medical and psychiatric reports
Episodes of prior assessment, treatment
Structured examination
Review of duty tour ("walk through")
Combat scales
Diagnostic scales
Mental status examination
Psychological assessment
MMPI:Keane's subscale, validity scales
Behavioral analysis
Psychophysiological testing
Peer review
Formulation, differential diagnosis

other specialized, structured procedures may also be invaluable. "Walking the veteran through" his or her tour of duty—a chronological review of military experience from basic training to discharge—may be illuminating to patient and investigating professional alike (Scurfield & Blank, 1985). Combat scales (for example, Egendorf *et al.*, 1981; Lund, Foy, Sipprelle, & Strachan, 1984; Wilson, 1978), more general stress scales (for example, Horowitz, Wilner, & Alvarez, 1979), and general diagnostic scales such as the Structured Clinical Interview for DSM-III (Spitzer & Williams, 1985) may be especially useful with patients who are imprecise or vague reporters, once good rapport has been established. The MMPI has proven useful to several workers in establishing the diagnosis of PTSD (Fairbank *et al.*, 1983; Foy *et al.*, 1984; Keane, Malloy & Fairbank, 1984) as have behavioral analyses (Keane, Fairbank, Caddell, Zimering, & Bender, 1985) and psychophysiological measures of arousal induced selectively by combat-related stimuli (Blanchard, Kolb, Pallmeyer, & Gerardi, 1982; Hyer, O'Leary, Elkins, & Arena, 1985; Malloy, Fairbank, & Keane, 1983). The clinician's willingness to make multiple diagnoses whenever justified, rather than insisting on a single diagnosis, may reduce Type 2 diagnostic errors (Atkinson, Henderson, Sparr, & Deale, 1982). Too often, in our experience, a clinician finding evidence for substance abuse, depression, or personality disorder fails to look further for less obvious signs of PTSD or else rules out the latter merely on "either/or" grounds despite awareness of PTSD signs in the case. This process also occurs in reverse when clinicians focus exclusively on PTSD. Peer review of preliminary diagnoses may also improve validity (Atkinson *et al.*, 1984).

Factitious PTSD

It is difficult to estimate prevalence of factitious PTSD: We believe that it is neither common nor rare. In our analysis of 207 compensation-seeking veterans, we established just 1 case of proven fabrication: Army discharge records showed that this veteran had never been in Vietnam. Lynn and Belza (1984) discovered 7 such cases in 5 months among 125 total patients (Vietnam veterans and others) admitted to a small VA psychiatric ward. Our group has collected about 10 factitious cases among several hundred Vietnam veterans in clinical settings. Determining the veracity of combat reports among veterans who did serve in Vietnam is more difficult. To confound matters further, symptoms suggesting PTSD can occur in veterans who had little or no combat exposure, especially those from unstable families (Boulanger, 1986).

There are several reasons why a person might falsify or exaggerate the story. Monetary compensation from VA (Atkinson *et al.*, 1982) and relief from criminal responsibility (Sparr & Atkinson, 1986; Sparr, Reaves, & Atkinson, 1987) are the two most often discussed motives. Family dynamics, guilt about not having served in combat, faulty self-esteem, and social labeling may also contribute to factitious combat accounts and PTSD claims (Lynn & Belza, 1984; Sparr & Pankratz, 1983). Some cases resemble the picture seen in extreme factitious medical disorders ("Munchausen's syndrome"). Historical and medical features that may assist in detecting factitious cases include the coexistence of purported episodes of major neurological illness and other hospitalizations for physical problems, criminal justice records, or evidence of disciplinary problems in the military suggesting prior fabrications, or other evidence of antisocial behavior, and extremely dramatic stories of very unusual events. For example, two patients said that their entire immediate families had recently been killed in disaster situations, stories later proven to be fabrications. Military discharge documents (DD214) should be obtained from military records in suspected cases, as the veteran may have altered his own copy. The MMPI Validity scales may also assist in these cases (Fairbank, McCaffrey, & Keane, 1985).

Concurrent Diagnoses

Substance abuse, although hardly mistakable for PTSD, is certainly a common coexisting disorder (Atkinson *et al.*, 1984; Lindy *et al.*, 1984; Sierles *et al.*, 1983). Although it has been popular to think that "self-medication" with alcohol or drugs may incompletely or temporarily suppress PTSD symptoms, based on clinical case reports (Lacoursiere, Godfrey, & Ruby, 1980), contrarily, continuing alcohol and drug use have been shown in community samples of combat veterans to coexist commonly with PTSD (Laufer *et al.*, 1985; Roth, 1986). Grief and depression can be profound enough to justify a concurrent diagnosis of an affective disorder (Breslau &

Davis, 1987; Escobar *et al.*, 1983; Lindy *et al.*, 1984; Sierles *et al.*, 1983). Although often meeting criteria for dysthymic disorder, symptoms in some more complex cases constitute a major depressive episode. Preservice deviant behavior and parental psychopathology have been shown to predict postwar depression (Helzer, Robins, Wish, & Hesselbrock, 1979; Helzer, 1981).

Because so many combat veterans encountered combat trauma at a developmentally impressionable age (late teen-age years), a number of workers believe that subsequent signs of personality disorder can represent either "exaggeration" of preexisting personality pathology (Blank, 1982b; DeFazio, 1978) or fixation of personality development at an adolescent level (Wilson, 1980). The general relationship of PTSD to personality disorder is not well understood (Green, Lindy, & Grace, 1985). Study of this question in Vietnam veterans has been hampered not only by the necessity for retrospective assessment but also by the lack of either a theory or measures to specify childhood or early adolescent behavioral precursors for adult personality disorders. The only exception is antisocial personality, for which preadolescent precursor behaviors have been well established empirically. Sierles and associates (1983) found postwar behavior patterns consistent with antisocial personality disorder in more than half of hospitalized Vietnam veterans also suffering from PTSD. However, in a number of cases, these behaviors had not been present prior to age 15, as required by DSM-III to justify the diagnosis. Behavior consistent with borderline (Arnold, 1985) and schizotypal (Wilson, 1985) personality disorders may also be associated with PTSD.

It is this quartet of problems—PTSD, affective disorder, substance abuse, and either personality disorder or behavior resembling personality disorder—in the most complex PTSD cases that requires the special treatment considerations to be discussed in the next two sections.

TREATMENT RESOURCES IN THE VA SYSTEM

Orientation of General Mental Health Services

At the outset, it is important for the reader who is unfamiliar with the VA health care system to realize that, contrary to some popular notions, it is not a monolithic organization in which the pattern of clinical services in every locale is determined by fiat from Washington. Local factors, for example, community demographics, the effectiveness and special interests of local VA hospital clinical and administrative leadership, congressional influence, medical school affiliation, and the number and calibre of applicants available for clinical jobs all tend to shape the nature and quality of services offered, more than do agencywide policies. Given this caveat, it can be said that in connection with most of the general hospital facilities in the system, there usually is found an acute psychiatric inpatient unit, a substance abuse program, a mental health or mental hygiene clinic, and an outreach center for Vietnam veterans. These programs are staffed by teams representing all or most of the mental health disciplines, although the discipline asserting primary iniative on behalf of Vietnam veterans will vary from one locale to the next.

Orientation of Services for Vietnam Veterans

In our surveys (Atkinson *et al.,* 1985; Reaves, Atkinson, Ponzoha, & Kofoed, 1988), we found that, just as mental health services in general vary from place to place, so also do specialized programs for Vietnam veterans. Certain generalizations are possible: Mental health staff in most medical centers we surveyed work in some degree of positive collaboration with local Vietnam veteran outreach teams, and most medical centers have created some treatment programs to meet the special needs of Vietnam veterans. However, the delivery style of even the best services can vary significantly: In one locale, a specialized inpatient program may be the predominant approach (for example, Berman, Price, & Gusman, 1982); in another, a specialized day-hospital program (Sineps, 1983); in still another, a consultation/liaison team (Dwyer & Pentland, 1983); whereas in a fourth locale, an outpatient multiservice center approach may be created (Buffalo VA Medical Center, 1984). Our own approach has been based on the principle of networking staff in existing programs, rather than developing separate programs for Vietnam veterans. Staff members who have a common interest in Vietnam veterans have been identified within the mental hygiene clinic, acute inpatient service, and substance abuse program, and close linkage of these key staff with the staff of the outreach center has been achieved. Outreach center staff conduct some of their work within the hospital-based programs, and hospital staff likewise spend time counseling clients at the outreach center (Atkinson *et al.,* 1985). These key staff members are also consulted, and all treatment programs are considered, in the comprehensive, sequential management of particularly complicated cases. Outreach center leadership also is involved in administrative oversight of the hospital-based mental health services.

These example are but a few among the many, varied strategies that have developed within a system in which local conditions and leadership determine programs. There are two major weaknesses of this decentralized system. First, we are aware that at some VA medical centers, little has been done to address the special treatment needs of Vietnam veterans. Second, systematic evaluation of the outcome of treatment is not required by the central VA administration and is viewed as an unaffordable luxury by most local facilities. It is only through local acquisition of systemwide, competitive research funds that the efficacy of treatment can be studied, Unfortunately, within the VA Medical Research Service, there has been very little funding of studies of the efficacy of psychosocial treatments in general and less for examining the treatment of post-traumatic stress disorders by any means. Consequently, in the discussion of various treatment modalities and settings that follows, our assertions about the usefulness of these cannot be broadly confirmed with empirical treatment outcome data.

Readjustment Counseling Centers ("Outreach Centers" or "Vet Centers")

These special programs for Vietnam veterans (Blank, 1982a, 1985) offer assessment, "rap" groups, and other forms of group counseling and psychotherapy (Smith, 1985b; Walker & Nash, 1981; Williams, 1980), individual counseling focusing on either war-related or current life issues (Smith, 1985a), and counseling services for mates (Harris & Fisher, 1985) and families (Williams & Williams, 1985). Specialized educational and skill-building groups, for example, on substance abuse awareness, communication skills, and self-assertion may be offered as well. Occasionally, more intensive psychotherapies may be offered, depending upon the availability of appropriately trained professional staff either on a salaried or volunteer basis. These programs are not intended to provide comprehensive psychodiagnosis, medication, or lengthy psychotherapies for treatment of associated mental disorders. A network of private mental health professional contract providers has also been established to deliver equivalent services to veterans living at remote distances from vet centers.

Mental Hygiene Clinics

These hospital-linked mental health clinics offer the traditional range of modalities for psychodiagnosis, psychotherapy, and pharmacotherapy. This setting is of particular value for comprehensive diagnosis and management of complex patients who have associated mental disorders. For many of these patients, conjoint treatment by vet center and mental hygiene clinic staff is preferable to treatment in either setting alone. Depending upon the case, staff of one discipline may have much to offer, for example, behavioral assessment and treatments by clinical psychologists (Fairbank & Keane, 1982; Keane, Fairbank, Caddell, Zimering, & Bender, 1985) or the work of VA nurse–practitioners with women who served as nurses in Vietnam (Rogers & Nickolaus, 1987). Medication prescribed by psychiatrists for management of depressive, reexperiencing, and arousal symptoms associated with PTSD may be a helpful adjunct to counseling conducted concurrently in the vet center (for example, van der Kolk, 1983). "Rap" groups have also been conducted in mental hygiene clinics (Atkinson *et al.*, 1985).

Acute Inpatient Psychiatry Units

These programs are indicated when veterans become overwhelmed by PTSD symptoms such as rage, grief, or self-reproach, when social supports break down precipitously, or when severe symptoms of associated disorders supervene. Rapid comprehensive diagnosis, crisis containment, control of disabling symptoms, and mobilization of family and other supports can be accomplished readily in the hospital. Education about war-related problems and planning initial engagement or reengagement with the vet center or mental hygiene clinic are facilitated by specialized group approaches for Vietnam veterans (Atkinson *et al.*, 1985; Reaves & Maxwell, 1987). More extensive special tracks for education and treatment have been created for Vietnam veterans in some VA general psychiatric inpatient units (for example, Starkey & Ashlock, 1984). A particularly strong aspect of these special tracks is the joint leadership of the efforts by hospital and vet center staff.

Entire inpatient units have been organized for treating Vietnam veterans with complicated PTSD; the count is about 14 such facilities at this writing. These programs require several months' time for assessment, acculturation to the unit milieu, working through of war-related problems, and preparation for more effective living upon discharge (Berman *et al.*, 1982). Such programs are costly, and the current resource allocation models in the VA system, which are oriented to very brief stays, make it difficult to sustain them. The trend is toward reducing length of stay on such specialized units to 2 months or less. Whether the objectives of longer programs can be achieved in briefer stays is conjectural.

Substance Abuse Treatment Programs

Typically in VA, these programs consist of detoxification, residential inpatient and outpatient components. Although the number of Vietnam veterans treated for substance abuse in the VA system is substantial, special approaches for treating Vietnam veterans for substance abuse associated with PTSD have been slow to develop (Atkinson *et al.*, 1985). Lacoursiere and associates (1980) have shown that treatment of alcohol dependence may unmask previously suppressed symptoms of PTSD. On the other hand, successful substance abuse treatment may be essential as a prerequisite to meaningful treatment of coexisting PTSD. The evaluation and treatment of veterans with PTSD and coexisting alcohol use disorders in a VA substance abuse treatment setting has been described by Schnitt and Nocks (1984). Screening of patients admitted to substance abuse treatment for combat involvement in Vietnam is a critical element in assessment, in order to anticipate possible treatment complications and needs (Jelinek & Williams, 1984; Schnitt & Nocks, 1984).

Having reviewed the major VA settings in which Vietnam veterans with PTSD may receive treatment, we will next present case vignettes that illustrate how these resources were marshaled in order to respond to the treament needs of three complex patients.

CASE REPORTS

Case 1

This Caucasian man was 34 years old when he first contacted the Portland vet center nearly 2 years ago, requesting help because of instrusive Vietnam memories, insomnia, nightmares, war-related guilt feelings, poor impulse control, and marital discord. He had recently lost a job. He made contact by telephone, for he lived in a rural community a hundred miles away.

He was one of seven children born to working-class parents and raised in small western towns. He found school "boring," dropping out in the ninth grade in order to work. He denied substance abuse and had no contact with legal authorities prior to enlisting in the Marines at age 17. He achieved his high-school GED while on duty. He spent 1 year assigned to a field artillery battalion in Vietnam, late 1968–1969. He consistently refused to discuss details of his duty tour, but it is clear from military records and his superficial reports that he was involved in extensive combat. Upon return, he married his former high-school girlfriend. After attending community college for 2 years to learn a trade, he then drifted from one job and town to the next, totaling perhaps 25 to 30 brief employment episodes over the next 12 years. However, his marriage remained intact, and the couple had two children. Three years before contacting the vet center, he had first asked for help at the mental hygiene clinic of another VA medical center. For his symptoms of anxiety, irritability, nightmares, and chronic headaches, he received medications that sedated him; he discontinued them and did not return for follow-up. His pattern remained as described, and, in addition, he drank up to a fifth of whiskey daily for periods of a week or longer, believing that this helped reduce his irritability. He did not see alcohol as a problem.

Because of his remoteness from the vet center, he was referred to a nearby clinical psychologist who was a contract provider with the vet center program. Individual psychotherapy over the next several months did not reduce his symptoms, and he was admitted to the Portland VA inpatient psychiatric unit. Diagnoses were PTSD and episodic alcohol abuse. He entered the special inpatient group for Vietnam veterans as well as other psychotherapeutic activities on the ward and received no medications. His course was marked by his provocative, intimidating style of interacting with staff and other patients, and there were frequent confrontations after he violated ward rules. Although he made obvious efforts to control himself, he was only partially successful. The night before discharge, when he discovered there was no medication to help him sleep, he became enraged and destroyed hospital property. Nevertheless, he accepted the treatment plan negotiated with inpatient and vet center staff, who had concluded that the pervasive nature of his problems required his treatment in a specialized PTSD inpatient program, once he became acculturated to an intensive, group-oriented treatment approach. He agreed to resume weekly psychotherapy sessions with the contract psychologist and also make the 200-mile round trip to attend a weekly rap group at the vet center. If he sustained his involvement in these treatment efforts for 4 months, this would demonstrate his readiness to enter a specialized PTSD inpatient unit at a VA hospital in a neighboring state.

The patient complied with the plan but also resumed heavy use of alcohol. He became depressed, and this deepened after a month, when he agreed not to drink alcohol. A consulting psychiatrist in the patient's home community prescribed an antidepressant, desipramine, 200 milligrams per day, and an antianxiety agent, alprazolam, 8 to 10 milligrams per day. For the next 3 months he remained sober and kept up his attendance at rap group meetings. Gradually he became less emotionally guarded; however, depressed mood and periodic suicidal ideation became worse. At the end of the 4-month rap group cycle, by prearrangement, he was readmitted to the Portland VA psychiatric inpatient unit for reevaluation and transfer to the specialized PTSD unit. Signs of depression justified the additional diagnosis of dysthymic disorder. At this writing, he has spent several months in the specialized PTSD unit, has made progress there, and is currently nearing discharge. Shortly after his transfer, his wife entered a support group for partners of Vietnam veterans conducted at the Portland vet center. She rarely missed a meeting over the following three months, despite the long drive. Currently the patient and his wife are collaborating with staff of the PTSD unit and local staff to plan postdischarge treatment.

Case 2

This Caucasian man was 34 when he first sought help at the Portland vet center 4 years ago. He complained of depression, "night terrors," insomnia, emotional constriction, intrusive recollections of combat, uncontrolled anger, and substance abuse.

He was the only child of East European immigrant parents. The family settled in a west coast city, where his father established a small business. His childhood adjustment was good; in high school he was active in several sports, dated regularly, and had friends. After high school, he attended a nearby state college briefly and then enlisted in the Army. Trained as an infantryman, he was sent to Vietnam in 1967 and assigned to a reconnaissance team of the 101st Airborne Brigade. He spent all but a few days of his 8 months in Vietnam in the field. The team sought to draw enemy fire in order to locate targets for artillery and counterassaults. Thus contact with the enemy was a nearly daily occurrence. Eventually, he was shot in the hand during a firefight and left behind when his unit was evacuated by helicopter. He was forced to make his way on foot to the unit camp, and he recalls vivid feelings of abandonment. After a series of military hospitalizations over the next 20 months, he was discharged with a 30% service connection for his wounds. Over the next 14 years, he was married and divorced twice, had a series of jobs, and abused alcohol often. The year prior to contact with the vet center, his employer required his participation in a community-based alcohol treatment program, but he resumed drinking the day treatment was concluded. He was again directed to enter treatment or lose his job, and this prompted his contact with the Portland vet center.

He attended one group and three individual counseling sessions, then failed to return. A week later he independently sought admission at the Portland VA Medical Center and was hospitalized on the psychiatric unit for suicidal ideas, insomnia, anhedonia, and depressed mood. Diagnoses were PTSD, major depressive disorder, and episodic alcoholic abuse. He responded to an antidepressant, amitriptyline, 150 milligrams per day, and engaged in individual and group therapy (his first admission occurred prior to formation of the special inpatient group for Vietnam veterans). Following discharge after 4 weeks, he initially complied with the outpatient treatment plan of individual counseling at the vet center and antidepressant medication monitoring at the mental hygiene clinic but then dropped out. His girlfriend joined a group for partners of Vietnam veterans at the vet center, attending three sessions before the patient came to the center and literally pulled her out of a group meeting. She said he had been abusing her physically. At this time, he was drinking on a daily basis but denied that this was a problem. He was also smoking marijuana regularly and occasionally using oral amphetamines.

A few months later, he was again hospitalized on the Portland VA psychiatric inpatient unit after losing a job. Diagnoses were PTSD, alcohol abuse, adjustment disorder with depressed mood, and borderline personality traits. He entered the special group for Vietnam veterans, in addition to other group and individual therapeutic activities, and again received amitriptyline, 150 milligrams per day, and an antianxiety agent, diazepam, 30 milligrams per day. He and his girlfriend also joined in brief couples' therapy. His acute symptoms resolved, and his general social situation improved. He was discharged after 2 months. Because he was reluctant to return to the vet center, follow-up in the mental hygiene clinic was arranged in order to maintain his medications and provide alcohol abuse-oriented group therapy. However, he did not follow through. Ten months later he set his girlfriend's car on fire after a spat while they were on a camping vacation. For this, he spent a month in jail and was released on the condition that he again seek psychiatric treatment.

Portland VA inpatient psychiatry staff collaborated with vet center staff to arrange the patient's admission to the specialized PTSD inpatient unit mentioned in Case 1. He remained there for 7 months and made progress despite a stormy course. He married his then-pregnant girlfriend during this period. After discharge, he returned to Portland, attended eight individual counseling sessions at the vet center according to the prearranged plan, but then discontinued, stopped antidepressant medication, and resumed drinking. Six months later he directly sought readmission to the specialized PTSD inpatient unit, where he was treated for another 3½ months. In addition to the usual intensive group therapy programs offered in this program, he was also treated with several modalities seldom used there, including intensive individual psychotherapy, and antidepressant and antianxiety medications. Because of underlying personality psychopathology, he was judged to need individual, long-term psychotherapy after discharge from the PTSD unit. With facilitation from the local VA inpatient psychiatry staff, individual psychodynamic psychotherapy was arranged at the Portland VA mental hygiene clinic. The patient entered psychotherapy here 7 months ago, augmented only by the sedative-hypnotic drug, triazolam, 1 milligram nightly.

With these arrangements, the patient experienced his most stable outpatient course yet over the following 6 months. Unfortunately, 1 month ago, a Vietnam veteran, whom he had befriended while the two were in the special PTSD unit, died after a heroin overdose while visiting the patient. The patient's symptoms of anxiety, depression, and anger rapidly escalated, and he required admission for the third time to the Portland VA inpatient psychiatric unit. Individual and group supportive treatment, including the special inpatient Vietnam veteran group, assisted him, aided perhaps by the addition of an antihypertensive drug with antianxiety effects, clonidine, 0.3 milligrams per day. After 3 weeks he was discharged and has just resumed outpatient psychotherapy at the mental hygiene clinic.

Case 3

This Caucasian man was 38 years old and recently separated from his fourth wife when he first contacted the Portland vet center 2½ years ago. He listed his problems as unemployment, emotional constriction, suicidal ideation with a recent intentional drug overdose, alcohol and drug abuse, faulty self-esteem, survivor guilt, uncontrolled anger, nightmares, insomnia, depression, and intrusive recollections of Vietnam experiences.

He grew up in rural towns in the western mountain states. His father was an alcoholic who severely beat the patient and his three siblings. He frequently ran away from home as a youngster, was declared a ward of the court for incorrigibility at age 15, and later was arrested for burglary and sentenced to a reform school for 15 months. At age 17 he joined the Army and was trained as an infantryman. He served less than a full tour in Vietnam, 1966–1967. As an infantry squad leader, he was involved in numerous firefights, engaging the enemy at least once weekly while on patrols. On at least two separate occasions, he requested artillery fire that resulted in the killing of South Vietnamese and U.S. troops. Although cleared of wrongdoing at subsequent investigations, he continued to feel responsible and thereafter was haunted by guilt about these incidents. He states that, subsequently, he threw his rifle at his commanding officer and was hospitalized on a military psychiatric ward. He claims to have had two other military psychiatric hospital admissions and two courts martial for insubordination and AWOL, all of which resulted in a general discharge in 1967. During his first few years as a civilian, he worked as a long-haul truck driver, was an active participant in Vietnam Veterans against the War, and used alcohol and street drugs daily. His experiences over the next 16 years included the following: four marriages, an 8-month incarceration for assault, at least six arrests for driving under the influence of alcohol, three suicide attempts, numerous fights, and admission to various VA medical centers on at least six occasions, two for substance abuse treatment and four for depression and suicidal ideation.

After evaluation at the vet center, he attended a rap group and an alcohol treatment and information group sporadically over the next 7 months, while continuing to abuse alcohol. He obtained service connection for the PTSD, began schooling sponsored by VA Vocational Rehabilitation but soon dropped out, experienced increasing depression, and spontaneously drove 200 miles to enter another VA medical center where he had been treated before. After 2 weeks, he returned to resume group treatment at the vet center and attend Alcoholics Anonymous. He also received follow-up medication at the Portland VA mental hygiene clinic. This had been arranged independently by the discharging inpatient program and was not coordinated locally with vet center staff. He did well for the next 6 months, attending meetings and receiving an antidepressant, amoxapine, 200 to 250 milligrams per day. He then obtained a truck-driving job and precipitously discontinued vet center and Alcoholics Anonymous meetings. He continued amoxapine sporadically, and as symptoms of depressed mood, suicidal thinking, and combat-related nightmares increased, his mental hygiene clinic physician added neuroleptic drugs, first perphenazine, 4 to 8 milligrams per day, later changed to chlorpromazine, 25 to 50 milligrams per day, but these did not help. Four months after discontinuing vet center treatment, after losing his job, he reluctantly complied with vet center staff requests that he enter the Portland VA psychiatric inpatient unit, where the diagnoses were PTSD, major depressive symptoms possibly secondary to alcohol abuse, and antisocial and dependent personality traits. During this 3-week stay, all medications were stopped, and he engaged in both the inpatient Vietnam veterans group and a rap group at the vet center. His depression rapidly improved, he arranged to sell a handgun that he had frequently thought of using to kill himself in the past, and he reinitiated contact with one of his children. He was discharged to continue group treatment at the vet center and medication management at the mental hygiene clinic, supervised by a new staff psychiatrist who had recently concluded a senior resident elective at the vet center. Initially low doses of the antidepressant, nortriptyline, were prescribed to help prevent recurrent depression and control nightmares. At first he did well, finding part-time work and complying with the treatment program. However, he returned to occasional abusive drinking, and 2 months after discharge he was arrested for driving under the influence of alcohol and attempting to assault the arresting police officer. Because of this event, a special staffing was conducted with representatives of the vet center, inpatient psychiatry unit, substance abuse program, and mental hygiene clinic. Following the group confrontation with the patient, a treatment plan was negotiated, requiring individual and rap group treatment at the vet center, monitored participation in Alcoholics Anonymous, and antidepressant drug management at the mental hygiene clinic.

For the past 8 months, he has had a stable outpatient course. He successfully completed two 4-month rap group cycles and maintained his individual treatment commitment. Nortriptyline was increased to 100 milligrams per day. The court ordered alcohol education and surveillance as a consequence of his arrest. On this regimen he has remained sober and is again employed part-time. Symptoms of depressed mood, insomnia, and war-related nightmares have abated, he has made new friends, has worked through intense feelings of survivor guilt, and is speaking with pride about his status as a Vietnam veteran for the first time in 15 years. At this writing he continues in outpatient treatment.

COMMENT

The stories of these three veterans do not have "successful endings." They are stories in progress, dominated by the veterans' turmoil and the profound challenge they have presented to the personnel who have undertaken their treatment. The vignettes do illustrate the importance of multiple alternative treatment settings, strategies, and staff to meet the changing needs of the patient. These patients can be extremely frustrating and intimidating (Fox, 1974; Rosenheck, 1985), producing profound feelings of fear and rage in those who treat them (Frick & Bogart, 1982; Newberry, 1985). The mutual support and advice exchanged when staff gather to discuss these most difficult patients is of inestimable value in reducing countertherapeutic responses and promoting persistence in attempts to be helpful. It is also essential at times that a fresh setting or therapist be arranged, at least temporarily, when patients have worn out their welcome elsewhere. These procedures are best arranged in a collective treatment network, and few institutions can support this network of staff and services as well as the VA. It is our hope that the potential for such coordinated efforts can be realized more uniformly throughout the VA system in the near future.

REFERENCES

American Psychiatric Association (1980). *Diagnostic and statistical manual of mental disorders* (3rd ed.). Washington DC: American Psychiatric Association.

Arnold, A. L. (1985). Diagnosis of post-traumatic stress disorder in Vietnam veterans. In S. M. Sonnenberg, A. S. Blank, Jr., & J. A. Talbott, (Eds.), *The trauma of war: Stress and recovery in Vietnam veterans* (pp. 99–123). Washington DC: American Psychiatric Press.

Atkinson, R. M., Henderson, R. G., Sparr, L. F., & Deale, S. (1982). Assessment of Vietnam veterans for posttraumatic stress disorder in Veterans Administration disability claims. *American Journal of Psychiatry, 139,* 1118–1121.

Atkinson, R. M., Sparr, L. F., Sheff, A. G., White, R. A. F., & Fitzsimmons, J. T. (1984). Diagnosis of posttraumatic stress disorder in Vietnam veterans: Preliminary findings. *American Journal of Psychiatry, 141,* 694–696.

Atkinson, R. M., Callen, K. E., Reaves, M. E., & Drummond, D. J. (1985). VA mental health services for Vietnam veterans. *VA Practitioner, 2*(5), 72–74, 77.

Berman, S., Price, S., & Gusman, F. (1982). An inpatient program for Vietnam combat veterans in a Veterans Administration hospital. *Hospital and Community Psychiatry, 33,* 919–922.

Blanchard, E. B., Kolb, L. C., Pallmeyer, T. P., & Gerardi, R. J. (1982). A psychophysiological study of post traumatic stress disorder in Vietnam veterans. *Psychiatric Quarterly, 54,* 220–229.

Blank, A. S., Jr. (1982a). Apocalypse terminable and interminable: Operation outreach for Vietnam veterans. *Hospital and Community Psychiatry, 33,* 913–918.

Blank, A. S., Jr. (1982b). Stresses of war: The example of Vietnam. In L. Goldberger & S. Breznitz (Eds.), *Handbook of stress* (pp. 631–643). New York: Free Press/Macmillan.

Blank, A. S., Jr. (1985). The Veterans Administration's Vietnam veterans outreach and counseling centers. In S. M. Sonnenberg, A. S. Blank, Jr., & J. A. Talbott (Eds.), *The trauma of war: Stress and recovery in Vietnam veterans* (pp. 227–261). Washington DC: American Psychiatric Press.

Boulanger, G. (1986). Predisposition to posttraumatic stress disorder. In G. Boulanger & C. Kadushin (Eds.), *The Vietnam veteran redefined: Fact and fiction* (pp. 37–50). Hillsdale, NJ: Lawrence Erlbaum.

Boulanger, G., Kadushin, C., Rindskopf, D. M., & Carey, M. A. (1986). Posttraumatic stress disorder: A valid diagnosis? In G. Boulanger & C. Kadushin (Eds.), *The Vietnam veteran redefined: Fact and fiction* (pp. 23–35). Hillsdale, NJ: Lawrence Erlbaum.

Breslau, N., & Davis, G. C. (1987). Post traumatic stress disorder: The etiologic specificity of wartime stressors. *American Journal of Psychiatry, 144,* 578–583.

Buffalo VA Medical Center. (1984). *Proposal for a multiservice center for Vietnam veterans with post traumatic stress disorder.* Unpublished manuscript.

Callen, K. E., Reaves, M. E., Maxwell, M. J., & McFarland, B. H. (1985). Vietnam veterans in the general hospital. *Hospital and Community Psychiatry, 36,* 150–153.

Card, J. J. (1983). *Lives after Vietnam.* Lexington, MA: Lexington Books.

DeFazio, V. J. (1978). Dynamic perspectives on the nature and effects of combat stress. In C. R. Figley (Ed.), *Stress disorders among Vietnam veterans: Theory, research and treatment* (pp. 23–42). New York: Brunner/Mazel.

Domash, M. D., & Sparr, L. F. (1982). Post-traumatic stress disorder masquerading as paranoid schizophrenia: Case report. *Military Medicine, 147,* 772–774.

Dwyer, J., & Pentland, B. (1983). Vietnam veterans liaison unit. West Los Angeles VA Medical Center. Various unpublished materials.

Egendorf, A. (1982). The postwar healing of Vietnam veterans: Recent research. *Hospital and Community Psychiatry, 33,* 901–908.

Egendorf, A., Kadushin, C., Laufer, R. S., Rothbart, G., & Sloan, L. (1981). *Legacies of Vietnam: Comparative adjustment of veterans and their peers* (Publication No. V 101 134P-630). Washington, DC: U.S. Government Printing Office.

Escobar, J. I., Randolph, E. T., Puente, G., Spiwak, F., Asamen, J. K., Hill, M., & Hough, R. L. (1983). Post-traumatic stress disorder in Hispanic Vietnam veterans. *The Journal of Nervous and Mental Disease, 171,* 585–596.

Fairbank, J. A., & Keane, T. M. (1982). Flooding for combat-related stress disorders: Assessment of anxiety reduction across traumatic memories. *Behavior Therapy, 13,* 499–510.

Fairbank, J. A., Keane, T. M., & Malloy, P. F. (1983). Some preliminary data on the psychological characteristics of Vietnam veterans with posttraumatic stress disorders. *Journal of Consulting and Clinical Psychology, 51,* 912–919.

Fairbank, J. A., McCaffrey, R. J., & Keane, T. M. (1985). Psychometric detection of fabricated symptoms of posttraumatic stress disorder. *American Journal of Psychiatry, 142,* 501–503.

Fox, R. P. (1974). Narcissistic rage and the problem of combat aggression. *Archives of General Psychiatry, 31,* 807–811.

Foy, D. W., Sipprelle, R. C., Rueger, D. B., Carroll, E. M. (1984). Etiology of posttraumatic stress disorder in Vietnam veterans: Analysis of premilitary, military and combat exposure influences. *Journal of Consulting and Clinical Psychology, 52,* 79–87.

Frick, R., & Bogart, L. (1982). Transference and countertransference in group therapy with Vietnam veterans. *Bulletin of the Menninger Clinic, 46,* 429–444.

Friedman, M. J. (1981). Post-Vietnam syndrome: Recognition and management. *Psychosomatics, 22,* 931–943.

Frye, J. S., & Stockton, R. A. (1982). Discriminant analysis of post-traumatic stress disorder among a group of Vietnam veterans. *American Journal of Psychiatry, 139,* 52–56.

Green, B. L., Lindy, J. D., & Grace, M. C. (1985). Posttraumatic stress disorder: Toward DSM-IV. *The Journal of Nervous and Mental Disease, 173,* 406–411.

Green, B. L., Wilson, J. P., & Lindy, J. D. (1985). Conceptualizing post-traumatic stress disorder: A psychosocial framework. In C. R. Figley, (Ed.), *Trauma and its wake: The study and treatment of post-traumatic stress disorder* (pp. 53–69). New York: Brunner/Mazel.

Harris, M. J., & Fisher, B. S. (1985). Group therapy in the treatment of female partners of Vietnam veterans. *Journal for Specialists in Group Work, 10,* 44–50.

Helzer, J. E. (1981). Methodological issues in the interpretations of the consequences of extreme situations. In B. S. Dohrenwend & B. P. Dohrenwend (Eds.), *Stressful life events and their contexts* (pp. 108–129). New York: Neale Watson Academic Publications.

Helzer, J. E., Robins, L. N., Wish, E., & Hesselbrock, M. (1979). Depression in Vietnam veterans and civilian controls. *American Journal of Psychiatry, 136,* 526–529.

Hendin, H., Pollinger, A., Singer, P., & Ulman, R. B. (1981). Meanings of combat and the development of post-traumatic stress disorder. *American Journal of Psychiatry, 138,* 1490–1493.

Hendin, H., Pollinger, A., & Haas, A. (1984). Combat adaptations of Vietnam veterans without posttraumatic stress disorders. *American Journal of Psychiatry, 141,* 956–959.

Horowitz, M. J. (1986). *Stress response syndromes* (2nd ed.) New York: Jason Aronson.

Horowitz, M., Wilner, N., & Alvarez, W. (1979). Impact of event scale: A measure of subjective stress. *Psychomatic Medicine, 41,* 209–218.

Hyer, L., O'Leary, W. C., Elkins, R., & Arena, J. (1985). PTSD: Additional criteria for evaluation. *VA Practitioner, 2*(9), 67–68, 73–75.

Jelinek, J. M., & Williams, T. (1984). Post-traumatic stress disorder and substance absue in Vietnam combat veterans: Treatment problems, strategies and recommendations. *Journal of Substance Abuse Treatment, 1,* 87–97.

Kadushin, C. (1985). Social networks, helping networks, and Vietnam veterans. In S. M. Sonnenberg, A. S. Blank, Jr., & J. A. Talbott (Eds.), *The trauma of war: Stress and recovery in Vietnam veterans* (pp. 57–68). Washington DC: American Psychiatric Press.

Keane, T. M., Malloy, P. F., & Fairbank, J. A. (1984). Empirical development of an MMPI subscale for the assessment of combat-related posttraumatic stress disorder. *Journal of Consulting and Clinical Psychology, 52,* 888–891.

Keane, T. M., Fairbank, J. A., Caddell, J. M., Zimering, R. T., & Bender, M. E. (1985). A behavioral approach to assessing and treating post-traumatic stress disorder in Vietnam veterans. In C. R. Figley (Ed.), *Trauma and its wake: The study and treatment of post-traumatic stress disorder* (pp. 257–294). New York: Brunner/Mazel.

Keane, T. M., Scott, W. O., Chavoya, G. A., Lamparski, D. M., & Fairbank, J. A. (1985). Social support in Vietnam veterans with posttraumatic stress disorder: A comparative analysis. *Journal of Consulting and Clinical Psychology, 53,* 95–102.

Keane, T. M., Zimering, R. T., & Caddell, J. M. (1985). A behavioral formulation of posttraumatic stress disorder in Vietnam veterans. *The Behavior Therapist, 8,* 9–12.

Lacoursiere, R. B., Godfrey, K. E., & Ruby, L.M. (1980). Traumatic neurosis in the etiology of alcoholism: Vietnam combat and other trauma. *American Journal of Psychiatry, 137,* 966–968.

Laufer, R. S., Brett, E., & Gallops, M. S. (1985). Symptom patterns associated with post-traumatic stress disorder among Vietnam veterans exposed to war trauma. *American Journal of Psychiatry, 142,* 1304–1311.

Lindy, J. D., Grace, M. C., & Green, B. L. (1984). Building a conceptual bridge between civilian trauma and war trauma: Preliminary psychological findings from a clinical sample of Vietnam veterans. In van der Kolk, B. A. (Ed.), *Post-traumatic stress disorder: Psychological and biological sequelae* (pp. 43–58). Washington, DC: American Psychiatric Press.

Lund, M., Foy, D., Sipprelle, C., & Strachan, A. (1984). The combat exposure scale: A systematic assessment of trauma in the Vietnam war. *Journal of Clinical Psychology, 40,* 1323–1328.

Lynn, E. J., & Belza, M. (1984). Factitious posttraumatic stress disorder: The veteran who never got to Vietnam. *Hospital and Community Psychiatry, 35,* 697–701.

Malloy, P. F., Fairbank, J. A., & Keane, T. M. (1983). Validation of a multimethod assessment of posttraumatic stress disorders in Vietnam veterans. *Journal of Consulting and Clinical Psychology, 51,* 488–494.

Newberry, T. B. (1985). Levels of countertransference toward Vietnam veterans with postraumatic stress disorder. *Bulletin of the Menninger Clinic, 49,* 151–160.

Penk, W. E., Rabinowitz, R., Roberts, W. R., Patterson, E. T., Dolan, M. P., & Atkins, H. G. (1981). Adjustment differences among male substance abusers varying in degree of combat experiences in Vietnam. *Journal of Consulting and Clinical Psychology, 49,* 426–437.

Reaves, M. E., & Maxwell, M. J. (1987). The evaluation of a therapy group for Vietnam veterans on a general psychiatric unit. *Journal of Contemporary Psychotherapy, 17,* 22–33.

Reaves, M. E., Atkinson, R. M., Ponzoha, C. A., & Kofoed, L. L. (1988). Trends in VA mental health services for Vietnam veterans. *VA Practitioner.*

Rogers, B., & Nickolaus, J. (1987). Vietnam nurses. *Journal of Psychosocial Nursing and Mental Health Services, 25*(4), 10–15.

Rosenheck, R. (1985). Malignant post-Vietnam stress syndrome. *American Journal of Orthopsychiatry, 55,* 166–176.

Roth, L. M. (1986). Substance use and mental health among Vietnam veterans. In Boulanger, G., & Kadushin, C. (Eds.), *The Vietnam veteran redefined: Facts and fiction* (pp. 61–71). Hillsdale, NJ: Lawrence Erlbaum.

Schnitt, J. M., & Nocks, J. J. (1984). Alcoholism treatment of Vietnam veterans with posttraumatic stress disorder. *Journal of Substance Abuse Treatment, 1,* 179–189.

Scurfield, R. M., & Blank, A. S., Jr. (1985). A guide to obtaining a military history from Vietnam veterans. In S. M. Sonnenberg, A. S. Blank, Jr., & J. A. Talbott (Eds.), *The trauma of war: Stress and recovery in Vietnam veterans.* (pp. 263–291). Washington, DC: American Psychiatric Press.

Sierles, F. S., Chen, J. J., McFarland, R. E., & Taylor, M. A. (1983). Posttraumatic stress disorder and concurrent psychiatric illness: A preliminary report. *American Journal of Psychiatry, 140,* 1177–1179.

Silver, S. M., & Iacono, C. U. (1984). Factor-analytic support for DSM-III's post-traumatic stress disorder for Vietnam veterans. *Journal of Clinical Psychology, 40,* 5–14.

Sineps, J. G. (1983). *Vietnam veterans program, day hospital, Minneapolis VA Medical Center, psychiatry and psychology services.* Unpublished manuscript.

Smith, J. R. (1985a). Individual psychotherapy with Vietnam veterans. In S. M. Sonnenberg, A. S. Blank, Jr., & J. A. Talbott (Eds.), *The trauma of war: Stress and recovery in Vietnam veterans* (pp. 125–163). Washington, DC: American Psychiatric Press.

Smith, J. R. (1985b). Rap groups and group therapy for Vietnam veterans. In S. M. Sonnenberg, A. S. Blank, Jr., & J. A. Talbott (Eds.), *The trauma of war: Stress and recovery in Vietnam veterans* (pp. 165–191). Washington, DC: American Psychiatric Press.

Sparr, L. F., & Atkinson, R. M. (1986). Post-traumatic stress disorder as an insanity defense: Medico-legal quicksand. *American Journal of Psychiatry, 143,* 608–613.

Sparr, L., & Pankratz, L. D. (1983). Factitious posttraumatic stress disorder. *American Journal of Psychiatry, 140,* 1016–1019.

Sparr, L. F., Reaves, M. E., & Atkinson, R. M. (1987). Military combat, posttraumatic stress disorder, and criminal behavior in Vietnam veterans. *Bulletin of the American Academy of Psychiatry and the Law, 15,* 141–162.

Spitzer, R. L., & Williams, J. B. W. (1985). *Structured clinical interview for DSM-III.* New York: New York State Psychiatric Institute, Biometric Research Department.

Starkey, T. W., & Ashlock, L. (1984). Inpatient treatment of PTSD: An interim report of the Miami model. *VA Practitioner, 1*(12), 37–40.

Sudak, H. S., Corradi, R. B., Martin, R. S., & Gold, F. S. (1984). Antecedent personality factors and the post-Vietnam syndrome: Case reports. *Military Medicine, 149,* 550–554.

van der Kolk, B. A. (1983). Psychopharmacological issues in posttraumatic stress disorder. *Hospital and Community Psychiatry, 34,* 683–684, 691.

van Putten, T., & Emory, W. H. (1973). Traumatic neuroses in Vietnam returnees: A forgotten diagnosis? *Archives of General Psychiatry, 29,* 695–698.

Walker, J. I., & Nash, J. D. (1981). Group therapy in the treatment of Vietnam combat veterans. *International Journal of Group Psychotherapy, 31,* 379–389.

Williams, C. M., & Williams, T. (1985). Family therapy for Vietnam veterans. In S. M. Sonnenberg, A. S. Blank, Jr., & J. A. Talbott (Eds.), *The trauma of war: Stress and recovery in Vietnam veterans* (pp. 193–209). Washington, DC: American Psychiatric Press.

Williams, T. (1980). A preferred model for development of interventions for psychological readjustment of Vietnam veterans: Group treatment. In T. Williams (Ed.), *Post-traumatic stress disorders of the Vietnam veteran* (pp. 37–47). Cincinnati: Disabled American Veterans.

Wilson, J. P. (1978). *Identity, ideology and crisis: The Vietnam veteran in transition.* The Forgotten Warrior Project. Cleveland: Cleveland State University.

Wilson, J. P. (1980). Conflict, stress and growth: Effects of war on psychosocial development among Vietnam veterans. In C. R. Figley & S. Leventman (Eds.), *Strangers at home: Vietnam veterans since the war* (pp. 123–165). New York: Praeger.

Wilson, J. P. (1985, February 27). *Differential diagnosis of PTSD and personality disorder.* Seminar. VA Region 5 and 6 Readjustment Counseling Centers Staff Training. Las Vegas NV.

Epilogue

In this book we have assembled some of the most recent perspectives on war-related extreme stress. The twentieth century has been marked by the most destructive wars mankind has ever witnessed and has ushered in the beginning of the nuclear era, especially as symbolized by Hiroshima. On a global level, the world wars of this century, the Nazi Holocaust, the Korean War, the Vietnam War, the Cambodian Holocaust as well as other more recent wars have produced a level of mass destructiveness and killing unparalleled in recorded history. Although conventional warfare has produced losses, death, destruction, and atrocities, the advent of nuclear warfare has changed the meaning of war forever and produced unprecedented destructive capabilities. It is obvious that events of this magnitude leave lasting and permanent imprints in the collective conscious and individual memories of those who survive and create legacies for future generations.

As Lifton suggested in the first chapter of this book, the concept of the death imprint and imagery is an important one for our times, especially in the specter of worldwide annihilation by nuclear weapons. Perhaps, in this regard, it is possible to speak of global trauma and begin to raise questions about the long-term effects of war in the lives of survivors and in the fabric of society and its cultures. If nothing else, the research in the area of post-traumatic stress disorder has made it clear that traumatized persons attempt to avoid or deny the painful aspects of their experiences; later they pay the price of reliving what happened in distressing images and feelings. Certainly, it is possible that whole nations, cultures, and societies may suffer traumatic stress reactions in ways that we only dimly understand at this time. Consider one example of societal avoidance—the fact that the cross-sectional research on Holocaust survivors reported in this book is but one of a few its kind and occurred 40 years after the Nazi Holocaust. Why did it take so long for social scientists to raise a broad range of questions about the impact of the Holocaust in the lives of the survivors and their children? Why was it presumed by most clinicians that Holocaust survivors must suffer only deleterious effects of that experience? What about the strong survivors who coped well with life-course development and raised successful families? How do persons transform extreme stress experiences? And what does it mean psychologically to be a survivor? Indeed, what aspects of personality, identity, character structure, and style of coping are altered by traumatic events? What are the vicissitudes and forms of survivorship? And in what ways do cultures either facilitate positive personal integration of extreme stress experiences or hinder the recovery process in one way or another? As noted by Silver and Wilson in their chapter on Native American perspectives of war trauma, how one "sees" traumatic events depends in large part on how one "sees" the world through the lenses of his or her culture. Part of the wisdom developed in many Native American tribes was the understanding that war alters warriors and those exposed to it. Thus, to integrate the war experience may require ritualized forms of experience to "see" what happened in a new way, one that is congruent with the traditions of the tribal group or world view.

The survivors studied in this book include persons who endured war-related extreme stress experiences from the Holocaust to Vietnam. These include veterans exposed to combat, death, destruction, and war attrocities, those who were interned in prisoner of war and concentration camps and those dislocated by war. It is these individuals who have encountered death and have lived to share the legacy of survival, both positive and negative, who point out the inadequacy of many theories based in "normal human experience." The poignancy of this legacy has compelled many academicians and clinicians to contemplate the impact of survival on the lifelong development of survivors.

Those who participated in or were affected by World War II are facing the experiences and challenges of aging; others are in the later stages of their adult life. They may be experiencing irreversible age-associated declines in health and functional status, changes in appearance and body image, reductions in economic resources, losses of family members and friends, and are consequently confronting the challenge of adjustment to these late-life changes and losses. It is critical that we have a better understanding of the ways that long-term consequences of extreme stress interact with and affect late-life adaptation, mental health, and adjustment to aging. It is also critical that stress researchers and gerontologists integrate their conceptual approaches to produce a better understanding of the factors that ameliorate and or moderate the long-range effects of stress on mental health and adjustment to aging.

In this book, there are significant explorations of some critical theoretical, conceptual, and methodological issues in the field of traumatic stress and gerontological studies. The critical issues explored in this book include human tendencies and capacity to observe, endure, struggle with, and actively participate in war attrocities; the mechanisms (e.g., doubling, serial self) that account for the transformation of individuals from peaceful family members to participants in attrocities; the deep impact and importance of death imagery and death encounters in the formation and reconstruction of the post-traumatic self; the ways that wars disrupt the process of identity development and lead to diffusion and fragmentation in the self-structure; the societal processes and forces that hinder the reintegration and identity reconstruction of war veterans and war victims; the ways that individuals endured and survived the extensive extreme stresses of combat exposure and internment in POW and concentration camps; the coping style, coping strategies, and coping responses that aid or hinder the processing and ultimate resolution of war stresses; and the manifestation of long-term symptom patterns and functional impairments in traumatized persons. The chapters in this book provide findings from empirical studies and address critical issues in the lives of victims of extreme stress. These include the long-range impact of combat and war-related stress on mental health and epigenetic life-course changes in identity; the long-range effects of captivity on the lives of former prisoners of war; the moderating effects of postwar experiences and adaptation (e.g., social and emotional support) on the psychological well-being of Holocaust survivors; the evolution of attitudes and relationships between Holocaust survivors and their children; and patterns of countertransference in therapists who work with war veterans, Holocaust survivors, children of Holocaust survivors, and former POWs.

This book stresses the need for sensitivity to the special status, concerns, and areas of vulnerability in survivors that may have emanated from a traumatic experience. In both research and treatment, emphasis needs to be placed on empathetic listening to the survivors narrative in a sensitive, open, and nonjudgemental manner that, in turn, can lead to rapport and trust that may increase the validity of research data as well as the effectiveness of treatment. The book notes that conceptual approaches employed in much of the research on consequences of war stress have serious limitations. For example, there are few longitudinal studies of survivorship, and most current studies are based on selected populations that come to the attention of mental health professionals or those who file for claims. Further, some of the major conceptual approaches are still anchored in the medical psychiatric literature and are accordingly limited. In both of these cases, there is limited generalizability of the findings unlike that afforded by more systematic cross-sectional and longitudinal studies. There is a lack of empirical evidence on the effects of military service during wartime on health, later life-course adjustment, and aging of veterans and war stress victims.

There is a beginning realization, however, that each combat exposure, participation in and exposure to war atrocities, and captivity or hostage experience may result in differing effects on survivors, depending on the duration and severity of the experience and the resources and the support received from others both during the war experience and in subsequent years. The more recent studies of extreme stress have begun to employ conceptual and methodological approaches anchored in the social and behavioral sciences, rather than being limited to clinical studies of individual cases. The empirical research reported on in this book is, therefore, significant for two major reasons: (a) it is anchored conceptually in the social sciences; and (b) the research reports on war veterans, POWs, and Holocaust survivors are based on conventional cross-sections of these populations. The chapter on children of Holocaust survivors is also unique in its identification of normative processes in parent–child relationships within this group.

Today the global news coverage in the various media show us that intergroup hostilities and war continue in all parts of the world (e.g., the Middle East, South America, Ireland, Central America, South Africa, the Far East). There can be little doubt that we currently live in a climate of global trauma that includes terrorism, guerilla warfare, torture, political persecution, bombings, and missile rockets that attack on military targets that bring us close to retaliatory war. Moreover, there are now in some countries several generations of children who have experienced constant warfare and social upheaval. What are the implications of these events for moral development, ideology, and self-esteem? How do they "see" their world now and in the future? On a broader scale, what are the implications of chronic conflict and warfare for the development of national character and social structure? Is it possible that such countries with enduring turmoil will establish patterns that lead to forms of revictimization and reenactment of long-standing conflicts that emanated from political, religious, economic, and ideological differences?

As noted by the authors of this volume, there are a range and variety of traumatic stress syndromes. However, there have been rather limited scientific efforts directed at the identification of the short, intermediate, and long-range effects of these experiences on those affected by them. Similarly, there have been very few questions raised concerning the role of environmental resources, including the homecoming climate, the availability of compensations, health, educational, and economic benefits, in aiding adjustment of war veterans and war victims. We believe that in the United States, our individualistic value system has affected and limited scientific inquiry into deeper understanding of traumatic stress reactions in society. Further, this same value system has affected our collective efforts to support, treat, and help integrate survivors into the necessary opportunity structures that lead to the healthy stress recovery process. Societies, like individuals, naturally avoid painful, distressing, and troubling consequences of war-related stress. Yet, traumatic events rarely, if ever, occur in a vacuum. The failure to implement policies designed to heal survivors further perpetuates the legacy of the trauma by denying the need for collective responsibility and caring. As noted in the chapter by Parson, narcissistic injury can exist at both the individual and the cultural level. The acceptance of collective responsibility and the creative implementation of policies and programs designed purposely to heal the wounds of war as well as other traumatic events is a first step toward a genuinely humanistic society. As painful and difficult as it is to face the often tragic consequences of war and extreme stress experiences, it is important that we do so because the opposite dimension of trauma and victimization is the discovery of deeper levels of human dignity and integrity.

Index